INTERVENTIONS: NEW STUDIES IN MEDIEVAL CULTURE

Ethan Knapp, Series Editor

Chaucer, Gower, and the Affect of Invention

STEELE NOWLIN

The Ohio State University Press • Columbus

Copyright © 2016 by The Ohio State University.
All rights reserved.

Library of Congress Cataloging-in-Publication Data
Names: Nowlin, Steele, 1976– author.
Title: Chaucer, Gower, and the affect of invention / Steele Nowlin.
Other titles: Interventions (Columbus, Ohio)
Description: Columbus : The Ohio State University Press, [2016] | Series: Interventions: new studies in medieval culture | Includes bibliographical references and index.
Identifiers: LCCN 2016023925 | ISBN 9780814213100 (cloth ; alk. paper) | ISBN 0814213103 (cloth ; alk. paper)
Subjects: LCSH: English poetry—Middle English, 1100–1500—History and criticism. | Invention (Rhetoric) | Affect (Psychology) in literature. | Chaucer, Geoffrey, –1400—Criticism and interpretation. | Gower, John, 1325?–1408—Criticism and interpretation.
Classification: ILCC PR311 .N69 2016 | DDC 821/.109—dc23
LC record available at https://lccn.loc.gov/2016023925

Cover design by Laurence Nozik
Text design by Juliet Williams
Type set in Adobe Minion and Caudex

♾ The paper used in this publication meets the minimum requirements of the American National Standard for Information Sciences—Permanence of Paper for Printed Library Materials. ANSI Z39.48–1992.

9 8 7 6 5 4 3 2 1

FOR VERNA, BETTY, AND JULIAN

CONTENTS

	Acknowledgments	ix
Introduction	The Emergence of Invention	1
Chapter 1	"Gooth yet alway under": Invention as Movement in the *House of Fame*	36
Chapter 2	"Ryght swich as ye felten": Aligning Affect and Invention in *The Legend of Good Women*	69
Chapter 3	A Thing So Strange: Macrocosmic Emergence in the *Confessio Amantis*	93
Chapter 4	"The Cronique of this fable": Transformative Poetry and the Chronicle Form in the *Confessio Amantis*	122
Chapter 5	Empty Songs, Mighty Men, and a Startled Chicken: Satirizing the Affect of Invention in Fragment VII of the *Canterbury Tales*	151
Conclusion	From Ashes Ancient Come: Affective Intertextuality in Chaucer, Gower, and Shakespeare	191
	Bibliography	213
	Index	227

ACKNOWLEDGMENTS

THE INVENTION of this book was a long process and one that I could not have completed without the help of many people. My own thinking about medieval invention began more than a decade ago in the graduate program at the Pennsylvania State University, and I am especially grateful to Robert R. Edwards for his mentorship over the years, and for graciously reading drafts and offering advice about my scholarly projects and the profession in general. I'm grateful too for graduate faculty at Penn State who worked with me at the early stages of my thinking about invention, especially Patrick Cheney, Caroline Eckhardt, Benjamin Hudson, Sherry Roush, and Alice Sheppard, whose seminar on medieval historiography first introduced me to the exciting possibilities that medieval literature offered the careful reader. Tim Arner provided constant help and advice during our frequent and often late-night conversations about Chaucer and medieval literature. My thanks go also to Jeff Pruchnic and Dustin Stegner for many discussions over the years and more recently for helpful advice during the final stages of this project. Annika Farber, Dan Hicks, Lindsey Jones, and Adam Miyashiro likewise helped to make my time at Penn State among the most intellectually rewarding of my life, and I'm deeply grateful to these faculty, colleagues, and friends for helping to make it so.

A wider circle of scholars also helped me to think about matters of late medieval literature and culture. I'm especially grateful to R. F. Yeager, who offered advice at various stages of my career and who graciously welcomed me into the thriving community of Gower scholars, including Stephanie Batkie, Craig Bertolet, Georgiana Donavin, Brian Gastle, Matthew Irvin, and Eve Salisbury, all of whose conversations with me about Gower over the years helped shape my thinking about Gower's English and Latin works. Seth Lerer and the participants in the summer institute on Chaucer at the National Humanities Center in 2008—still referred to fondly as "Chaucer Camp"—made me a better teacher and scholar. I am especially thankful to Eugene O'Connor and Ethan Knapp at The Ohio State University Press for their support of this project, and to Glenn Burger and the anonymous reader whose thoughtful and exacting comments greatly strengthened this book. For conversations, advice, and a supportive word here and there, I'm grateful also to J. Allan Mitchell, Alex Mueller, Myra Seaman, and Lynn Shutter.

Incredibly supportive colleagues and friends in the Department of English at Hampden-Sydney College helped me with innumerable discussions of teaching and writing, and I'm especially grateful to my department chairs over the years, Katherine Weese, Evan Davis, and Cristine Varholy. Faculty colleagues from other departments read very early drafts of some of these chapters: my thanks go to Eric Dinmore, James Frusetta, J. Michael Utzinger, and Daniella Widdows for their helpful comments during our faculty writing-group meetings. The students in my Chaucer and medieval literature classes frequently helped me to discover—and rediscover—vital nuances in the texts discussed in this book, and as they shared their own writing with me and their peers, the students in all of my undergraduate courses reminded me of the importance of considering the affective components of processes of invention. Research for this book could not have been completed without the tireless help of the Interlibrary Loan staff of the Bortz Library at Hampden-Sydney: Maureen Culley, Bret Peaden, and especially Gerry Randall. My thanks go as well to Jane Holland, for all of her help.

Travel and research grants from several sources also helped make this book possible. The English Department at Penn State helped fund travel during my graduate career, and a fellowship from the Rock Ethics Institute at Penn State allowed me to share my early work on medieval invention and poetry with an interdisciplinary group of graduate colleagues. My sincere thanks go to the deans of the faculty at Hampden-Sydney, Earl Fleck, Robert Herdegen, Walter McDermott, and Dennis Stevens, for never failing to fund my frequent requests for research and travel grants for work on this and related projects. A semester-long sabbatical in the spring of 2014 likewise gave me the opportunity to focus on completing the manuscript. The Mednick Research Fellowship from the Virginia Foundation for Independent Colleges allowed me to travel to and work at the Folger Shakespeare Library, and I am grateful to the library staff for their help.

Chapters 2 and 4 of this book revise and expand previously published material: Chapter 2 is derived, in part, from an article published in *Exemplaria* on 12 Nov. 2013 (available online: http://www.tandfonline.com/doi/full/10.1179/1041257312Z.00000000023); and Chapter 4 from "Gower's Chronicles of Invention: Historiography and Productive Poetry in Book 4 of the *Confessio Amantis*," *Modern Philology* 110 (2012): 182–201, © 2012 by the University of Chicago Press. All rights reserved. I am very grateful to the editors and publishers of these journals for their kind permission to reprint this material here.

Heartfelt thanks go to my family, especially my parents and grandparents for their support—both emotionally and financially!—of my education, and to my brother and sister for their unceasing and unquantifiable support. As this project on affect and invention grew, so did my own family, and I could not have completed it without their love. I am grateful to Tessa for our daily, thought-clearing walks over the years. I miss them. My deepest thanks and love go to Verna Kale and to our children, Betty and Julian, to whom this book is dedicated. A short sentence in an acknowledgments page can't hope to convey my love for them and how grateful I am for the life we share together.

INTRODUCTION

THE EMERGENCE OF INVENTION

THIS BOOK EXAMINES the process of poetic invention as it is conceptualized and expressed in the poetry of Geoffrey Chaucer and John Gower. Specifically, it examines how these poets present invention as an affective force, a process characterized by emergence and potentiality, and one that has a corollary in affect—that is, a kind of force or sensation distinct from emotion, characterized as an "intensity" that precedes what is only later cognitively understood and expressed as feeling or emotion, and that is typically described in a critical vocabulary of movement, emergence, and becoming. Itself a force of movement and emergence, poetic invention includes not only the formal rhetorical structures and methods traceable to Cicero and Boethius, for example, and transduced through the medieval *ars poetica* tradition, or only the corresponding ways of negotiating the social, literary, and linguistic power struggles that comprise authorial politics, but also the movements and energies that occur before, but result in, the more formal activities of invention. This book studies the "affect of invention," a self-reflexive process that conceptualizes affect and invention in terms of each other and that understands invention as a process concurrent with the movements of affective emergence.

As I will show, Chaucer and Gower mobilize this conception of invention in culturally productive, though ultimately different, ways. Chaucer works in his narrative poetry to simulate and externalize necessarily inaccessible moments of affective emergence in order to demonstrate how dominant cultural narratives, especially of gender, maintain their power through a pervasive attachment to affective experience. He explores inventional and affective emergence by linking structural aspects of his narrative poetry to descriptions of the emotional experiences of characters. Gower takes a similar approach in the *Confessio Amantis* but extends his reach beyond depictions of individual experience and directs it toward his poem's larger project of revitalizing a corrupted and disordered world. Working to make poetic treatments of invention something constitutive of culture, his long English poem fictionalizes a rejuvenating transformation not only of individual readers but of "the world" as a whole.

I thus use the term "affect" somewhat differently than much of the work in the recent "turn to affect" in medieval studies, focusing not on the representation of emotion or desire, or on efforts to engage medieval alterity, but on the movement and emergence that precede emotional experience. I likewise argue for a broader understanding of invention in late medieval English literature that includes the dynamism and sense of potential that characterize inventional activity. In short, I wish to think about how the relationship of affect to emotion functions analogously to the relationship of invention to invented text. My goal in this introduction will be to clarify my terms, explaining exactly what I mean when I use the term "affect" and what I mean by an "expanded understanding" of poetic invention throughout this study by contextualizing those terms within a discussion of recent affect theory and scholarship on the medieval rhetorical tradition. I then turn my attention to explaining why Chaucer and Gower in particular are the focus of this exploration.

Before proceeding, however, I want to offer two examples, brief close readings of small portions of poems written at about the same time by Chaucer and Gower, in order to sketch how I plan to examine affect and invention throughout this book, and moreover to suggest how this approach offers a dynamically different way of thinking about poetic invention and what is at stake in doing so. My examples are of two paralyzed dreaming narrators: Chaucer's in *The Parlement of Foules,* and Gower's in the opening book of the *Vox Clamantis.* Each passage presents a moment of paradoxically fixed mobility, a scene teeming with movement and potential transformation that somehow renders the narrator-persona immobile, and each results in a more formalized articulation of a tentative, nebulous poetics whose very indeterminacy and ambiguity mark its productive, transformative potential.

SOM THYNG AND THE *MIDDEL WEIE*

In my first example, the narrator of Chaucer's *Parlement* finds himself stuck in front of a gate that leads to the Garden of Nature, in which he witnesses, dramatically performed in the histrionic bird parliament, the tensions of love, desire, governance, ethics, and common profit that inform the diverse array of *Parlement*'s source texts, ranging from Macrobius's commentary on Cicero, to Boccaccio and Alan of Lille. The narrative process of *Parlement* is inseparable from its progress through its own literary sources, and reading the dream vision means experiencing what Robert Worth Frank Jr., once called the "shocks" and "jolts" of the transitional moments that form the "pattern of the poem's movement."[1] As a transfer point between conceptual sections of the poem, the gate draws attention to itself as an intertextual artifact and hub of inventional transit, doubly inscribed with a Dantean recalibration of the erotic polarities of the *Roman de la Rose*.[2] The first inscription, written in "vers of gold" (141), promises those who enter the relief and tranquility, the "cure" and "grace," which the dreamer initially experiences in Nature's garden (128–29).[3] The second inscription promises the "strokes" of "Disdayn and Daunger" (135–36), evoking the darker side of erotic love thoroughly represented in the *Rose*.

---

1. Robert Worth Frank Jr., "Structure and Meaning in the *Parlement of Foules*," *PMLA* 71 (1956): 534 and 537. Criticism of *Parlement* has traditionally traced some kind of metanarrative—or the frustration of one—in its use of sources and traditions. *Parlement* is, as Theresa M. Krier describes it, an experiment in the "fusions of genres" ("The Aim Was Song: From Narrative to Lyric in the *Parlement of Foules* and *Love's Labour's Lost*," in *Refiguring Chaucer in the Renaissance*, ed. Theresa M. Krier [Gainesville: University Press of Florida, 1998], 172), an effort to bring together different literary forms and traditions—Latin, Italian, French; philosophical treatise, allegory, lyric; see also Krier, *Birth Passages: Maternity and Nostalgia, Antiquity to Shakespeare* (Ithaca, NY: Cornell University Press, 2001), in which she notes that lyric poetry itself is inherently characterized by "forward momentum and generativity" (118); Leslie Kordecki likewise argues that the poem "has a peculiar feel of travel about it" (*Ecofeminist Subjectivities: Chaucer's Talking Birds* [New York: Palgrave, 2011], 54). For a survey and analysis of Chaucer's use of his sources along this intertextual progression, see especially Robert R. Edwards, *The Dream of Chaucer: Representation and Reflection in the Early Narratives* (Durham, NC: Duke University Press, 1989), 130–37; and Alistair J. Minnis, *The Shorter Poems*, Oxford Guides to Chaucer (Oxford: Clarendon, 1995), 265–307.

2. Daniel Pinti, "Commentary and Comedic Reception: Dante and the Subject of Reading in *The Parliament of Fowls*," *Studies in the Age of Chaucer* 22 (2000): 311–40, argues for an additional level of intertextuality in the gate, reading the inscription on Chaucer's gate as a "mediation on writing, and therefore on reading, specifically on reading and writing Dante in the fourteenth century" (315), and that refers in particular to the commentary tradition through which any reader of Dante in the fourteenth century engages the poet (339–40).

3. All Chaucer quotations are taken from *The Riverside Chaucer*, gen. ed. Larry D. Benson (Boston: Houghton Mifflin, 1987). Line numbers are cited parenthetically in the text.

The scene, however, distills this intertextual cross-chatter into the physical sensation of affective forces intersecting at the site of the narrator's body:

> Right as betwixen adamauntes two
> Of evene myght, a pece of yren set
> Ne hath no myght to meve to ne fro—
> For what that oon may hale, that other let—
> Ferde I, that nyste whether me was bet
> To entre or leve.
>
> (148–53)

The simile of competing magnetic fields captures viscerally a moment of bodily stasis created by invisible forces that are themselves detectable not by their inherent natures but by how they move and what they displace. Like a lab experiment intended to simulate conditions for analysis, the scene artificially and impossibly prolongs a moment of emergence (that of walking through the gate) by, paradoxically, rendering stasis as the result of movement. It conceptualizes a stage of narrative process not as a point retrospectively defined along an inventional trajectory already understood to have been completed, nor even as a horizon of topical possibilities among which a writer chooses material for poetic production, but instead as a sensation of unstructured potential, here registered affectively by the narrator. The scene generates an impression of impending emergence by vacillating between incorporeal magnetic fields and the felt reality of embodied experience.

Africanus, the narrator's corporeal guide, explicitly emphasizes the literalness of this experience, and the drama that follows enacts as narrative a process by which these more nebulous sensations of potential collapse into more recognizable and definable structures. The narrator reports that "Affrycan, my gide, / Me hente and shof in at the gates wide" (153–54), and then more tenderly, "myn hand in his he tok anon, / Of which I confort caughte, and wente in faste" (169–70). Africanus first grabs the narrator, shoves him "at" the gate itself (154)—a motion sudden, unexpected, and registered only as physical displacement—before then taking his hand to lead him through—a soothing maneuver that regulates displacement via discourses of emotion. If, as Kurt Olsson suggests, "here" Chaucer's "invention begins," then it occurs at the very moment at which affective intensities collapse into emotional understanding under the structural archway of an explicitly self-conscious intertextual junction.[4] The narrator is momentarily

---

4. Kurt Olsson, "Poetic Invention and Chaucer's 'Parlement of Foules,'" *Modern Philology* 87 (1989): 19. For Olsson, *Parlement* fictionalizes the process of invention by mining

fixed in a field of movements, the experience of which is inseparable from the process by which the poem itself is written. The gate is at once an affective and textual transfer point, and the narrator's experience passing through it registers intertextuality affectively and gestures toward a representation of invention as movement and emergence that is almost instantaneously encoded as emotional retrospection. As if to amplify the scene's already exaggerated gesture toward this complicated sensation of something about to emerge, Affricanus's words of comfort further displace the narrator's initial reaction: "dred the not to come into this place," he tells the narrator, "For this writyng nys nothyng ment bi the" (157–58). The narrator will feel neither the "grace" nor the "mortal strokes of the spere" promised by the gate (129, 135). It turns out he has undergone an affective occurrence he wasn't supposed to have undergone, had an emotional experience that was meant for somebody else. As if being stuck between "adamauntes two" weren't bad enough, now he is caught among other people's affects, has felt somebody else's emotions, and Affricanus' actions displace again a process that itself was already about the experience of displacement.

This brief, potent scene at the gate, doubled like the inscription that hovers above it, gestures back to an initial and necessarily unrepresentable moment of emergence. Following the narrator through the gate reveals how what he sees around the Temple of Venus enacts a similar gesture via exaggerated contrast. The figures of Pleasaunce, Lust, Delyt, and Desire (among many others) that he observes there appear as culturally specific codifications: belated, particularized, scripted, and personified manifestations of the more nebulous occurrence from moments before. At the same time, these figures stand in as static inventional topics to be used and arranged according to more formal rhetorical practices: that is, things to write about, places from which to expand.

But the poem's concluding experience of deferred narrative resolution again emphasizes a sensation characterized by emergence and potential rather than by determinedness and fixity. Nature's decision to grant the formel a year to make her choice transfers Nature's own affective potential—her "prike" of "plesaunce" (389)—into a mandate that concludes without resolving, installing the deferred resolution of Chaucer's poem with its defining sensation of potential.[5]

---

seemingly unrelated topics and combining them with other sources to create a "confusion of shapes" (18) that leads to new inventions not discovered before and to a new kind of knowledge. Edwards argues that Chaucer's inventional quest in *Parlement* involves an effort to locate "a pragmatic middle term on which to ground poetry as a form of knowledge" in its own right (*Dream of Chaucer*, 125), and that it ultimately succeeds in finding that "the same process joins aesthetic creation and natural production," and that "poetry is part of the world it represents and thus that its claims, though always problematic, have real authority" (146).

5. Nature herself has been identified as a locus of potential and possibility defined in affective terms. Theresa Tinkle, "The Case of the Variable Source: Alan of Lille's *De Planctu*

The ensuing roundel sung by the birds replaces a figure of formal regulation with a celebration of sensation, describing a process of movement and transformation. Like the inscription over the garden gate, the lyric resonates with pain as well as joy. Blatantly ignoring the narrative it has translated into song—four members of the highest order of birds have in no way "recovered" their mates as the roundel claims (688)—its voiced elation echoes with the threats of death that await the year's end when the assembly reconvenes: the "batayle" threatened by the tercels who would fight to possess the formel, for example (539), or the suicidal despair of the unrequited tercel who will "lyve or sterve" by the formel's choice (420).[6] The roundel is packed with potential for pain and death as well as for invention and renewed life. The song is thus not so much a sign of lyric fusion or "release" as a more general portent of impending emergence.[7] Like Africanus's initial shove, the roundel pushes the narrative "at"—but not transcendently through—its thematic contraries, finally emphasizing not resolution but the feeling of potential, registered at once in terms of affect and invention.

Appropriately, then, the inventional prize wordlessly articulated in the sudden rush of flapping wings that wakes the dreamer and sends him back to his books is the tentative promise of finding "som thyng for to fare / The bet" (698–99)—presumably a novel poetic epistemology that can somehow wrangle competing conceptualizations of desire and productively navigate the

---

Naturae, Jean de Meun's *Roman de la Rose*, and Chaucer's *Parlement of Foules*," *Studies in the Age of Chaucer* 22 (2000): 341–77, notes that Nature's "sentences," like the intertexts of *Parlement* itself, "delineate a wide array of spiritual, affective, and sexual pleasures. No single 'sentence' is presented as dominant, and none excludes the others" (375). Kordecki argues that Nature is an unstable figure, characterized by "shifting designations for this creature, this power outside the dreamer," though eventually in the poem this subjectivity "slides, after a few bumps, into constructing easy formulations of nature, the other, the nonself, intricately intertwined with the female" (69–70). Edwards argues that Nature becomes a sign of "Chaucer's artistic and conceptual achievement" that "consists in defining a unified poetic substance without refining away the singularities and discordant individualism of the particulars" (*Dream of Chaucer*, 141). Edwards's reading of Nature implies an unceasing associational motion, one indicated by the back-and-forth between universal and particular, genus and species, that is inherent in her function in the poem.

6. The hardships could be prolonged even further: D. S. Brewer in his edition of the poem asks whether the two tercels who aren't eventually chosen are "to remain faithful" indefinitely, "with the absolute certainty of no reward" (*The Parlement of Foulys* [London: Thomas Nelson, 1960], 12).

7. Krier, *Birth Passages*, 112. Critics do not agree on whether the roundel fully synthesizes the poem's competing viewpoints in a moment of absolute lyric beauty, or whether it merely masks intractable irresolution at the heart of the poem. For the former, see ibid., 135–36. For the latter, see David Aers, "*The Parliament of Fowls*: Authority, the Knower, and the Known," in *Chaucer's Dream Visions and Shorter Poems*, ed. William Quinn (New York: Garland, 1999), 293–94; and Edwards, *Dream of Chaucer*, 129–30.

muddled entanglement of experience and literary traditions cited intertextually and enacted in the bird parliament. Part of the point of the poem's deferral of narrative resolution seems to be that, in order to retain its potentially productive characteristics, any such poetics must remain unrealized, and Chaucer seems less concerned with the possibility of reconciling the competing genres, philosophies, and cultural traditions his poem represents than with exploring the sensation of potential itself that characterizes the effort.

In this way, *Parlement,* especially the scene beneath the gate, conceptualizes poetic invention in terms of affective movements, presenting moments of affective occurrence and inventional discovery—that is, in Middle English, *fyndyng*—emerging simultaneously. Movement in the poem does not simply become a metaphor for a rhetorical process of topical invention—that is, an allegory for moving among possible topics, for example—but also functions literally, as a flash of the action of poetic emergence, a felt gesture toward the always imminent discovery of the "som thyng" of invention. As it is articulated in *Parlement,* then, poetic invention includes the forces implicit in the term *inventio* as a sudden coming-upon, forces that resonate alongside those of the narrator's experience amid the "adamauntes," pulled and pushed toward "som thyng": a moment of unstructured potentiality, emergent discovery, an event of *fyndyng*.

What my reading I hope conveys is that when Chaucer discusses the process of poetic invention in this highly explicit scene of poetic making, he does so by presenting invention in a way that emphasizes potential and a sense of becoming. This sense is achieved in the poem by linking via narrative a process in which initial, indescribable affective occurrences (like the startled stasis at the gate) transform into recognizable emotions, and in which the energies that precede formal poetic invention transform into the more stable mental constructs that mark the formal beginnings of the generation of poetry. The final promise of discovery that concludes the poem, the active and hopeful quest to find some way of faring better, then explicitly links this dual process of affective and inventional transformation to a world of social reality, suggesting, however nebulously, that the narrative representation of how affect becomes emotion and invention becomes poetry is a crucial part of coming to understand how to live in the world. This complex, doubled exploration, I want to argue, characterizes Chaucer's consideration of invention throughout his poetic career, and examining it is the subject of this book.

A similar scene of paradoxically fixed mobility punctuates a transitional moment in Book 1 of Gower's *Vox Clamantis,* as the dreaming narrator, on the run from legions of metamorphosing *rustici* or *vulgari* (as Gower variously refers to them) storming London, finds himself momentarily stuck in the middle of the road. In this *visio,* apparently appended to the rest of the *Vox* only after the events of the Rising of 1381,[8] the narrator sees field workers transforming into beasts, marching into the streets of London-as-*Troia nova,* and attacking the city and its inhabitants. Panicked at their murder of the archbishop, he flees the city for harsh wilderness and is eventually rescued by a ship that fluctuates between being a sailing vessel and the Tower of London. Onboard, he hears of the defeat of the rebels and the death of their leader, and he disembarks at the "Isle of Brutus"—that is, Britain itself—a place whose diverse ethnic population is always divided against itself. Despairing yet again, he is finally calmed by a voice that commands him to write down what he has dreamed. He wakes and does so.

The scene just before the narrator's rescue by the ship—describing how he "ran away across alien fields and became a stranger in the wild woodlands"[9]—is depicted as a narrative moment alive with the narrator's affective experiences of terror but also sensations of movement and emergence that characterize the world beyond the narrator's interiority. Relating a cascading historical present whose outcome, in the fiction of the dream at least, is completely uncertain, the narrator's account creates the impression of a ceaselessly unfolding, never fully coalescing emergence of event in its figuration of the metamorphosis of the *vulgari* and in the way in which traditional structures of meaning—especially allegory and "historical" precedent—are shown to be inadequate for understanding and even representing the situation of the present.[10] The field workers, for example, become not only animals or animal-

---

8. For a discussion of the composition and transmission histories of the *Vox,* see Maria Wickert, *Studies in John Gower,* trans. Robert J. Meindl (Washington, DC: University Press of America, 1981), 1–26. The rift between the dream vision of the Rising and the rest of the estates satire has also been ascribed to the shocking nature of the events it describes. Gower, as R. F. Yeager argues, must have suddenly found himself "overtaken by events of the sort he had hoped, through his writing, to ward off"; for Yeager, "that Gower would 'change his plan' to comment directly on these events is less surprising than that he should stick unwaveringly to it as the chickens came home to roost" (*John Gower's Poetic: The Search for a New Arion* [Cambridge: D. S. Brewer, 1990], 204).

9. "Tuncque domum propriam linquens aliena per arua / Transcurri, que feris saltibus hospes eram." All quotations from Gower's Latin poetry are from *The Latin Works,* vol. 4 of *The Complete Works of John Gower,* ed. G. C. Macaulay (Oxford: Clarendon Press, 1899-1902). English translations are by Eric W. Stockton, *The Major Latin Works of John Gower* (Seattle: University of Washington Press, 1962), with my revisions. Parenthetical citations refer to book and line numbers in Macaulay and page numbers in Stockton, here, 1381–82; 80.

10. Andrew Galloway argues that in the *visio* Gower clearly demonstrates the inadequacy of supposedly straightforward historical exemplarity. Instead, Gower's "vigorous and relentless use of historical antecedents does not seek simply to show historical alignments; rather he remains acutely conscious of the differences between the contexts of his source texts and of his own narrative." For Galloway, this historical perspective helps Gower "define his own authority

human hybrids but also entities whose final physical form never seems to be fixed but instead is always in flux. "They who had been men of reason before" now "had the look of unreasoning brutes," the narrator reports,[11] but the transformation does not end there: men who were now oxen nevertheless "did not remember [their] own nature" as oxen, and Nature "forsook their transformed shapes and had caused the oxen to be like monsters."[12] Likewise, for people who had transformed into swine, "Nature wandered so far from her regular course that a pig did not keep to the behavior of a pig, but rather of a wolf."[13] Gower's kinetically unstable allegory ruptures the representational commonplace of rendering peasants as animals, resulting in doubled narrative process—one literal and physically perceptible by the narrator, the other metapoetic and occurring at the level of allegorical representation—that flushes the narrative of the *visio* with an overbearing feeling of unceasing and radically unstructured movement.

Similarly, the London-as-New-Troy allegory shifts unsettlingly, as Gower's representation of the city and its components flutters between Trojan and fourteenth-century referents. John of Gaunt and the Savoy, for example, are not portrayed through Trojan analogues; instead, Lancaster is the "longum castrum"—the "long camp" or "march" that "did not know which path to take"—and the Savoy the "via salua"—the "safe way" that now "burned fiercely in flames."[14] When the Londoners do become Trojan, the analogy is as unfixed as the field workers' physical forms. Archbishop Sudbury, for example, is only

---

outside of the traditions he so massively invokes" in the *Vox* ("Gower in His Most Learned Role and the Peasants' Revolt of 1381," *Mediaevalia* 16 [1993]: 336).

11. "Qui fuerant homines prius innate racionis, / Brutorum species irracionis habent" (177–78; 54).

12. ". . . set bouis ipsum / Constat naturam non meminisse suam" (293–94; 56); "Sic transformatas formas natura reliquit, / Et monstris similes fecerat esse boues" (253–54; 56).

13. "Deuia natura sic errat ab ordine, mores / Porcus quod porci non habet, immo lupi" (319–20; 57). Others have also noted the multiplicity of the peasants' change: Steven Justice, *Writing and Rebellion: England in 1381* (Berkeley: University of California Press, 1994), calls the peasants' transformation "a horrible double metamorphosis" (208). Kim Zarins, "From Head to Foot: Syllabic Play and Metamorphosis in Book I of Gower's *Vox Clamantis*," in *On John Gower: Essays at the Millennium*, ed. R. F. Yeager (Kalamazoo, MI: Medieval Institute Press, 2007), 144–60, notes how Gower takes the metamorphoses a step beyond Ovid, from people to animals to hybrid monsters: "His peasants change not once but twice, which allows Gower to contrast a more conventional metamorphosis with the monstrous one that is arguably the main focus of the book" (144). The peasants gain agency and identity through this play in Gower's version of events (150–51): Gower "metaphorically casts the peasants as destructive manipulators of language" (152). See also Wickert, 35–36.

14. "Que via salua fuit, furit ignibus impetuosa, / Quo longum castrum ductile nescit iter" (929–30; 70). See Stockton, 356n7, who argues, based on Macaulay's hesitant speculation, that Gower surely refers to Lancaster here.

for a moment "the high priest Helenus, who served Troy's Palladium at the altar," before becoming another Thomas Becket, murdered in his church, until the narrator finally collapses on a heap of unsatisfactory allusions: "O who knows of such infamies in time past to be compared to the deeds which are mirrored in the Primate's murder?"[15] The lack of stable allegory narrates how poetic and social structures break down simultaneously, how each informs and impinges on the other. The narrative of his vision is woven out of lines borrowed from Ovid,[16] yet events replace *auctores* as the authoritative signposts of historical meaning: "Even Nestor's years do not know of the commission of such a crime."[17] Galloway argues that the "bookish style" of the *visio* "creates 'history' by providing the temporal depth of source texts against which attentive and knowledgeable readers can chart a range of possible historical correspondences and differences" in the narrative context of a specific historical event.[18] Yet Gower's rendering of this allegory-in-flux provides no stable system of allegorical referentiality, and the result is the sensation of movement and of occupying a narrative moment amid an extended and seemingly unceasing process of transformation.

It is in the rush of this complex intershifting of unfolding eventuality and the apparent sudden irrelevance of historical and literary precedent that the narrator finds himself faltering in his movement and, like the *Parlement*'s

---

15. "O qui palladium Troie seruabat ab ara, / Helenus Antistes" (1.1001–2; 72); "O proba transacto quis tempore talia noulit, / Que necis in speculo presulis acta patent?" (1105–6; 74). Galloway notes that Sudbury also becomes a Christ figure ("Gower in His Most Learned Role," 335). See Galloway's discussion of the precedents for Sudbury's murder (335–36).

16. Critics now generally agree that Gower's interlacing of Ovidian quotations is purposeful and contributes meaningfully to a larger poetic vision. R. F. Yeager, "Did Gower Write Cento?" in *John Gower: Recent Readings*, ed. R. F. Yeager (Kalamazoo, MI: Medieval Institute, 1989), 113–32, argues that Gower might have modeled his use of Ovid on the *Cento Virgilianus* of A. Faltonia Proba, both through the work's popularity and through reference to her and the form in Isidore and Boccaccio. Galloway argues that Gower's use of Ovid here "is unusual, if not unique" ("Gower in His Most Learned Role," 343). Eve Salisbury sees a cultural logic of monstrosity operating in Gower's *cento* composition method as a whole, arguing that as "Gower's monster," the *Vox* "recombin[es] fragments from Ovid and others" in a way that "startles and instructs simultaneously" ("Remembering Origins: Gower's Monstrous Body Poetic," in *Re-Visioning Gower*, ed. R. F. Yeager [Asheville, NC: Pegasus Press, 1998], 162). For Maura Nolan, Gower's Ovidian allusions import material and affective experience as a countermeasure to the authoritative generic structures of estates satire and prophecy that shape the *Vox* and *visio*, and they allow Gower to establish, via the aesthetic field they construct, links between himself, his readers, and the larger community his poetry attempts to restore ("The Poetics of Catastrophe: Ovidian Allusion in Gower's *Vox Clamantis*," in *Medieval Latin and Middle English Literature: Essays in Honour of Jill Mann*, ed. Christopher Cannon and Maura Nolan [Cambridge: D. S. Brewer, 2011], 113–33).

17. "Tale patrasse malum non norunt Nestoris anni" (1109; 74).

18. Galloway, "Gower in His Most Learned Role," 332.

narrator, articulating a new kind of inventional poetics. "Hoc michi solliciti certissima causa timoris," the narrator reports in one of many declarations of the emotional effects of his dream experience: "This was to me the most certain cause of anxious fear."[19] Siân Echard shows that Gower's "anxiety about his poetic voice and its political dimensions" is "an anxiety he kept throughout his poetic career,"[20] and Maura Nolan discovers in these passages of personal feeling woven from Ovidian allusions a reference to Arion, whose poetics "will offer to readers a participatory relationship, one in which the poet's experience is shared in order to create points of connection between the narratorial 'I' and individual readers."[21] In addition to conjuring the artistic figure whose poetics Gower would elaborate later in the Prologue of the *Confessio Amantis*, the "anxious fear" experienced by the dreaming narrator leads to Gower's first expression of what would become the explicit methodology of his poetic project in the *Confessio*: the poetics of the *middel weie*. "My steps wandered," he writes, lost amid a forest of Ovidian phrases, "and my lips were silent; my eye was struck with amazement and my ear was in pain; my heart trembled and my hair stood stiffly on end."[22] Then he explains, "Si qua parte michi magnis expediens foret ire, / Perstetit in media pes michi sepa via"—"Even if it were more expedient for me to go somewhere, my foot often stood fixed in the middle way."[23] Here, in an earlier form in the *Vox*, the *media via*—the middle way—emerges alongside the narrator's anxious worry.[24] Later, in the Prologue of the *Confessio*, Gower will figure the *media via* as a path between

---

19. 1373; 79. In addition to meaning "anxious," Gower's adjective *sollicitus* also carries with it connotations of unceasing motion.

20. Siân Echard, "Gower's 'bokes of Latin': Language, Politics, and Poetry," *Studies in the Age of Chaucer* 25 (2003): 128. Echard sees Gower's attitude toward language, both Latin and vernacular, as one of "genuine anxiety" (134).

21. Nolan, "Poetics of Catastrophe," 126; the allusion to Ovid's Arion occurs in lines 1771–74. Others have seen in the *visio* a similar nexus of emotion and participation: see, for example, Galloway, who argues that the *visio* prefigures "the more metaphysical or 'psychological' focuses" of the *Confessio* and represents one of Gower's first forays into imaginative literature ("Gower at His Most Learned," 329); and Matthew W. Irvin, who argues that Gower's "clerkly readers are motivated by his affective poetry not merely to seek wisdom, but to apply their prudence, through advice, to action" (*The Poetic Voices of John Gower: Politics and Personae in the* Confessio Amantis [Cambridge: D. S. Brewer, 2014], 43; see 37–43). Both Nolan and Galloway see the *visio* as a transition point in Gower's poetic career that moves finally to the richly complex treatments that constitute the *Confessio*.

22. "Pes vagat osque silet, oculus stupet et dolet auris, / Cor timet et rigide diriguere come" (1.1393–94; 80).

23. 1399–1400; 80.

24. In her analysis of Gower's grammatical play, Zarins argues that the metamorphosed peasants "not only swap their *pedes* for better ones; they cause the narrator's feet, metrical and physical, to stumble" ("From Head to Foot," 156).

two kinds of narrative: "I wolde go the middel weie," he writes, "And wryte a bok betwen the tweie, / Somwhat of lust, somewhat of lore" (17–19). While it describes an approach to narrative content and register, the *middel weie* also encapsulates a poetics of movement and potentiality at work throughout the *Confessio* and one that also imagines how, like Chaucer's *Parlement*, the work of poetic invention and the felt realities of emotional experience intersect to suggest ways of living in the world. Gower's articulation in the *Vox* of this poetics that will later organize the whole of the *Confessio* emerges alongside his narrator's *timor sollicitus* within an unstable narrative field characterized by flux, movement, transformation, and emergence. Moreover, his experience at the end of the *visio*, washed up on the shore of the Isle of Brutus and receiving from an old man a brief history lesson of the island and its diverse peoples, demonstrates not only that internal discord is, for Gower at least, the chief criterion of England as a historically imagined geopolitical entity but also that Gower's poetry itself is somehow present at that very moment of historical origin, somehow constitutive of the discordant historical reality that his own poetry will, once he "returns" to his own present in the fourteenth century, take as its ostensible subject matter.[25]

Parlement and the *Vox* are, of course, radically different poems, but both locate their discussions of inventional emergence—that is, of the explicit representation of things about to come into being, about to emerge—in the physical bodies of dreaming narrators who are overwhelmed by emotion and find themselves suddenly immobilized in narrative settings characterized by unceasing motion. Chaucer's "som thyng for to fare / The bet" and Gower's *media via* conceptualize *inventio* as an extended and indeterminate process of *fyndyng* in the broadest sense, one that involves not only source texts and emotional experiences, particularly those dictated by the erotic discourses of court poetry and culture, generic conventions of the dream vision, and the traditions of morally and ethically instructive poetry, but also more nebulous affective emergences that generate those experiences and the sudden and unexpected movements inherent in processes of *inventio*, of *fyndyng*. In examining this broader formulation of invention, I attempt in this book to demonstrate some of the links in the poetry of Chaucer and Gower between the processes of invention and affective experience, seeking to understand better how the emergent qualities of each inform the other. For both writers, gestures toward what I term "the affect of invention" are momentary and fleeting,

---

25. Echard argues that this moment in the *Vox* shows Gower asserting that his multilingual poetic career "suits him, then, to speak to his nation—a nation that is mixed, and still in search of the mutual love necessary to bind it" ("Gower's 'bokes of Latin,'" 155).

but they posit, however tentatively, ways in which the emergence of poetry coalesces with the discourses and patterns that construct cultural understanding and that, for all intents and purposes, make reality. Both Chaucer and Gower locate the productively transformative potential of poetry—its ability to somehow affect people and the historical points in which they live—in moments of inventional emergence.

AFFECT, INVENTION, AND THE AFFECT OF INVENTION

As I hope is evidenced by these brief close readings, while I am interested in Chaucer's and Gower's representations of emotional experiences, I use the term "affect" not as a synonym or near-synonym for emotion, passion, or desire, but as a term relating much more broadly to the kinds of indefinite sensations of movement, intensity, and emergence described in recent work by social and cultural theorists building on Deleuzian and Guattarian considerations of affect, as well as Eve Kosofsky Sedgwick's work on the embodied "texture" of affective occurrences.[26] I am most interested in condensing, from the various permutations of affect and emotion that constitute what Pansy Duncan calls the subfield of "feeling theory," ideas of imminence, emergence, and movement as a way of understanding Chaucer's and Gower's conceptualizations of poetic invention.[27] As Eric Shouse succinctly describes it, affect is "a non-conscious experience of intensity [and] a moment of unformed and unstructured potential."[28] The term thus refers not only to the neuropsychological processes of individual brains and bodies (that is, to an embodied, post-Cartesian notion of processes of emotion and cognition) but also to the intersubjective and nonhuman networks that comprise the habits, practices, and engagements of everyday life in which feeling, sensation, and movement are essential parts of living in an always-emerging present moment. "Affect" is distinct from "emotion," then, and refers to the "intensity" that precedes what is only later cognitively understood and expressed as feeling or emotion. In his frequently cited work on affect, Brian Massumi studies the affective processes that occur between the body and the mind in the micro-moments

---

26. Eve Kosofsky Sedgwick, *Touching Feeling: Affect, Pedagogy, Performativity* (Durham, NC: Duke University Press, 2003).

27. Pansy Duncan, "Taking the Smooth with the Rough: Texture, Emotion, and the Other Postmodernism," *PMLA* 129 (2014): 205. Duncan is interested in locating evidence of emotional investment in the ostensibly unemotional work of postmodern theorists of aesthetics.

28. Eric Shouse, "Feeling, Emotion, Affect," *M/C Journal* 8 (2005), <http://journal.media-culture.org.au/0512/03-shouse.php>.

that precede the recognition of affective experience *as* affective experience. Affects, Massumi argues, are registered autonomically, in breathing and heart rate, and ensuing "depth reactions" involve both body and mind: "Modulations of heartbeat and breathing mark a reflux of consciousness into the autonomic depths, coterminous with a rise of the autonomic into consciousness. They are a conscious-autonomic mix, a measure of their participation in one another."[29] This intensity is never fully registered through cognition; rather, "it is only when the idea of the affection is doubled by *an idea of the idea of the affection* that it attains the level of conscious reflection."[30] Appropriately, then, affect is neither fully bodily nor fully transcendent; it is "not directly accessible to experience," Massumi writes, but "it is not exactly outside experience either. It is immanent to it—always in it but not of it."[31] In the framework sketched by Massumi, "emotion is qualified intensity."[32] It is the almost instantaneous and internal act of narrating (remembering, perhaps fictionalizing) the experience of affect, but *not* the affect itself. For Massumi, emotion is "the most intense" form of the "*capture*" of affect.[33]

"There is no single, generalizable theory of affect," Gregory J. Seigworth and Melissa Gregg write, but it can be said that affect "arises in the midst of *in-between-ness*: in the capacities to act and be acted upon." It is "found in those intensities that pass body to body (human, nonhuman, part-body, otherwise), in those resonances that circulate about, between, and sometimes stick to bodies and worlds, *and* in the very passages or variations between these intensities and resonances themselves."[34] It is, as Ruth Leys summarizes in her recent critique of "the turn to affect," "the name for what eludes form,

---

29. Brian Massumi, *Parables for the Virtual: Movement, Affect, Sensation* (Durham, NC: Duke University Press, 2002), 25.
30. Ibid., 31.
31. Ibid., 33.
32. Ibid., 28. For a useful survey of the differences between affects, as conceptualized by Silvan Tomkins, and Freudian "drives," see Sedgwick, 19–21.
33. Massumi, 35; emphasis in original. For helpful summaries of this view of affect as potential and intensity, see also Deborah Gould, "On Affect and Protest," in *Political Emotions*, ed. Janet Staiger, Ann Cvetkovich, and Ann Reynolds (New York: Routledge, 2010), 25–28, and Ruth Leys, "The Turn to Affect: A Critique," *Critical Inquiry* 37 (2011), 436–43. Part of Massumi's project is to define being in terms of becoming, to offer a more dynamic and promising structure by which to understand identity and culture than is provided by older (historicist) models of positioning people on grids of power and discourse.
34. Gregory J. Seigworth and Melissa Gregg, "An Inventory of Shimmers," in *The Affect Theory Reader*, ed. Melissa Gregg and Gregory J. Seigworth (Durham, NC: Duke University Press, 2010), 3, 1; emphasis in original. See Seigworth and Gregg for an excellent, if necessarily emergent, definition of what affect means across a number of disciplines and a categorization of "orientations" or approaches to affect (1–9).

cognition, and meaning," the "subliminal affective intensities and resonances that so decisively influence or condition our political and other beliefs," and what Duncan labels "a mobile, organic, nonsubjective, and noninterpretive mode of feeling."[35] Citing André Green's characterization of affect as "a metapsychological category spanning what's internal and external to subjectivity," Lauren Berlant argues that the study of affect examines a field far broader than just neuropsychological activity and opportunities for political control: "the moment of the affective turn brings us back to the encounter of what is sensed with what is known and what has impact in a new but also recognizable way."[36] The "activity" of affect, as she puts it, "saturates the corporeal, intimate, and political performances of adjustment that make a shared atmosphere something palpable and, in its patterning, releases to view a poetics, a theory-in-practice of how a world works."[37] Indeed, the "unfixed and polygenerative" state of affect that is "bursting with potential," as sociologist Deborah Gould describes it,[38] also becomes a means through which forms of social repression are made not only to seem natural but to feel that way as well, and cultural and social theorists locate in the study of affect a potential for new forms of agency.[39] It also invites entry into what Sedgwick calls "a conceptual realm that

---

35. Leys, 450, 436; Duncan, 205. Leys's critique centers on some theorists' apparent rejection of the very cognitive methods used to construct their arguments and their slipping into the same reason–passion, mind–body binaries their work purports to explode. Patricia Ticineto Clough broadly defines affect in terms of its application to the social sciences as referring "generally to bodily capacities to affect and be affected or the augmentation or diminution of a body's capacity to act, to engage, and to connect, such that autoaffection is linked to the self-feeling of being alive—that is, aliveness or vitality" ("Introduction," in *The Affective Turn: Theorizing the Social,* ed. Patricia Ticineto Clough and Jean Halley [Durham, NC: Duke University Press, 2007], 2).

36. Lauren Berlant, *Cruel Optimism* (Durham, NC: Duke University Press, 2011), 16, 53.

37. Ibid., 16. Berlant's project works to understand the present moment from within that moment, the present as affective emergence. Hers "is a kind of proprioceptive history, a way of thinking about represented norms of bodily adjustment as key to grasping the circulation of the present as a historical and affective sense" (20).

38. Gould, 26.

39. Sara Ahmed, for example, demonstrates how dominant cultures erase the ways in which affects become assigned—"stuck"—to particular people or groups in order to define them in terms of the other (*The Cultural Politics of Emotion* [New York: Routledge, 2004], 11–12). Teresa Brennan has shown how such affective "dumping" has in particular shaped the West's view of the feminine in terms of masculinist narratives (*The Transmission of Affect* [Ithaca, NY: Cornell University Press, 2004], 6). Ahmed focuses on the discourses that enable these processes of "erasure" and becoming "stuck" (11). Brennan argues that affects are biologically and chemically transmittable between individuals independently of the "linguistic and visual content, meaning the thoughts" subsequently attached to them (7). For Brennan, the acknowledgement of the biochemical realities of affective transmission "liberates" subjects "scientifically" and "physically" by encouraging means of healing and extending consciousness (95). In this way, realizing the processes by which these sorts of erasures and assignments occur—and, moreover, how

is not shaped by lack nor by commonsensical dualities of subject versus object or of means versus ends."[40]

What Berlant describes as a "poetics" of world making and living involves both preconscious affective movements and historical forces: "Laws, norms, and events shape imaginaries, but in the middle of the reproduction of life people make up modes of being and responding to the world that altogether constitute what gets called 'visceral response' and intuitive intelligence."[41] For Berlant, then, this "intuitive intelligence" or "intuition" manifests as a sort of sudden, preconscious invention characterized by potential emerging into forms, the origin of which typically goes unnoticed by the inventor. This notion of the manifestation of affect—as something that is embodied, pre-emotional, pre-cognitive, and conceptualized in terms of movement, emergence, and becoming that informs the formation of intuitive practices for getting through life—suggests an analogous relationship to the activities of poetic invention. Indeed, poetic invention functions similarly: its processes deal with existing and imagined forms, with texts already written and those arranged in the mind. Like affect, however, invention is also about imaginative potential and about the energies leading to discovery—their movements and Deleuzian "lines of flight," the "shift in thought happening to the writer" that is only later captured as writing,[42] and that occur between, but not necessarily in, the narratives that inform or even inspire invention.[43] Indeed, the significance that Kathleen Stewart sees in affects—lying in "the intensities they build and in what thoughts and feelings they make possible," and "where they might go and what potential modes of knowing, relating, and attending to things are already somehow present in them in a state of potentiality and resonance"—is also what is significant about invention.[44] Berlant's "activity" of affect reverberates in this formulation of the activity of invention. Affect and invention overlap in their existence as felt potential, and in, as Stewart puts it, the impression that "*something* throws itself together in a moment as an event and a sensation;

---

affects may be manipulated by those in power to generate forms of control through precognitive means—is, for some theorists, nothing short of liberating.

40. Sedgwick, 21.

41. Berlant, 53.

42. Clough, 14.

43. This image of invention as potential shares characteristics of what Nicholas Watson calls the "threats" and "energetic potentialities" of medieval concepts of the imagination ("The Phantasmal Past: Time, History, and the Recombinative Imagination," *Studies in the Age of Chaucer* 32 [2010]: 13), a prime metaphor for which is Chaucer's *House of Fame* (13–18). I take up Watson's reading later in chapter 1.

44. Kathleen Stewart, *Ordinary Affects* (Durham, NC: Duke University Press, 2007), 3.

a something both animated and inhabitable"[45]—perhaps even, as the narrator of *Parlement* might put it, the sudden discovery of "som thyng for to fare / The bet."

By considering affect in terms of potential, movement, and emergence, I aim also to redirect the discussion of affect from more typical uses of that term in medieval studies, in which affect often becomes a synonym for emotional experience more generally or desire more specifically. As such, my consideration of affect diverges from important recent studies in the history of emotion and the ways in which emotional understandings and performances build both communities and subjectivities, as in the work of Barbara H. Rosenwein, as well as that of Sarah McNamer, who traces the development of emotion "scripts" in medieval spiritual writing; my study differs too from work on the literary representation of emotional experience, such as that of Guillemette Bolens.[46] This book, of course, builds on those studies, as well as on recent work that attempts to develop affective models for engaging with texts and discourses of the past, to which the writing of Carolyn Dinshaw and L. O. Aranye Fradenburg remains vital, and I engage with their work in the chapters that follow.[47] I also want to direct recent work on the concept of

---

45. Ibid., 1; emphasis in original. Indeed, the pursuit of this "something" in both senses of Berlant's "poetics"—that is, how a poem works and the ways in which people intuitively work through an always-emerging, unfolding present life—leads many theorists back to what we might call the "literary" as the means of pursuit: Massumi, for example, advocates the short narrative form of the "parable" or "example" as the method of inquiry and academic discourse (18, 21); Stewart writes short, narrative essays to produce a "contact zone for analysis" (5); and Berlant analyzes aesthetic representations of "situations" and "impasses" (4–5).

46. Barbara H. Rosenwein, *Emotional Communities in the Early Middle Ages* (Ithaca, NY: Cornell University Press, 2006); for a discussion of both the importance and challenges of tracing the history of emotions in the Middle Ages, especially working to recover the emotional content typically neglected in historical narratives more generally, see especially the Introduction and chapter 1. Sarah McNamer, *Affective Meditation and the Invention of Medieval Compassion* (Philadelphia: University of Pennsylvania Press, 2010); for a summary of emotional scripting, see Keith Oatley and Jennifer M. Jenkins, *Understanding Emotions* (Oxford: Blackwell, 1996), 98–124. See also the important work of the Australian Research Council Centre of Excellence for the History of Emotions, <www.historyofemotions.org.au>. Guillemette Bolens, *The Style of Gestures: Embodiment and Cognition in Literary Narrative* (Baltimore: Johns Hopkins University Press, 2012); Bolens analyzes "kinesis" in literary works and argues that the representation of emotion and gesture comprises the key linkage between texts and readers. My study does share with Bolens's an emphasis on the affective event: Bolens writes that the "elicitation and manifestation of an emotion constitute an intersubjective and progressive *event*, not a circumscribed reifiable and static *object*" (44; emphasis in original).

47. See especially Carolyn Dinshaw, *Chaucer's Sexual Poetics* (Madison: University of Wisconsin Press, 1989), and *Getting Medieval: Sexualities and Communities, Pre- and Postmodern* (Durham, NC: Duke University Press, 1999); and L. O. Aranye Fradenburg, *Sacrifice Your Love: Psychoanalysis, Historicism, Chaucer* (Minneapolis: University of Minnesota Press, 2002); "Beauty and Boredom in *The Legend of Good Women*," *Exemplaria* 22 (2010): 65–83; and "Living

the event in medieval literature to a more focused consideration of invention. J. Allan Mitchell, for example, has recently shown how medieval notions of Fortune "give conceptual priority to the singularity of the *event*" and emphasize the sense of "the immanence of events" and "potentiality" as an aspect of the understanding of an ethical subject;[48] I want to turn the direction of such examinations "back" to a study of fictions of poetic origins to understand how such ethical potentialities are expressed as an aspect of poetic invention. My overall project of redirecting such diverse (if related) critical approaches as these consists in studying how Chaucer and Gower conceptualize invention in particular; doing so, I will argue, reveals how these poets' own investigations of how cultural discourses shape experience are bound up in the very action of poetic invention.

Consequently, I work in this book to broaden the understanding of medieval invention to refer not only to formal processes that characterize rhetorical poetics but also to the sensations of movement and emergence that precede and impel those processes. By "movement," then, I refer not to the rhetorical power of a text to somehow "move"—that is, persuade or influence—an audience, or simply to the Aristotelian notion of emotions as "movements" of the soul, but rather to the necessarily unrepresentable processes of emergence commonly discussed in studies of affect, acknowledging sensations of movement and emergence as inherent components of inventional activity.[49] By the

---

Chaucer," *Studies in the Age of Chaucer* 33 (2011): 41–64. Nicholas Watson's recent efforts to posit alternative forms of engagement with the past based on empathy and imagination draw in part on the work of Caroline Walker Bynum; see especially "Phantasmal Past," and "Desire for the Past," *Studies in the Age of Chaucer* 21 (1999): 59–97. My focus is also different from recent studies of how classical and early medieval formulations of desire, emotion, and ethics develop through the later Middle Ages. See especially Robert R. Edwards, *The Flight from Desire: Augustine and Ovid to Chaucer* (New York: Palgrave, 2006); Jessica Rosenfeld, *Ethics and Enjoyment in Late Medieval Poetry: Love after Aristotle* (Cambridge: Cambridge University Press, 2011).

48. J. Allan Mitchell, *Ethics and Eventfulness in Middle English Literature* (New York: Palgrave, 2009), 3; emphasis in original. Mitchell works to recover the sense of eventuality and emergence that characterizes classical and medieval notions of Fortune, and he interprets eventuality in the Middle Ages in a way that registers several of the issues noted above by affect theory: "That events are not just facts in the objective order but rather significant moral pressures, cognitive possibilities, and emotional affects, could be said to represent the general picture medieval thinkers inherited from Aristotle and Boethius" (20); for love especially as an "affective force" for late medieval writers, see 6. Mitchell also deftly summarizes the sense of "belatedness" shared by much modern thinking about the event: as he puts it, "To speak of the event is already to say too much, too late" (25), and, moreover, "Events amount to the coming to pass of what has been; literary form is future-tending in this way" (26). See 11–26 for a consideration of how modern theories of the event relate to medieval philosophical considerations of Fortune.

49. For a recent analysis of persuasive movement involving emotional appeals in late-medieval English interpretations of Aristotle's *Rhetoric*, see Rita Copeland, "*Pathos* and Pastoralism: Aristotle's *Rhetoric* in Medieval England," *Speculum* 89 (2014): 96–127.

fourteenth century, invention was a well-developed theoretical and practical concept, and medieval texts about invention were essentially derived from Cicero's "rhetorics," the *De inventione* and the *Rhetorica ad Herennium*, which was attributed to him. In these, *inventio* meant quite simply looking for things in terms of "topics": as Cicero explains in the *Topica*, "that is the name given by Aristotle to the 'regions,' as it were, from which arguments are drawn."[50] "From Aristotle onwards," as Rita Copeland puts it, "the task of finding something to say is constituted mainly through a system of logical inquiry."[51] Intended originally for the creation of arguments to be used in various loci of Roman public life, this conceptualization of invention provided a framework onto which medieval writers grafted methods of poetic invention. Typically understood as a component of medieval rhetorical poetics, invention is traditionally traced in modern scholarship along a well-rehearsed trajectory from classical and early medieval sources (especially Boethius), then to the *artes poetriae*—the twelfth- and thirteenth-century "arts of poetry and prose" that variously instruct students on how to compose poetry, letters, and sermons— and finally to the work of French, Italian, and English vernacular poets.[52]

While it was once believed that invention as a theoretical concept essentially disappeared in the Middle Ages in favor of imitation and augmentation,[53] recent scholarship has shown that discussions of invention in fact shifted focus from the social, juridical, and political environs that defined classical rhetoric onto the texts themselves (and their commentaries), as well as onto the individuated experiences of writers *as* writers. For example, in her analyses of the artificial structures for thinking and remembering that defined

---

50. "enim appellatae ab Aristotele sunt eae quasi sedes e quibus argumenta promuntur." All references to Cicero are to *De inventione, De optimo genere oratorum, Topica*, ed. and trans. H. M. Hubbell (1949; repr. Cambridge, MA: Harvard University Press, 1993), 1.2.7, pp. 386–87.

51. Rita Copeland, *Rhetoric, Hermeneutics, and Translation in the Middle Ages* (Cambridge: Cambridge University Press, 1991), 151.

52. Copeland charts the development of concepts of invention from antiquity through the *artes poetriae* of the Middle Ages (*Rhetoric, Hermeneutics, and Translation*, 151–78); I discuss her important work in more detail below. See also James J. Murphy, *Rhetoric in the Middle Ages: A History of Rhetorical Theory from Saint Augustine to the Renaissance* (Berkeley: University of California Press, 1974). The most thorough survey of the medieval *artes poetriae* is Douglas Kelly, *The Arts of Poetry and Prose*, Typologie des Sources du Moyen Age Occidental 59 (Turnhout: Brepols, 1991); Kelly coins the phrase "arts of poetry and prose" as a more inclusive (and accurate) term for the *artes poetriae*.

53. In an important early study of Chaucer's rhetorical poetics, Robert O. Payne traces the supposed disappearance of *inventio* from the regimen of medieval poetics, arguing the medieval "revision" of the classical system of rhetoric "shows first of all the tremendous decrease in importance of that component which the modern critic would probably consider the most transferable from rhetoric to poetic—*inventio*" (*The Key of Remembrance: A Study of Chaucer's Poetics* [New Haven: Yale UP, 1963], 43).

medieval practices of organizing texts, thought, and experience, especially in religious contexts and communities, Mary Carruthers shows how invention as a method of finding and discovering, at least in terms of conscious efforts to organize information, is an implicit and central component of memory and thinking.[54] Invention, in other words, defines the way in which formal thinking and remembering happen. For the production of poetic texts specifically, *inventio* in the Middle Ages essentially came to include description, augmentation, and elaboration as well as discovering things to write about. As Douglas Kelly has shown in his important work on the medieval *artes poetriae* and French vernacular poetry, these practices of invention corresponded to the imaginative work of the writer: imagination—as a mental faculty and a location in the mind—essentially produces "images," which themselves require intellection to be understood, and the work of invention thus occurs internally, within the conscious (and unconscious) mind of the writer.[55]

This "inward" turn manifests textually as well. In her influential study of medieval practices of translation, Copeland shows how invention moves from being linked to dialectic and logical disputation (as it was in ancient rhetoric) to being an aspect of hermeneutics. Locating the origins of this transformation in Augustine, she argues that in the Middle Ages, *inventio* becomes "hermeneutical performance" or "hermeneutical action," an act of inventing material from the interpretation of source material in such a way that the text itself becomes the source for locating topics.[56] Invention is thus reformulated "as hermeneutical inquiry, as the discovery of meaning in inherited textual matter," and rhetorical praxis moves to literary interpretation, giving readers—rather than orators or writers—"the power of invention."[57] This inward, exegetical turn also obtains in the secular *artes poetriae*, which "teach the art of composition through the art of formal literary analysis," and which, by "transforming invention into a hermeneutical procedure . . . prize the ingenuity of the exegetical performance that can disguise its own moves through a consummate act of

---

54. Mary Carruthers, *The Book of Memory: A Study of Memory in Medieval Culture* (Cambridge: Cambridge University Press, 1990), and *The Craft of Thought: Meditation, Rhetoric, and the Making of Images, 400–1200* (Cambridge: Cambridge University Press, 1998). For a concise description of the role of invention in "locational memory," see *Craft of Thought*, 10–24.

55. Douglas Kelly, *Medieval Imagination: Rhetoric and the Poetry of Courtly Love* (Madison: University of Wisconsin Press, 1978), 30–31; Kelly briefly analyzes the importance of imagination to the *artes poetriae* in *The Arts of Poetry and Prose*, 64–68. I take up the relationship between affect, invention, and medieval concepts of the imagination in my discussion of Chaucer's *House of Fame* in chapter 1.

56. See *Rhetoric, Hermeneutics, and Translation*, 151–58, for Copeland's summary of this change.

57. Ibid., 222, 158.

textual appropriation."⁵⁸ This developmental trajectory culminates by the later Middle Ages in the hermeneutical performances of "secondary translation," in which vernacular texts actively work to disguise their origins as translations. In this reading, Chaucer's *Legend of Good Women* and Gower's *Confessio* consciously establish themselves as vernacular replacements for the Latin sources they displace, achieving *auctoritas* through the "vernacular appropriation of academic discourse."⁵⁹ In Copeland's schema, invention leads ultimately to replacement, the assimilation of an original text in a way that disguises the act of translation and sets up the new text as the authoritative original. Copeland refers to this process as displacement, a term I also use throughout this study. For Copeland, this term describes the replacement of a Latin or previously authoritative text by a vernacular or newer text; as will become clear in the following chapters, I use the term far less technically to refer more generally to a sense of movement—a kind of "rush" of displacement rather than a conscious act of textual appropriation—that, as I will show, many of the works of Chaucer and Gower embed thematically as an aspect of narrative structure.

In what remains the most subtle examination of the aesthetic implications of how an inward inventional turn plays out among theoretical and poetic texts in the high and late Middle Ages, Robert R. Edwards argues succinctly that "the theory of aesthetic invention is, in short, a theory of intertextuality," since, in the development of invention through Ciceronian rhetoric, Augustinian hermeneutics, and twelfth- and thirteenth-century *artes poetriae*, "imagination and reading are reciprocal functions."⁶⁰ For Edwards, poetry becomes the means by which both the ambiguous images of the imagination, and the disparity between personal experiences and "authorized systems of understanding" can be integrated into a self-consistent larger structure, thereby making them into objects that can be analyzed rationally.⁶¹ If, for Copeland, invention is an arm of authorial politics and intertextual territorialization, then for Edwards (like Kelly) it is the method by which poets transform the images of the imagination into the components of self-contained, self-sufficient, self-coherent, and self-reflexive systems, which themselves interact with the worlds of personal experience, emotion, and authoritative cultural discourses. In this way, as Edwards shows, poetry becomes an aspect of experience and a kind of knowledge.

But what exactly happens in those apparently ineffable moments that lead up to the more formal, structural processes of invention that are prescribed

---

58. Ibid., 161, 174.
59. Ibid., 3.
60. Robert R. Edwards, *Ratio and Invention: A Study of Medieval Lyric and Narrative* (Nashville: Vanderbilt University Press, 1989), 86.
61. Ibid., 74; see 34–74 for the full discussion.

so precisely in Cicero's rhetorics or the *artes poetriae*? Critics have tended to offer only cursory gestures toward these pre-inventional phenomena. Copeland notes, for example, that the "hermeneutical performance" she describes took on for medieval inventors "the character of event," as "the power of cognition and explanation unite[d] with the power of application."[62] Edwards too notes that though medieval texts on invention prescribe that "the poet intentionally imagines the conceptual architecture of his poem, . . . the 'purpose' he intends sometimes gives way in the process to chance."[63] These are the inventional analogues to the kinds of "shifts" and "activities" that modern theorists locate in the movements of affect, and it is exactly such movements that my own study seeks to explore. Though affect, as a kind of emerging potentiality, occurs outside of or before its congealment into form, imagining affect, much less representing it, requires structures of narrative, and narrative is the very indication that affect has already been transformed into something else. A similar paradox characterizes the activity of poetic invention: the artificial (that is, consciously structured and activated) strategies for organizing memory and thought more generally, and the guidance for generating poetic texts more specifically, essentially treat the aftereffects of initial inventional activity. I want to turn our attention to the sensation of emergence and potential, the notion of something becoming, something about to emerge as a form, that is also a part of invention.

It is in the concept of the *archetypus*—the "main idea," central meaning, or structural archetype that guides poetic composition, and that precedes the actual act of writing—that medieval accounts of invention come closest to discussing this pre-inventional movement. Perhaps the most well-known metaphor for the structural archetype to which all inventional activity should be directed is Geoffrey of Vinsauf's equating the work of a writer to the work of a house builder in the *Poetria nova*:

> If a man has a house to build, his impetuous hand does not rush into action. The measuring line of his mind first lays out the work, and he mentally outlines the successive steps in a definite order. The mind's hand shapes the entire house before the body's hand builds it. Its mode of being is archetypal before it is actual. Poetic art may see in this analogy the law to be given to poets: let the poet's hand not be swift to take up the pen, nor his tongue be impatient to speak; trust neither hand nor tongue to the guidance of fortune.[64]

---

62. Copeland, *Rhetoric, Hermeneutics, and Translation*, 20.
63. Edwards, *Dream of Chaucer*, 159.
64. "Si quis habet fundare domum, non currit ad actum / Impetuosa manus: intrinseca linea cordis / Praemetitur opus, seriemque sub ordine certo / Interior praescribit homo, totamque figurat / Ante manus cordis quam corporis; et status ejus / Est prius archetypus quam

This metaphor is not original to Geoffrey, and the central concept it presents is in fact a commonplace in medieval thinking about poetic production.[65] I focus here on this example, not because Chaucer cites it explicitly in his later poetry (to describe Pandarus's plotting in *Troilus and Criseyde*), but because it is now, at least, the most famous figurative representation of this kind of inventional thinking.[66] As Edwards summarizes, "Geoffrey's *archetypus* is an imaginative construct that conveys the poet's intentions and informs the aesthetic plan of the work."[67] Kelly writes that the faculty of imagination allows for "the projection in the mind, and thence into matter, of the artist's conception of the work to be written,"[68] and he shows that this formulation of invention is the result of the application of neoplatonic ideas about divine Creation to the theory of poetic invention.[69] This view of artist as creator, of course, has deep roots in medieval thinking, including expressions in Augustine, Anselm, and Bernardus Silvestris. Plato's *Timaeus* is another, which, as Kelly summarizes, establishes

> a parallel between the activities of God, Nature, and the artist. God conceives and thereby creates archetypes; Nature stamps these into matter through procreation; the artist re-creates them by invention and imitation of the images presented by Nature. . . . Artists—any artist from architect to poet—conceived of the work to be written, then planned it out carefully in his or her mind; the poet proceded [*sic*] to put the plan into words and, then,

---

sensilis. Ipsa poesis / Spectet in hoc speculo quae lex sit danda poetis. / Non manus ad calamum praeceps, non lingua sit ardens / Ad verbum: neutram manibus committe regendam / Fortunae." The Latin text is from *Les Arts Poétiques du xxe et du xxiiie siècle*, ed. Edmond Faral (Paris: Champion, 1924), 1.43–52; the translation is by Margaret F. Nims, in *Poetria Nova of Geoffrey of Vinsauf* (Toronto: Pontifical Institute of Mediaeval Studies, 1967), 16–17.

65. Kelly notes that the architectural metaphor was common before Geoffrey's famous formulation ("Theory of Composition in Medieval Narrative Poetry and Geoffrey of Vinsauf's *Poetria Nova*," *Mediaeval Studies* 31 [1969], 126); see also Rita Copeland and Ineke Sluiter, eds., *Medieval Grammar and Rhetoric: Language Arts and Literary Theory, AD 300–1475* (Oxford: Oxford University Press, 2009), 596n14.

66. For a survey of the importance of Geoffrey's treatise to Chaucer and evidence that Chaucer probably did not discover the *Poetria nova* until later in his career, see Martin Camargo, "Chaucer and the Oxford Renaissance of Anglo-Latin Rhetoric," *Studies in the Age of Chaucer* 34 (2012): 173–207.

67. Edwards, *Ratio and Invention*, 85.

68. Kelly, *Arts of Poetry and Prose*, 65.

69. This understanding of invention "derives from the adaptation of neoplatonic . . . notions of Creation and procreation to poetic creation, or invention" (ibid., 38), and while the equation of the artist with God or Nature may not be stated explicitly in the *artes poetriae*, "the image is elsewhere presented matter-of-factly and consistently enough to be considered commonplace and generally received" (55). This application, Kelly argues, is "the factor that made possible a new and coherent art of literary composition—a *poetria nova*" (56).

to clarify the words in a manner consonant with the original 'archetypal' conception.[70]

The *artes poetriae,* then, focus on how to regulate and direct inventional and imaginative energy toward the elucidation of an archetype, ultimately portraying it in terms of negation and restraint—even when they implicitly liken the creative work of the poet to that of God. Yet this very process of redirection gestures toward a powerful sense of potential, one that precedes not only the finished poems themselves but also the more formal, structured mental acts (like building an *archetypus*) of thinking about invention. Before they move on, passages like Geoffrey of Vinsauf's house-building analogy refer to something just prior to the moment of invention, obliquely conveying the potential, the movement, the sensation of what we might call inventional emergence.

Indeed, perhaps one of the most interesting aspects of Geoffrey's metaphor is how much it works to *stop* exactly this kind of movement: "If a man has a house to build," Geoffrey writes, "his impetuous hand [*impetuosa manus*] does not rush into action." What Geoffrey describes as "impetuous" is in fact the radically unstructured and pre-conscious movements of something coming together just prior to a moment of archetypal organization, the sensation of impending inventional emergence that precedes more formal inventional activity. Geoffrey's metaphor also registers this movement in the liminal space occupied by affect: it is at once embodied—the *manus* is the "impetuous" agent here—but also unfixed, since the hand is actually only one of the vehicles of the house-building metaphor. Geoffrey returns to his regulatory directive more explicitly toward the end of his treatise, when, in his section on ornamentation and style, he warns the student against moving like a *scurra,* a "buffoon":

> You know what is fitting, and you say the fitting thing, yet you may be guided by chance, not by a principle of art. You do not understand what to look for in a subject at first glance, and on what aspect to concentrate your attention; at what point you should begin applying your efforts, and what source gives rise to the adornment of words. Your mind wanders over one part after another, and your aimless steps betray a mind unsure of itself, like the steps of a blind man feeling out where or what his way is—one whose staff is his

---

70. Ibid., 65; Kelly writes, "The great medieval example of such 'recreation' was Bernardus Silvestris' *Cosmographia,* a work that displays Creation in neoplatonic images and language, with Nature and, as metaphor, the artist at work" (65).

eye and whose guide is fortune. What then? By the precepts of art you may curb your mind so that it will not wander like a buffoon.⁷¹

Geoffrey's "precepts of art," then, work to structure and redirect movements that here manifest as the excited anxieties of novice writers. This emotional manifestation becomes the affective residue of a pre-inventional movement that, if not channeled properly through formal dicta, makes the student into a bad writer (and a buffoon). The *Poetria nova* is very much about recognizing these movements and then consciously reflecting on them, training oneself to make productive poetic use of them. And while his treatise obviously concerns itself with strategies for doing just that, it also, indirectly but consistently, evokes this anterior inventional movement, gesturing toward a sense of emergence by conflating the student-writer's emotions with formal poetic figures that he or she should use to regulate the action of invention.

This kind of prescriptive instruction is of course typical of the *artes poetriae*, and it is possible to trace similar gestures toward inventional emergence in their efforts to compel student-readers to channel inventional activity along sanctioned lines.⁷² But if twelfth- and thirteenth-century *artes poetriae* work to avoid discussion of inventional movements, then the treatment of invention in English vernacular writing *does* interest itself in representing just such movements. In their influential anthology of Middle English texts that self-consciously discuss what they label a kind of "vernacular literary theory," Ruth Evans, Andrew Taylor, Nicholas Watson, and Jocelyn Wogan-Browne show that such texts, often in so-called prologues or prefaces to longer works, conceptualize aspects of poetic composition in more expansive, amorphous,

---

71. "Quid deceat nosti dicisque decentia dici, / Forte tamen casu ductus, non arte. Nec in re / Sentis quid primo visu speculeris et in quo / Praefundes studium, quis sit locus unde studendi / Anticipes cursum, quae gignat origo decorem / Verborum; sed mens hac parte vagatur et illa, / Et vaga sunt dubiae mentis vestigia, tanquam / Caeci palpantis qua vel quae sit via, cujus / Est oculus baculus et dux foruna. Quid ergo? / Arte domes animum, qui quasi scurra vagetur . . ." (Faral 4.1588–97; Nims, 72–73).

72. For example, Matthew of Vendôme had earlier described inventional movement in his *Ars versificatoria* using the same negative terms. He warns students against "stray[ing] shamefully from the path of proper doctrine," either because they are "poorly instructed," "crackbrained," or "are being misled by misleading teachers" (". . . male disciplinati solent plerumque delirare et a semita doctrinali turpiter exorbitare. . . . forsitan cum perversis doctoribus pervertuntur." Latin text of the *Ars versificatoria* from Faral, ed. [Paris: Champion, 1924], 180; translation by Roger P. Parr, *Ars versificatoria* [Milwaukee: Marquette University Press, 1981], 93). Much might also be made of the unwieldy memory system developed by John of Garland in his *Parisiana poetria*—called "garbled" and its author "confused" by Carruthers (*Book of Memory*, 123)—as he advises students to move, almost frantically, back and forth among authoritative texts, formal structures of artificial memory, and personal experience. See the discussions in Carruthers (123–26), Copeland (*Rhetoric Hermeneutics, and Translation*, 160–66), and Edwards (*Ratio and Invention*, 76–81).

noncentralized, and ultimately figurative ways. Arguing that English vernacular treatments of composition are not limited to displacing Latin authorities,[73] they show how this expansive consideration of vernacular literary self-awareness is accompanied by a sense of being "embodied" in specific social relationships between writers, readers, and texts, and "immediate" in the sense of being in "a language with immediate access to people's feelings and easily comprehensible—as Latin is not, even to those who can understand it."[74]

Robert R. Edwards and Nicolette Zeeman furthermore observe that when invention is discussed in Middle English narrative poetry, it is typically presented metaphorically and tropologically. Edwards shows that fourteenth-century vernacular narratives (*Sir Gawain and the Green Knight* and *The Squire's Tale*, for example) figuratively take up the meta-topic of invention by depositing within narrative poems metaphorical "emblems" of invention (that is, objects, characters, or discourses that, in the fiction of the text, symbolize processes of invention), and thus point to themselves as the "sources" of their own composition. Moreover, Edwards shows that the site for investigations of the nature and work of poetic invention is vernacular narrative itself, especially the "internalization of invention" that often characterizes late medieval vernacular poetry.[75] Zeeman likewise notes how such texts stage moments of discovery as a component of plot: dreaming narrators, for example, literally "find" or "discover" texts or songs within the narratives, Chaucer's *Book of the Duchess* providing one well-known example.[76] These sorts of figurative representations essentially constitute a self-conscious commonplace about the theorizing of poetic composition within English vernacular writing. In other words, when Middle English writers discuss the work of invention, they tend to do so by making figurative renderings of inventional action contingent on narrative development. The movement of invention in Middle English, then, is increasingly inseparable from the movement of narrative process.

---

73. Ruth Evans, Andrew Taylor, Nicholas Watson, and Jocelyn Wogan-Browne, "The Notion of Vernacular Theory," in *The Idea of the Vernacular*, ed. Jocelyn Wogan-Browne, Nicholas Watson, Andrew Taylor, and Ruth Evans (University Park: Pennsylvania State University Press, 1999), 314–30, argue that while the relationship between Latin and English is of course important, the treatment of "literary theory" in Middle English is "far wider" than this, and "Middle English writers were concerned with a range of more detailed theoretical issues, having to do not simply with authority but with reading and audience, instruction, pleasure and truth in history and fiction, and theories of meaning" (322).

74. Ibid., 324, 325.

75. Edwards, *Ratio and Invention*, 115.

76. Nicolette Zeeman, "Imaginative Theory," in *Middle English*, ed. Paul Strohm (Oxford: Oxford University Press, 2007), 230–35, and 230–31 in particular for English vernacular assimilations of, and alternatives to, Latinate composition practices.

A similar entrenchment within literary structures characterizes how Middle English writers tend to conceptualize form in terms of the relationship between poetic text and the *archetypus*. Christopher Cannon argues that English vernacular writing posits invention in terms of a transition from Platonic to Aristotelian views of form:

> At the border between the view that form is the idea that precedes the thing [Platonic] and the view that form is the attribute that gives things their distinctive being [Aristotelian] is a way of conceiving the process of creation or making as a movement from one of these states to the other, as the *in*forming of raw materials according to the script of some idea, as the *forming* of an object guided by some thought.[77]

Again, however, theories of composition in Middle English writing "are more usually *embedded* than stated," and "such a theory is, necessarily, more steadily present in poetic *activity*—in the making of texts and the texts themselves."[78] The difficulty in identifying and itemizing discussions of form or invention posed by Middle English texts, as Cannon notes, can be traced in part to the fact that if such discussions are systematized, then they are done so only ambiguously through the particularized narrative and figurative demands of individual works.

English vernacular poetry, especially that of the late fourteenth century, when "a developed literary consciousness" first "make[s] itself felt in Middle English writing,"[79] becomes the ideal location for exploring the ways in which affect and invention work together. More than that, though, the intermingling of affective and inventional work becomes for late-fourteenth-century English poetry a formative aspect of that poetry's aesthetic and cultural work. The kinds of formal ambiguities traced by these critics in English writing, and the kinds of motional displacements that characterize adoption and redeployment of classical rhetoric and neoplatonic thought in the *artes poetriae*, parallel what modern theorists identify as constitutive of affect itself. Form retrospectively reveals the ways in which affect has already emerged in the

---

77. Christopher Cannon, "Form," in Strohm, *Middle English*, 177; emphasis in original.

78. Ibid., 179; emphasis in original. As Cannon puts it, "The form of a Middle English text could be described as lying somewhere between what might be said about it and what it actually was" (184).

79. Kevin Brownlee, Tony Hunt, Ian Johnson, Alastair Minnis, and Nigel F. Palmer, "Vernacular Literary Consciousness c. 1100–c.1500: French, German, and English Evidence," in *The Cambridge History of Literary Criticism*, vol. 2, ed. Alastair Minnis and Ian Johnson (Cambridge: Cambridge University Press, 2005), 423.

motions of everyday life; as Seigworth and Gregg put it, there is something that "emerges, overspills, exceeds: *a form of relation* as a rhythm, a fold, a timing, a habit, a contour, or a shape [that] comes to mark the passage of intensities."[80] There is something, then, in the formal composition of Middle English texts in particular, at least as these critics approach them, that is "affective" in the sense that form must be experienced in some way (rather than prescribed as it is in formal—and Latin—treatises on composition), performed in the act of reading and relating the specific back to larger thematic ideas, in order to be detected. It is for this reason that looking at Middle English texts for an affect of invention makes sense, and for looking at Gower's and Chaucer's explorations in particular, since these two poets consciously work to explore the potential of this more ambiguous discussion of invention.

CHAUCER, GOWER, AND THE AFFECT OF INVENTION

The phrase "affect of invention" as I use it in this book, then, refers more generally to the analogous relationship of affective and inventional movement: I argue, that is, that the way in which affect emerges and "collapses" into emotion parallels the way in which invention emerges and collapses into poetic forms. Furthermore, I use the phrase "affect of invention" to refer also to the ways in which affective and inventional movement inform each other. Not only are these analogous movements, but the potential for poetry to reveal in startling ways the affectively binding power of authoritative discourses (as Chaucer's poetry does) or even to attempt to productively transform culture in an effort to somehow rejuvenate it (as Gower's poetry does) also requires aligning affective emergence with inventional emergence and showing how the world-making abilities of the latter can impinge upon those of the former. In the poetry of Chaucer and Gower that I study in this book, examining the ways in which aesthetic productions emerge through processes of invention (defined broadly, as I have explained it in this introduction) creates ways in which poetry can intervene in the discursive constructions of reality that exist outside of poetic worlds. As such, this book also joins the recent renewed interest in aesthetics and the revaluation of sensory, sensual, and nonrational ways of coming to knowledge, including, for example, Peggy A. Knapp's work explaining how "ideological intuitions [are] immanent to aesthetic effects," and Maura Nolan's careful analyses of how aesthetic form registers and regulates relationships between individual subjectivities and ideas

---

80. Seigworth and Gregg, 13; emphasis in original.

of temporality, historicity, and the divine.[81] By focusing in particular on the movements of invention, however, this book offers a new way of understanding how the poetry of Chaucer and Gower might have imagined itself impinging on cultural reality by examining the ways in which that poetry attempts to activate the transformative potential that characterizes not only affect but also the energetic processes inherent in invention.

I have chosen to focus my study on the English vernacular poetry of Chaucer and Gower in particular for several related reasons. Both writers explicitly articulate a desire to do something "more" with their poetry than fulfill the duties of courtly *makyng* (in the case of Chaucer) or offer straightforwardly moralized exemplary instruction (in the case of Gower). In their discussions of the distinction between "poets" and "makers" in the work of Chaucer, for example, Glending Olson and Lee Patterson show how Chaucer self-effacingly inserts himself into a canon of classical and continental European "poets," a strategy that, by the time Chaucer is referred to by Lydgate a generation later, has proven successful.[82] Although in a very different way, Gower—long ago rescued by critics from his stultifying "moral" label—likewise takes the ostensibly moral-ethical project of the *Confessio* and directs it at once inward and outward, not simply to generate ethical subjects who can make sound

---

81. Peggy A. Knapp, *Chaucerian Aesthetics* (New York: Palgrave, 2008), 6; Knapp continues that "a surface respect for the power of ideology blinds us to that of aesthetics, a deeper respect for it informs aesthetic effects. While ideology critique relies solely on the intelligible reduced to concept, the mode of imagination through which we respond to art calls upon the sensible and the intelligible in tandem" (8). Nolan's exploration of aesthetics spans several important essays, including "Historicism after Historicism," in *The Post-Historical Middle Ages*, ed. Elizabeth Scala and Sylvia Federico (New York: Palgrave, 2009), 63–85; "Agency and the Poetics of Sensation in Gower's *Mirour de l'Omme*," in *Answerable Style: The Idea of the Literary in Medieval England*, ed. Frank Grady and Andrew Galloway (Columbus: The Ohio State University Press, 2013), 214–43; and "The Poetics of Catastrophe," cited above. For a general description introducing theoretical methods for locating the representation of multiple temporalities within medieval texts, see Nolan, "Making the Aesthetic Turn: Adorno, the Medieval, and the Future of the Past," *Journal of Medieval and Early Modern Studies* 34 (2004): 549–75. Other important recent studies of aesthetics in medieval literature include those by Linda Tarte Holley, who charts metaphors of space and movement in her examination of how late-medieval poetry enacts a kind of movement through fields of knowing. Holley writes that "we place ourselves here and there by memory, imagination, map or metaphor. By this motion of mind—this pedagogical exercise—we begin to understand" (*Reason and Imagination in Chaucer, the* Perle-*Poet, and the* Cloud-*Author: Seeing from the Center* [New York: Palgrave, 2011], 13). Focusing on different medieval texts, Mary Carruthers, *The Experience of Beauty in the Middle Ages* (Oxford: Oxford University Press, 2013), reevaluates the ways in which sensual and situational understanding of aesthetics is central to even the most apparently stolid of medieval spiritual writing.

82. Glending Olson, "Making and Poetry in the Age of Chaucer," *Comparative Literature* 31 (1979): 272–90; Lee Patterson, "'What Man Artow?': Authorial Self-Definition in *The Tale of Sir Thopas* and *The Tale of Melibee*," *Studies in the Age of Chaucer* 11 (1989): 117–75; see also Brownlee et al., 468–71.

choices in the social world, but also to in some way reinvigorate, re-energize, and otherwise rejuvenate what he sees to be a fallen present moment characterized by division and decay. An aim across their poetry is not simply vernacular *auctoritas* or legacy, but also an attempt to demonstrate how (or, perhaps, whether) English poetic productions can in some way impinge upon the discourses that establish culture—historical, political, sexual—not simply by way of critique but also, somehow, productively. Invention, the process by which writers find the things they wish to write about, becomes for Chaucer and Gower the means by which the productive potential of this kind of cultural impingement can be most fully imagined and most powerfully articulated.

The exploration of this productive potential also depends on the expanded definition and broader understanding of invention that I have worked to outline in this introduction. The late-fourteenth-century vernacular explorations of that expanded conceptualization of invention—that is, not only articulating but also conceptualizing invention by making it an aspect of narrative plot and thematic meaning—constitute a vernacular "tradition," or at least a commonplace, of which Chaucer and Gower are very much part.[83] Their poetry explores invention in these same terms, as an aspect of narrative structure and a component of the imaginative material of poetry, even while Chaucer and Gower present themselves as conscious interlopers into what Lynn Arner labels a "Greco-Roman" poetic tradition.[84] Moreover, they consciously sustain and develop this treatment of invention over what we now have come to term literary "careers": that is, they make the exploration of invention an aspect of the shape they consciously give to their larger poetic opus. They also appear to have talked to each other about invention in these terms, and while the nature of their poetic relationship is still famously ambiguous, it is clear that they borrowed, shared, and developed ideas mutually. Studying Chaucer and Gower together, not simply as a compare-and-contrast case, but also as an opportunity to see how the treatment of invention as a topic for poetry developed mutually and explicitly as an aspect of narrative poetry and the idea of giving shape to a poetic "career," is thus essential to understanding how the concept operated in the late fourteenth century and how it might have then been taken up by fifteenth- and sixteenth-century English writers.

---

83. Evans et al., 330.

84. Lynn Arner, *Chaucer, Gower, and the Vernacular Rising: Poetry and the Problem of the Populace after 1381* (University Park: Pennsylvania State University Press, 2013). I agree with Arner in that one of the characteristics that separate Chaucer and Gower from their contemporaries is not simply their engagement with classical and continental material, but the explicitly self-referential way in which they articulate those engagements.

Chaucer and Gower also explore affect and invention in expressly secular terms. As we have seen, the critical conversation about invention tends to focus on its development through classical-rhetorical, scholastic, and theological traditions, and much of the important work in medieval affect studies focuses on spiritual writing and practices. It has long been noted that imagining the experiences of characters operating in the cosmological constructs of antiquity allows Chaucer to contemplate the nature of being and experience without directly appealing to Christian theological principles as means of explanation, and the same is true for Gower: the contemplations of Chaucer's Dido, Troilus, or Criseyde resemble, in this cosmological capacity at least, those of Gower's Medea or Apollonius. The projects of both writers, then, actively work to understand the relationship between affective occurrence and inventional activity in a similar way, appealing not simply to scholastic rhetorical traditions or neoplatonic notions of poetic creation. The intersection of internal and external worlds, of cosmological concerns with the particular social, cultural, and political realities of lived experience that make both Chaucer's and Gower's writings so appealing to us today, constitutes the same conceptual realms in which they explore the relationship of affect and invention.

To examine these ideas, I look in this book primarily at Chaucer's *House of Fame*, *Legend of Good Women*, and selected tales from Fragment VII of the *Canterbury Tales*, and at selected narratives from Gower's *Confessio Amantis*. But why these particular works when, of course, representations of affective experience and metapoetic commentary on the generation of poetry can no doubt be located anywhere—and, indeed, *everywhere*—else in Chaucer's and Gower's writing? First, as narratives, each of these works explores the nature of invention in the imaginative, metaphorical, and ultimately narratological terms common in late-fourteenth-century English vernacular poetry. I have chosen not to focus on Chaucer's or Gower's lyrics since, as I will show, the formulation of invention that I explore in this book is dependent upon *process*—that is, the Middle English term for the progression of events that create narrative trajectory—to unfold and develop. In the same way, I have chosen these texts because of the ways in which they concentrate on the sensations of movement, emergence, potentiality, imminence, and becoming that characterize affect (as I use the term in this book) rather than emotion. *The Book of the Duchess*, of course, organizes its entire plot around the experience of emotion and the understanding of particular emotional experiences in others. But the *House of Fame*, and the Prologue and individual narratives of the *Legend of Good Women*, as I will show in chapters 1 and 2, are more interested in exploring ideas of movement and displacement than empathy—that is, these poems explicitly study affect more than emotion. Similar reasons apply to my consideration of Gower's *Confessio* as a collection of narratives in English. Gower explores the relationship of affect and invention within specific narratives and linking segments, and I focus in this book on the Prologue, the tales of "The Three Questions," "Constantine and Sylvester," and "Medea and Jason," as well as some of the "historical" material involving famous inventions and the development of world religions in Books 4 and 5. What is more, the slow burn that is the cumulative effect of reading the *Confessio* and considering how these individual narratives contribute to a larger, whole, and complete formal structure is essential for, as I argue in chapters 3 and 4, understanding how Gower most fully explores how the imaginative treatment of poetic invention can productively impinge on cultural realities. In my reading of Fragment VII of the *Canterbury Tales,* in chapter 5 I argue that Chaucer satirizes the kind of explorations examined in the preceding chapters, while at the same redirecting a project of critique toward a vision of productive invention.

I also have chosen to focus on narrative poems that in particular posit moments of affective and inventional emergence. By this I mean passages that in some way represent—often metaphorically, but sometimes literally—the seemingly ineffable process by which affective and inventional movement collapse to become emotion and invented poetry. The passages I study in this book represent such processes in various ways, sometimes as aspects of physiological and emotional experiences, sometimes as aspects of narrative form, sometimes as aspects of genre, and sometimes as more nebulous, non-localized renderings of sensations of emergence. They are, however, moments when emergence itself becomes in some way a poetic topic in its own right. Furthermore, I have chosen these particular texts by Chaucer and Gower because both of them, to different extents, function in some way as "treatises" on the relationship of invention to affective experience. Chaucer's dream visions operate as *artes poetriae* in which theoretical principles about invention are discussed and then "dramatized" through narrative process. Gower's *Confessio* makes self-commentary a formal aspect of the poem's *compilatio* structure, embedding self-conscious analysis of its own making as a central component of its structure and development. To put the point even more straightforwardly, the texts selected here are appropriate not simply because they are "about" invention or affect, but because they consciously depict the meta-analysis of those concepts as aspects of their narratives.

As they explore Chaucer's sustained efforts to map a relationship between affect and invention, chapters 1 and 2 show how Chaucer's poems continually work to "get behind" the discourses and emotions that structure experience by examining parallel efforts to investigate pre-inventional movements that result in the production of poetry. As they move the discussion to Gower's *Confessio*, chapters 3 and 4 argue that in exploring similar issues, Gower's poem works to move the potentially productive emergent qualities that characterize the affect of invention into the world outside of poetic fiction. These chapters thus also trace a trajectory of cultural engagement and imaginative praxis that manifests generically. They begin with Chaucer's contemplative dream visions, in which the coemergence of affect and invention is explored in the relatively enclosed spaces of fictional characters' personal experiences and formal poetic structures. These poems not only expose the ways in which pervasive cultural discourses construct identity and power relationships but also attempt to represent poetically what the sudden realization—the rush of *fyndyng*, we might call it—of that exposure might feel like, as a way of moving beyond critique and toward larger cultural reinvention. The chapters then proceed to Gower's concerted effort to deploy the imaginative potential latent in inventional activity to the world outside of the poetic fiction, ultimately concentrating on the chronicle as the generic vehicle through which this imaginative deployment might take place. The final chapter reveals how Chaucer's critique of both of these approaches—contemplative dream vision and imaginatively prescriptive chronicle—allows for yet another potentially productive way of conceptualizing the relationship between affect and invention.

My study begins, then, with Chaucer's initial experiments in the *House of Fame* to represent invention as movement and emergence. Chapter 1 examines how the poem formulates Dido's and the narrator's act of co-invention in Book 1 as a moment of affective and inventional emergence that the rest of the poem works to unpack via the representation of *tydynges* in Book 3 and the eagle's lecture on sound in Book 2, both of which work in different ways to generate impressions of movement and emergence. *The House of Fame* also offers Chaucer's most detailed exploration of the work of the imagination, the swirling energies that writers of medieval *artes poetriae* work so hard to regulate and even condemn, and that match in profound ways what modern theorists have discovered to be the energies of affect. I argue finally that in representing Dido's inventional self-insertion into the masculinist literary tradition that she sees will define her, Chaucer conflates the inventional and affective processes of emergence in order to explore how the movements that precede both inventional action and emotional experience are vital to understanding particular patterns of cultural power. Chapter 2 traces Chaucer's development of these ideas to his final formal dream vision. *The Legend of Good Women* presents a theory-and-application model in the form of the dream Prologue and subsequent legend narratives that links the processes of emergence that precede the conscious recognition of emotion with the inventional processes that culminate in poetic art. The *Legend* is Chaucer's fullest narrative treatise on the affect of invention, and my examination of its poetics provides a new perspective on the vexed question of how the *Legend* positions itself within a literary tradition characterized by antifeminism and misogyny. Ultimately, I argue, the poem attempts to gesture behind both the discourses that shape late medieval ideas of gender and the affect that infuses those discourses with their personal and cultural power.

The next two chapters turn to the *Confessio Amantis* and examine Gower's more expansive deployment of affect and invention. Chapter 3 studies how Gower thematizes affective and inventional emergence—that is, composes narrative episodes that represent metaphorically the transformative power of affect and invention—within three significant *Confessio* narratives—the tales of Jason and Medea in Book 5, Constantine and Sylvester in Book 2, and Peronelle and the Three Questions in Book 1—to suggest an analogue for how the poetics of transformative emergence that he postulates in the Prologue might revitalize the physical world as much as transform the individual reader. The examples of these tales, three among many in the poem, culminate in a gesture toward a gesture: an imagined representation of how a poem like the *Confessio* might work to jumpstart cultural rejuvenation at the macrocosmic level. Chapter 4 builds on this argument by studying two sets of chronicles that Gower inserts at the heart of the *Confessio*—the history of famous inventions in Book 4 and the history of religions in Book 5—to demonstrate how he transduces the affect of invention thematized in his poem's narratives to an authoritative genre that purports to reflect and shape culture. Gower effectively transforms the *Confessio* into a kind of affective chronicle of inventional emergence: a poem that formally embeds affective and inventional potential as a part of its poetic structure.

The final chapter returns to Chaucer, arguing that in Fragment VII of the *Canterbury Tales,* Chaucer satirizes both his own and Gower's gestures toward the affect of invention. *The Prioress's Tale* presents explicit moments of affective and inventional emergence only to nullify them through a process of exaggeration that uses the very same movingly inventional language that generated them in the first place, ultimately suggesting how easily this kind of poetic exploration can become nothing but a vacant echo chamber of apparent movement. Similarly, the *Monk's Tale* presents the Monk as a poet-chronicler figure whose historical tragedies critique the poet-chronicler figure that Gower works to establish for himself in his poetry. Taken as a whole, the chronicle of the Monk's tragedies demonstrates this poetic model to lead ultimately not to the possibility of a culturally restorative inventional movement, but rather to its termination. In no way, however, does Chaucer finally condemn Gower's project and abandon his own. Instead, he follows these tales with the self-reflexive *Nun's Priest's Tale*, which comically resituates representations of affective emergence and chronicle narrative, finally suggesting that a project of critique is itself part of a much larger exploration that can be redirected toward the work of productive invention.

The more speculative Conclusion looks briefly at Shakespeare's use of Chaucer and Gower respectively in his famously enigmatic lyric "The Phoenix and Turtle" and his sprawling late romance *Pericles: Prince of Tyre* (co-written, most critics believe, with George Wilkins). I argue that these two texts recognize—and consciously perpetuate—what they posit to be distinctly "Chaucerian" and "Gowerian" conceptions of invention. As this lyric and play explicitly reformulate Chaucer and Gower, they do so in terms of how these poets' earlier works formulated creative invention as an aspect of affective emergence. My goal in this final section of the book is to demonstrate how the patterns of metapoetic exploration I chart in this book are in fact the same as those registered by a writer in the early seventeenth century. Furthermore, as a way of looking forward to future studies of the affect of invention, I wish to suggest that the result of Shakespeare's treatment of Chaucer and Gower is the generation of a kind of "affective intertextuality" that offers modern critics new ways of thinking about how early-modern writers engaged medieval poetry, as well as how the expansive conceptualization of invention in late-medieval vernacular poetry informs later English writers' thinking about how poetry comes into being.

This introduction began with the striking images of two stuck dreamers, narrators who suddenly found themselves in their respective dreamscapes frozen amid complex overlapping fields of affective occurrences and discursive networks, the resulting effect of which was the imaginative rendering of inventional emergence—a feeling or sensation, more than an emblem, symbol, or literary figure, of a process by which emotions and poetry both come into being. The first chapter of this book returns to a similar image, as the dreaming Geffrey of the *House of Fame* finds himself caught in similarly complex networks. Chaucer's focus this time, however, is on movement itself, a sustained, literalized metaphor that most explicitly begins his examination of the affect of invention.[85]

---

85. I borrow the idea of the "literalization of metaphor" from Ursula K. Le Guin in her introduction to *The Norton Book of Science Fiction: North American Science Fiction, 1960–1990*, ed. Ursula K. Le Guin and Brian Attebery (New York: Norton, 1993), 30.

CHAPTER 1

"GOOTH YET ALWAY UNDER"

Invention as Movement in the *House of Fame*

IN THE INTRODUCTION I argued that the critical vocabulary of movement, emergence, and becoming that is typically used to describe phenomena of affect can also be used to describe medieval concepts of poetic invention, specifically the movements and sensations of emergence that precede more formal compositional activity. Invention, then, isn't simply the structured process of discovering ways of best expressing a preconceived *archetypus*; it is also a phenomenological process of coming-into-being experienced as movement from invention to invented poetry. This inventional process, I argued, parallels a similar movement as affect collapses into structured and recognizable emotional experience. Over the next five chapters, I will show how Chaucer and Gower variously explore the productive potential of this alignment of affect and invention, beginning first with Chaucer's *House of Fame*—one of the most explicit and prolonged imaginative representations of the affect of invention. As D. Vance Smith argues, the poem's depictions of *tydynges* and the whirling wicker basket comprise Chaucer's "first truly invented scene" in that "it describes his *own* scene of invention rather than the treasury of European literature, as in the *Book of the Duchess*."[1] Moreover, what we see in the *House of Fame* are the beginnings of Chaucer's correlation of affect and invention

---

1. D. Vance Smith, "Chaucer as an English Writer," in *The Yale Companion to Chaucer*, ed. Seth Lerer (New Haven, CT: Yale University Press, 2006), 87; emphasis in original.

through his almost clinical dissection of the work of the imagination and the source texts that provide the *materia* within which poetic *fyndyng* can occur. In this chapter, I want to explore how the poem carefully and deliberately uses the theme of movement to align depictions of affective and inventional emergence. In doing so, it gradually folds the aesthetic into the political, establishing the basics of a poetics that probes how the affective movements that precede both inventional action and emotional experience are vital to understanding particular patterns of cultural power.

Itself long recognized as one of his early articulations of an *ars poetica*, Chaucer's dream vision conceptualizes invention in terms of movement almost to an exaggerated degree. As Steven F. Kruger succinctly puts it, "a consistent, if complicated, pattern of movement" unifies the poem literally and thematically, and, as with the *Parlement of Foules*, charting metanarratives of movement in the *House of Fame* is a chief characteristic of criticism on the poem.[2] Indeed, the narrator's careful progress—through the images of the Dido-Aeneas story in the Temple of Glass, through the upper atmosphere in the clutches of the eagle, and finally through the whirling basket of *tydynges* in which any claims to cultural, historical, or textual authority seem to be undermined—traces a rapid acceleration away from the hope of meaningful structure to a hopeless whirlwind of floating signifiers. Winds blow, waves ripple, eagles fly, a pudgy poet reels, Fame shrinks and expands, wickerbaskets spin, guns (at least metaphorically) fire, and *tydynges* wriggle, coalesce, and mutate. Dreams turn (or do not), epistemologies shift, and critical vantage points rocket toward philosophical abstraction and barrel down to the physically concrete—and all of this happens as a component of the poem's conscious imitation, revision, and deconstruction of its authoritative sources in Virgil, Ovid, and Dante. The poem moves even after it stops, its abrupt ending arriving so suddenly as to create a narrative inertia that extends its movement

---

2. Steven F. Kruger, "Imagination and the Complex Movement of Chaucer's *House of Fame*," *Chaucer Review* 28 (1993): 117. Sheila Delany, for example, traces a general movement from inner to outer worlds (*Chaucer's House of Fame: The Poetics of Skeptical Fideism* [Chicago: University of Chicago Press, 1972], 36–37); Thomas Kennedy sees a movement from literature to philosophy to theology ("Rhetoric and Meaning in the *House of Fame*," *Studia Neophilologica* 68 [1996]: 9–23); Kathryn L. Lynch sees the *House of Fame* appealing to imagination, then to reason, and finally to memory as it moves through its books (*Chaucer's Philosophical Visions* [Cambridge: D. S. Brewer, 2000], 62–63); Leslie Kordecki sees the concept of "becoming" in a Bakhtinian sense as important in the poem in terms of the "emergence of a subjectivity," in this case, of Chaucer's poetic self-representation (30); Linda Tarte Holley sees physical movement in the poem as a parallel for the dreamer's efforts to locate himself among fields of knowledge (55–70); Piero Boitani, *Chaucer and the Imaginary World of Fame* (Cambridge: D. S. Brewer, 1984), characterizes the poem as a representation of Chaucer's own imaginative faculty, emphasizing movement more generally.

beyond the limits of the poem itself, throwing readings into an unsettled speculative realm that exists only as possibilities of historical and textual contingency. It is a poem "teetering on the brink of formless energy and flux," as John Fyler describes it,[3] though it ultimately celebrates this formlessness and energy as decidedly "generative."[4] *The House of Fame* also moves between an effort to represent literally the abstract activities of *tydynges* and the emotional experience that the dreaming narrator imagines for Dido. In doing so, it establishes a careful parallel between affect and invention, exploring how the former's emergence into emotion aligns with the latter's generation of poetry.

Like would-be eel stompers in Book 3's spinning house of twigs, critics have long worked to trap meanings in the poem's teeming representational ecosystem, seeing in it not only the destabilization of textual and cultural authority, but also Chaucer's implicit but self-conscious movement from one poetic tradition to another, a dramatization of the work of the senses, imagination, and memory, and even new models for how modern scholars might engage the past.[5] Critics have also studied the tenuous way in which the poem

---

3. John M. Fyler, *Chaucer and Ovid* (New Haven, CT: Yale University Press, 1979), 24.

4. John M. Fyler, *Language and the Declining World in Chaucer, Dante, and Jean de Meun* (Cambridge: Cambridge University Press, 2007), 154. Fyler attributes this generative potential in part to Chaucer's "comically invert[ing] the pretensions of the *Commedia*" (152). See also Fyler, *Chaucer and Ovid*, 63–64. Recent criticism that sees "generative" potential in the *House of Fame* is indebted to the shift in perception, inaugurated by Delany, that reads the poem's pervading incompleteness and "incongruity" as productive (*Chaucer's House of Fame*, 35).

5. See David K. Coley, "'Withyn a Temple Ymad of Glas': Glazing, Glossing, and Patronage in Chaucer's *House of Fame*," *Chaucer Review* 45 (2010): 61n7, for a helpful survey of recent criticism that extends Delany's original argument of the de-authorizing work of the *House of Fame*; Coley himself argues that the poem's presentation of authority is not necessarily as tenuous as often thought. See Susan Schibanoff, *Chaucer's Queer Poetics: Rereading the Dream Trio* (Toronto: University of Toronto Press, 2006), for a summary and critique of scholarship that tends to view the *House of Fame* as the escape of Chaucer's poetics from an effete French court tradition via Dante and Italian poetry. Several recent studies of the *House of Fame* develop the poem's representation of artificial memory systems and the work of imagination: Beryl Rowland, "The Art of Memory and the Art of Poetry in *The House of Fame*," *Revue de l'Université d'Ottawa* 51 (1981): 162–71, and "Bishop Bradwardine, the Artificial Memory, and the *House of Fame*," in *Chaucer at Albany*, ed. Russell Hope Robbins (New York: Burt Franklin, 1975), 41–62; Mary Carruthers, "Italy, Ars Memorativa, and Fame's House," *Studies in the Age of Chaucer: Proceedings* 2 (1987): 179–87; Ruth Evans, "Chaucer in Cyberspace: Medieval Technologies of Memory and the *House of Fame*," *Studies in the Age of Chaucer* 23 (2001): 66; Edwards, *Dream of Chaucer*, 99–106, 116; Watson, "Phastasmal Past," 13–18. Fyler argues that the poem represents "in some sense thought itself" (*Language and the Declining World*, 152), and Kruger claims that the poem "figures a mediate realm akin to that of imagination" ("Imagination and the Complex Movement," 117). See Watson and Evans for how the poem imagines new models for thinking about the past. *The House of Fame* is often seen as a harbinger of postmodern life: see Minnis, *Shorter Poems*, 219–23 and 248–50, for a survey of the poststructuralist implications of the poem.

explores poetic invention specifically. Robert R. Edwards, for example, notes that an inventional *besinesse* occupies the narrator, as "Geffrey is continually enmeshed in details and preparation for a poetic topic that remains inaccessible" as Chaucer works in the poem to negotiate the relationship between poetry and knowledge, and Fyler remarks that the especially "confusing" nature of the *House of Fame* arises "largely because it explores something equivalent to the Ovidian conflict of *ratio* and *impetus,* that is to say in poetic terms, of the structuring impulse, and the forces in the self and the world that work to subvert its efforts."[6] My own stomping effort targets not how the poem represents forces that threaten to frustrate invention wholesale or how Chaucer explores the possibility of establishing a vernacular literary authority against Latin and Italian writers, but instead how the poem gestures toward the necessarily impossible act of representing the moments of emergence that culminate in invention, articulating this gesture through a complex pattern of shifts and displacements occurring along several narrative levels.

To track the poem's variegated exploration of the affect of invention across its three books, I want to show first how the explicit language of beginnings in the invocation and proems establishes movement and emergence as the defining conceptual framework for the poem's thinking about invention. Chaucer stages an act of co-invention explicitly in Book 1, when Geffrey composes Dido's complaint without recourse to any "other auctour" (314), formally staging a moment of affective and inventional emergence that the rest of the poem works to unpack. To understand this moment more fully, I take a cue from critics who read the poem "backwards," arguing first that Book 3 represents inventional work in terms of movement, doing so by using the mental faculty of imagination as a corollary for the process of poetic invention, but defining the nature of each not as objects or organizational systems, but as movement itself. In Book 2, the eagle's lecture on the behavior of sound develops an analogy that shifts between literal and figurative representations of movement in an effort to generate a sensation of displacement that signals inventional and affective movement. Finally, Dido's inventional self-insertion into the masculinist literary tradition that she sees will define her conflates the inventional and affective emergences that characterize Geffrey's engagement with Dido's story and suggests how the aesthetic concerns of invention impinge on cultural discourses of power and identity. Establishing a poetics that Chaucer would develop throughout his poetry, the *House of Fame* ultimately offers not simply a remarkable narrative treatise on how affect and invention parallel each other, but also the first example of Chaucer's sustained effort to examine

---

6. Edwards, *Dream of Chaucer,* 108; Fyler, *Chaucer and Ovid,* 24.

how pairing affect with invention plays a vital part in thinking about the world of experience outside of the poem.

GYNNYNGES: MOVEMENT AS INVENTIONAL TOPIC AND CONCEPTUAL FRAME

At its outset, the *House of Fame* establishes the sensation of anticipated movement as the primary conceptual framework within which to engage its subject matter, effectively setting the stage for the poem's examination of invention as movement by making a nonlocalized feeling of impending discovery a component of its own poetic topic. The Proem's opening request that God might "turne us every drem to goode!" (1), with its inherent "feeling of breathlessness and confusion,"[7] sets the conditions of the dream vision investigation in a way that deemphasizes what dreams might mean in favor of conceptualizing them first and foremost as movement. The repeated desire that a God who "mover is of al" (81) might "turne" dreams to "goode" not only bookends the survey of medieval dream theory but effectively dismisses it—"For I of noon opinion / Nyl as now make mensyon" (55–56)—emphasizing instead, for the duration of the poem at least, that dreams do not have meanings so much as trajectories, even if the origins and destinations of their trajectories cannot be predicted with any regularity.[8] Though Chaucer lists several different types of dreams and their causes, the Proem is unified not only by its overwhelming sense of uncertainty—or even outright "futility," as Sheila Delany argues[9]—but also by its presentation of dreams as affective forces: full of potential and always in a state of becoming, dreams are first and foremost forces and movement, even before they are narratives with (or without) some kind of meaningful content. What is more, the "air of good humour [that] pervades the poem," as Alistair Minnis puts it,[10] originates in this happy dismissal and dispels any real sense of anxiety, effectively transforming what might be a feeling of trepidation about a perceived lack of definite authority into a broader sense of displacement that is registered in the seemingly effortless sweeping away of the whole

---

7. Fyler, *Chaucer and Ovid*, 27.

8. Edwards suggests that the Proem "proposes, by shifting to the optative [mood], that some kind of intention ought to be at work" (*Dream of Chaucer*, 98), but the poem famously never fulfills this wish. See also Boitani, *Chaucer and the Imaginary World of Fame*, 180; and William A. Quinn, "Chaucer's Recital Presence in the *House of Fame* and the Embodiment of Authority," *Chaucer Review* 43 (2008): 173–74.

9. Delany, *Chaucer's House of Fame*, 41.

10. Minnis, *Shorter Poems*, 165; Kathryn Lynch argues that in the poem Chaucer's poetry is "playful" and "does not devolve into certainties" (78).

of medieval dream theory.¹¹ The "air of good humour" here extends even to the resulting urge to laugh at the ease with which serious dream theory is cast aside, a viscerally affective reaction that rushes in to fill a realm explicitly voided of rational meaning. Yet even this laughter is tenuous at best, significant for the sense of rupture that it registers rather than for its complexity as an intertextual joke. In establishing the topic and tone of the *House of Fame*, the Proem of Book 1 also performs the process of displacing feeling—anxiety, laughter—with a broader, less identifiable sensation of movement.

The opening call to "turne" dreams capitalizes at once on that term's double meaning as an act of movement and a process of poetic making and shaping. Geffrey assimilates these meanings and acknowledges dreams as vectors by calling his Proem "my gynnynge" (66), that is, the poem's *incipit*, its textual starting point, but also Geffrey's own action of beginning. The opening gerund works grammatically—and paradoxically—to capture and hold a sense of movement by seeming to stretch out for a prolonged length of time the process of beginning. The term also puns on "engyn" and in doing so reaches forward to the *gynnynge* of Book 2, where Geffrey replaces *gynnynge* with *engyn*:

> O Thought, that wrot al that I mette,
> And in the tresorye hyt shette
> Of my brayn, now shal men se
> Yf any vertu in the be
> To tellen al my drem aryght.
> Now kythe thyn engyn and myght!
> (523–28)

"Thought" here is Chaucer's term for the imaginative cell of medieval faculty psychology, and "engyn" in this context emphasizes the multivalent vibrancy of that faculty: an intellectual capacity for creativity, the structure of creative output, and a productive machine.¹² As it links the capacity for inventional movement with the process of starting to move—*engynes* and *gynnynges*—the Proem to Book 2 rewrites Dante's own invocation in the *Commedia* in a way that, as critics have often noted, keeps its muses rooted in a physical world of lived experience and human agency rather than the celestial realm of the

---

11. Lynch goes further, calling the *House of Fame* "a thoroughgoing parody of classical literary vision" (61).

12. For a concise discussion of the "creative power" ascribed to *engyn* as the imaginative faculty, see Minnis, *Shorter Poems*, 175–76; and Knapp, 32.

divine.[13] Relegation to the sublunary world further emphasizes the sensation of movement, not simply in terms of instability or decay, but as a productive alternative to the inventional stasis and inaccessible sublimity of celestial bodies and agencies. As rebuttals to Dante's poetics, which, the *House of Fame* suggests, implicitly purports to end inventional movement by directing it toward theological truth, these *gynnynges* can be seen to join the rest of the poem in identifying the poetics of the *House of Fame* as contingent and unstable, and in suggesting the tenuous nature by which we claim knowledge at all. But to jump to such hermeneutic conclusions so quickly—to assume that the *gynnynges* function mainly as indicators of a larger *archetypus* of indeterminacy that the rest of the poem expresses metaphorically, allegorically, or even intertextually via the deconstruction of authoritative texts—is essentially to skip to the end of the poem's trajectory in spite of its own efforts to slow down exactly this sort of "forward" interpretational movement. First and foremost, as the initial step of any such reading, the *gynnynges* of the *House of Fame* ask readers to linger within the motion of that trajectory in order to explore how it moves, before making an interpretive leap to another level of signification. Accordingly, the poem's language of beginnings does not figure this act of lingering simply as a kind of straddling of an ambiguous, liminal threshold, characterized by authorial anxiety and textual indeterminacy, but foremost as a kind of impending emergence. These *engynes* and *gynnynges* explicitly link the movement of dreams to the movement that precedes poetic invention, calling for an examination not of where but of how the poem moves.

Through their invocations of *thought, engynes,* and *gynnynges,* the proems furthermore make Chaucer's early exploration of the affect of invention an aspect of the work of the imagination as much as that of "translating" Virgil and Dante. Moreover, by explicitly linking *thought*—the mental faculty of the imagination—with *engynes* and *gynnynges,* the poem emphasizes the motional characteristics of the work of imagination and connects them with the work of invention. Looking at how the *House of Fame* represents imagination thus reveals how the poem synthesizes the affective and inventional movements I outlined in the Introduction: not simply how the one functions as an analogue

---

13. See, for example, Edwards, *Dream of Chaucer,* 99, 103–5. Kruger argues that the poem "embraces neither revelation nor the world of matter," opting instead to remain in "the intermediate realm of imagination" (128). Helen Cooper traces the poem's focus on secularity and skepticism to Chaucer's reaction to Dante's poetics, which she characterizes as "a poet who cannot leave Dante alone, but who disagrees with the very basis of the poetic of Dante's greatest work" ("Four Last Things in Dante and Chaucer: Ugolino in the House of Rumor," *New Medieval Literatures* 3 [1999]: 52); for Cooper, moments like Chaucer's replacement of Dante's "mente" with "Thought" in the Proem show Chaucer trying to "break free" from Dante's model (57).

for the other, but how affective and inventional processes are inherently linked in the generation of both feeling and poetry.

THOUGHT, ENGYN, AND IMAGINATION

The swirling *tydynges* in the wicker basket of Book 3's House of Rumor indeed seem to be modeled on how images were thought to circulate, combine, and emerge into consciousness in medieval understandings of imagination. Reading the House of Rumor as an allegory for the imagination, Nicholas Watson builds on studies by Mary Carruthers and Ruth Evans, who stress the active, dynamic, inventive, and imaginative work of medieval memory practices, and he understands *tydynges* to be datapoints in Chaucer's "characteristic[ally] extreme" metaphor for cellular imagination.[14] While perhaps not quite as extreme as Watson suggests, Chaucer's model nevertheless emphasizes the motional quality of imagination. Before moving to a reading of the *tydynges* of Book 3 as a literalization of the work of invention, I want to contextualize Chaucer's depiction within broader medieval conceptualizations of the imagination, but I do so with a focus on how Chaucer uses such commonplace conceptualizations as a way of explicitly linking affect with invention.

Indeed, conventional medieval understandings of how the imaginative faculty works implicitly combine the movements of affect with those of invention. In fact, what Brian Massumi intends to be a description of how forces of affect are reflected on the body also encapsulates important tenets of medieval imagination: "To think the body in movement," Massumi argues, "means accepting the paradox that there is an incorporeal dimension *of the body*. Of it, but not it. Real, material, but incorporeal. Inseparable, coincident, but disjunct . . . as energy is to matter. Energy and matter are mutually convertible modes of the same reality."[15] Similarly implicit in the medieval concept of the imagination—as both a kind of memory storehouse and an active faculty of perceiving in which images are combined, recombined, and called upon to remember or to invent, and in which distinctions like those between the felt and the known, the real and the fictional, the physical and the psychic, the bodily and the spiritual, are articulated in terms of constant motion and circulation—are notions of movement and emergence.[16]

---

14. Watson, "Phantasmal Past," 16.
15. Massumi, 5.
16. See Stewart, 1–7, for perhaps the most forceful impression of how affective movements of twenty-first-century, neoliberal everyday life might be seen to correspond to the everyday movements that constitute the medieval imagination. Seigworth and Gregg's summary of the

Though the general schema of medieval faculty psychology has been well traced, as Murray Wright Bundy succinctly put it almost a century ago in words that themselves parallel Gregory J. Seigworth and and Melissa Gregg's description of affect theory, "There is no consistent mediaeval theory of imagination."[17] Always acknowledged to be a component of the mind and the process of thinking, imagination constitutes one of the three cells of the brain, alongside the estimative or rational cell and memory. In this schema, the imaginative cell, located in the front of the head, stores images collected by the five "external senses" into the *sensus communis*; then, depending on the treatise describing the process, either the imaginative "power" or *vis*, or the estimative or cogitative power, or some sort of combination of both, combines, divides, and otherwise draws on the images of the imagination in order to aid in the work of rational thinking. The specifics about the location and power of the imagination change as they develop from their Galenic and Aristotelian roots, through Avicenna, and into the late Middle Ages. For example, in Albertus Magnus's influential thirteenth-century schema, the imagination, located in the frontmost cell of the brain, holds images taken into the *sensus communis* after the actual object sensed is no longer present, but the imagination doesn't hold those images as long as memory does. The imagination's images are brought to the estimative cell, where they are somehow infused with *intentiones*, initial evaluations made that determine the way in which images should be viewed. The recombinative work of inventing ideas then happens not in the imagination, but in the *phantasia*, a cell and power located at some liminal threshold between imagination and memory that has the ability variously to draw on, fuse, and parse images from the imagination and

---

capacity for affect theory to reveal "promise or threat," especially the very tentative hope that "we live in a world ceaselessly recomposing itself in unforeseen passages through the best of all possible impasses," also suggests a contemporary instantiation of the good–bad binary of imagination as leading one either to divine truth or to sinful distraction, inherent in the contingency of imaginational circulation (13).

17. Murray Wright Bundy, *The Theory of Imagination in Classical and Mediaeval Thought* (Champaign: University of Illinois Press, 1927), 177. Common sources for the medieval psychology of imagination include Avicenna, Albertus Magnus, Thomas Aquinas, Bartolomaeus Anglicus, and Roger Bacon. For especially cogent syntheses of late-classical and medieval ideas about faculty psychology and imagination especially, in addition to Bundy, 177–98, see Alistair J. Minnis, "Langland's Ymaginatif and Late-Medieval Theory of Imagination," *Comparative Criticism* 3 (1981): 71–103, and "Medieval Imagination and Memory," in *Cambridge History of Literary Criticism*, ed. Alastair Minnis and Ian Johnson, vol. 2 (Cambridge: Cambridge University Press, 2005), 239–74; V. A. Kolve, *Chaucer and the Imagery of Narrative: The First Five Canterbury Tales* (Stanford, CA: Stanford University Press, 1984), 20–24; Carolyn P. Collette, *Species, Phantasms, and Images: Vision and Medieval Psychology in* The Canterbury Tales (Ann Arbor: University of Michigan Press, 2001), 5–13; and Watson, "Phantasmal Past," 9–13. My summary below draws on these sources.

intentiones stored in memory. Aquinas collapses these into the single faculty of the *imaginatio* but argues also for the *vis imaginativa* as an active power of the mind.[18] In the best of circumstances, and under the proper control, the images that occupy the imagination are subjected to the estimative faculty, where they can be directed toward good ends—like thinking about a tough problem or about prudent actions for the future or about God. In the worst of circumstances, imagination's tempestuous movement cannot be controlled and leads thinkers into intellectual pride or sin or debilitating, self-consuming fantasy.[19] As Alistair Minnis puts it, "The imagination is, it would seem, as potentially misleading as it is wonderful"; imagination allows for the appreciation of beauty, Peggy A. Knapp argues, "but against a backdrop of distrust."[20]

Moreover, though classification seems to be the main focus of medieval commentators, faculty psychology is itself understood to be a field of movements, vectors, trajectories, and becomings. In her studies of medieval memory practices, Mary Carruthers emphasizes that the processes of "human cognition" ought to be thought of "in terms of 'ways,'" rather than "faculties," just as the work of formal invention (in her view, essentially "recollection," a function of memory) is about "mov[ing] 'things' into relationships with one another."[21] Ruth Evans likewise argues that it is much more accurate to think of the cellular model of medieval brains "less as a static map of the brain . . . and more like a dynamic flowchart of our desires." The cellular map "is an attempt to represent diagrammatically a set of mobile spatial and temporal relationships."[22] Indeed, medieval conceptions of imagination seem in part to involve an almost infinite regression of movements. As Aquinas notes, the images reeling around in the imaginative cell are "movements started by actual sensations," and memory, in part the storehouse of such images, is "delayed motion

---

18. Minnis, "Medieval Imagination and Memory," 242.

19. Minnis, "Langland's Ymaginatif," calls interest in ends and means "one of the basic tenets of medieval Aristotelianism" (74).

20. Minnis, "Medieval Imagination," 243; Knapp, 26; see Knapp, 26–41, for a discussion of imaginative work as well as medieval aesthetics and modern understandings of the philosophy of cognition. Knapp notes that Chaucer's use of the term *engyn* for imagination has a range of meanings but also denotes "imagination as an active, even aggressive, intellectual process" (32). For a summary of the embodied and motional nature of sense images and knowledge, see Carruthers, *Book of Memory,* 54–60; and Watson, "Phantasmal Past," 5.

21. Carruthers, *Craft of Thought,* 70, 34. Likewise, Carruthers writes that the rhetorical term *ductus* refers not merely to the "flow" of a written work but also to "a thinking mind on its *way* through a composition" (77): "Every composition, visual or aural, needs to be experienced as a journey, in and through whose paths one must constantly *move*" (81; emphasis in original); for the relationship of this movement to the work of medieval imagination, see also Holley, esp. 4–10.

22. Evans, 61.

that continues to exist in the soul."[23] In addition to the movements inherent in the *vis imaginiativa*, the images themselves are fused with *intentiones*, "a kind of judgment," as Mary Carruthers describes them, "but one that is not simply rational."[24] *Intentiones* are not merely "opinions" formed about things taken in through the senses, but also "those inherent qualities of animals, people, and things that are real but beyond the power of the five external senses to determine," as Carolyn P. Collette describes them, or "gut feeling[s]" and "emotional direction[s]," as Carruthers characterizes them, a kind of affective residue determined by the internal and external conditions of the senses' first experience of them, images "of things as they were *when they appeared to and affected us.*"[25] They characterize every image of the imagination, infusing it with a kind of attraction or revulsion.[26] *Intentiones*, then, are judgments or evaluations only insofar as they are movements.[27] An image's intention is not so much a category or label as it is an energy or a hum, a being-in-trajectory. Their nature is defined by affective valence. What they are is in large part determined by how they move.

Adding to this complexity, emotions—which themselves attach to or somehow "charge" the *intentiones* of images—are also understood as movements, aspects of a soul that is itself also essentially movement,[28] hence the medieval commonplace of the motional relationship between emotions and artistic expression: lyric poetry, for example, has the power to move the soul by synchronizing its movements with that of the verse, toward either good or ill, themselves resonant echoes and reflections of larger cosmological

---

23. Qtd. in Carruthers, *Book of Memory*, 56
24. Carruthers, *Craft of Thought*, 15.
25. Bundy, 189; Collette, *Species, Phantasms, and Images*, 9; Carruthers, *Craft of Thought*, 45, 97; *Book of Memory*, 54. *Intentiones* are in part produced biologically, as when sheep are afraid of the image of a wolf, for example, in part socially, as when different people and different communities experience different attitudes toward the same object. See Carruthers, *Craft of Thought*, 39, 45. As Carruthers puts it, they are "partly personal, partly emotional, partly rational, and mostly cultural" (ibid., 15).
26. Carruthers, *Experience of Beauty*, 43; for Cicero, this is the *vis aestimativa*; for Augustine, it is *intentio* (42–43).
27. Carruthers emphasizes the movement inherent in *intentio* and distinguishes the different emphases in the *intentio* of faculty psychology and the *intentio* within a work of art (ibid., 48–53 and 167–72). In the classical and early medieval traditions, *intentiones* are tensions of the soul and of physical strings, as Augustine and Cicero describe them, (Carruthers, *Craft of Thought*, 15).
28. Emotions are movements for Aquinas, for example, but not for his teacher, Albertus Magnus, who described them as "qualities," but qualities nevertheless "generated by movements" (*De bono*, qtd. in Simo Knuuttila, *Emotions in Ancient and Medieval Philosophy* [Oxford: Clarendon Press, 2004], 238).

movements.²⁹ But medieval philosophy also worries over those initial moments of affective emergence, inheriting and developing these anxieties from classical precursors. Stoic philosophers' concerns about "first movements"—the *propassio* or "pre-emotion" that will eventually emerge as an emotion—provide a good example. While essentially introduced as a way of reconciling the reality of affective experience with the philosophical desire to control that experience, the *propassio* formulation attempts to identify something—"an agitation of the mind," in Seneca's words, *delectatio* in Augustine's—that resembles affect in the way discussed by some modern theorists.³⁰ This movement is not mystical or spiritual but embodied, carried through a liquid medium of "neural spirits," and representative of the larger humoral reality of the human body as "a compound," as Carruthers puts it, "of matter and animation."³¹ The beginnings of "first movements" are, to reassign Massumi's words, neither inside nor outside of experience, but "immanent to it—always in it but not of it."³²

It is little wonder, then, why "no consistent mediaeval theory of imagination" ultimately emerges out of what Watson calls in his discussion of the *House of Fame* the inherently "ambiguous standing of images and the faculty that generates and recombines them," especially given that the imagination "exists so close to the boundary between corporeal and spiritual, crossing and recrossing that boundary" as a matter of its very nature.³³ Imagination is, Watson writes, a consummately "liminal" entity.³⁴ It is at once a space and a force, at once physical and intangible. It stores and it acts, sometimes with

---

29. Knuuttila provides an invaluable survey of the evolution of thought in the medieval philosophy of emotion; for a concise synthesis, see his earlier "Medieval Theories of the Passions of the Soul," in *Emotions and Choice from Boethius to Descartes*, ed. Henrik Lagerlund and Mikko Yrjonsuuri (Dordrecht and Boston: Kluwer Academic Press, 2002), 49–83. For a discussion of the generation of poetry in these terms, see especially Edwards, *Ratio and Invention*, interchapter 1 through chapter 3.

30. Seneca, *On Anger*, 2.3.5, qtd. in Kuuntilla, *Emotions in Ancient and Medieval Philosophy*, 64; see 170 for Augustinian *delectatio* as an "initial state" of affective reaction to the *suggestio* of an object, which is not in itself necessarily sinful. Medieval thinking about this emergent emotional occurrence ultimately centered on whether such movements should be identified as sins, and if so, to what degree, especially since they seem to have occurred even in Christ himself. For a discussion of *propassio*, its precursors in ancient thought and its influence on medieval philosophy of emotion, see ibid., 63–65, 178–95.

31. The "Neural spirit" is the medium of transfer in Avicenna, for example (ibid., 220); Carruthers, *Experience of Beauty*, 31; see 31–35 for a brief discussion of the body as movement in medieval medical theory, and 45–53 for a summary of the movement inherent in sensation and forming images.

32. Massumi, 33.

33. Watson, "Phantasmal Past," 10.

34. Ibid., 12; Edwards notes that Petrarch also presents the imagination in a liminal position, "located between perception and understanding" (*Ratio and Invention*, 39).

the will and sometimes without it. Movement defines imagination's nature, its function, and even its biography in the history of philosophy: the very form of imagination itself shifts through its own written history as if somehow understanding itself to be a collection of images phasing in and out of the carnal and rational powers of management and combination.[35]

As Massumi, drawing on Henri Bergson, writes about an example of a flying arrow, "The transition from bow to target is not decomposable into constituent points.... The points or positions [of the arrow in its flight path] really appear *retrospectively,* working backward from the movement's end."[36] Distinguishing the notion of "possibility" from "potential," Massumi writes that "Possibility is back-formed from potential's unfolding.... Potential is unprescribed. It only feeds forward, unfolding toward the registering of an event: bull's-eye."[37] Medieval concepts of imagination construct the faculty similarly, gesturing—however indirectly amid classifications and anxieties about the sinful destinations of unchecked thinking—toward an anterior sensation of movement and emergence. Yet, for all its dynamism, imagination is only as shifting and liminal as it is ordinary: it is, finally, "an essential part of the normal process of human thinking."[38] It works constantly, everywhere. Its actions may be mysterious and at times ineffable, but the imagination is not sublime: it is decidedly ordinary.

When Chaucer conjures his own reeling image of the imagination in Book 3 of the *House of Fame,* he casts imagination as an unstructured field of perpetually emerging *gynnynges,* emphasizing liminal, motional qualities of imagination even more so, I will argue, than the perennial question of whether the images culled from imagination's swirling repository can be trusted as truthful or valuable. But Chaucer's kinetic allegory is not fixed solely on imagination; rather, it folds imagination's inclusion of the untraceable movements of emergence and becoming, literalized as they are across and among parts of the body, into a consideration of similar aspects of poetic invention. Like imagination, invention becomes a kind of movement, and through this conceptualization the *House of Fame* ultimately examines how the relationship of affect and invention informs cultural constructions of power and identity.

---

35. Watson argues that the ambiguity of the nature of imagination "constitutes an organizing principle for medieval imaginative theories" ("Phantasmal Past," 10).

36. Massumi, 6; emphasis in original.

37. Ibid., 9.

38. Minnis, "Langland's Ymaginatif," 76. As Collette shows in her discussion of vision in late-medieval thought, these ideas of images and movement were not exclusive to a Latinate elite but were "part of the common, received knowledge of educated people in late-fourteenth-century England" (*Species, Phantasms, and Images,* 31).

TYDYNGES FULLY SPRUNG: CAPTURING INVENTION AS MOVEMENT

Superimposing an allegory for invention over this model for imagination, the House of Rumor in Book 3 literalizes and anatomizes the process of invention itself by parsing moments of *gynnynge* as finely as possible and presenting *tydynges* as filaments of inventional movement. The eagle takes Geffrey to the twig house so that he might acquire some new material for invention, "somme newe tydynges for to lere, / Somme newe thinges, y not what, / Tydynges, other this or that, / Of love or suche thynges glad" (1886–89). The *tydynges* that slip into the spinning twig house arrive there "naturally" because of their nature as sound, as "air ybroke" (770).[39] Their initial appearance in the poem, strange as it may seem, is in fact conventional enough. Wriggling their way into the twig house through one of the countless gaps that punctuate its rickety exterior, the *tydynges* instantly transform from sound into corporeal bodies identical to those of the human agents who first uttered them, clothed variously in red and black as "letters come to life," as Christopher Baswell puts it, according to the commonplace medieval conflation of the spoken and written word, the heard and the seen.[40] In the deauthorizing chaos of the basket-house, the *tydynge*-people talk to and variously coalesce with one another before wriggling back out to fly toward the House of Fame. The fact that individual *tydynges* are variously "fals and soth" (2108), and that each kind routinely—and happily—coalesces to link false and true together into a single *tydynge* of indeterminate veracity, has rightly been read as the central epistemological and poetic quandary of the poem, destabilizing claims not only to poetic and cultural authority, but also to whether it is possible to know anything at all.

On the surface, *tydynges* appear to be data items, ranging from the most basic images and their attending *intentiones* recorded from sensory stimulation, to fragments of discourse, to fuller items of "news" (that is, little

---

39. As Martin Irvine notes, it is the nature of *tydynges* as sound, not as discourse, that causes them to float upwards to the realm of Fame ("Medieval Grammatical Theory and Chaucer's *House of Fame*," *Speculum* 60 [1985]: 868).

40. Christopher Baswell, *Virgil in Medieval England: Figuring the Aeneid from the Twelfth Century to Chaucer* (Cambridge: Cambridge University Press, 1995), 238; see also Minnis, *Shorter Poems*, 196–99, and Irvine. The poem generates an intentional ambiguity as it conflates visual and aural sense impressions as a consequence of dramatizing through the transformation of the *tydynges*, what Irvine calls "an allegory of reading and writing" (869); Rowland also links this corporealization to the writing process ("Art of Memory," 169–70). Boitani reads the transformation of the *tydynges* from sounds into people in terms of the ways in which meaning is instilled in a word, and he does so by contextualizing the passages within the Modistae tradition (*Chaucer and the Imaginary World*, 212–16).

narratives) regarding the entire range of human experience. As *materia* for invention, they are, literally, up in the air for anyone to grab. In fact, the *House of Fame* might have proceeded to cast this entire *tydynge* system as an allegory for invention and the formal rhetorical canons that follow: topics whirl around and are fused and augmented through the work of imagination, after which they are siphoned to Fame's castle where they are variously ordered, ornamented, and finally pronounced to the earth below with the help of Fame's blaring trumpets, and then finally, as "published" texts, they float back upwards as fragmented *materia* to undergo the process again. But by reverse-engineering this process, by making the *tydynges* the last topic of the poem instead of the first, the *House of Fame* directs us consider *tydynges* in their own right before assigning them a position in a larger structural analogue, observing these whirling inventional filaments first as elements of being-in-trajectory before situating them as components of a larger hermeneutical process, defined retroactively, like Bergson's arrow, by their eventual destinations. Put another way, their presentation in Book 3 depicts *tydynges* not so much as topics for invention as inventional *gynnynges*.

Watson's reading of Book 3 emphasizes in particular the motional relationship between *tydynges* and the events they purport to encode: "Coming between events and their afterlife, 'tidinges' generate differences between one moment and the next by recasting the 'soth' of an event within an endless array of alternative versions whose very variance makes its own impact on what happens next. This is an unpredictable process in which, despite the persistence of cause and effect, any ability to *track* causality is soon lost."[41] *Tydynges,* Watson argues, like the images described by other dream and religious vision writers, have a kind of "*power,*" a "potential efficacy, contained in the image."[42] While he relegates *tydynges* to the programmatic position of representing phantasms and their conventional medieval benefits and dangers, Watson also recovers the "radical" energy inherent in Chaucer's rendering of the House of Rumor. Indeed, as Beryl Rowland notes, the first *tydynges* of the poem "are represented mainly in kinetic images. They are given human traits

---

41. Watson, "Phantasmal Past," 17; emphasis in original.
42. Ibid., 18. Emphasizing *tydynges* as signs of potential, Watson's reading, in which the sensation of historical unfolding depends upon the generation of alternative possibilities and histories, resonates with the patterns that Jeffrey Jerome Cohen and Maura Nolan find operating in other medieval writing about the past, and, he argues, might provide modern scholars with new ways of engaging history. See Cohen, "Time Out of Memory," in *The Post-Historical Middle Ages,* ed. Elizabeth Scala and Sylvia Federico (Houndmills: Palgrave, 2009), 37–61,and Nolan, "Historicism after Historicism."

but they remain visually unrealized, and their content is not described."[43] But the dynamism of Chaucer's *tydynges* extends even further. As metatextual filaments that gesture toward an event's unfolding as a kind of felt potential rather than as retroactive textualization, *tydynges* become figures for the movements of inventional emergence that occur before the collapse of that movement into more formal activities of invention.

Representing this sensation of emergence begins the moment that Geffrey sets eyes on the basket spinning behind Fame's castle. As he approaches, the house whirls noisily, "As dooth the rowtynge of the ston / That from th'engyn ys leten gon" (1933–34), and it spins around "as swyft as thought" (1924). His description, offered just as he is about to enter the house itself, recasts the terms of *gynnynge* that marked the formal entry into Book 2 of the poem. "Engyn" now refers to something like a catapult that would throw a stone, and "thought" is now relegated to serving as the comparative term of a simile describing the speed of the house's motion rather than the lauded dedicatee of a proem's apostrophe. These subtle shifts in usage transform the formal inventional themes of the poem—the process and imaginative capacity of invention—into a more nebulous registration of displacement, converting explicit topics into less distinct but no less important sensations of movement. *Engyn* and *thought* are no longer simply "creativity" and "imagination." They no longer stand apart from the narrative as they do when they appear in the Proem to Book 2, but now work instead as elements of the descriptive apparatus that builds the fictional dream world of Chaucer's poem, infusing its fabric with a kind of residual vibration that, on the one hand, echoes their earlier heralding of the poem's second *gynnynge* and, on the other hand, energizes the narrative action of Geffrey's imminent entry into the House of Rumor.

At this point, the *House of Fame* seems to stage poetic invention using a narrative device that, as we have seen, Nicolette Zeeman shows to be a commonplace of Middle English narrative poetry: a protagonist literally discovers or finds something to be invented within the plot of a poem.[44] But Chaucer's rendering of this Middle English metatextual commonplace transforms it by blurring the very conventions of metaphor on which the trope depends. The passages detailing Geffrey's experience in the House of Rumor attempt nothing less than making literal what conceptualizing invention as movement and emergence *might actually look like,* were someone able to observe it physically. Indeed, though critics have tended to note the way in which the poem moves

---

43. Rowland, "Art of Memory," 170.
44. Zeeman, "Imaginative Theory."

from emphasizing sight in Book 1 to sound in Book 3 and the overwhelming "noyse" of the spinning house,[45] in fact we get very little reporting about what the people-*tydynges* actually have to say. "The wondermost" thing of Geffrey's entire adventure in the twig basket turns out to be the protracted process he views in which individual corporealized *tydynges* combine with and augment one another (2059). The process by which *tydynges* exchange information and variously "eche" and "encres" refers, of course, to the ways in which tales grow in the telling (2065, 2074). Chaucer, however, takes pains to represent this process visually rather than aurally—he sees the *tydynges* grow and combine, rather than simply hearing stories expand and change—and this process casts the *tydynges* as emergent phenomena, as things that are about to happen, rather than merely as the personifications of discourse. It is worth looking with Geffrey in some detail at what he witnesses. When a *tydynge*

> was ful yspronge,
> And woxen more on every tonge
> Than ever hit was, [hit] wente anoon
> Up to a wyndowe out to goon;
> Or, but hit myghte out there pace,
> Hyt gan out crepe at som crevace,
> And flygh forth faste for the nones.
> And somtyme saugh I thoo at ones
> A lesyng and a sad soth sawe,
> That gonne of aventure drawe
> Out at a wyndowe for to pace;
> And, when they metten in that place
> They were achekked bothe two,
> And neyther of hem moste out goo
> For other, so they gonne crowde,
> Til ech of hem gan crien lowde,
> "Lat me go first!" "Nay, but let me!
> And here I wol ensuren the,
> Wyth the nones that thou woldt do so,
> That I shal never fro the go,
> But be thyn owne sworen brother!
> We wil medle us ech with other,
> That no man, be they never so wrothe,

---

45. John Finlayson, "Seeing, Hearing and Knowing in *The House of Fame*," *Studia Neophilologica* 58 (1986): 47–57; see also Kordecki, 31–32.

> Shal han on [of us] two, but bothe
> At ones, al besyde his leve,
> Come we a-morwe or on eve,
> Be we cried or stille yrounde."
> Thus saugh I fals and soth compouned
> Togeder fle for oo tydynge.
> Thus out at holes gunne wringe
> Every tydynge streght to Fame.
> (2081–111)

The speech that Geffrey reports hearing is not the content or "text" of actual tidings of love, war, gossip, or whatever else, but the conversations that the *tydynge*-people have about how they are planning to move and their announcements of their intentions to "medle" with one another before wriggling out of the basket. In other words, when the *tydynge*-people talk, they do not talk about the content of their *tydynges* but about how they plan to move, comingle, and transform. The "text" of *tydynges,* then, is not about material, but about movement. Appropriately, when Geffrey finds himself surrounded by *tydynge*-people particularized according to their vocations,[46] their climactic wrestling match as they scrap for a love *tydynge* is a visual spectacle of piled bodies and foot stomping, a mess of literalized, embodied movement. A side effect of this movement is that false and true *tydynges* blend indistinguishably together, but even more wondrous is the literal representation of that process of fusion: What, after all, does it *look* like when two *tydynge*-people "medle . . . ech with other," are "compouned," and "wringe" themselves out of a window toward Fame's castle?[47]

Geffrey never provides a clear description, instead roughing out an image indirectly by expressing it in terms of displacement. As they *wringen* from the holes in the walls, twisting and writhing, the *tydynge*-people also presumably morph from their *medeled* humanoid forms back into "Wynged wondres" that "faste fleen, / Twenty thousand in a route, / As Eolus hem blew aboute" (2118–20), in a manner that computer-generated images have made an almost tedious commonplace for modern moviegoers. *Wringen* conjures images of

---

46. Rowland, "Art of Memory," 170.
47. To "medle" in Middle English can mean to blend together, as these *tydynges* do, as well as to have sex, as the comingling of the bodies of the *tydynge*-people also implies. William Langland furthermore uses the term "medle" to describe his own process of vernacular composition when Ymaginatif accuses Will of "medel[ing] with makynges" (*Piers Plowman,* B-Text, 12.16–19), as Minnis notes in "Langland's Ymaginatif," 86–87. The term, as Chaucer uses it in the *House of Fame,* neatly conflates all of these resonances.

liquid being squeezed out of a cloth,[48] and the verb connects *tydynges* thematically to the larger watermill-like circular motion of the entire earth-to-sky-to-earth cycle of the *tydynges'* ecosystem,[49] as well as to the water analogy the eagle uses in Book 2 to describe sound in terms of water waves: phenomena that, like "eyr ybroken" (765), are observable only in terms of the medium they displace. When Geffrey encounters them, then, *tydynges* are marvelous because of what they look like, even though their direct, literal representation proves impossible. For this reason, Geffrey's visual account describes *tydynges* by how they move, perceiving them finally not as sound or texts or images, but as movement. He triangulates sensory data to gather an impression not of what *tydynges* are, nor even what they look or sound like, but of where they might be heading and how they might be *medelyng* with one another. Geffrey enters the basket looking for inventional topics. What he discovers instead is the ceaseless movements of inventional emergence.

Appropriately, then, the ultimate origin given for the *tydynges* is "Aventure" or chance (1982). *Aventure* is their mother, Geffrey reports, but only as much "As the see [is] of welles and sprynges" (1984). In other words, *tydynges* are made of the exact same "substaunce" as *aventure* (768), just as the sea and wells and springs are all made of water.[50] In this formation, *tydynges* become significant not because they are the "raw discourse" of events, as Leslie Kordecki describes them, but because they are something like fragments of unfolding eventuality, their motional natures resonating with movements of emergence like wells and springs echoing the sea.[51] "Coming between events and their afterlife," as Watson puts it, *tydynges* may still ultimately function as threads of discourse, reports of things that did or did not happen. As Piero Boitani rightly notes, "Reality as told is different from reality as it existed before it was told,"[52] and Chaucer's emphasis on their movement attempts to gesture back toward a moment of emergence, of both the text and the event, rendering *tydynges* as not only fragments of utterance but also phenomenal filaments. Put another way, the *House of Fame* here functions as the best

---

48. Indeed, most uses of the word reflect this liquid meaning; the *Middle English Dictionary* (*MED*) cites *wringen* in the sense of squirming or writhing in definitions 4, 7, and 8; 1–2 record its "liquid" meanings. All citations from the *MED* are taken from the online edition, <http://quod.lib.umich.edu/m/med/>.

49. See Carruthers, *Craft of Thought*, 92–94, for the watermill origin for the work of the imagination; see Watson, "Phantasmal Past," 14, for its application to Chaucer's poem.

50. Boitani, *Chaucer and the Imaginary World*, 164.

51. Kordecki, 48.

52. Boitani, *Chaucer and the Imaginary World*, 210; for Delany, "the House of Rumor reveals the present fast becoming history" (*Chaucer's House of Fame*, 106), providing a glimpse of that process itself.

science fiction might, representing the sensation of impending emergence as something that can be observed, touched, and interacted with, an entity whose existence extends well beyond a metaphorical or allegorical signification and comes into its own as an essential part of a fictional narrative world. As in Massumi's discussion of Bergson's arrow, Chaucer's *tydynges* are an attempt to represent the condition of being-in-trajectory without the retrospective construction of points of origin and destination. It is finally not the fact that the "soth" and "fals" *tydynges* cannot be distinguished that makes these powerful images of inventional action, but that their nature is determined by their movement, making them remarkable instances in processes of inventional emergence.

Rather than a strict allegory for the *fyndyng* of topics in poetic invention or the combination of images in new and productive ways, *tydynges* become gestures toward the sensations that impinge upon the more formal processes of invention. They are strings of inventional action, physical entities characterized only by movement; they cannot be directly observed but need to be sensed indirectly, by observing the shapes of displacement. They are finally interesting to Geffrey not as specific, historical things that are said or heard but as undifferentiated phenomena of emergence that indirectly indicate imminent action of poetic invention. Book 3 of the *House of Fame* thus presents Chaucer's most literalized rendering of invention as a *gynnynge* that will eventually result in the generation of things like archetypes and poetic figures but that is first and foremost a process of movement and becoming.

GOING ALWAYS UNDER: RIPPLES AND THE SENSATION OF DISPLACEMENT

Reading *tydynges* as filaments of movement traceable via what they displace rather than what they actually "say" emphasizes the emergence of inventional discovery—the event of *fyndyng*—as opposed to the content of that discovery itself, be it "soth," "fals," or a bit of both. Indeed, this is precisely what Geffrey's flight with the eagle in Book 2 takes as a topic: not an arrival at a site for the empirical observation of stellar bodies and its concordant, Dantean epiphanies about the nature of language and reality, but a gesture toward the sensation of the experience of coming into a moment of discovery in an inventional sense. The eagle's lecture on the nature of sound emphasizes displacement first by talking about language as sound and sound as displaced air, and second by embodying and enacting displacement through its genre as a satire of academic discourse. As the lecture straddles two levels of representation—the eagle's formal lecture topic of displacement is of course known to him and to Geffrey, but its genre as satire is not—it works to generate a complex sensation of displacement whose motional origin is finally untraceable but must be located somewhere in the gap between those levels.

As "air ybroke" (770), the eagle tells Geffrey, not only does sound float upward because of the "kyndely enclynyng" in an Aristotelian universe in which like seeks out like (734), but it also travels in the same way as water waves, as the "litel roundell" created by throwing a stone in a pool that "wol cause another whel, / And that the thridde, and so forth, brother, / Every sercle causynge other / Wydder than hymselve was" (791–97).[53] Despite the analogy's accuracy by modern standards—as it turns out, sound *does* travel like this—critics have been quick to point out the flaws in the eagle's lecture to Geffrey: It is not a real lecture but a satire of scholarly philosophical discourses;[54] "It is not science but a parody of science";[55] it "confuses levels of argument by mixing analogy and proof,"[56] and it ultimately turns out to be "irrelevant to the central problems of the poem."[57] For Edwards and Fyler, at the center of the eagle's failure as a debater is his resorting to the literal, taking Boethius' idea of ripples in the water as real ripples in real water, "reducing metaphor to a physical literalism,"[58] and, in equating language with sound, revealing a "reductiveness, which erases categories of meaning and levels of style to no purpose."[59] But it is precisely the lecture's function as a satire of scientific, philosophical, and poetic authority that enables Chaucer's poem to gesture further toward the sensations of displacement rendered most fully in Book 3. As a satire of academic philosophical debate, a parody of Dante's eagle and poetics, a misapplication of the methods of logical proof, and perhaps even an

---

53. For a discussion of Aquinas's characterization of sound as movement and change, see Fyler, *Language and the Declining World*, 154; Delany surveys Aristotelian views of movements and causes, noting that "by Chaucer's time the work of Ockham, Buridan, and others had already stripped Aristotelian science of much of its earlier prestige" (*Chaucer's House of Fame*, 75), thus allowing Chaucer to emphasize the comic nature of the eagle (71–79).

54. For a critique of the eagle's logic, see K. Lynch, 71–75. Joseph E. Grennen argues that the humor of the eagle's speech extends beyond parody to "a pastiche of terms and ideas drawn from contemporary scientific writing" ("Science and Poetry in Chaucer's *House of Fame*," *Annuale Mediaevale* 8 [1967]: 42).

55. Delany, *Chaucer's House of Fame*, 74.

56. Edwards, *Dream of Chaucer*, 109.

57. Fyler, *Language and the Declining World*, 147.

58. Edwards, *Dream of Chaucer*, 109.

59. Fyler, *Language and the Declining World*, 148. Fyler furthermore argues that "the Eagle's naturalism" undermines Boethius's philosophy, "shrink[ing] the world by emptying it of intelligibility and human meaning. The alternative, inescapable below the moon, is fog and confusion" (*Chaucer and Ovid*, 56).

extended fart joke,⁶⁰ the eagle's speech for most critics refers to the physics of sound only as much as it refers to something that stands apart from but looks back to its subject: a dramatization of interpretive error referring not to physics or sound but to the discourse used to contemplate those topics. Indeed, the most compelling lesson about the way things move in the sublunary world comes not from the eagle's incorporation of Aristotelian notions of movement, nor even from what John Leyerle calls the "forced experience" the eagle gives to Geffrey "by acting out the theory he describes . . . actualiz[ing] his theory of sound, parallel to the way the eagle himself actualizes a metaphor,"⁶¹ but from the way in which the genre of the eagle's lesson generates a sense of movement apart from the content of the lesson itself. This tertiary action of displacement occurs behind the lecture's overt topic of elemental displacement (air and water) and the blazingly literal and "physical rapture" of Geffrey's flight into the upper atmosphere, compliments of the transubstantiation of Boethius's feathers of philosophical knowledge.⁶² The genre of the satirical lecture thus signals displacement more subtly, running parallel to the grander literalization of movement through the eagle's atmospheric flight. It thus gestures toward a sensation of movement that seems to be occurring just beside these other examples of displacement, one that, in contrast, appears more difficult to trace and pin down and that is best understood not in representational terms but as movement itself. As we feel compelled to snicker at Chaucer's eagle, we find ourselves belatedly registering ripples of affective displacement.

The tripartite matrix of displacement that constitutes the eagle's lecture—the topic of sound as displacement, the physical flight through the air, and the momentary generic shift to satire that generates the entire scene, characterizing it with an *intentio* of gleeful vibration and oscillation—is hardly a reduction, then. Instead, it performs the difficult work of transforming the process of talking about displacement into a process of experiencing it, and of finally using the feeling of displacement to conceptualize affect, an imminent movement signaled at a structural level. The eagle's "proof" about how sound moves becomes little more than "persuasion" (872),⁶³ moving Geffrey to a position of declared concordance, if not actual acceptance or understanding. Taken

---

60. See Delany, *Chaucer's House of Fame*, esp. 74–75; see John Leyerle, "Chaucer's Windy Eagle," *University of Toronto Quarterly* 40 (1971): 255, for the eagle's lecture on sound as a joke about flatulence, and Minnis's summary (*Shorter Poems*, 223–24).

61. Leyerle, 256.

62. "Physical rapture" is Schibanoff's term for the flight, which she sees as "connoting the Chaucerian narrator's anxiety about poetic deviance" (152); on Boethian feathers, see Leyerle, 252–53, and Fyler, *Chaucer and Ovid*, 46–47.

63. Edwards, *Dream of Chaucer*, 109.

as a whole, however, the passage—whatever the eagle may have intended for it—moves in a very different way, extracting affective movement from other fields of meaning and trying to generate sensations of movement itself. Book 2 uses the inherent sensation of displacement generated by its generic choices to blur the line between the literal and the figurative, creating resonances that, as we have seen, echo well into Book 3. In the wicker basket, the transformative coagulation of *tydynges* is represented as affectively separate from Geffrey: he sees that this transformation is wondrous, but he does not take part in it in the same way he that takes part in the journey of sound from the ground to the upper atmosphere. Similarly, the emotional registration of affective movement—laughter—caused by the satire of academic lectures goes unfelt by Geffrey, even as it is felt almost immediately by his readers.

Moreover, the eagle's lecture and its accordant movements have implications for narrative invention that extend far beyond the ostensible denigration of speech as mere broken air. If sound emerges as rupture concurrent with the gaps between sections of "air ybroke," then the action of invention emerges in exactly the same way. The *ars poetica* tradition encouraged poets to find the gaps in established narratives and fill them in with new narrative inventions; sites for invention were to be located in places where narrative was "ybroke." Like *tydynges,* which are observable in terms of displacement, moments of inventional emergence are identified in terms of narrative breaking, observable, as in the eagle's analogue of water waves, only in the appearance of "litel roundell" after "litel roundell" (791). As the eagle puts it, "Although thou mowe hyt not ysee / Above, hyt [sound] gooth yet alway under, / Although thou thenke hyt a gret wonder" (804–6). This movement goes always under, unseen from above not because it is hidden but because it is perceptible only as displacement. By extension, the same principle applies to invention, which the poem works to describe not in terms of finding topics or reappropriating or replacing authoritative discourse, but as a force of movement itself perceptible only by the sense of displacement it leaves in its wake.

But the *House of Fame* does not leave the discussion of inventional emergence floating about in a whirlwind of affective abstraction or unfathomable gaps. Indeed, missing from this consideration so far are the emotional corollaries that in Chaucer's poetry tend to shape the representation of inventional emergence and move any consideration of invention beyond the merely imaginative, metafictional, and metaphysical into social, cultural, and political realms. The Dido passages of Book 1 consider topics of movement, invention, and emergence in the explicit context of emotion, suggesting how the alignment of affect with invention reveals the two concepts not simply to be analogous processes of emergence but essentially linked processes by which inventional action is made real—that is, becomes a component of living in the world.

AT A TURNING: DIDO, GEFFREY, AND THE AFFECT OF INVENTION

Geffrey's stroll through the Temple of Glass's "mnemonic *Aeneid*," as Baswell calls it,[64] emphasizes narrative gaps, places where parts of the story go missing and which generate in Geffrey increased levels of emotional engagement with the story. Creusa's sudden disappearance provokes Geffrey's first serious investment in the Trojan images, registered as "pitee" (180) and causing him to switch for the first of several times in this narrative sequence from emphasizing what he sees to emphasizing what he hears. Baswell notes the conflation of emotional and aesthetic shifts at the appearance of women among the images: Geffrey sees everything, but he then begins, "in a surprising piece of sympathetic perception," to "hear" at the moment Creusa is introduced: "It is symptomatic that this penetration of aesthetic levels and conventions occurs at a moment of heightened sympathy for a feminine character."[65] While the "pitee" he feels seems automatically to prompt Geffrey to engage more deeply with the images, Creusa's vanishing "At a turnynge of a wente" also creates the first sensation of displacement in the narrative, causing Geffrey to note "How Creusa was ylost, allas, / That ded, not I how, she was" (183–84). Creusa's ghostly reappearance a few images later fuses the earlier sense of displacement with explicit metacommentary: her function now is to impart to Aeneas "hys destinee, sauns faille" (188), which, in narrative terms, is essentially a preview of the series of images Geffrey can see lining the walls of the temple. Geffrey's encounter with this first narrative gap aligns affective and inventional emergence.

His own explicitly dramatized effort of poetic invention emerges with Dido's, and critics have long pointed to both the emotional and aesthetic entanglement of Dido and Geffrey.[66] The "sententious, if not directly proverbial"

---

64. Baswell, 233; Baswell also notes that the complex reception history of the *Aeneid* makes Virgil's texts, and thus the images in Chaucer's Temple, full of "potential meanings" for medieval readers (230).
65. Ibid., 233.
66. Baswell argues that "the act of reading itself" by both Geffrey and Dido "occupies the emotional high point of the first book of the *House of Fame*" (234); Marilynn Desmond argues that Chaucer uses the figure of Dido to explore "the relationship between authorial positions [that Chaucer's narrator] adopts as reader and translator . . . and the textualized desire" she

lines, as Delany describes them, are entrenched in the "overt sentimentality" registered by the narrator's emotional response,[67] and Geffrey links Dido's "grete peyne" (312) to his own refusal to "alegge" any "other auctor" (314). Dido is often assigned the role of importing emotional substance into the narrative of the Trojan story,[68] but Chaucer's point does not seem to be the simple equation of feeling with poetic utterance, merely suggesting how experiencing or even thinking about powerful emotions can generate powerful poetry. Instead, the passage points toward an effort to simulate a distance from the emotion and the poetry in order to glimpse not origins, but moments of imminent materialization, the very production process of emotion and poetry. Chaucer performs this dynamic investigation using expressly traditional materials: Book 1 aligns Geffrey's process of invention not only with Dido's but also with conventional medieval ideas about inventing and ordering narratives, all while framing the inventional action within the culturally conventional emotional context of Dido's suffering and Geffrey's "pitee" for her. The *medelyng* here of fields of affect and invention is what the subsequent two books of the *House of Fame* work to unpack and anatomize, and examining this passage closely reveals most fully how Chaucer works to conceptualize the affect of invention in the poem.

Chaucer was, of course, not the first poet to rewrite the *Aeneid* for different ends, as Baswell's and Desmond's comprehensive studies make clear. As with the example of Chaucer's transformation of Dante's eagle in Book 2, my argument here is not so much concerned with how Chaucer might be assimilating, critiquing or working to replace with his own vernacular *makyng* Virgil's authoritative Latin poem. Rather, I am interested in how Chaucer makes Dido, as a component of Virgil's authoritative, teleological, and masculinist narrative (at least, as it is presented as such in Chaucer's Temple of Glass), a nexus for thinking about affect and invention in terms of each other. The fact that Chaucer's Dido is presented as at once a Virgilian and Ovidian construct is important to me in particular because those authoritative texts provide the site from which Chaucer

---

represents (*Reading Dido: Gender, Textuality, and the Medieval Aeneid* [Minneapolis: University of Minnesota Press, 1994], 129).

67. Delany, *Chaucer's House of Fame*, 53.

68. Emotion is traced even to historical inquiries about whether Dido actually met Aeneas, presumably in an effort to rescue her from Aeneas's betrayal. Fyler identifies an "emotional impetus for these defenses of Dido," one rooted in the *Aeneid* itself, citing readers' apparently natural inclination to sympathize with Dido when she turns away from Aeneas in the underworld (*Chaucer and Ovid*, 34). Schibanoff argues that "Geffrey does not vicariously fall in love with Dido; he tells us that he remains an outsider to such emotion" (178). See Minnis for surveys of medieval writers who doubt the veracity of Dido's encounter with Aeneas (*Shorter Poems*, 232–34). Minnis raises the question of whether the fact that a story is "demonstrably false" potentially reduces "the emotional force" of the story for Chaucer (233).

gestures "backwards": that is to say, Virgil provides not a source text, a formal "place" for invention, but the idea, the imaginative construct, of a final invented narrative (and a culturally authoritative one at that) that fictively serves as a reference point for gestures back toward moments of imagined inventional emergence. In other words, the *Aeneid* here is not a textual "place" for the discovery of *materia* from which to invent, but rather a moment within an imagined trajectory of inventional process, a point along the flight path of the Massumian/Bergsonian arrow that the *House of Fame* works carefully to understand in terms of movements of becoming rather than in terms of origins and destinations.

Geffrey's catalogue of images suddenly stops at the moment he sees "al the dispence" that Dido lavishes on Eneas after she "demed / That he was good, for he such semed" (260, 263–64). What then follows, introduced by his sudden exclamation of "Allas!", is a rapid-fire procession of conventional moralization, terse plot summary, and proverbial expression:

> Allas! What harm doth apparence,
> Whan hit is fals in existence!
> For he to hir a traytour was;
> Wherefore she slow hirself, allas!
> Loo, how a woman doth amys
> To love hym that unknowen ys!
> For, be Cryste, lo thus yt fareth:
> "Hyt is not al gold that glareth."
> (265–72)

Next, Geffrey amplifies his interpretation of the two-sentence plot summary, mixing advice with more moralization in which he argues essentially that the lesson to be learned from this experience is that no one should be "so nyce" (276) as

> To take a love oonly for chere,
> Or speche, or for frendly manere,
> For this shal every woman fynde,
> That som man, of his pure kynde,
> Wol shewen outward the fayreste,
> Tyl he have caught that what him leste;
> And thanne wol he causes fynde
> And swere how that she ys unkynde,
> Or fals, or privy, or double was.
> (277–85)

He concludes this section by formally introducing a proverb that summarizes the whole point: "Therefore I wol seye a proverbe, / That 'he that fully knoweth th'erbe / May saufly leye hyt to his yë'" (289–91). The "moral" that this passage illustrates for Geffrey is only as straightforward as it is impossible: hold off on falling in love with someone until you know more fully what that someone is really like. This cannot be followed simply because of the very nature of the "faculte" of love itself (248), of which Geffrey, in his defense, professes to be ignorant anyway. The rest of his summary of the Aeneas story is terse and literal, and this "renewed passivity marks the shock," as Fyler calls it, "of being betrayed by his source halfway through its retelling."[69]

The passage gestures toward two different but coalescing forces: one of invention—the processes that result in poetry—and one of affect—the processes that precede their ultimate manifestation as emotions recognized as such. Geffrey articulates his invention through the voice of Dido, and however original his efforts are, Dido's cannot be. Her complaint, especially her professed realization that "Now see I wel, and telle kan, / We wrechched wymmen konne noon art" of the kind that traitorous men like Aeneas work (334–35), essentially voices in the guise of lived experience exactly what Geffrey has already stated explicitly and formally, through his earlier moralizing. But Dido's invention then extends beyond the range of Geffrey's stated topics and proverbial interpretations, extending outward to the larger theme of "wikke Fame" itself (349), the topic of Chaucer's larger work.[70] Dido ventriloquizes what future readers—readers like Geffrey himself—will say, that "Loo, ryght as she hath don, now she / Wol doo eft-sones, hardely" (358–59). Dido not only laments what she correctly sees to be her future infamy; she also essentially "invents" Geffrey as a future reader-inventor who, in composing her lament, uses it as an opportunity to explore the process of invention. Geffrey invents Dido's complaint, then, which itself is ultimately about inventing Geffrey as an inventor. For Dido, however, the gap of narrative displacement from which Geffrey invents is an expressly affective space in which the "shock" of realization and betrayal crystallizes into emotions of grief and anger. For her, this process is not simply a complex, recursive feat of metatextual acrobatics, but her own life, her own future. In his fiction of dramatized invention, Geffrey imagines an inventor occupying a space of inventional emergence affectively, transforming the narrative gap in a formal process of invention into a realm of affective experience, all while maintaining a narrative distance despite his emotional entanglement, observing how an inventor might think to find

---

69. Fyler, *Chaucer and Ovid*, 39.
70. Kruger, "Imagination and the Complex Movement," 119.

herself immersed in a field of emergence in which moments of affect and invention are indistinguishable. Geffrey, imagining backward in time, invents Dido imagining forward, as each inventor sees "utterly" the subsequent images of the Aeneas story (296). Their crisscrossing inventional gestures generate a sensation of displacement that occurs alongside their emotional experiences and their inventional efforts.

For all its metatextual subtlety, this process of carefully structuring metatextual material to create sensations of displacement in fact occurs according to the traditional strictures of formal invention practices. For example, in the *Poetria nova*, lyrically amplifying a medieval convention for finding a way to start a poem, Geoffrey of Vinsauf identifies selecting a proverb as an effective way of beginning a work:

> If a still more brilliant beginning is desired (while leaving the sequence of the material unchanged) make use of a proverb, ensuring that it may not sink to a purely specific relevance, but raise its head high to some general truth. See that, while prizing the charm of the unusual, it may not concentrate its attention on the particular subject, but refuse, as if in disdain, to remain within its bosom. Let it take a stand above the given subject, but look with direct glance toward it. Let it say nothing directly about the subject, but derive its inspiration therefrom.... It is reluctant to appear, unless, indeed, it is compelled to do so. Proverbs, in this way, add distinction to a poem. [71]

Dido does not simply become an example of the importance of following the advice of Geffrey's opening proverb to know the properties of something before you make it a part of your life, nor is she simply an example of someone who does not follow the advice of that specific proverb. She also becomes a kind of proverb herself by acting like one with respect to the narrative in which she explicitly finds herself. Moreover, she is not merely *this* proverb— about herbs and eyes—but *any* proverb, based on her relationship to the narrative *materia* that will become her fame. She laments not only her betrayal and the actions leading up to it but also the results of future inventions, and she imagines what future readers will say about her love for Aeneas. Like Geoffrey of Vinsauf's proverb, Dido struggles to "stand above the given subject" of the invented narrative that will characterize her for posterity, and her own

---

71. "Si pars prima velit majus diffundere lumen, / Thematis intacta serie, sententia sumpta / Ad speciale nihil declinet, sed caput edat / Altius ad quoddam generale; novoque lepore / Materiae formam nolit meminisse, sed ejus / Abneget in gremio, quasi dedignata, sedere: / Supra thema datum sistat, sed spectet ad illud / Recta fronte; nihil dicat, sed cogitet inde ... [V]enit invite, nisi forte venire coactus. / Sic opus illustrnt poverbia." Faral, 2.126–42; Nims, 20–21.

historical position mirrors that of the proverb: in terms of how future reader-inventors will remember her and her "nyce lest," Dido "is reluctant to appear" until she is "compelled to do so." Dido functions analogously to a proverb, at once encapsulating and looking back on the matter she introduces; in this function, she registers the displacement that characterizes both affective and inventional emergence, conceptualizing each in terms of the other and linking both in a single narrative of the process of poetic invention.

My argument here is not that Geoffrey of Vinsauf provides a direct source for the *House of Fame;* indeed, as Martin Camargo has shown, it is less likely that Chaucer knew the *Poetria nova* earlier in his career than later, when he discovered Geoffrey's treatise at Oxford as part of a wider interest in rhetorical texts in circulation there, though Camargo does leave open the possibility that Chaucer may have known the treatise when he wrote the *House of Fame.*[72] Whatever the case, Geoffrey of Vinsauf's ideas about proverbs and artificial and natural narrative order were, like his house-building metaphor, commonplaces of compositional theory; as Camargo puts it, "By Chaucer's day, the contents of the arts of poetry and prose by Matthew of Vendôme and Geoffrey of Vinsauf are likely to have been absorbed into standard teaching materials and practices, even if the treatises themselves no longer were readily available."[73] Indeed, Matthew of Vendôme, writing before Geoffrey, and John of Garland, writing after, similarly note the benefits of beginning compositions with proverbs, particularly when finding things to say about people.[74] As Marjorie Curry Woods notes, the *Poetria nova* itself was quickly mined by commentators who extracted proverbs from their context as inventional

---

72. Camargo introduces Cooper's argument for the possibility of a later composition date for *House of Fame,* during which time Chaucer may well have known the *Poetria nova* (198–99). The specific dating of *House of Fame* with regard to the other early dream narratives, however, does not affect my argument about its earlier position with regard to the *Legend of Good Women* and the *Canterbury Tales.*

73. Ibid., 197.

74. As is characteristic of these *artes poetriae,* Matthew and John provide copious examples of proverbs for different subjects. Matthew likewise notes the benefits of beginning with proverbs, in particular because they introduce "a general idea, to which credence is customarily given, common opinion readers assent, and by which the integrity of uncorrupted truth is undisturbed" [id est communis sententia, cui consuentudo fidem attribuit, opinio communis assensum accomodat, incorruptae veritatis integritas adquiescit] (Faral, 1.16; Parr, 22). John defines proverbs even more succinctly as "a brief statement, moral in purpose, setting forth what is good or bad in an important matter" [sententia breuis ad instructionem dicta, comodum uel incomodum grandis materie manifestans] (Latin and English translation in *The* Parisiana *poetria of John of Garland,* ed. and trans. Traugott Lawler [New Haven, CT: Yale University Press, 1974], 12–13); even his concise definition introduces the immense cultural weight that proverbs were meant to embody and convey.

strategies.[75] I quote Geoffrey here because of the way in which his personified rendering of the rhetorical figure in fact theorizes it more fully, revealing the concepts that underwrite even the most commonplace compositional prescriptions, like using proverbs.

Chaucer's Geffrey makes Dido into a formal figure for the coemergence of affect and invention, created through sensations of displacement and residual emotional and inventional effects. As a figure for the processes of invention, she resonates at several metapoetic levels. She is the subject of the dreaming Geffrey's first formal invention, and that invention is itself Dido's own invented lament. The focus of her lament is on the future reception of the false narrative that Aeneas's actions themselves have invented, and in inventing and being invented in this way by Geffrey, Dido "proverbially" encapsulates and looks back on the experience she is made to represent. Like Creusa, who "was ylost, allas," very suddenly "At a turnynge of a wente," Dido becomes a figure of perpetual emergence able to be seen only through a kind of perturbation, unknowable except through the plainly fabricated narratives of Fame and the emotions obligatorily assigned to her narrative. Like a *tydynge* in the house of twigs, Dido is at once a figure for, and yet composed of, the same *substaunce* as the unfolding event of which she is a part. She is not only a figment of discourse manipulated by future speakers but also a filament of inventional emergence, traceable, ultimately, only in terms of motional displacement.

None of this complex representational work mapping intersecting fields of affective and inventional movement does Dido any good, however. For all this talk of inventional potential, she is still as trapped in the Aeneas narrative as she ever was. In fact, this dynamic figuration of affect and invention relies on keeping Dido in stasis and essentially exploiting her as a means by which Chaucer can explore an affective poetics of invention. As such, this project becomes an inventional corollary to what Elaine Tuttle Hansen sees to be the larger project of Geffrey's becoming "feminized" through his entanglement with the story of Dido: "it is in this man's likeness to women, in his femininity or perhaps androgyny, that the narrator differs from, and is superior to, Dido," who, in her lament against Fame, "firmly endorses her own subjugation within the totalizing category of women," while Geffrey, "the unmanly, sympathetic narrator, by contrast, articulates in his self-representation the ambiguity and fluidity of gender, which become readable as the possibility of transcending the problems of gender and heterosexual relations altogether."[76] Geffrey con-

---

75. Marjorie Curry Woods, *Classroom Commentaries: Teaching the* Poetria nova *across Medieval and Renaissance Europe* (Columbus: The Ohio State University Press, 2010), 44–47.

76. Elaine Tuttle Hansen, *Chaucer and the Fictions of Gender* (Berkeley: University of California Press, 1992), 104. "Feminization" for Hansen is "a dramatized state of social, psychological,

structs for himself a dominant masculine identity by enacting the realization of the fluidity of gender, an enactment that relies for its demonstration on the more static understanding explicitly expressed by Dido.[77] Figuring Dido as a proverb may make her into a text with a special interpretive prerogative in Geoffrey of Vinsauf's formulation—one in which inventional potential is a necessary characteristic of existence—but it is still, ultimately, just a text. At the same time, however, Dido becomes an inventor, an imposer of form. Whereas Geoffrey's proverb "stand[s] above the given subject . . . look[ing] with direct glance towards it" but "say[ing] nothing," Dido says *something*, and this takes her characterization beyond what Catherine Sanok has called the key marker of medieval misogyny, figuring women as matter onto which form is imposed, or as Marilynn Desmond puts it, "the sexual politics of reading and the unrepresentability of woman, except as representation."[78] Indeed, proverbs, as quintessentially precise texts, reify; they simulate the particulars of experience in their very gestures toward the representation of larger cultural "truths." At the same time, however, the affective relationship—one of reluctance, resistance, and disconnection—that Geoffrey of Vinsauf establishes especially for proverbs would seem to challenge that reification because of the sense of movement and emergence they represent. In the same way that, in the Proem to Book 1, Geffrey suggests more broadly that dreams, as a topic for poetic invention, be thought of in terms of movement and trajectory rather than meaning or signification, Dido's transformation into a proverb emphasizes not her reification but her displacement, her standing apart from that process even as it occurs.

Ultimately, though, any agency that Dido has is limited and contingent. To argue that the inventional efforts in some way dispel the forces that have prompted those particular efforts in the first place is to ignore the inventional and affective realities of her position: available to her is a range of inventional

---

and discursive crisis wherein men occupy positions and/or perform functions already occupied and performed, within a given text and its contexts, by women or normatively assigned by orthodox discourses to Woman" (16).

77. Several critics variously engage Hansen's compelling argument. Baswell argues that Aeneas himself displays "feminine" qualities normally assigned to Dido (390n10); Desmond argues that Geffrey ultimately "resists . . . feminization" and the "dangers" it poses to totalizing masculinist narratives like the *Aeneid* (151); Kordecki is "not convinced that Chaucer's dreamer is capable of actually embodying the subversive female voice" represented in part by Dido (41); and Schibanoff argues that Geffrey's focus never actually shifts from Aeneas to Dido (177–79).

78. Catherine Sanok, "Reading Hagiographically: *The Legend of Good Women* and Its Feminine Audience," *Exemplaria* 13 (2001): 328; Desmond, 141. Desmond furthermore ascribes the breaking down of Geffrey's control of the narrative at the point of Dido's suffering not to emotional intensity but to his sense of "the female character whose sexuality threaten[s] the mythic program of the *Aeneid*," and his further inability "to fit her into an objectifying category" (146).

topics and emotional experiences limited to despair, betrayal, and the realization of perpetual misunderstandings of her own words. Her acts of invention finally relegate her to the limited and contingent inventional material pithily captured in the couplet, "Dido, and hir nyce lest, / That loved al to sone a gest" (287–88). It is possible to argue that this entire metatextual process represents the imposition of masculine form on the feminine matter of Dido: making Dido an inventor only makes her say what Geffrey is already thinking. In this way, Dido becomes again little more than a vivid example of loving a guest too easily—an *exemplum* itself. The same formal mechanism that grants the Dido passage its status as the most affectively and inventionally charged moment of the *House of Fame* also renders Dido in masculinist terms, even at this abstracted level of metacommentary on invention: her connection to the emergent potential of proverbs is realized only in the larger context of Aeneas's masculinist narrative.

Yet even in this reading, the *House of Fame* does not, at least at the metatextual level of inventional reflection, shut down Dido's resiliency as an agent of emergence and potential. One of the extant manuscripts of the *House of Fame* records a variant in its analysis of Dido's tragic flaw. In the Pepys 2006 manuscript, she "loved al to sone a gost," not a "gest."[79] That is to say, Dido, in the context of the twig house's metaphorical references, falls in love not with a guest newly arrived from burned-out Troy, but a ghost—a "fantome," the potentially dangerous and uncontrollable species of image that swirls in the vortex of the imaginative cell of medieval faculty psychology.[80] In loving all too easily a phantasm, the Dido of Pepys 2006 falls in love not with a person, but with the patriarchal, phantasmal image that Aeneas represents, the whole force of masculinist perspective that characterizes the cultural reception of both the *Aeneid* and the Ovidian texts that, traditionally, are read to destabilize the Virgilian tradition.[81] This one variant distills not only the whole destabilizing theme of the *House of Fame* into a singular, anthropomorphized phantasm but also acknowledges the movement at work in both Dido's affective entanglement with Aeneas and the vying inventions that characterize him

---

79. See Nicholas R. Havely's edition of the poem, (Durham, UK: Durham Medieval Texts, 1994), 106, note to line 288. William Caxton's edition of the poem assumes this reading, printing "ghost" for "gest."

80. For a summary of the resonances of "fantome" in *House of Fame,* see Quinn, "Chaucer's Recital Presence," 172; Quinn refers in passing to Aeneas as a "phantom" (175), identifies the *tydynge*-people of Book 3 as "re-formed phantoms of the speakers" (183), and calls the text of the *House of Fame* itself "a phantom of Chaucer's recital of the work" to a live audience of listeners (190).

81. This Ovid-versus-Virgil binary reduces the reality of the reception history, as many critics have noted. See especially Baswell; and Desmond, 261n2.

and the tradition he represents. It is likewise tempting to see a pun at work in the standard version of the line, "loved al to sone a gest," reading *gest* not merely as "guest" but also *geste,* that is, the English *turnyng* of the Latin *gesta,* at once a deed, an event that happened, and the poetic-historical discourse that records or creates (that is to say, lies about) the deed, a play on words that Chaucer seems to develop elsewhere as well.[82] In loving too quickly a *geste,* Dido finds herself becoming entangled with the discourse-event, the *tydynge* itself, the always-emerging emotional-inventional phenomenon that is Aeneas. In this specially charged metatextual environment, Dido can never function as a mere *exemplum.*

I have argued in this chapter that the *House of Fame* works carefully and deliberately to represent literally (as far as that is possible) the processes by which invention functions as a kind of movement and emergence. At the same time, the poem yokes this emphasis on invention-as-movement to the imagined emotional experience of Dido, representing her as a fictive construct and poetic figure, but also as a feeling human agent who imagines herself as such—all in an attempt to gesture toward the ways in which affect and invention together emerge into emotional experience and poetry. Throughout his poetic career, Chaucer takes up the ideas that he works through in the *House of Fame,* and the poem functions as a kind of starting point for charting the development of these ideas. Indeed, Geffrey follows his own invention on the topic of Dido with a list of suffering women that becomes, in retrospect, a preview of the *Legend of Good Women,* "a sort of chain reaction concerning other wronged women of the past," including Phillis, Ariadne, Hypsipyle, and Medea.[83] In an important sense, this catalogue implicitly acknowledges that what Geffrey is doing is not really different from the actions of other male writers who "usen here . . . women for to" advance their own literary fame.[84] The question remains whether the space of emergence that Geffrey and Dido open together provides any sort of escape from this misogynistic trope of masculinist invention. I think that the answer is ultimately yes, but it is in the *Legend of Good Women* that Chaucer more fully explores both the processes by which this can occur and also the significance of such processes for poetry and the culture it engages.

---

82. See, for example, the *Miller's Tale* for a similar pun, one in which the Miller deliberately echoes the language of the Knight as he transitions immediately from the Knight's "noble storie"—that is, a narrative *geste*—into a story about a "riche gnof, that gestes heeld to bord" (3188).

83. Minnis, *Shorter Poems,* 244.

84. *Troilus and Criseyde,* 4.182.

CHAPTER 2

"RYGHT SWICH AS YE FELTEN"

Aligning Affect and Invention in *The Legend of Good Women*

IN THE PREVIOUS CHAPTER, I argued that the *House of Fame* represents poetic invention in terms of movement by drawing on medieval commonplaces about imagination as a component of medieval faculty psychology that itself emphasizes movement, and then literalizing in the *tydynge*-house of Book 3 a process by which the movements and sensations of coming to a discovery collapse and transform into invented forms and texts. The *House of Fame* also explicitly links this abstracted examination of invention to the emotional experience that the dreaming narrator imagines for Dido. By constructing Dido at once as a feeling subject and as an inventional agent operating in narrative gaps, the poem powerfully illustrates the relationship between affect, invention, and culturally pervasive discourses of gender and power. The *House of Fame*, however, never suggests how its alignment of affective and inventional processes might result in productive alternatives for thinking about such cultural forms. *The Legend of Good Women*—itself forecast in the images that Geffrey sees in the Temple of Glass—does take this next step, actively working to trigger in readers a sudden awareness of the pervasiveness of cultural constructions of gender and power.

The *Legend* is a dream vision immediately awash in feelings. As the poem begins, this new Geffrey defines himself from the outset in terms of the "condicioun" brought about by his intense "affeccioun" for the May daisy (F 40, 44).[1] At the same time, virtually nothing can turn him from his books, not simply because he has the "feyth," "ful credence," and "reverence" one ought to have for "olde appreved stories," but also because of the sheer "delyte" the stories offer him (31–32, 21, 30). The legends likewise wrench their protagonists between radical extremes of love and despair, and even the poem's opening epistemological quandary presents itself in emotional terms: its example of knowledge that can be reported only in texts is nothing short of the "joy" of heaven (2). Among these affective currents, the *Legend* navigates its relationship to literary tradition and the conditions of its own invention to such a degree that critics have long identified the poem as yet another Chaucerian *ars poetica*, though in a form very different from that of the *House of Fame*.[2] Given what we have seen in that earlier poem, it is perhaps not a surprise that Chaucer's revised, sustained treatment of poetics occurs alongside one of his most explicit explorations of affective experience. Indeed, the *Legend* takes up affect and invention together as components of a single poetic project. Whereas the *House of Fame* gestures fragmentarily and abstractly toward affective elements of invention, coming closest to an articulation of the concept in its complex but refracted depiction of Geffrey's contemplation of Dido, the *Legend* most fully reformulates invention as an affective force. Reading the poem with this focus reveals how the operation of its poetics provides a new perspective on the vexed question of how the *Legend* positions itself within a literary tradition characterized by antifeminism and misogyny, and in doing so, how it develops more fully the productive potential of the inventional poetics first dissected and examined in the *House of Fame*.

As a palinode responding to the anger of the God of Love, the *Legend* generically assumes emotion to be central to the fictional account of its invention, and emotional experience has since been a vital, if not always acknowledged, part of the critical reception of the poem. Indeed, the central question of that reception—whether the *Legend* undermines or exacerbates antifeminist tradition—often centers on readers' affective responses: Does it ultimately feel like Chaucer is being ironic or sincere?[3] While some critics contend that the

---

1. Like most critics, I assume the F *Prologue* to be the earlier text and G a revision.

2. Important discussions of the *Legend* as an *ars poetica* include Robert O. Payne, *The Key of Remembrance: A Study of Chaucer's Poetics* (New Haven, CT: Yale University Press, 1963), 91–111; Lisa J. Kiser, *Telling Classical Tales: Chaucer and the* Legend of Good Women (Ithaca, NY: Cornell University Press, 1983); and Russell A. Peck, "Chaucerian Poetics and the Prologue to the *Legend of Good Women*," in *Chaucer in the Eighties*, ed. Julian N. Wasserman and Robert J. Blanch (Syracuse, NY: Syracuse University Press, 1986), 39–55. I treat their work more fully in what follows.

3. For summaries of this tradition, see William A. Quinn, ed., *Chaucer's Dream Visions and Shorter Poems* (New York: Garland, 1999), 299–302; Carolyn P. Collette, "Rethinking the

Legend introduces emotions only to dismiss them,[4] Robert Worth Frank, Jr., argues that its representation of emotions rescues the poem from oversimplification and exemplary moralizing, and Sheila Delany finds its affective material to be richly ambiguous and "subversive of easy assumptions."[5] Moreover, critics have acknowledged the important role that the depiction of emotional experience plays in the *Legend*'s discussion of poetic invention—though often arriving at opposite conclusions. Lisa J. Kiser and Russell Peck, for example, see emotion as integral to a transcendent species of vernacular poetry symbolically imagined in the *Prologue*, while Carolyn Dinshaw sees it as ultimately halting poetic production.[6] Most recently, L. O. Aranye Fradenburg argues

---

Legend of Good Women: Context and Reception," in The Legend of Good Women: *Context and Reception*, ed. Carolyn P. Collette (Cambridge: Brewer, 2006), vii–ix; and the bibliographies in Minnis, *Shorter Poems*. See also Nicola F. McDonald, who argues that fourteenth-century female readers would have understood the poem in the context of playfully erotic courtly games, arguing that in this context, it is difficult to take the *Legend* as seriously as those fifteenth-century readers who treated it as conduct literature ("Games Medieval Women Play," in Collette, The Legend of Good Women, 176–97; and "Chaucer's *Legend of Good Women*, Ladies at Court and the Female Reader," *Chaucer Review* 35 [2000]: 22–42).

4. Arguing that this dismissal is a necessary step toward achieving a kind of rational transcendence or to humiliate its protagonists further, Donald Rowe sees the poem demonstrating how the "poet's rationality" "frees" readers from the "blindness" of the legends' emotion (*Through Nature to Eternity: Chaucer's* Legend of Good Women [Lincoln: University of Nebraska Press, 1988], 139); see Jill Mann's response to Rowe in *Geoffrey Chaucer* (Atlantic Highlands, NJ: Humanities Press International, 1991), 40–41. Alcuin Blamires sees emotions as components of "an idolatrous empiricism" that Chaucer dismisses in favor of textual authority ("A Chaucer Manifesto," *Chaucer Review* 24 [1989]: 36).

5. Sheila Delany, *The Naked Text: Chaucer's* Legend of Good Women (Berkeley: University of California Press, 1994), 235. For Frank, "feeling is at once more complex and more ambiguous than moralization, which normally oversimplifies an action and narrowly limits the range of reaction" (*Chaucer and* The Legend of Good Women [Cambridge, MA: Harvard University Press, 1972], 174), and Minnis argues that the "the *Legend* may be regarded as the poet's most consistent and sustained experiment" in pathetic verse (*Shorter Poems*, 344). See also Dorothy Guerin, "Chaucer's Pathos: Three Variations," *Chaucer Review* 20 (1985): 90–112, and Steven F. Kruger, "Passion and Order in Chaucer's *Legend of Good Women*," *Chaucer Review* 23 (1989): 219–35.

6. For Kiser, who offers the most thorough analysis of the *Legend* as an *ars poetica*, the poem models how literature can provide a crucial "indirect vision" for regulating overpowering experience; Chaucer, when "faithful to the spirit of his source . . . is able to reproduce and convey whatever emotional power it contains" (145), and this transfer of emotional authenticity contrasts sharply with the "emotional wasteland" of court poetry (146). Peck argues that the *Prologue* establishes emotion as the means of achieving visionary poetry beyond the binary of text and experience: "the poetic vision [the narrator] encounters through the daisy is in its own way empirical, albeit proven on the heart and seen only through the eye of affection" ("Chaucerian Poetics," 50). Dinshaw argues that "it's clear from the abandoned series of legends that reading like a man leads to no literary activity at all" (*Chaucer's Sexual Poetics*, 87). Payne argues in passing that Chaucer represents his relationship to old books as the product of "some *mysterious* compulsion in the attraction of . . . shifting forms of beauty and desire"

that the poem sustains both extremes by evoking two contrasting emotions: the beauty of the *Prologue*'s daisy is charged with a transformative representational power to encode and transmit the "joy" inherent in artistic creation and appreciation, while the legends themselves evoke an anxiety of trauma that halts the very imaginative processes the figure of the daisy represents.[7] In this reading, the legends thus work to perpetuate the misogynistic traditions that prescribe the fates of their protagonists and define feminine identity only in terms of masculinist constructions of gender.[8]

Rather than read the legends as being in affective opposition to the *Prologue*'s potential, or how the *Legend* generates sublimely transcendent poetry or abject poetic failure, I aim instead to show how the two parts of the *Legend* sustain a concerted effort to articulate the forces that shape emotion and poetry. Amid its interest in the representation of emotional experience, the *Legend* also works to represent affect as something distinct from emotion—those initial visceral responses that, in the context of the *Legend*'s narratives, precede emotions before their recognition and interpretation by the mind as emotions. As part of the same effort, the poem works to represent the movement of invention, the actions and energies that occur before but result in invented poetry. The *Legend* studies not only emotion itself but also its emergence as affect, not only poetry but also its emergence as invention, and it does so by blending together both of these trajectories of collapse within the narrative arc of its prologue and the experiences of individual characters within the legends.

My focus here, then, offers something of a change in direction from much recent discussion of poetic process in the *Legend*. In addition to yoking together the *Prologue* and legends as part of a wholesale effort to investigate invention, I turn my attention momentarily away from Chaucer's efforts to validate his own poetry in the face of authoritative tradition. For example, Rita Copeland has thoroughly demonstrated how in the *Prologue* especially, Chaucer "invents his own authorship" by treating his own poetic works in the way exegetes treat those of Ovid, thus displacing the texts of Latinate tradition with self-authorized vernacular inventions.[9] While Chaucer's relationship to

---

which Chaucer finally "must register . . . emotionally, whether or not he can account for them" ("Making His Own Myth: The Prologue to Chaucer's *Legend of Good Women*," *Chaucer Review* 9 [1975]: 207–8; emphasis in original).

7. Fradenburg, "Beauty and Boredom," 73.

8. See also Fradenburg, *Sacrifice Your Love*, 195–97; and "Beauty and Boredom," 79–80.

9. Copeland writes, "For Chaucer to use the critical vocabulary normally applied to Ovid and to apply it to himself in his translations of Ovid and other *auctores* is to carry through on the motive of displacement always at work in exegesis and in exegetical translation: in the *Legend of Good Women* Chaucer invents his own authorship out of the conventional *topoi* of

his sources is very much central to the *Legend*—this relationship, after all, is what constructs "the key" of "remembraunce" (26)—the poem also, and quite consciously, works to express the creative process of writing poetry in terms other than authorial politics. I begin this exploration in the *Prologue* of the poem, showing how the manipulation of narrative form and intertextual borrowings introduces a theoretical method for reconceptualizing invention as an affective force, articulated in terms of shifts and motions, as were sketched out earlier in the *House of Fame* but theorized here more fully as a kind of poetics. The individual legends then apply that theory to short narrative cases. They develop the method laid out in the *Prologue*, dramatizing the process by which affect and invention are transformed into emotion and poetry and working to simulate the experience of affect and invention, ultimately turning that experience to political ends. *The Legend of Good Women* functions as Chaucer's fullest narrative treatise on the affect of invention. It works carefully and thoroughly to define affect and invention in terms of each other, to formulate invention as a process concurrent with the movements of affective emergence, and, as a consequence, to destabilize the antifeminist literary and cultural traditions its narratives would seem to represent.

AFFECTIVE AND INVENTIONAL EMERGENCE IN THE *PROLOGUE*

The *Prologue* first generates a sensation of displacement through its use of source texts about poetic invention, and then enacts through the narrator's reported experience the process by which initial movements of affect and invention collapse into emotion and narrative. The narrator's emotional devotion to the daisy at first appears to be the result of commonplace medieval practices of the production of emotion through the internalization and performance of the kind of "intimate scripts" that Sarah McNamer has shown to be vital to the cultivation and expression of emotional experience via vernacular religious texts.[10] The narrator's overwhelming emotional "condicioun" (40)—his "gret affeccioun" at the "blisful sighte" of the daisy that "softneth al [his] sorwe," makes him "so glad," and causes him to declare of the daisy, "I love it, and ever ylike newe, / And evere shal til that myn herte dye" (44–57)—is in fact "learned" (and here translated) from the texts of Froissart,

---

Ovidian exegesis" (*Rhetoric, Hermeneutics, and Translation*, 195); as I noted in the Introduction, I also use the term "displacement" differently than Copeland.

10. See McNamer, *Affective Meditation*, and my discussion in the Introduction.

Deschamps, and Machaut.¹¹ Chaucer's borrowing is typically viewed as the conflation of text and experience, a view ironically compounded by the narrator's explicit separation of each from the other as he bids "Farewel" to his books (39)—a separation that, as Florence Percival notes, is illusory but, as Catherine Sanok suggests, questions "the very possibility of differentiating between life and literature."¹² Learned emotions also seem to inform the narrator's reading habits. His first affective admissions refer not to May or daisies, but to his books. He confesses that "in myn herte [I] have hem in reverence / So hertely" that almost nothing can divert him from them (32–33). Borrowing the terms McNamer uses to analyze how devotional texts generate conditioned emotional responses in spiritual settings, we might say that the narrator's library becomes the "intimate script" that, if not teaching him wisdom, has taught him how to feel. He then literally performs the affective habits he has learned, returning "hom" at day's end to recreate the experience of the field, commanding his servants to "strawen floures on my bed" that he might reenact not only his own experience but also the French texts that structured the initial performance in the first place (200, 207). The cyclical motion of the narrator's own "besy gost" that "thursteth alwey newe" further emphasizes and internalizes this process. His *gost*—the aspect of his self that registers affect and is separate from reason and the mind¹³—churns repeatedly through an endless series of affective motions, "experiencing and re-experiencing" the daisy,¹⁴ that neither textual meditation nor direct experience will satisfy. Texts and their performance would thus appear to "make feeling" in the way McNamer describes.¹⁵

The affective *besinesse* of the narrator's *gost* is not simply overwhelming emotion, however, but also an indication of the "conscious-autonomic mix" that, as we have seen, Brian Massumi argues precedes emotional experience as such, the nonlocalized potential for emergence that is "immanent" to experience.¹⁶ While the scripting process seems to describe the experience of the narrator, at the metanarrative level the *Prologue* defies this sort of inscription,

---

11. For accounts of Chaucer's borrowings from this tradition, see John L. Lowes, "The Prologue to the *Legend of Good Women* as Related to the French *Marguerite* Poems and to the *Filostrato*," *PMLA* 19 (1904): 593–683; James I. Wimsatt, *Chaucer and His French Contemporaries: Natural Music in the Fourteenth Century* (Toronto: University of Toronto Press, 1991), 161–68; Minnis, *Shorter Poems*, 349–54; and Florence Percival, *Chaucer's Legendary Good Women* (Cambridge: Cambridge University Press, 1998), 24–46.
12. Percival, 25; Sanok, 333.
13. See *MED*, "gost," 3a.
14. Peck, "Chaucerian Poetics," 45.
15. McNamer, "Feeling," in Strohm, *Middle English*, 248.
16. Massumi, 25, 33.

and through this defiance it gestures toward the more nebulous inventional movements that precede formal activities. The narrator first speaks of invention in expressly borrowed terms. After lamenting that he cannot "make of sentement" in "Englyssh, ryme or prose, / Suffisant this flour to preyse aryght" (66–69), he explains how an initial moment of affect results in the generation of the very poetry he narrates. The daisy would seem to pluck his heartstrings, "as an harpe obeieth to the hond / And maketh it soune after his fyngerynge," and "Ryght so mowe ye oute of myn herte bringe / Swich vois, ryght as yow lyst, to laughe or pleyne" (90–93). For Delany, the passage "is a perfect example of self-reflexive subversion," ironically demonstrating that the poet "is a world-class maker."[17] This *makyng*, however, is a translation, but one deriving not from Latin *auctores* but from the opening stanzas of Boccaccio's *Filostrato*. The lines describe metaphorically the simultaneous process of affective and poetic invention—a muse whose affective manipulation is registered physiologically and results in the poetic conversion of affect into emotion—and do so as a translated vernacular text. It is not a flower that plucks the narrator's heartstrings, but a Florentine.

Examining more closely how this textual borrowing works, however, reveals that the passage does much more than simply demonstrate how easy it is for Chaucer to counterfeit authentic emotion;[18] it also reveals how the *Prologue* generates a sense of displacement—that is, a sensation of movement akin to those registered in the *House of Fame* rather than an authoritative replacing of Boccaccio's text with Chaucer's—that works to gesture toward the sensation of pre-inventional movements coming into some kind of poetic form. Drawing on the opening stanzas of the *Filostrato* in which Boccaccio seeks poetic inspiration from Fiammetta, Chaucer borrows an invocation that calls for aid through an explicit project of affective displacement:

Tu se' nel tristo petto effigiata
con forza tal, che tu vi puoi più ch'io;
pingine fuor la voce sconsolata
in guisa tal che mostri il dolor mio
nell'altrui doglie. . . .

---

17. Delany, *Naked Text*, 58.
18. Blamires, 38–39; Blamires suggests that the veiled citation of Boccaccio may constitute a "labyrinthine joke," rewriting the opening of the *Troilus* as Cupid would have liked, but using a source of which Cupid is unaware (38–39). For David Wallace, Chaucer's use of Boccaccio is "a secret betrayal of his imagined audience" (*Chaucerian Polity: Absolutist Lineages and Associational Forms in England and Italy* [Stanford, CA: Stanford University Press, 1997], 350).

Thy image is fixed so strongly in my sad breast that thou hast greater sway there than I myself. Drive forth from it my despairing voice in such guise that my grief will show itself in another's sorrow.[19]

The *Filostrato* identifies its muse by her ability to relocate the poet's feelings inside Troiolo's. As Chaucer's lines convert Boccaccio's transfer of affect into a transfer of invocation, they also invoke the displacement of affect that is the subject of Boccaccio's text. Chaucer's passage reverberates with textual shifts and movements: someone else's poetry provides the narrator's description of his authentic experience, and at the same time the subject of these borrowed words is the switching of affect with poetic invention. Operating always beneath the narrative of emotional experience that determines the surface topic of Chaucer's dream vision, this metatextual sensation of movement is how the *Prologue* constructs its gestures toward affect and invention. As Peck and David Wallace note, for a moment the narrator appears to become "nothing": no one, finally, plays the narrator's heartstrings, not even the narrator himself.[20] They appear to resonate on their own.

Moreover, they resonate in English. Chaucer overloads his translation with words of English (as opposed to French) origin, and the rapid succession of "wynt," "ledeth," "hert," "sorwfull," "brest," "dredeth," "word," "werk," "knyt," "bond," and, most significant, "harpe," "fyngerynge," and "soune" (85–91), supports Delany's sense of "the Englishness that pervades" the poem and marks its "sensibility."[21] The vocabulary also establishes a residual impression of something preceding both Boccaccio's text and its translation and conveying a feeling—though not the reality—of authenticity. The music of the narrator's plucked heartstrings *sounds* English. Through the doubled movement between Boccaccio's text and Chaucer's, and between each text's topics of affective and inventional displacement, this action simulates the "echo" of affect, resulting in a sense that some anterior force "gooth yet alway under" (*House of Fame*, 805) these lines.[22] My point here, then, is not that Chaucer disguises his use of Boccaccio, but that this highly metapoetic process of textual borrowing is a way of pointing toward a necessarily inaccessible affective occurrence, a moment that is only ever retrospectively articulable in the discourses of emotion. Likewise, the *Legend*—or indeed any poem—cannot represent the

---

19. Boccaccio, *Filostrato*, quoted from *Tutte le opere*, ed. Vittore Branca, vol. 2 (Milan: Mondadori, 1964), 1.5.1–5; the English translation is by R. K. Gordon, *The Story of Troilus* (New York: Dutton, 1964), 31.
20. Peck, "Chaucerian Poetics," 44; Wallace, 350.
21. Delany, *Naked Text*, 229.
22. Massumi, 14.

affect of invention directly, but it can only ever gesture toward it, thematizing displacement and movement to generate the feeling that something is in motion behind and before these already-invented and already-felt narratives. This passage thus also suggests a very different kind of intertextuality than is usually traced by modern readers of the *Legend,* one in which a process of poetic invention appears to occur outside of—but not independently of—the politics of authorial self-presentation and cultural appropriation. I do not mean to suggest that Chaucer is not interested in issues of authority, of course, but I do want to emphasize that there seems to be something else going on inventionally in the Prologue, a carefully crafted sensation of a kind of poetry coming into being, that cannot be explained only by appealing to strategies of authorial politics.

That something is the way in which the *Legend* works to align affect and invention, and the daisy would seem to be an icon of that alignment, a figure that appears at once to capture without halting this intensely metapoetic sensation of movement. Indeed, it has often been seen as a figural panacea for the problems of representing representation. For Kiser, the daisy's poetic lexical origins (a "dayesye" is the "ye of day" [184]) fuse metaphor and etymology, allowing the daisy to work like poetry: "it names clearly yet indirectly the thing it symbolizes."[23] In so doing, the daisy, as James Simpson puts it, "can represent nothing but figuration itself," the reading of which Peck argues constitutes "a religious experience" for the narrator, one in which "imagination functions both naturally and mythically."[24] For Fradenburg, the daisy captures but also expresses movement (its opening and closing), and it becomes an almost ideal aesthetic object that generates communities among people by compelling the transfer and reproduction of its transformative beauty.[25] Again, however, such figurative fusion depends on cultural fission: the daisy is a remarkable flower primarily because it is *not* a French flower but an English one. Its etymology is likewise remarkable not merely for its accuracy or ability to collapse figurative and literal meanings but also because it is exclusively English. Paradoxically, the daisy relies on its separateness in order to achieve its acts of representational synthesis. This back and forth—a figure that demands to be read as standing for "figuration itself" but that takes the

---

23. Kiser, 50.

24. James Simpson, "Ethics and Interpretation: Reading Wills in Chaucer's *Legend of Good Women,*" *Studies in the Age of Chaucer* 20 (1998): 88–89; Peck, "Chaucerian Poetics," 46. See also Fyler, *Chaucer and Ovid,* 116–19. Both Peck (46, 50–51) and Kiser (47–48) note the equation of the daisy to the Virgin Mary. Delany too notes the narrator's religious devotion to the daisy (*Naked Text,* 66–68), but she finds Alceste to be "deeply ambiguous" (107).

25. Fradenburg, "Beauty and Boredom," 66–74.

shape demanded by the literary tradition that informs it—likewise gestures toward, if not representing outright, the sensation of movement that Chaucer had linked with the processes of inventional discovery far more explicitly in the *House of Fame*. In the case of the daisy, the result of this back-and-forth movement is not the assertion of linguistic or cultural authority but the generation of a felt sense of something moving underneath conventional patterns of both textual representation and emotional experience.

As these metatextual resonances echo through the *Prologue*, on the surface level the narrator's recognition of Alceste dramatizes the collapse of affect and invention into emotion and narrative. When he describes his feelings for Alceste, the narrator expresses them not in terms of the sense of inventional and affective potential indexed through the daisy, but rather in terms of the masculinist narratives that construct gender identities in the tradition of courtly lyric. The God of Love reminds the narrator that he should recognize his advocate from a textual source: "Hastow nat in a book," he asks, "The grete goodnesse of the quene Alceste, / That turned was into a dayesye?" (510–12). "Yis," the narrator replies immediately, "Now knowe I hire" (517–18), and, before reciting the life and afterlife of Alceste, he articulates the moment of recognition in terms of affect: "Now fele I weel the goodnesse of this wyf," and "Wel hath she quyt me myn affeccioun" (520, 523). The narrator's description of his emotional transaction with Alceste is coded with characteristic fourteenth-century constructions of gender. Alceste's "goodnesse" is her willingness "to goon to helle" in place of her husband (514) and is compounded by the fact that, unlike the other heroines of the *Legend*, she is "rescowed" from death and "stellyfye[d]" (515, 525). But the *affeccioun* that the narrator feels she *quyts* is his own objectifying devotion, and her contribution to his immediate plight is *pité*, the emotion that the dreaming Geffrey of the *House of Fame* feels when he sees the story of Dido, and that in fourteenth-century discourse defines the feminine in order to define the masculine.[26] Alceste here is *founde* to be part of an already-invented narrative. The narrator only comes to "knowe" her, even feelingly, when he—in conversation with another man—situates her, despite her markedly different biography, comfortably within already-existing literary and cultural narratives.[27]

---

26. See Mann, 39–43; Fradenburg, *Sacrifice Your Love*, 182–84; and Dinshaw, *Chaucer's Sexual Poetics*, 70–72. McNamer, *Affective Meditation*, demonstrates the connection between the performance of compassion and gender performance.

27. V. A. Kolve argues alternatively that the *Legend of Good Women* was originally intended to conclude with the *Legend of Alceste* and thus lead to "a typological adumbration of release and transcendence" because Alceste ultimately stands in as a figure for Christ (*Telling Images: Chaucer and the Imagery of Narrative II* [Stanford, CA: Standford University Press, 2009], 58).

At the same time, however, the narrator's immediate narrative encoding of what he sees and feels allows Chaucer to gesture toward something outside the *Prologue*'s fictional frame, and the precise order of events in the recognition scene is especially important to realizing this process. As Delany notes, "no single named generative text" can be found in the *Legend*, unlike in Chaucer's earlier dream visions.[28] The *Prologue* does not depict the narrator's falling asleep while reading a book about Alceste and then having a dream derived from that story. Moreover, the narrative order suggests that the book to which the God of Love refers—and which the narrator has already read—is itself produced *by* the dream. As Percival argues, the passage "enacts and celebrates the act of poetic imagination which results in the Prologue to the *Legend of Good Women*" itself.[29] Robert O. Payne goes further, arguing that this "book" refers to all of Chaucer's own previous work and that Alceste existed always "*in potentia*" in them, essentially reading Alceste as the textualized emergence of potential somehow imminent in Chaucer's corpus.[30] In addition to rendering as narrative the process of its own making, however, the narrator's invention (his dream) produces the text ("Hastow nat in a book?") that originally inspired invention, and it posits as a source the narrative of Alceste that Chaucer himself created. But the poetry invented in this narrative fiction is not simply the *Legend of Good Women*; it is some other specific "book." In none of his potential sources for Alceste does she metamorphose into a daisy in an Ovidian sense,[31] and if "Chaucer invents a myth," as Fyler puts it, or "a new meaning for the daisy," as Fradenburg suggests, then he does so in the modern, not the medieval, sense of the term: not discovering, but creating.[32] What is more, the fiction of the dream vision refuses to acknowledge this moment of invention, instead forever obscuring an unknowable and removed textual antecedent—a text, in other words, that is neither Chaucer's nor that of some distant *auctor* and that can only ever be understood in terms of emergence. By gesturing toward some nebulous text that exists only as potential and structuring that gesture through sensations of displacement, the *Prologue* presents poetic invention in terms of movement and potential. Furthermore, by aligning this inventional gesture with the affective echoes registered explicitly in Geffrey's *affeccioun*, the *Prologue* finally narrates what experiencing invention as a kind of potential might actually feel like.

---

28. Delany, *Naked Text*, 43.
29. Percival, 55.
30. Payne, "Making His Own Myth," 207.
31. Percival, 49–51.
32. Fyler, *Chaucer and Ovid*, 116; Fradenburg, "Beauty and Boredom," 72. Percival argues that Chaucer may have been inspired more generally by Ovid, Froissart, and the entire French love poetry tradition (33–35, 49–50).

Before I proceed to the legends themselves, one point is worth emphasizing again here. While the sensations of movement and displacement of the *Prologue* are similar to those of the *House of Fame*, a key difference lies in the way in which Chaucer embeds them more completely within what appears to be a more courtly dream narrative. My claim is not simply that by the time he writes the *Legend*, Chaucer represents himself as a more confident and assertive vernacular poet—an argument almost routinely made about the *Legend*'s relationship to the other dream visions and about the differences between the F and G versions of the *Prologue*—and that, consequently, we should expect a far more subtly synthesized treatment of the affect of invention in this later poem. While this may very well be the case, Chaucer's revised approach in the later dream poem brings emotional experience more fully into his consideration of invention. Moreover, the dream frame of the *Legend* is thoroughly coded in courtly, gendered language, and it brings into sharp focus the issues raised less directly, if no less powerfully, in Book 1 of the *House of Fame*. It is for this reason especially that the legends ought to be read not as breaks from, but rather continuations of, the examination of invention begun in the *Prologue*. Indeed, it is through the legends' extreme representations of pathos that Chaucer not only gets closest to representing the conversion of affect and invention into emotion and poetry but also, and most significantly, situates this complex representation squarely within the potentially misogynistic and antifeminist literary framework that his poem explicitly introduces.

ALLAS, ELISION, AND EMERGENCE IN THE LEGENDS

Far from failing to fulfill the imaginative potential of the *Prologue*, then, the legends continue its very gesture, and the first two legends provide contrasting perspectives on this process. Frank views the legends of *Cleopatra* and *Thisbe* as polar opposites in their treatment of emotion. For him, *Thisbe* is organized around emotion, while *Cleopatra* "lacks a strong central emotion to make it coalesce."[33] Indeed, after establishing a back story of intercontinental epic romance—Antony's abandonment of his wife, his treason against Rome, and his falling in love with Cleopatra—the legend delivers on its promise "to make shortly" (614) by eliding the narrative of Cleopatra and Antony's courting and marriage, saying simply that she "wax his wif, and hadde hym as hire leste" (615). The reason for the elision, the narrator declares, is that poets too often "may overlade a ship or barge" (621), and he instead elects to "skyppe" "al the

---

33. Frank, *Chaucer and* The Legend of Good Women, 50, 45.

remenaunt" (622–23). Fyler notes that this image of an overloaded ship conflates Cleopatra with narrative structure: "Ships are common enough metaphors for poems; but an overloaded barge inevitably brings to mind some of the more luxurious events in Cleopatra's life."[34] By translating an iconic image of Cleopatra's medieval reception into a narrative pattern intended to transmit "th'effect" of invention (622), the legend explicitly removes the "strong central emotion" from the strategy of invention. It skips the wooing and the wedding, but it encapsulates emotions involved in those events within an empty ship, making the evacuation of emotion a symbol for narrative composition.

Cleopatra herself reinserts this lost affective material through an act of *makyng*: Antony's burial "shryne" (675), the monumental function of which is to entomb an emotional *condicioun* of Antony known only by Cleopatra. The hearts of the two lovers engage in an affective entanglement apparently independent of poetic utterance, and Cleopatra conceptualizes her marriage to Antony as a bond of complete affective reciprocity. After constructing the shrine, she describes her marriage vow in fully affective terms:

> "in myself this covenaunt made I tho,
> That ryght swich as ye felten, wel or wo,
> As fer forth as it in my power lay,
> Unreprovable unto my wyfhod ay,
> The same wolde I fele, lyf or deth."
>
> (688–92)

The "covenaunt" that Cleopatra establishes in her own heart is not only what Jill Mann calls a "passionate identification with his being"[35] but also the pledge that she will "fele" exactly what Antony does, a description of the mutual internalization not of texts but of bodily affects that link the two lovers. As the tomb memorializes her "unreprovable" devotion, it also entombs that reciprocity, the affective mobility of which the legend implicitly describes as unrepresentable: Antony's going "out of his wit" after Actium, for example (660), echoes in Cleopatra, but "tonge non" is able to "telle" of the "routhe"

---

34. Fyler, *Chaucer and Ovid*, 100. Fyler notes that the "barge" goes from being the ship associated with Cleopatra to literal ships at Actium (100), a battle that Laura J. Getty argues is a metaphor for wrestling with textual sources ("'Other smale ymaad before': Chaucer as Historiographer in the 'Legend of Good Women,'" *Chaucer Review* 42 [2007]: 57–58). For the relevance of barges in medieval accounts of Cleopatra's life, see Fyler (*Chaucer and Ovid*, 188–89n7) and Percival (223). Vincent of Beauvais also characterizes Cleopatra by "her golden ship, and her purple sail" (qtd. in Minnis, *Shorter Poems*, 354).

35. Mann, 42.

she "mad" (669–70). Chaucer's technical language of *makyng*—she "made her subtyl werkmen make a shryne" (672)—doubly emphasizes the connection between the construction of a physical shrine and the impossibility of representing affect. Indeed, the shrine itself becomes an *occupatio*. As it locks away Antony's corpse, it also promises to lock away affect, indicating—but not representing—the nebulous process by which affective emergence is *made* into emotional narrative. *The Legend of Cleopatra* refracts the image of affect twice: first, eliding the narrative of the protagonists' wooing, and second, encasing affect in the shrine. It then gives us the resulting inventions—the tomb and the legend—which themselves gesture toward but never represent the process of inventing.

The Legend of Thisbe takes the opposite approach, drawing out the affective experiences of the protagonists and describing in detail both the physiological changes that precede the recognition of emotions and key moments of narrative development. Arriving late to the rendezvous, Piramus gradually detects narrative clues that lead to Thisbe's bloody wimple:

> His eyen to the ground adoun he caste,
> And in the sond, as he byheld adoun,
> He sey the steppes brode of a lyoun,
> And in his herte he sodeynly agros,
> And pale he wex; therwith his heer aros,
> And ner he com, and fond the wimpel torn.
> "Allas," quod he, "the day that I was born!"
> (827–33)

Piramus's heartbeat quickens, the blood rushes away from his face, and his hair stands up. These physiological responses occur *before* his discovery of the wimple as he follows the "steppes brode" of the lion, themselves traces of a narrative that he has yet actually to read, let alone experience. Piramus's body registers affective emergence before his mind realizes exactly what is happening, and because readers, unlike Piramus, already understand fully what he will discover through his misreading of the text he finds in the moonlight, the physiological description emphasizes those moments before his full understanding of what he (mistakenly) will later understand to have happened. Piramus's affective processes coincide with a bodily process of invention, the sensation of participating in the emergence of a narrative. This emergence folds into a narrative of invention once Piramus has "fond the wimpel torn," *fyndyng*—that is, inventing—the story of which he is already a part. Thisbe likewise emerges from the cave to a moment of discovery, *fyndyng* the dying Piramus:

> And at the laste hire love thanne hath she founde,
> Betynge with his heles on the grounde,
> Al blody, and therwithal a-bak she sterte,
> And lik the wawes quappe gan hire herte,
> And pale as box she was, and in a throwe
> Avisede hire, and gan hym wel to knowe,
> That it was Piramus, hire herte deere.
>
> (862–68)

Thisbe starts backward, her heartbeat accelerates with an undulating intensity, the blood rushes from her face, and she looks at him "in a throwe," that is, in an instant of bodily anguish triggered by a narrative she has "founde" independently of what she eventually "gan to . . . knowe."[36] Thisbe's and Piramus's bodies anticipate the narrator's invention before they themselves do, and their bodies register that invention as affect: that is, detectable not in terms of the conscious acknowledgement of emotional experience but in terms registered physiologically in and between their own physical bodies.

Piramus punctuates his *fyndyng* by crying, "Allas . . . the day that I was born!" Appearing 27 times in the *Legend of Good Women*, the interjection "allas" signals the moments at which affect and invention collapse into emotion and narrative.[37] *Allas* first accompanies the narrator's explicit longing for invention in the *Prologue*: "Allas that I ne had Englysh, ryme or prose, / Suffisaunt this flour to preyse aryght!" (66–67), appears once in the *Legend of Cleopatra*, and then saturates the *Legend of Thisbe*, appearing ten times in the 217-line story. Piramus's cry parrots Antony's exactly (658), and both utterances compound a sense of narrative self-awareness as they attempt to dispel the accumulation of experience that leads to the tragic situations from which the speakers long to extract themselves. Likewise, in the legend following *Thisbe*, Aeneas echoes both Piramus and Antony when he literally sees his place in the story of Troy's fall, painted on the wall in Carthage (1027). Dido herself explicitly links *allas* to affect and poetic making. She utters it twice when she suddenly discovers Aeneas's efforts to insert her into the Trojan story and confronts him about his plot to abandon her:

> "Allas, what woman wole ye of me make?
> I am a gentil woman and a queen.

---

36. Chaucer here conflates two meanings of the noun *throu*, referring to a span of time and a moment of extreme pain. See *MED*, "throu," lemmas 1 and 2.

37. Once, the word appears as "alas" (756).

> Ye wole nat from youre wif thus foule fleen?
> That I was born, allas! What shal I do?"
>
> (1305–8)

Dido uses the terminology of invention to indict Aeneas as the source of her infamy: he will "make" her into a particular kind of woman. What is more, Dido's figuring of Aeneas as the would-be *maker* captures him in a moment of perpetual inventional emergence. Whereas in the *House of Fame,* Dido imagines her infamy as a text already invented, here her words—phrased, moreover, as questions rather than as statements or exclamations—hold out the moment of invention as something at once unrealized and coterminal with the affective realization of Aeneas's impending decision to abandon her. The narrator refuses to relate the text of Dido's complaint, using his own impending emotional reaction as an excuse: "I may nat wryte" of that, he claims, "So gret a routhe I have it for t'endite" (1344–45). Of course, Chaucer has already written of this in the *House of Fame,* and in the *Legend of Dido* he replaces his earlier account with an absence characterized by impending *routhe.* The narrator precedes his refusal with the last declaration of "allas" in the legend (1341), reserving it for the discussion of his own previous inventional actions rather than as an emotional harbinger of the scene of Dido's suicide. Similar uses of *allas* can be catalogued throughout the *Legend.* As a metapoetic and emotive marker, it functions as a kind of morpheme that points backward to emergent processes that, by the time the word has been uttered, have already transformed into emotional anguish and narrative entrenchment.

The legends' use of elision, on the other hand—rhetorical *abbreviatio, occupatio,* and *praeteritio*—works to elicit affective responses in readers by destabilizing expected patterns of invention. The sudden elision of narrative material produces an affective response—a surprise—and an immediate impulse to investigate the narrative structure that triggered that response, thereby attempting to externalize affect as something to be investigated. In the *Legend of Hypsipyle* for example, Jason conspires with Hercules to "bedote" or trick Hypsipyle (1547), wooing her, marrying her, and then abandoning her even as she bears his children. The brevity with which Chaucer presents the betrayal is striking:

> The somme is this: that Jason wedded was
> Unto this queen and tok of hir substaunce
> What so hym leste unto his purveyaunce;
> And upon hire begat he children two,
> And drogh his sayl and saw hir nevere mo.
>
> (1559–63)

The emphasis on summation—"The somme"—is sharpened further by the extensive historical background that characterizes the narrative as a whole. The legend does not elide the story of Jason's origin and his quest for the fleece; rather, its narrative grows out from the historical apparatus that begins the medieval versions of the Troy story no less, before ever getting to Hypsipyle, who herself seems to wander into Chaucer's version of the story almost as effortlessly as Jason wanders out of her life. The sudden intensification of brevity simulates through narrative form the sense of abandonment felt by Hypsipyle, even though readers know exactly what the narrative outcome will be before they begin. By omitting the narrative that would both represent and elicit emotion, the legend creates a narrative vacuum that is instantly filled by affect, by an initial response, a reaction to the fact of elision. The legend itself soon follows suit, transforming the initial moment of affective elision into Hypsipyle's letter, which is likewise then elided. "Ye gete namore of me," the narrator declares just before describing Hypsipyle's abandonment, "but ye wole rede / Th'origynal, that telleth al the cas" (1557–58). In this way, the legend simulates the emergence of affect, pairing the fact of elision with the recognition of the narrative material that has been elided. The affective response to Hypsipyle's plight occurs both inside and outside of the text, marked by its simultaneous separateness from, and entrenchment in, acts of narration. Subsequent efforts to analyze the origin of the affective emergence are always directed back to the narrative structure itself, again blurring and confounding moments of affective and inventional emergence. Narrative elision simulates an initial, unrepresentable sensation of the movements of affect in a state of becoming something else that demands analysis but boils away at the moment of analytic engagement.

These figures—*allas* and elision—would seem at first to propagate masculinist traditions by which feminine interiority emerges only in the service of defining masculine subjectivity.[38] *Allas* is formulaic and traditionally feminizing: it marks a loss of agency and defines its speaker through an emotional call for *pité* and compassion. Likewise, elision abandons the interiority that the legend might otherwise render more fully, and it is the chief criterion for the critical tradition of Chaucer's "boredom" regarding the *Legend*. But even as they import masculinist rhetoric to the legends, *allas* and elision respectively signal and generate moments of narrative rupture, creating again a sense of displacement that both registers affect and invention in terms of sensations of

---

38. See Holly A. Crocker's discussion of affect in the *Reeve's Tale*, in which, she argues, the affective exchanges among the men in the tale define feminine subjectivity only to posit masculine subject positions ("Affective Politics in Chaucer's *Reeve's Tale*: 'Cherl' Masculinity after 1381," *Studies in the Age of Chaucer* 29 [2007]: 225–58).

movement and establishes the inaccessibility—but indisputable existence—of the moments of impending emergence in which these movements culminate. Looking finally at the *Legend of Lucrece*, I wish to show exactly how Chaucer's poem uses moments like these to attempt to gesture "behind" both the discourses that shape late-medieval ideas of gender and the affect that infuses those discourses with their personal and cultural power.

"TH'EFFECT" OF THE AFFECT OF INVENTION

The Legend of Lucrece in particular demonstrates the ramifications that Chaucer's poetics has for the masculinist narratives of gender that inspire the *Legend of Good Women*. Like the *Prologue*'s daisy, Lucrece seems at first to synthesize processes of affect and invention: "Hyre contenaunce is to hire herte dygne, / For they acorde bothe in dede and sygne" (1738–39). While they indicate the depth of "hire wifly chastite" by denying any gap between what Lucrece feels and what she expresses (1737), these lines also gesture toward a perfect alignment of affect and invention; the "dede" of her "herte" accords completely with the "sygne" of her "contenaunce." Yet the legend suggests that this alignment is culturally produced, a result of Lucrece's complete internalization of the "intimate scripts" enacted by virtuous Roman wives.[39] Lucrece's "teres, ful of honeste" that "embellished hire wifly chastite" (1736–37), however, seem to be neither the vacuous performance of a social role nor a "pure," nonnarrative reflection of affect. Rather, like her "blysful chere" at the unexpected return of Colatyn (1743), they suggest the extent to which the internalization of texts disintegrates the distinction between affective emergence and learned response. By setting this process in pagan Rome, moreover, Chaucer separates it from the affective religious practices of his own time and provides readers with a kind of critical distance that enables close study.[40] The legend's emphasis on the apparent seamlessness between Lucrece's internal affective state and its external registry, between her "herte" and her "sygne," invites analysis of initial moments of emergence.

But that invitation is precisely what compels Tarquinius to rape Lucrece: the apparent synthesis of affect and its representation is the same impetus

---

39. Contextualizing Chaucer's version among other English versions of the story, Andrew Galloway argues that only at the moment before her suicide, as the men forgive her, "does Lucrece realize the assumptions... her culture" holds about gender ("Chaucer's *Legend of Lucrece* and the Critique of Ideology in Fourteenth Century England," *ELH* 60 [1993]: 828); building on Galloway's analysis, Guillemette Bolens argues that Lucrece ultimately refuses to submit to any available social script (116–17).

40. Minnis, *Shorter Poems*, 410.

by which Tarquinius "caughte to this lady swich desyr" (1750).⁴¹ The legend then would seem to link acts of invention with acts of rape, and Percival suggests that the narrative goes so far as to invite readers "to empathize with Tarquinius, if not to approve" of his actions.⁴² The metaphors of penetration that characterize the legend and foreshadow Tarquinus's raping of Lucrece—the siege of Ardea, the Roman soldiers' imaginative incursion into their wives' unobserved lives, Colatyn's surprise appearance in Lucrece's domestic space⁴³—imply that accessing a moment of affective emergence is an act of masculine violation of the feminine. The legend's initial allusion to Augustine encloses the entire legend in this speculative frame. As many critics have noted, Augustine's "gret compassioun / Of this Lucresse" appears ironic in light of the fact that Augustine not only condemns Lucrece's suicide but furthermore suggests (though finally rejects) that she may have killed herself because she was complicit in her own rape (1690–91). Augustine's reading of Lucrece becomes for many critics the central issue in determining the legend's own stance on the narrative.⁴⁴ Despite their varying conclusions about Chaucer's intentions, these readings often assume by default an interpretive stance parallel to the legend's initial allusion to Augustine: the scholarly effort to penetrate Lucrece's heart and mind, to know what she was feeling and thinking, to discover, externalize, and narrate the exact relationship between her "herte" and "sygne." Moreover, the legend's narrative makes this interpretive action immediate and unavoidable, suggesting an equation between such efforts and Tarquinius's. Indeed, Chaucer assigns the legend's vocabulary of invention to Tarquinius himself, who, after "recordynge" Lucrece again and again in his mind, declares to himself, "What ende that I make, it shal be so" (1760, 1774)—explicit inventional terminology that does not punctuate Lucrece's final act covering "hir fet or suche thyng" as she dies (1859).⁴⁵ In portraying Tarquinius

---

41. See also Fradenburg, "Beauty and Boredom," 68–69.
42. Percival, 273.
43. See Minnis, *Shorter Poems*, 363–64.
44. See the discussions in Galloway, "Chaucer's *Legend of Lucrece*," and Bolens (111–16); Frank (*Chaucer and* The Legend of Good Women, 93–110) and Minnis (*Shorter Poems*, 382) argue for the legend's sincere commitment to its emotional "effects," and Frank reads the ending of the legend as refusing to "intellectualize" into some moral principle the suffering and death of Lucrece (103). Kathryn L. Lynch, however, argues that Chaucer's citation of Augustine does exactly that, drawing the legend into the realm of academic debate, making Lucrece "an instrument of analytic thought" (135), and Delany sees Lucrece as inadvertently complicit in her existence as a "sygne" and thus "bent to authorial will, like any material" (*The Naked Text*, 206). Crocker notes that this masculine academic tradition informs a similar process occurring in the *Reeve's Tale* (240).
45. Dinshaw furthermore argues that in "the patriarchal context" of *Lucrece*, "the self-defining or self-signifying act—the only strong act of the heroines—is a sin, and is, furthermore,

as the poet figure in the legend, Chaucer installs the act of invention with an affective charge, but links the legend's image of invention not to the representational symmetry of Lucrece's "herte" and "sygne" but to the inventional and violative "ende" made by Tarquinius.

This, however, is expressly *not* the image of invention that the legend finally produces. Just before Tarquinius rapes her, Lucrece faints "and wex so ded / Men myghte smyten of hire arm or hed; / She feleth no thyng, neyther foul ne fayr" (1816–18). The crucial narrative moment lacks both affect and invention: Lucrece feels nothing, and contrary to what Augustine suggests, she has no conscious or preconscious part in the construction of this point of her narrative. There is finally nothing to feel and nothing to speculate about, and the vacuum quickly fills with the narrator's invocation of the cultural, discursive constructions of knighthood and chivalry, masculine "intimate scripts" that a "verray knyght" like Tarquinius (1821) should have internalized long ago to preempt his actions.

In addition to removing the object of this Augustinian investigation, the legend presents a final image of invention that actively defies traditional gendered interpretations of the masculine inventor shaping feminine form. One of the reasons the narrator claims to have told the story of Lucrece is to characterize invention as the discovery—the *fyndyng*—of feminine interiority: "I telle hyt . . . for the stable herte, sadde and kynde, / That in these wymmen men may alday fynde. / There as they kaste hir herte, there it dwelleth" (1874–78). The language would at first seem to describe invention in the familiar gendered terms of the literary tradition of which the *Legend* is a part. Masculine authors repeatedly shape the feminine in order to define the masculine—"men may alday fynde" the "herte" that women "kaste"—that is, set—firmly in place.[46] This *fyndyng* of *caste* hearts reflects the doubled cultural tradition of medieval legendaries of "good women" that, on the one hand, praise virtuous women but, on the other, articulate that virtue in solely masculinist terms and only so far as it helps to construct masculine identity.[47] In addition to "setting," however, *casten* can mean to throw away or expel; it also can mean

---

both overdetermined by men's actions and completely self-destructive" (*Chaucer's Sexual Poetics*, 77); more broadly, the narrator's poetic art is "a record of his continual exercise of control over the feminine" (86). Getty reads Lucrece as a textual "source" violated by acts of writing (63–64). Other critics have noted the equation of the poet to the male villains of the legends: see, for example, Kiser, 114–15; Percival, 283, 291–95; and Edwards, *Dream of Chaucer*, 159–60.

46. See *MED*, "casten," 14.

47. See, for example, Boccaccio's closing words on Lucretia in *De mulieribus claris*, in which her virtue is praised but defined in tandem with "romana libertas," the "freedom for Rome" (*Famous Women*, ed. and trans. Virginia Brown [Cambridge, MA: Harvard University Press, 2001], 198–99).

to think about, perceive, decide, to make, and to construct.[48] Indeed, given the range of meanings of the verb, what men *fynde* in this process of invention is not merely a fixed *herte* but also the action of its displacement. Through the ambiguous reference of "they" to either "men" or "wymmen" in the preceding sentence, Chaucer activates the multiple senses of the term simultaneously. The "kaste" heart captures the notion of fixity that characterizes the Lucrece tradition for Chaucer's readers, but it also generates the sense of inventional displacement that we have seen throughout the *Legend of Good Women*. The act of inventing Lucrece's heart occurs simultaneously with the act of conceptualizing it as movement. The legend thus demonstrates the impossibility of representing inventional emergence at the same time that it defies what Sanok calls "the signal gesture of (medieval) misogyny: designating the feminine as the object of literary representation."[49] Figuring Lucrece's heart as a locus for invention within a "fixed" tradition, the legend finally characterizes invention as a movement of emergence that necessarily precedes and defies all narrative attempts to shape it or situate it within a specific narrative.

Ultimately then, the legend does not implicate its readers in a program of Tarquinian invention.[50] Instead, it uses a motional conceptualization of affect and invention to demonstrate just how quickly—almost instantaneously—the processes of emergence (of both emotion and poetic forms) can be folded into traditional narratives of gender and emotion. Unable to access this Lucrecian site of invention through his *makyng*, the narrator tries to account for the unstructured movement he suddenly discovers in terms of traditional masculinist narratives of "brotel" and "stable" hearts (1885, 1876)—that is, a behavior code violated by Tarquinius and a fantasy of infinitely devout women sanctioned by reference to the New Testament. Contrary to the narrator's (perhaps well-intentioned) authorial efforts, what is expressly not *founde* in the legend

---

48. See *MED*, "casten," 20–25
49. Sanok, 328.
50. Nor does it implicate them in the narrator's efforts to empathize with the plight of the legends' protagonists. As Simpson ("Ethics and Interpretation") and Elizabeth D. Harvey show, the narrator's implied claim of allegiance to women who suffer under dominant masculine cultural narratives because his own poetry has been misunderstood by the tyrannical God of Love merely renews the masculinist paradigms that such an allegiance would attempt to overcome. As Harvey argues, "to assume the voice of a silenced woman or to act as advocate for a group of women unable or unwilling to speak on their own behalf entails a power that can easily become despotic" ("Speaking in Tongues: The Poetics of the Feminine Voice in Chaucer's *Legend of Good Women*," in *New Images of Medieval Women: Essays Toward a Cultural Anthropology*, ed. Edelgard E. DuBruck [Lewiston, NY: Mellen, 1989], 57). See also Lynn Arner, who argues that the *Legend* co-opts women's voices as part of an effort to "obviate the need for female participation in the generation of knowledge, ultimately defining and controlling female contributions" (115).

is a feminine interiority created as an object for masculine self-definition, nor a conventional complaint that, however sincerely meant by the narrator, defines femininity only in terms of suffering and the ability to elicit *pité*.

The work of the affect of invention in the *Legend of Good Women* is thus not only aesthetic, gesturing toward irreducible moments of poetic emergence—that strange flash in which an *archetypus* or artistic object distills into a shape. Its work reveals what Sara Ahmed shows to be a common tactic by which dominant cultures erase the ways in which affects become assigned—"stuck"—to particular people or groups in order to define them in terms of the other, as well as what Teresa Brennan argues is an affective "dumping" that has in particular shaped the West's view of the feminine in terms of masculinist narratives.[51] By manipulating the traditional processes of invention in order to rupture gendered patterns of narrative, Chaucer's legends elicit an affective response that forces a resistance to participation in those narratives and compels a different kind of investigation, one that examines not merely alternative constructions of gender but also how and why we might fold ourselves into any construction so quickly.

This point is worth emphasizing, since it differs from readings that see the *Legend* as inviting alternative formulations of gender narratives through empathy with the protagonists. Depicting a set of emotional experiences that readers "are invited to feel," for example, necessarily results in critical interpretations that reproduce gender norms and transform the protagonists into objects of study.[52] Similarly, the affect of invention also gestures outside of the gendered structures that Sanok sees as allowing alternative interpretations of gender in the poem. The *Legend* "carefully inscribes women as audience into its own rhetoric" through hagiography, Sanok argues, a genre gendered feminine because of the late-medieval "cultural fiction" that connects it with women readers.[53] Such formal inscriptions enable the poem to counteract misogynist tradition by generating an "extraordinary openness . . . to radically different interpretations."[54] Only "the category of the feminine" can best formulate such interpretations,[55] and the *Legend* resists misogynistic traditions by categorizing itself feminine through this gendered connection. Instead, the poem gestures behind such structures and their culturally assigned genders and emotions. The sensations of displacement that the *Legend* repeatedly generates call attention to the typically unremarked means of erasure that

---

51. Ahmed, 11–12; Brennan, 6. See also my discussion in the Introduction.
52. Minnis, *Shorter Poems*, 324; see also Watson, "Phantasmal Past," 2.
53. Sanok, 352, 326.
54. Ibid., 344–45.
55. Ibid., 346.

Ahmed describes, forcing readers to experience the moments of disassociation between the affects elicited and the narratives that immediately rush in to transform them. The *Legend* finally signals a possibility of alternative formulations not through empathy but in the potential to which the poem gestures. In this way, the *Legend of Good Women* attempts to "get behind" both the constructions of traditional narratives and the collapsing of affect that makes those narratives pervasive.

The *Legend*'s gesture thus "entangles us," as Holly A. Crocker puts it in her recent discussion affect in the *Reeve's Tale,* and does so in a way that preserves both the alterity of the past and its connection to the narratives of gender—and the possibility of their overthrow—still experienced by readers.[56] The *Legend* gestures beyond cultural narratives without either transcending them or locking away alternatives. It asks questions about how the narratives of emotion, invention, and gender are formed, but it also charges this asking with an affective urgency. The impulse to discover alternatives happens before we realize why it needs to happen, as we find ourselves moving among textual displacements, cries of *allas,* narrative elisions, and cast hearts. Chaucer's gestures are necessarily structural, but "th'effect" of those gestures is not. Nor is the effect merely empathic, inviting a sharing of emotional narratives that reiterate the gender conventions that produce them. In the end, the *Legend* makes received cultural narratives *feel wrong*—not only ethically wrong, but affectively *incorrect,* mismatching emotional and narrative understandings to the affect they would represent.[57] In so doing, the *Legend of Good Women* casts its poetics beyond critique and toward invention—a new kind of invention, moreover, whose processes of discovery apply not to written texts but to the pervasive and intangible forces that construct cultural experience.

It is precisely this new focus of inventional action—directed at cultural experience, at the life and the world that exist outside of the fictional worlds rendered in narrative poetry—that John Gower develops in the *Confessio*

---

56. Crocker, 251. Crocker importantly emphasizes the negative affects that emerge in a critical stance in which "we leave ourselves unprotected from the negative feelings we engage through such study" (252). Indeed, as the critical reception of the *Legend* indicates, the narrative alternatives that the poem offers are in no way necessarily positive.

57. Because the *Legend*'s generation of displacement requires the back-and-forth between affect and cultural narratives, we even find in the poem the potential for reconciling an affective approach with what D. Vance Smith sees as the narcissistic anti-intellectualism in the turn toward affect in medieval studies ("The Application of Thought to Medieval Studies: The Twenty-First Century," *Exemplaria* 22 [2010]: 85–94), and what Ruth Leys sees as the exclusionary fault of cultural theorists' turns toward affect at the willful expense of the very intellectual constructs that allow for such analyses. The affect of invention, as Chaucer presents it in the poem, shows how affect and its intellectual and institutional others cannot, at the levels of analysis and the lasting work of poetry, be separated out.

Amantis, and far more fully than Chaucer. As I will show in the following two chapters, Gower's conceptualization of invention in the *Confessio* shares with Chaucer's the explicit effort to make the aesthetic impinge on the cultural, using discourses of affect as a way of articulating how processes of invention can *fynde* things to write about, but also ways of living within specific social and cultural realities. Chaucer's *House of Fame* introduces in a somewhat unbridled form the ways in which affect and invention are first and foremost movements; his *Legend of Good Women* distills that motional representation by embedding it within a narrative treatise and short, individual narrative cases in a way that works to startle readers into a belated—but decidedly felt—realization of enfolding narratives of cultural power. Gower's *Confessio*, as I will show, goes one step further, consciously working to harness the energetic potential inherent in a motional conceptualization of affect and invention, and putting it in service of a larger, explicit project of widespread cultural rejuvenation.

CHAPTER 3

A THING SO STRANGE

Macrocosmic Emergence in the *Confessio Amantis*

I SUGGESTED at the end of Chapter 2 that in the *Confessio Amantis,* Gower develops to a much fuller extent than Chaucer the ways in which exploring the relationship between affective and inventional movements can be used to imagine widespread cultural rejuvenation. In the next two chapters, I trace how Gower's poem develops this project. Like Chaucer, Gower thematizes affect and invention within individual narratives, representing these concepts in ways that emphasize their capacities for movement and transformation. At the same time, however, Gower also dramatizes how this conceptualization leaks into the physical realities of narratives' fictive worlds—and even into what the poem posits to be the "real" world outside of its own fictive frame—imagining how the transformative potential inherent in motional understandings of affect and invention can enable the *Confessio* to somehow trigger the beginnings of a macrocosmic cultural revivification that the poem establishes as one of its explicit goals. As I will show, Gower achieves this imaginative representation in two ways. First, the *Confessio* narrates through several important tales how aligning affective and inventional movements results in the rejuvenation of tales' social and physical worlds. Second, the *Confessio* shifts its narratives generically, blending the shorter, self-contained narrative *exempla* that populate the poem with historical chronicles, which Gower posits as an authoritative genre that purports to reflect and shape culture. These chronicles essentially function as a kind of generic extension of the *Confessio*'s own inventional poetics into the world it explicitly seeks to reshape. In this way, the *Confessio* not only offers new ways of thinking about how dominant cultural narratives enfold readers but also shows how those new ways of thinking can themselves reshape cultural narratives. This chapter explores in detail the first of these two stages of Gower's representation of invention, emphasizing how Gower thematizes affect and invention within narratives in order to generate imaginative analogues for how his poem might effect large-scale macrocosmic change.

HANDS, WAYS, AND CHANGE: REINVENTING ARION'S "LUSTI MELODIE"

The explicitly macrocosmic focus of the *Confessio*'s initial frame establishes the broad parameters of Gower's restorative project. Moreover, from the outset of his poem, Gower emphasizes that such potential restoration can result only from aligning inventional action with affective movements. Book 1 of the *Confessio Amantis* opens with a gesture of poetic invention that paradoxically purports to abandon its macrocosmic efforts even before it begins. After carefully outlining in the Prologue an estates satire reminiscent of his earlier works of social critique, the *Mirour de l'Omme* and *Vox Clamantis*, Gower announces that he must "lete . . . overpasse" any attempts to address macrocosmic transformative change, unable, he feels, to "strecche up to the hevene / Min hand" to "setten al in evene / This world" (1.1–6).[1] As Götz Schmitz writes, Book 1 "begins on a note of resignation," and James Simpson argues that the opening of the book "puts a very sudden and unexpected brake" on the Prologue's project.[2] Instead, Gower writes, "Fro this day forth I thenke change / And speke of thing is noght so strange" (9–10), grounding this new poetic effort in the topic of "love," a force that is only as overwhelming and "out of reule" as it is commonplace (15, 18). In reality, of course, by switching his inventional

---

1. All quotations from the *Confessio* are taken from *The Complete Works of John Gower*, ed. G. C. Macaulay, and are cited parenthetically in the text by book and line number. Like many modern readers, however, I have benefited greatly from reading the *Confessio Amantis* in Russell Peck's three-volume edition (Kalamazoo, MI: Medieval Institute, 2000–2004).

2. Götz Schmitz, "Rhetoric and Fiction: Gower's Comments on Eloquence and Court Poetry," in *Gower's* Confessio Amantis: *A Critical Anthology*, ed. Peter Nicholson (Cambridge: D. S. Brewer, 1991), 117; James Simpson, *Sciences and the Self in Medieval Poetry: Alan of Lille's* Anticlaudianus *and John Gower's* Confessio amantis (Cambridge: Cambridge University Press, 1995), 140. For a survey of the major differences between the *Confessio* and Gower's other two major works, see Peter Nicholson, *Love and Ethics in Gower's* Confessio Amantis (Ann Arbor: University of Michigan Press, 2005), esp. 3–40.

topic, Gower does not abandon a project of cultural rejuvenation but instead refocuses it at the level of the individual. As Peter Nicholson shows, Gower's approach in fact "broadens the scope of his subject," creating "a comprehensive ethic that is conscious of its own foundations and that embraces the entire range of the experiences that are designated by 'love.'"[3] Much recent scholarship on the *Confessio* focuses on how the poem works to produce an ethical subjectivity in readers, all the while self-consciously testing the efficacy of its own poetics to do so. In complicating Gower's supposedly "moral" project, this important critical work argues that the goal of the *Confessio* is to prepare readers "to accept the gift of good governance," as Kurt Olsson puts it, and "to bring its readers to an ideal form" by "revealing the subtle interrelations between ethical and political experience on the one hand, and the structure of the cosmos on the other," as Simpson argues.[4] Moreover, Gower advocates an active, emergent ethics in the poem, emphasizing, as J. Allan Mitchell describes, "a *pragmatic* orientation to ethics that is improvisatory even as it remains imitative,"[5] and while no critics examine affect in the *Confessio* as I do here, several have noted the importance of Gower's representation of emotion to his complex ethical project.[6] My study of the *Confessio* works in part to

---

3. Nicholson, *Love and Ethics*, 45. J. Allan Mitchell argues in passing that this conception of love amounts to "a medieval understanding of affect: indeed a commonplace in most discussions of the fortunes of love is that it has a legitimate and happy affective *force*, compelling the individual will to stand outside the subject" (*Ethics and Eventfulness*, 6; emphasis in original).

4. Kurt Olsson, *John Gower and the Structures of Conversion: A Reading of the* Confessio Amantis (Cambridge: D. S. Brewer, 1992), 24; Simpson, *Sciences and the Self*, 7, 12.

5. J. Allan Mitchell, *Ethics and Exemplary Narrative in Chaucer and Gower* (Cambridge: D. S. Brewer, 2004), 39; emphasis in original; Mitchell furthermore reads the poem's process of encouraging personal, ethical decision making in individual readers a kind of "invention" in "the old rhetorical sense" of selecting from a field of possible reader responses, culminating in "strategies of inventional reading" that the poem presents to its individual readers (60, 6). For similar readings that see the *Confessio* emphasizing an active, intentional ethical subject, see especially William Robbins, "Romance, Exemplum, and the Subject of the *Confessio Amantis*," *Studies in the Age of Chaucer* 19 (1997): 157–81; Elizabeth Allen, "Newfangled Readers in Gower's 'Apollonius of Tyre,'" *Studies in the Age of Chaucer* 29 (2007): 419–64; and Russell Peck, "John Gower: Reader, Editor, and Geometrician," in *John Gower: Manuscripts, Readers, Contexts*, ed. Malte Urban (Turnhout: Brepols, 2009), 11–37. These approaches work to revitalize the "classic" approach to Gower as working to establish ethical authority in English as he had previously done in French and Latin; see especially Alistair Minnis, *Medieval Theory of Authorship: Scholastic Literary Attitudes in the Later Middle Ages*, 2nd. ed. (Philadelphia: University of Pennsylvania Press, 2010), 177–90. Others reject the idea that the *Confessio* presents a holistic, comprehensive ethical project: see especially David Aers, "Reflections on Gower as 'Sapiens in Ethics and Politics,'" in Yeager, *Re-Visioning Gower*, 185–201; and Diane Watt, *Amoral Gower: Language, Sex, and Politics* (Minneapolis: University of Minnesota Press, 2003).

6. Nicholson argues that the *Confessio* establishes "pathos as a way of binding our emotional response to the lives of characters" (*Love and Ethics*, 93) and that this empathic connection is Gower's method of demonstrating how vice and virtue are real forces affecting the world,

shift a scholarly tradition that has focused on individual ethical subjectivity outward to the macrocosmic frame that the poem first establishes as its inventional topic. At the same time that he concerns himself with shaping readers' interiority, Gower also stretches forth his hand to address macrocosmic concerns, presenting throughout the poem moments that fictionalize how the *Confessio* might produce a larger, macrocosmic restorative transformation.[7] In these moments, Gower suggests how the purportedly restorative poetics of the *Confessio* might transform, if only imaginatively, "tout le monde," the entire world.[8]

Gower's Prologue links the microcosmic with the macrocosmic in very traditional ways, explicitly blaming human beings—not Fortune or the stars—for causing the "divisioun / Which moder of confusion / Is" and characterizing the present moment as corrupted and decayed from a more idealized past (Pr. 851–53). He labels each human being a "lasse world" and "a world in his partie" (947, 956), and it is humans' suffering in this regard that causes, "in comparisoun," the suffering of "othre creatures" on the planet (916–17); likewise, it is "A mannes Senne . . . Which makth the welkne to debate," sometimes "clowdy," and sometimes "clier" (925–28). However, Gower's call at the end of the Prologue for "An other such as Arion" (1054), the Ovidian singer whose music rejuvenates the world, explicitly demonstrates the potential effect that his poem might have at a level that extends beyond the individual. As R. F. Yeager shows, the poetry of Gower's Arion brings peace to both the macrocosmic

---

rather than abstract moral concepts (89–93); Charles Runacres argues that the particulars delivered through exemplary narratives are what elicit emotional involvement with narrative situations and thus allow for ethical engagement ("Art and Ethics," in *Gower's* Confessio Amantis: *Responses and Reassessments*, ed. Alistair J. Minnis [Cambridge: D. S. Brewer, 1983], 134); and Georgiana Donavin argues that the *Confessio* elevates the status of "Rethorique," since emotional appeals allow Amans to approach reason, "when passion moves the Will toward Intellect" ("Rhetorical Gower: Aristotelianism in the *Confessio Amantis*'s Treatment of 'Rethorique,'" in Urban, *John Gower*, 172).

7. Others have emphasized the macrocosmic interests of the *Confessio*. Watt, for example, argues that rather than providing clear ethical guidance, the *Confessio* offers readers "an aesthetic experience of the disorder of the world" (xiii). Critics locate politics at the intersection of the micro- and macrocosmic worlds in the *Confessio*, where individual decisions can reshape society: see especially Elizabeth Porter, "Gower's Ethical Microcosm and Political Macrocosm," in Minnis, *Gower's* Confessio Amantis, 135–62; and Simpson, *Sciences and the Self*.

8. The quotation is from the last of the balades in Gower's *Traitié* (18.22), in which he "envoie" "ceste Balade" "Al univérsité de tout le monde" [sends . . . this balade . . . to the community of the entire world]. Text from Macaulay, *Complete Works*, 4.391; translation by R. F. Yeager in *The French Balades* (Kalamazoo, MI: Medieval Institute, 2011), 31. While Gower may have imagined his French lyric poetry reaching a broader audience than his English work (Yeager, *French Balades*, 5), his closing envoy demonstrates that his reformative aspirations are never limited to individual readers alone but to a wider, though only imagined, space.

and the microcosmic worlds simultaneously.[9] In this fantasy, Arion does not simply "inform" a single human listener who then, by spreading the good news, "informs" other humans who eventually rejuvenate the entire world.[10] Rather, Arion cancels discord at a macrocosmic level *first*, convincing, via his music, deer, sheep, and rabbits to live happily alongside lions, wolves, and dogs (1059–61), and then moving on to lords and commons, melodically convincing them to live happily as well.[11] The image is not one of ethical instruction but of something like the Augustinian power of lyric "ratios" to realign disjointed spheres of reality.[12] Furthermore, as it is imagined at the end of the Prologue, the culturally rejuvenating power of Arion's poetry manifests affectively, not rationally, ethically, or even, at first, emotionally. "That was a lusti melodie," Gower recounts, "Whan every man with other low" (1070–71).[13] Laughter not only registers the successful creation of peace from discord but also somehow generates that peace.[14] Despite its obvious nostalgia and wishful thinking, this moment of rejuvenating transformation relates a moment of sudden affective transposition: as laughter suddenly replaces "malencolie" (1069), the passage gestures toward some kind of anterior movement that collapses almost immediately into recognizable emotion and invented "melodie." This movement occurs somewhere between the lines that describe it—a kind of shift, the aftereffect of which registers as macrocosmic and microcosmic, social and ethical, realignment. Arion's song imagines at the moment when the *Confessio* is about to formally begin a poetry whose rejuvenating effect

---

9. Yeager, *John Gower's Poetic*, 241. For Yeager, love in all its forms is the means of Arion's rejuvenation of the world (244–46), and "all creation finds itself at peace" (278). Elliot Kendall argues that Gower's Arion has the power to forestall apocalypse by reforming earth ("Saving History: Gower's Apocalyptic and the New Arion," in *John Gower, Trilingual Poet: Language, Translation, and Tradition*, ed. Elizabeth M. Dutton, John Hines, and R. F. Yeager [Cambridge: D. S. Brewer, 2010], 46–58).

10. For Genius's "information" of Amans and Gower's "information" of the reader of the *Confessio*, see Simpson, *Sciences and the Self*.

11. The social model that Arion patches up is restorative and "radical, but not revolutionary," as Kendall describes it: lords are still lordly, and commons are still common, but neither any longer sees that social disparity as a site of discord ("Saving History," 56; see 56–58).

12. For a discussion of early medieval lyric poetry in this regard, see Edwards, *Ratio and Invention*, 3–33. Helen Cooper argues that through Arion Gower imagines the balance that he works to enact metrically and thematically throughout the poem ("'Peised Evene in the Balance': A Thematic and Rhetorical Topos in the *Confessio Amantis*," *Medieavalia* 16 [1993]: 114).

13. Yeager sees Arion's "lusti melodie" as representing Gower's "middel weie" (*John Gower's Poetic*, 242).

14. Linda Barney Burke reads Arion as an example of Gower's subscription to "natural laughter," demonstrating "harmony with man's original dignity, his faculty of reason, and his ultimate salvation" ("Genial Gower: Laughter in the *Confessio Amantis*," in Yeager, *John Gower: Recent Readings*, 47–50, qt. from 47).

occurs as an embodied but nonlocalized sensation of emergence at the level of the entire world.[15]

The image of Gower's imagined, impetuous hand that opens Book 1 becomes a powerful symbol of how this kind of emergent potential can be registered and generated through poetic invention. Remarkable about this image is not its ability to realign macro- and microcosmic realms, but rather its express inability to do so. "I may noght strecche up to the hevene / Min hand" to "setten al in evene / This world," Gower writes, and his reluctant utterance itself gestures toward an initial urge to dive right into a poem that would do exactly that. In the conventional terms of medieval invention, Gower here renders an *archetypus* that fails to coagulate into a form; all that is ultimately represented in this image is an embodied urge to move and that movement itself, not the poetic forms or larger meanings that such a movement might work to achieve. Gower gestures literally, with a hand, toward a moment of inventional emergence—that is, an imaginative space characterized by things coming into form but not yet formed, essentially a space of movement and becoming, like that in which Arion's rejuvenative invention seems to have occurred. Book 1's haptic opening image parallels the work of Arion's music, but it does so only dimly, indirectly, and as an echo. The opening image is a kind of shadow of a gesture, a resonance of potential action not taken, the figurative embedding of an unrealized inventional impetus. In creating this moment of impending emergence, Gower's gesture generates a sensation of productive potential that contrasts the destructive potential of the boulder of Nebuchadnezzar's dream that threatens to smash the world into apocalypse via its own always-imminent movement.[16] In these opening lines, Gower momentarily imagines the potential, if not the form, that a world-transforming poetry might possess, this abstract, macrocosmic "thing . . . so strange," as he puts it, that seems impossible to represent, let alone enact.

Yet it is exactly this "thing" toward which the *Confessio* gestures throughout its books: its exploration of affect and invention occurs at this larger scale,

---

15. Cooper notes that the Arion passage "is crucially placed" in the Prologue "to show how one poet could generate" balance via words ("'Peised Evene in the Balance,'" 114). Critics have emphasized the representational gap between this "other Arion" and Gower himself: for Yeager, Arion "is not Gower the poet, but the poet's minstrel, working toward an identical goal" in a "poetic strategy as intense and self-conscious as Chaucer's in the *Canterbury Tales*" (*John Gower's Poetic*, 244); Kendall suggests a similar ambivalence, arguing that Arion "might bear a passing resemblance to John Gower," whose poem might be read "itself as an imitation of Arion's song" ("Saving History," 58).

16. Indeed, the apocalyptic boulder resting on the hilltop in Nebuchadnezzar's dream, poised to destroy the world, is not an image that the poem ever fully dispels, establishing what Peck describes as "an apocalyptic mood which is crucial to the overall effect" of the *Confessio* ("John Gower and the Book of Daniel," in Yeager, *John Gower: Recent Readings*, 160).

in moments where affective and inventional emergence seem to impinge upon macrocosmic structures themselves. Through the narratives of the *Confessio*, then, Gower works to replicate the macrocosmically transformative potential epitomized in the example of Arion. His challenge, however, is to do so in the thoroughly secular, nonallegorical, and ultimately "realistic" worlds that constitute the poem's individual narratives. He accomplishes this by showing how the collapse of inventional movements into poetic forms parallels the transitional movements of affect, generating subtly, and as an aspect of narrative form, the kinds of transformative energies that emerge more explicitly and fantastically in mythical stories like that of Arion. Indeed, his famous formulation to "go the middel weie" in the *Confessio* "And wryte a bok betwen the tweie, / Somwhat of lust, somwhat of lore" (Pr. 17–19), not only refers to poetic topics and registers but also casts the work of invention as a *weie*— at once a path and a process, a place for moving and movement itself, that results in the coming of something into being, rather than the meaning of that something itself. What is most remarkable about the *Confessio*, then, is how its treatment of affect and invention as poetic topics merges with the manipulation of narrative form and generic characteristics to create a pervasive sensation of something new emerging.

In the rest of this chapter, I will show how this Gowerian formulation of invention as movement—as *weie*—operates thematically and metatextually in three significant and representative tales from the *Confessio*. My goal is to demonstrate how in these narratives Gower both conceptualizes and enacts this poetics of transformational emergence. In the "Tale of Jason and Medea" from Book 5, Gower not only explores movements of affect and invention in ways familiar from Chaucer's *Legend* but also fictionalizes how Medea's magical inventions literally revitalize the physical world of the tale in a felt, embodied, and discernible way. The "Tale of Constantine and Sylvester" from Book 2 uses the metaphor of flowing liquids to sketch how the alignment of affective and inventional movements in the pre-conscious transformation of Constantine collapses into emotional, discursive, and institutional structures that construct the culture and social reality of that tale's fictive—but also expressly historical—world. Finally, the "Tale of the Three Questions" from Book 1 imagines the poetry of the *Confessio* itself emerging into the historical world via the tale's "surprise" revealing of its source in a lost Spanish chronicle. These three tales have in common an explicit effort to make the *Confessio*'s poetics of emergence constitutive of culture, imagining an entire world undergoing a process of rejuvenation. In chapter 4, I will argue that Gower then further develops this effort generically, inserting chronicles themselves into the fabric of the poem as a way of imagining how this restorative effort might, almost incarnationally, implicate itself in the social and historical world outside of the *Confessio*. Lingering first, though, on the tales of Medea, Constantine, and Peronelle, I want to show how these narratives represent fictionally how a poem like the *Confessio* might work to foment cultural rejuvenation at the macrocosmic level, a process that the Prologue of the *Confessio* labels a "thing . . . so strange."

"HERE TALE NEWE ENTAMED": MEDEA AND JASON

The tale of Medea and Jason presents an imaginative analogue for the way in which poetic invention, aligned with the movements of affective emergence, can impinge upon and radically transform the physical world itself. As he retells the story, Gower alters his sources in Benoît and Ovid considerably, and critics have noted in particular how his changes completely reshape the presentation of Medea. Not only is she no longer the "schizophrenic witch" of Ovid but she is also a capable administrator and devoted partner.[17] Moreover, she is entirely abused by Jason, whom the tale makes out to be the villain, despite even her murder of Creusa and her own children. Ellen Shaw Bakalian calls Gower's sympathetic revision of Medea "remarkable," and Elliot Kendall argues that Gower does not represent Medea "as surface and sign for inscription by male desire"; rather, "her personality and will dominate the telling" of the tale.[18] Yet, for all of the ways in which Gower's version attempts to reverse a tradition that locates monstrosity in Medea rather than in Jason, Gower, as Ruth Morse argues, "is not impervious to the temptations to ramify," and his efforts to transform Medea into a typically swooning character from medieval romance essentially rob her of the agency that characterizes other Medeas.[19] Kendall also argues that by the end of the tale, Medea's "will has been figured as profoundly transgressive, its exceeding of, and otherness from, household order inextricable from disruption of the natural order."[20] At the same time, Medea's story appears in what Nicholson argues to be the most self-aware book of the entire *Confessio*, in which Gower "seems to have

---

17. *John Gower: Confessio Amantis*, ed. Peck, 3:14.
18. Ellen Shaw Bakalian, *Aspects of Love in John Gower's* Confessio Amantis (New York: Routledge, 2004), 86; Elliott Kendall, *Lordship and Literature: John Gower and the Politics of the Great Household* (Oxford: Clarendon Press, 2008), 147; Kendall likewise notes that Gower adds to Benoît to amplify "Medea's powerful emotion" (ibid.). Derek Pearsall sees in the tale Gower's "moving away all the time from stereotypes of epic and romance towards the human situation" ("Gower's Narrative Art," *PMLA* 81 (1966): 475–84, rpt. in Nicholson, *Gower's Confessio Amantis*, 75).
19. Ruth Morse, *The Medieval Medea* (Cambridge: D. S. Brewer, 1996), 222.
20. Kendall, *Lordship and Literature*, 151.

become particularly alert to the possibilities of his own fiction."[21] Indeed, like Chaucer's *Legend*, Gower's tale builds in explicit metanarrative moments that work to "get behind" the discursive constructions by which literary and cultural traditions have characterized Medea. In Gower's tale, Medea becomes an active inventional agent in her own story, and her inventions establish a model for the rejuvenating project of the *Confessio*.

Medea and Jason "fall in love at first sight," as Bakalian puts it, and their initial meeting reveals the affect that constructs and defines their relationship.[22] Their first encounter is especially notable for its wordless intimacy, and Russell Peck suggests that the two seem to be pulled toward each other "apparently by the magnetic attraction of desire alone."[23] While their first meeting certainly depicts their love as mutual and sincere, it also emphasizes the shifting ambiguity of their entanglement. Jason, for example, "Whan he hire sih, ayein hire goth" (3371), approaching Medea the moment he sees her. As an adverb, however, *ayen* can mean not only to approach, but also to be put "against" in an oppositional placement, and furthermore even "anticipating or expecting" an imminent event.[24] Indeed, hanging over their entire first encounter is an overwhelming sense of impending event, of readers' knowledge of how the Jason and Medea story always ends. The wordlessness of their tactile exchange amplifies this sensation by attempting to stave off any language that will move their narrative forward to its inevitable conclusion:

> Thus ech of other token hiede,
> Thogh ther no word was or record;
> Here hertes bothe of on acord
> Ben set to love, bot as tho
> Ther mihten be no wordes mo.
>
> (3388–92)

---

21. Nicholson, *Love and Ethics*, 292.

22. Bakalian, 88; Yeager notes the importance of literal sight in their discovery of love, contextualizing the scene in the medieval concept of love entering through the eyes (*John Gower's Poetic*, 120). Critics often note that the love between Medea and Jason is mutual: in addition to Bakalian, see, for example, Kathryn McKinley, "Lessons for a King from Gower's *Confessio Amantis* 5," in *Metamorphosis: The Changing Face of Ovid in Medieval and Early Modern Europe*, ed. Alison Keith and Stephanie Rubb (Toronto: Centre for Reformation and Renaissance Studies, 2007), 114.

23. Peck, *Kingship and Common Profit in Gower's* Confessio Amantis (Carbondale: Southern Illinois University Press, 1978), 110. Matthew W. Irvin also notes that "Gower emphasizes the wordlessness of this encounter," but he concludes that the nature of their relationship is "shallow" (220).

24. For spatial positions, see *MED* entries for "ayen" (adv.), esp. 5 and 6; for anticipating an event, see "ayen" (prep.), 8.

As it represents an ideal aristocratic love in which the lovers' "hertes both of on acord / Ben set to love," the passage also, with its mention of "wordes" and "record," anticipates the narrative that promises to spring forth from this moment of impending emergence. The gesture is momentary as their speechless alignment is quickly coded into typical literary conventions: Jason, unable to sleep, finds himself "stered to and fro / Of love" (3412–13), deciding finally to "ferst beginne / At love," before going after the fleece (3417–18); Medea spends the night "riht the same wise" (3421), her thoughts finally dwelling on how she "mihte wedde" Jason "Be eny weie" possible (3425).

Gower then uses Jason and Medea's time together as an opportunity to align the collapse of affect and invention into emotion and poetry. Medea, promising to help Jason if he pledges himself to her, explains to him what he can expect to encounter in his quest for the fleece.[25] Medea sends a servant to bring Jason to her chamber, where "he fond" Medea "redi to bedde" (3478), and as they see each other, "Tho was here tale newe entamed" (3482). The terms of their entanglement are those of the composition of poetry: Jason "fond" Medea, and their love is a "tale," but one "newe entamed," that is, "opened up," but in the sense of reopening an old wound,[26] "newe" for Medea and Jason, but only newly rendered for Gower's readers. After a formal pledge of love and a sleepless night as "Thei hadden bothe what thei wolde" (3499), Medea plays the role of narrator, relating to Jason "fro point to point . . . al the forme, / Which as he scholde finde there, / Whan he to thyle come were" in search of the fleece (3501–4). As she explains what he can expect at each stage "of the pas" (3505), Medea essentially writes for Jason a narrative that he merely has to move through. Especially significant here, however, are the nature of the narrative invention she generates and her own particular relationship to it. As she explains the trials awaiting him on the island, she gives him a ring of invulnerability and invisibility. The ring functions at once as a symbol of their mutual pledge and as a kind of marker of the affective force by which Jason will move through the events of the narrative that Medea unfolds for him. It makes Jason literally untouchable and unseeable; he becomes a magical indicator of affect, an entity defined by movement that, like a *tydynge* in the House of Rumor, cannot be seen or sensed directly. With the ring, he moves among and through the events of the narrative while remaining separate from them, operating magically as an entity immanent to, rather than embedded in, the narrative of which he appears to be a part. As Andreea

---

25. Kendall argues that Medea "supplies most of the initiative and momentum to the pair's affair until it is established" (*Lordship and Literature*, 147).

26. See Peck's gloss, *John Gower: Confessio Amantis*, 3:112, and the MED definition of "entamen."

Boboc puts it, whatever Jason accomplishes during his quest for the fleece, "Readers know ... that Medea is in charge of Jason's ventures."[27] Yet her own concern for his safety, notable as she waits tensely for sight of his ship on the horizon, positions Medea as an inventor affectively immanent to her own invented narrative: even though she has written it already, she cannot be certain how this "tale newe entamed" will actually turn out. If displacement is the phenomenon by which affective and inventional movements are registered, then displacement is multiplied here: Medea invents Jason's narrative, which he performs as a magically invisible agent emerging into events, but his performance occurs beyond the stretch of Medea's ability to observe it. We are left with a sense of impending inventional emergence, one that waits along with Medea for an imminent emotional collapse into joyous relief with the appearance of Jason's ship.[28]

In his description of Medea's sorcery, Gower applies this quality of emergence to an explicit project of material rejuvenation. The "mydnyht" setting with the world "stille on every side" establishes a liminal space for her efforts to restore the youth of Jason's father, Eson, (3961–62), and Medea is "Al specheles" as she begins the ritual (3966). She moves like an animal, first "as an Addre" that "glod forth" (3967) until she reaches the "freisshe flod" of the ocean (3969), where she cries out to Hecate, who answers by providing a chariot pulled by dragons, allowing her to range all over the world to collect materials necessary for the invention of her spell. The "travaile" of her elaborate work of searching for material lasts "nyhtes Nyne" (4019–20), and as she begins the work of incantation, she makes "hirselven invisible, / As sche that was with Air enclosed" (4028–29). Her words to the gods as well as to attendants whom she commands to bring "olde Eson ... forth" (4059) must thus seem to emerge from nowhere at all, save for an atmospheric distortion and pressure change, a site of shimmeringly displaced "Air." She continues her practice of "that craft" (4055), running frantically around the fires she has lit on the altars, and Genius remarks that "Ther was no beste which goth oute / More wylde than sche semeth ther" (4080–81): her hair hangs "Aboute hir schuldres ... As thogh sche were oute of hir mynde / And torned in another kynde" (4082–84). After sprinkling a circle of water around Eson, she "ran so up and doun" and

---

27. Andreea Boboc, "Se-duction and Sovereign Power in Gower's *Confessio Amantis* Book V," in Dutton, Hines, and Yeager, *John Gower, Trilingual Poet*, 132.

28. The scene of the visual triangulation of Jason, Medea, and the fleece is in fact the one singled out by C. S. Lewis and R. F. Yeager as evidence of Gower's innovative, plain-style poetics (Lewis, *Allegory of Love* [Oxford: Oxford University Press, 1936], rpt. as "Gower" in Nicholson, *Gower's* Confessio Amantis, 22–25; Yeager, *John Gower's Poetic*, 26–27).

> made many a wonder soun,
> Sometime lich unto the cock,
> Sometime unto the Laverock,
> Somtime kacleth as a Hen,
> Somtime spekth as don the men:
> And riht so as hir jargoun strangeth,
> In sondri wise hir forme changeth,
> Sche semeth faie and no womman.
> (4097–105)

The passage is ambiguous about the nature of Medea's physical transformation, noting that while her "forme changeth" like her language, Medea never actually becomes "faie," but rather only "semeth" to. Medea's acting and sounding like animals makes her appear as animals to an observer, rather than relating a physiological transformation. This careful hedging frames even the description of Medea's transformative powers in the language of imminence. The poetic lines themselves contribute to this sensation, invigorating, as Yeager describes them, "the Protean energy of Medea's sorcery" by "reshap[ing] themselves rapidly."[29] Medea's magic is thus figured in terms almost absolutely of affective movement—a performed but not biological transformation, but also that of a force that is never transcendent but always acting in and among bodies, always immanent to the materiality of experience. Her movements also invoke invention: "Ful many another thing sche dede," Genius declares to Amans, "Which is noght writen in this stede" (4095–96), indicating and providing an explicit invitation for the work of future poetic invention.[30]

Medea's actions are literal, their application corporeal, and their effects measurable in the physical world. "To make an ende of that sche gan," as Genius puts it (4113), again invoking the language of poetic composition to describe her craft, Medea produces a medicine capable not only of restoring Eson's youth but of restoring life in general. The withered olive branch she

---

29. Yeager, *John Gower's Poetic*, 26. Nicholson argues similarly that the Eson episode "is one of the most picturesque passages in the entire *Confessio*, . . . relentlessly building momentum" (*Love and Ethics*, 293).

30. Magic and sorcery become ways for Gower to comment on a variety of metatextual issues. Claire Fanger argues that "Gower's treatment of magic is intrinsic to his concern with power, both erotic and political, and . . . is represented simultaneously as a form of knowledge and a form of coercion" ("Magic and the Metaphysics of Gender in Gower's 'The Tale of Circe and Ulysses,'" in Yeager, *Re-Visioning Gower*, 204). Larry Scanlon notes that magic "raises, in all its ambiguity and complexity, the question of how authority is constructed from within history" (*Narrative, Authority, and Power: The Medieval Exemplum and the Chaucerian Tradition* [Cambridge: Cambridge University Press, 1994], 277).

dips into her cauldron "gan floure and bere / And waxe al freissh and grene ayein" (4144–45), and in the spot where "the leste drope of alle" falls to the ground, "Anon ther sprong up flour and gras . . . And wox anon al medwe grene, / So that it mihte wel be sene" (4147–52). The ritual culminates in what is essentially a kind of blood transfusion in which Medea slices open Eson's side, letting "slyde" out all "The blod withinne, which was old / And sek and trouble and fieble and cold," replacing it with the potion she makes, "Of which his youthe ayein he cauhte" (4158–68). As the liquid comes into physical contact with his body, Eson's youthful features return to his face, and he "recovereth . . . his floures" just "lich unto the freisshe Maii, / Whan passed ben the colde schoures" (4172–74). Medea does literally what Gower's poem attempts to do figuratively, canvassing creation for material for productive invention, the "hole entente" of which is to somehow restore or rejuvenate a world that, like Eson, has grown so old it can do little more than "awaiten every day" for the time when it "scholde gon away" (4038, 3943–44)—a time represented as starkly imminent by the huge boulder threatening to pulverize the Statue of Time in Nebuchadnezzar's dream. Furthermore, like Gower in his opening gesture of Book 1, Medea, in her prayer to Hecate, "hield up hir hond" (3980), resulting ultimately in the restoration of a world of winter to the world of May. The reference to May likewise conjures from Medea's steaming cauldron the opening dream frame of *Confessio* itself, making literal the conventional generic framework that at once structures and thematically enacts, via its springtime imagery, the poetic project of the *Confessio*. Medea's magic makes literal the movement that characterizes invention as an activity of emergence. The ritual is rife with undulating bodies, speechless sounds, invisible movements, flowing waters, and impending, if not actual, metamorphoses. Indeed, Medea seems to act out the pervasive narrative metaphor of Ovid's *Metamorphoses* as if it were a kind of dramatic script, literally performing what Gower's own text does as it channels and repurposes Ovid for its own program. Enacting a ritual that gestures structurally toward emergence, Medea performatively invents the force of what it feels like to move through a narrative, to "pas" from one event to the next, to shift out of one moment and emerge into the next. The result is the generation of a material substance, a potion, with the capability of making "newe" anything it touches. Medea becomes, then, an analogy not for transformative text—that is, she is not feminine matter waiting to be shaped by the imposition of masculine form—but for the inventor whose text can magically alter physical reality. While her focus is the individual subject of Eson, the global scope of her movements suggests the application of this transformative movement to an entire world, restoring it, as if by magic, to youth.

It is exactly this promise of imminent newness that prompts Genius's own invention of the sorcery passage in the first place: "What sche dede in that matiere," he tells Amans, "It is a wonder thing to hiere, / Bot yit for the novellerie / I thenke tellen a partie" (3953–56).³¹ At the same time, however, the "novellerie" that thrills Genius is exactly the stuff that negatively characterizes Medea as an occult seducer of men and a child-murderer, and some critics view Medea's animalistic magical rituals as the foreshadowing of the "inhuman" act that readers know she will commit at the end of her tale.³² Similarly, when he finishes narrating the "wonder thing" to Amans, Genius immediately directs the 200-line passage back to the late-medieval cultural script that defines Medea in terms of her heartfelt contractual obligation to Jason and an object worthy of *pité*, the literary commonplace into which, as Morse argues,³³ Gower ultimately places Medea:

> Lo, what mihte eny man devise,
> A womman schewe in eny wise
> Mor hertly love in every stede,
> Than Medea to Jason dede?
>
> (4175–78)

Genius casually relegates the "novellerie" of Medea's dynamic agency back to courtly *pité*: Given these kinds of "wonder" powers, he asks, what other woman in time and space could possibly define her interiority in terms of a male lover more spectacularly than Medea could? Amans continues this masculinist relegation, asking at the end of the tale about the fate of the golden fleece itself, rather than inquiring about this singular example of "Hou the wommen deceived are" by "men" (3236–38), the ostensible exemplary purpose of the tale, at least as Genius introduces it. Genius happily obliges, and in their desire to follow Jason and the fleece, Amans and Genius perform the roles of

---

31. Nicholson emphasizes the wondrous and novel qualities heralded by Genius (*Love and Ethics*, 293).

32. For examples of such readings see Nicholson, who argues that the "purpose" of the scene is to present "the darker side of Medea's character that emerges in the tale's grim conclusion" (ibid.); Kendall, who argues that during the ritual, "Medea abandons humanity linguistically and bodily in lines reminiscent less of Ovid than of Gower's own anxiety-ridden metamorphism of the rebels of 1381 in *Vox clamantis*" (*Lordship and Literature*, 151); and Morse, who notes more generally that whatever novel changes Gower makes to Medea, he still writes a tale in which feminine revenge, even more than masculine perjury, "ultimately injures the state" (222). For other readings of the tale as an exemplum against destabilizing the state, see McKinley, and Boboc.

33. Morse, 222–23; Bakalian argues furthermore that Medea's "magic is an outward sign of her love for Jason" (94).

masculinist *makers*, converting Medea's affective and inventional movements into the scripted movements of Jason's ship through the waves of the Mediterranean, the cultural discourses of courtly *pité*, and, at the intersection of both, the imperial foundation narratives of the Troy story.[34] Culturally speaking, then, Genius and Amans convert new movements into tired old ones.

The narrative form of the tale, however, thwarts the efforts of Genius and Amans to collapse the story and its protagonist into any such emotional and historical scripts. In a conclusion often noted for its shocking brevity, Medea kills Creusa with a cursed shirt and then brings her sons before her husband, where she kills them. What follows is a sweeping act of narrative compression:

> With that sche bothe his Sones slouh
> Before his yhe, and he outdrouh
> His swerd and wold have slayn hir tho,
> Bot farewel, sche was ago
> Unto Pallas the Court above,
> Wher as sche pleigneth upon love,
> As sche that was with that goddesse,
> And he was left in gret destresse.
>
> (4215–22)

As it extracts Medea from the world of Jason, the passage ends the tale with the shocking displacement of affect. The entirety of the scene is handled in a single, breathless sentence, sweeping Medea from earth to heaven in the space of two short clauses—so quickly that we are left with a sense that *something* must rush into the newly evacuated space. Nicholson reads this ending as "bespeak[ing] its own lack of comprehensibility in view of all that precedes" it, and he concludes that Gower's intention must be to enact "a moral distancing" on the part of the reader, "a suspension of the precise moral weighing of each

---

34. Morse reads Gower in Book 5 as "circling around a history of Troy which he does not tell," a strategy that allows him to fall back on commonplace gendered readings in which the emotions and actions of women destabilize the state (222). For a discussion of Gower's complex treatment of *pité* within the contexts of ethical kingship, see Yoshiko Kobayashi, "*Principis Umbra*: Kingship, Justice, and Pity in John Gower's Poetry," in *On John Gower: Essays at the Millennium*, ed. R. F. Yeager (Kalamazoo, MI: Medieval Institute, 2007), 71–103; and for Gower's *pité* in the context of the political factionalism of 1388, see Andrew Galloway, "The Literature of 1388 and the Politics of Pity in Gower's *Confessio Amantis*," in *The Letter of the Law: Legal Practice and Literary Production in Medieval England*, ed. Emily Steiner and Candace Barrington (Ithaca, NY: Cornell University Press, 2002), 67–104. Irvin sees the central tension between the social virtue of charity and an overwhelming emotional distraction as defining Gower's treatment of *pité* (114–56).

act for the sake of a more important lesson," that of realizing the severity of the characters' intensely cruel actions.[35] Olsson likewise argues that the subject of the story is "too 'large' to be accommodated by the genre of the exemplum, if the purpose of that form is simple 'pointing' of a moral."[36] Working to understand this shocking narrative form in terms of the ethical project of the *Confessio*, readings such as these acknowledge the sense of something "too 'large'" for, but impinging on, the realms of representation and experience.[37]

The narrative rupture has potentially productive effects. In a reversal of the masculinist narrative of abandonment, it is now Jason who is abandoned, frozen in a moment of emergent action, and "left in gret destresse," the sword he intended to use on Medea—in a powerfully precise flash of emasculating imagery—now gripped uselessly in his hand. If this is part of the narrative that opens the Troy saga, here it is ripped from its historical moorings in order to leave a visceral residue and a sense of something still in motion, an image-in-flux that consists of emotions about to be formed and actions about to be committed. Even as it presents, however briefly, the image of Medea as a monstrous feminine threat to masculine identity and patriarchal lineage, Gower's tale works to gesture behind such pervasive cultural narratives, using gaps rent by its affective movements to signal something else, something more productive and radically unstructured. The affective and inventional potential of the tale resonates in the impending emotional response that is always about to emerge as Medea's narrative progresses, the knowledge that the visceral conclusion to this story is always imminent. Playing with this notion, Gower's ending temporarily removes Medea from the physical reality of the world of the tale and thus removes the inventional agent whose inventions a masculinist literary tradition works to bend to its own purposes. The resulting sense of affective and inventional decompression has the potential power to jolt readers into examining how quickly negative emotions characterize Medea in the literary tradition that defines her, but it also captures the activity of invention itself, the movement of emergence that only later becomes narrative and cultural forms. Medea's magic provides an imaginative analogue for Gower's *Confessio*, and the sudden narrative machinations that structure the ending of her

---

35. Nicholson, *Love and Ethics*, 291, 292.

36. Olsson, *John Gower and the Structures of Conversion*, 161; Olsson here refers to Avarice in the tale of Tereus, but in the context of Medea's story.

37. T. Matthew N. McCabe argues more generally that Gower expresses as grace the "surplus of meaning" that characterizes the experience of poetry as a whole (*Gower's Vulgar Tongue: Ovid, Lay Religion, and English Poetry in the* Confessio Amantis [Cambridge: D. S. Brewer, 2011], 230). Irvin argues that "The tale produces conflicting affects" between "pity for Medea" and "fear and disgust" at her "unnaturalness," which, he concludes, leads readers toward a better understanding of "trouthe" (225).

tale simulate, as far as is possible, the experience of transformative emergence that "An other such as Arion" might impart to the world.

"AS WHO SEITH ABREIDE OUT OF HIS SLEP": LIQUID, ENVY, AND CONSTANTINE

"The Tale of Constantine and Sylvester" offers a similarly complex treatment of the affect of invention at both microcosmic and macrocosmic levels, describing how a moment of personal transformation marked by pre-cognitive and pre-emotional movements unfolds as an inventional process at a wider social level. As the tale opens, the Roman emperor Constantine, on the advice of his doctors, plans to murder hundreds of innocent children and infants in order to cure his leprosy by bathing in their blood. When Constantine is first faced with the hundreds of people he plans to murder, weeping and wailing along with their families outside his window, he has a change of heart that leads to a change of mind. Disbursing both a philosophical revelation about the shared status of human beings in the larger cosmos and a financial compensation to the stricken families, Constantine is finally converted to Christianity by Sylvester, who in a long speech recodifies Constantine's apparently "natural" understanding of his place in the great chain of being and the common virtue of all humans by placing it within a larger context of Christian history. The tale thus serves as a textbook dramatization of the transformative power of ethical subject making, and as Larry Scanlon and T. Matthew N. McCabe have argued, it demonstrates this claim by privileging lay authority over clerical power and increasing access to the kind of "wisdom" that *Confessio* narratives purport to provide.[38] Powerful though it is, the tale's emphasis on ethical subject formation as central to the deployment of charity in the world comes almost as an elaborate afterthought to its intense scrutiny of processes of affective and inventional emergence. The tale locates the source of Constantine's transformation and the Christian conversion of Rome in a stunningly brief moment of affective ambiguity, when the emperor first takes in the rush of tears and moans of his weeping victims-to-be. To represent the implications of

---

38. Scanlon argues that the story presents a personal transformation independently of clerical authority figures, as Constantine undergoes an "entirely secular conversion," and that he is the focus of the story rather than Sylvester (*Narrative, Authority, and Power*, 265); McCabe argues for a similar privileging of lay authority in the tale, as Gower draws on English traditions of affective piety and emotional rhetoric as a way of granting access to lay readers (130–44). Olsson sees the tale as making "explicit" the pity and charity that were "only implicit in the tale of Constance" (*John Gower and the Structures of Conversion*, 103); see 103–6 for the tale's alignment of Christian and natural law.

this moment's motional work at both macro- and microcosmic levels, the tale draws on images of liquid and its movement, both the literal liquids present in the tale as well as more figurative impressions of movements and flows, in order to conceptualize metaphorically the rejuvenating and transformational potential that the *Confessio* imagines for its poetics.

Indeed, the "Tale of Constantine and Sylvester" teems with liquids: it is sprinkled with the breast milk and tears of weeping mothers, the blood of their children, and restorative baptismal water. Alongside literal fluids, other objects in the tale behave like liquids: Constantine's treasures flow out of his palace to the families he has summoned, his leprosy washes away like the scales falling from a fish, and the "venym" of materialism that Constantine's Donation "shad / In holi cherch" (3490–91) spills forth into the narrative reality of the tale's historical world. Other images of liquid dissolve the literal into the figurative, as when Constantine's sudden reaction to the wailing masses of families whose children he has summoned to slaughter combines the literal tears of "modres" and "yong babes" with his own groggy sloshing between waking and sleeping (3236–38). Such liquid moments coincide with key moments of invention in the tale: Constantine's sudden affective transformation results in the generation of poetry that is meant to be profoundly moving, including his own speech on the common connection of all human beings and, later on, Sylvester's history of the Church. Similarly, the *venym* of his donation gushes forth at the conclusion of the tale not only from divine pronouncement but also from the chronicle that Genius suddenly introduces, only at the end of the tale, as his source for the story's conclusion. These literal and thematic uses of liquid enable Gower to articulate the rejuvenating potential of a poetics that purports to be culturally restorative. Moreover, in the tale's larger context of Book 2's treatment of the sin of Envy, Gower presents liquid as a thematic metaphor simultaneously for how Envy operates, how discord leaks into and accrues in the historical world, and how an affective process of poetic invention might somehow jumpstart productive, transformative change.

As McCabe notes, "the decisive event" of Constantine's own profound change "has already occurred" well before Sylvester's long speech that leads to his conversion.[39] Indeed, it comes only some fifty lines into the tale when, outside of his window, the summoned

> Modres wepe in here degre,
> And manye of hem aswoune falle,

---

39. McCabe, 132.

> The yonge babes criden alle:
> This noyse aros, the lord it herde,
> And loked out, and how it ferde
> He sih, and as who seith abreide
> Out of his slep,
>
> (3236–42)

he launches into a soliloquy declaring that, despite their disparate social positions, "alle men" are "aliche fre" in the face of Fortune, death, virtue, and vice (3263, 3253). As the experience congeals for him, Constantine eventually develops a sympathy for his would-be victims, which Simpson argues is the fundamental first step to his eventual arrival at wisdom, and which McCabe attributes in large part to the "rhetoric of the body" and the "affective uses of bodily suffering" indicative of the rhetorical and hermeneutic traditions of affective piety on which Gower draws in his version of the tale.[40] The emotional development of Constantine's sympathy occurs some fifty lines later, however. Something else preceding that collapse happens in these seven short lines, and unpacking Gower's presentation of this moment reveals the subtle intricacy with which he suggests the potentially productive power of aligning affect and invention.

In a single overpowering rush, Constantine takes in the entire teeming scene of tears and moans, the mothers and suckling infants, the young children summoned to the city as walking bags of blood for him to pierce and drain: "how it ferde" indeed. The passage explicitly represents Constantine as being in a sudden state of emergence, like someone "who seith abreide / Out of his slep." The instant of Constantine's transformation takes place well before he is aware that it is even happening. The language of the sentence itself is charged with sensations of emergence generated by its complicated syntax and rapid succession of puns. The verb, *abreiden*—to move violently or suddenly—most obviously registers the severity and abruptness of the experience, the sudden jolt into a new state of being.[41] But its placement in the sen-

---

40. Ibid., 131, 130; McCabe further argues that Gower "enlarges the role of mothers" in his version of the tale, genders pity as feminine, and puns on childbirth in his description of Constantine's transformation (136–37). Simpson argues that the tale shows how sympathy, via Constantine's imagined identification with the suffering mothers and children, leads to reason, which leads to a fuller understanding of the self and the self's place in the macrocosm (*Sciences and the Self*, 265–66). McCabe makes a similar point, noting that "pathos ... produces spiritual insight" (144).

41. Similarly, *abreiden* refers to his being startled out of sleep while at the same time gesturing toward his forthcoming speech on the common plight of human beings, in which he essentially *abreideth*, that is censures, himself. See both separate entries for "abreiden" in the *MED*.

tence, at once part of an adverbial phrase and a clause following a coordinating conjunction, amplifies the sensation of affective displacement triggered by the sights and sounds of "how it ferde." Puns conflate aural and visual stimuli, as "sih" denotes Constantine's seeing the crowd while also intoning the sounds of the sighs of the mothers and children gathered outside his palace. Likewise the "seith" of "seith abreide" folds together both seeing and saying and links Constantine's own subsequent soliloquy with his act of seeing, thus making his later poetic invention a component of this field of affective emergence. The fluidity between these emergences is emphasized through a further pun on *sien* and *sethen*, meaning to drip, flow, boil, or roil.[42] The complex network of possible and potential meanings, pulling together seeing, hearing, flowing, moving, and speaking, conflates affective and inventional emergence in the potently brief passage. As the sentence stacks clause upon clause, it cascades through its own eventuality before collapsing into the formal invention of Constantine's words. The enjambment and combination of clauses in this passage give the impression of the lines rushing forward like a liquid, but also of collapsing in front of our very eyes from a moment of emergence into highly structured discourse. Moreover, it is not a dream from which Constantine seems to awaken, but rather sleep itself; this is not a strange set of signs requiring interpretation, as in the case of Nebuchadnezzar, or the prophetic dream Constantine has later in the tale, when he is told by Peter and Paul that "Silvestre schal thee teche" (3363), but a sudden phase shift from one state of being to another. This is a moment not of epiphany but of disorienting emergence.[43]

What follows is a series of emotions and formal inventions that spills forth into the tale and includes Constantine's *pité* for the families, both Constantine's and Sylvester's speeches on natural charity and Christian history, and the founding of new churches in Rome. Constantine's church-building project ostensibly aligns the microcosmic interiority of Constantine with the macrocosm of Christian history, demonstrating by analogy how restoring the one restores the other. This institutionalization is rendered in the explicit language of invention, as "This Emperour, which hele had founde, / Withinne Rome anon let founde / Tuo cherches, whiche he dede make" (3475–77). Both the miracle of Constantine's healing from leprosy and his establishment of churches in Rome are described as things *founde,* that is, things invented or

---

42. See the second entry for "sien" in the *MED*.
43. Andrew Galloway discusses, in another context, Gower's tendency to use a "waking sleep" motif in his dream visions, which "epitomizes his difficult balance between a writer's own desires and those of the disruptive social world he is analyzing, and between self-conscious emphasis on control and a claim to transcendent inspiration" ("Reassessing Gower's Dream Visions," in Dutton, Hines, and Yeager, *John Gower, Trilingual Poet,* 298).

discovered as much as "founded," and his order to begin construction of the churches, like Cleopatra's orders to her workmen in Chaucer's *Legend*, constitutes an act of *makyng* that transfers discursive invention to cultural infrastructure. The language connects Gower's *makyng* of poetry to the *makyng* of cultural history: *fyndyng* one allows for the *fyndyng* of the other, and the poetics of the *Confessio* seeps into and becomes constitutive of the historical reality it seeks to reform. These infrastructural inventions, however, are just as much formal codifications as Constantine's own emotional connection with the weeping families outside his palace. After both his initial start as if from sleep and his speech, Constantine looks again at "how it ferde" to "sih also the grete mone, / Of that the Modres were unglade, / And of the wo the children made" (3286–88). His "herte" then "tendreth,"

> And such pite withinne engendreth,
> That him was levere for to chese
> His oghne bodi for to lese,
> Than se so gret a moerdre wroght
> Upon blod which gulteth noght.
>
> (3289–94)

The sympathy that he feels is something separate from his experience of *abreidynge*; it is an emotional development that occurs only some fifty lines later. Indeed, the *pité* he reports to feel—the word is repeated three times in ten lines—indicates not an additional layer of emergence so much as the collapsing of his initial affective occurrence into cultural scripts of emotional expression, a collapse that, moreover, performs normalizing social work, "reinforc[ing]," as Larry Scanlon puts it, "the very class boundary that it crosses."[44] It furthermore encloses in the vocabulary of medieval estates the bodily rhetoric observed by McCabe and applies it to the conventional masculinist patterns immanent in Gower's "Tale of Jason and Medea" and in Chaucer's *Legend*.

The tale's subsequent inventions—of emotions, of speeches, of buildings, and of new cultural institutions—all gesture back toward their original site of emergence in Constantine's *abreidynge*, but they also stretch forward toward a second, macrocosmic jolt that arrives at the end of the tale when a voice from heaven announces that Constantine's final act of charity, his institutionalization of Christianity, will ultimately corrupt the Church: "'To day is venym schad / In holi cherche of temporal, / Which medleth with the spirital'"

---

44. Scanlon, *Narrative, Authority, and Power*, 265.

(3490–92). Genius closes the tale by telling Amans that he need only look around at his own world to understand the implications of this cryptic proclamation. While the ending provides further proof that all human institutions corrupt and degrade over the passing of years,[45] particularly striking is the metaphor this heavenly voice uses to describe the nature of the corruption and the method of its "worchinge" (3485). As *venym*, Constantine's gift flows forward through history as society continues its inevitable decline, moving across and among human institutions in the liquid way the poetics of the *Confessio* purports to operate. What Russell Peck calls the "chilling conclusion" of Constantine's tale emphasizes the precariousness of affective, Arionic invention:[46] the liquid means by which Constantine's *venym* seeps into history are the same means by which the *Confessio* fantasizes jumpstarting cultural rejuvenation.

In fact, Constantine's *venym* works at the level of chronicle history much as the sin of Envy itself works at the physiological level. In his transition to the final section of Book 2, Genius introduces a metaphor from Seneca that describes Envy in liquid terms:

> Senec witnesseth openly
> How that Envie proprely
> Is of the Court the comun wenche,
> And halt taverne for to schenche
> That drink which makth the herte brenne,
> And doth the wit aboute renne,
> Be every weie to compasse
> How that he mihte all othre passe,
> As he which thurgh unkindeschipe
> Envieth every felaschipe
>
> (3095–104)

Envy pours a "drink which makth the herte brenne," a liquid that "doth the wit aboute renne," which causes a similar running about of the imagination "to compasse"—we might say, invent or find—ways of acting on Envy in the social world. In medieval physiological traditions, however, Envy has a drying effect. As Genius himself describes it,

> thilke blod which scholde have ese
> To regne among the moiste veines,

---

45. *John Gower: Confessio Amantis*, ed. Peck, 2:27.
46. Ibid.

> Is drye of thilke unkendeli peines
> Thurgh whiche Envie is fyred ay.
> (3122–25)

George G. Fox cites Averroes on the physical processes and ramifications of the condition, which include not only fevers but also abscesses resulting from the drying effect.[47] Paradoxically, though, as it fires out humors and desiccates the body, Envy in the *Confessio* operates like a liquid. In Gower's description, it displaces the blood that would otherwise naturally "regne among the moiste veines," moving into the physical space of veins through a visceral act of liquid displacement, pushing out the blood and taking over its work. Its effects—fevers, or fires that "makth the herte brenne"—are the physical and emotional indicators of this initial displacement. Envy becomes a kind of physical substance that is perceivable because of its movement in places where liquids ought to flow, and its movement through the veins of the body parallels its movement through the matrix of inventional entanglements along which Envy flows through the social world. Gower conflates the physiological and social characteristics of Envy via a humoral materiality. Envy operates as a liquid that is defined by its actions of displacement and motion and that flows between the microcosm of the veins and the macrocosm of human social relations. The liquidness of Envy, then, bears an uncanny resemblance to the movements of Arionic poetry.

The Senecan metaphor of Envy's liquidness perfectly captures Envy as a force registered via sensation and movement, and one whose indeterminate origins are lost in a cascade of fluctuating matrices of emotional and narrative entanglement. Presented in this way, the topic of Envy becomes an ideal site for the articulation of Gower's Arionic poetics of affective invention—a poetics that is registered and moves in the same way as Envy but whose effects are, it is hoped, transformative and productive rather than recursive and corrosive. In the context of the bodily rhetoric of the "Tale of Constantine and Sylvester," it also flows between literal and figurative manifestations, at once a fluid moving within and among bodies, as well as a pan-historical *venym* seeping forward through time. If Medea's liquid potion represents the productive potential of the *Confessio*'s poetics of emergence, then Constantine's *venym* stands in as its destructive contrary, one that effectively reverses its restorative project, rushing into the veins of the poem and firing out is restorative poetic blood. The danger with a poetics of affective invention, then, is the reality that

---

47. George C. Fox, *The Mediaeval Sciences in the Works of John Gower* (New York: Haskell, 1966), 32–33.

any moment of becoming will always collapse into its discursive aftereffects—things like emotions, poems, or religions institutions—essentially evaporating the liquid potentiality and the promise of transformative change as a necessary aspect of its very gesture toward that potentiality.

Appropriately, Constantine's *venym* leaks into the world from a chronicle, a literary form that generically introduces the degenerative progression that characterizes the *Confessio*'s conceptualization of the historical world.[48] Genius's casually quick mention of his source at the end of the tale—"in Cronique this I rede" (3486)—is distinct from the more general identification of a source from "Among the bokes of latin" with which he first introduces the story of Constantine (3187), and it appears in the narrative as suddenly as the *venym* itself. The chronicle represents a collapse into historical narrative of the affective and inventional emergence explored elsewhere in the tale, and it furthermore suggests, if by way of a negative example, the structural significance of the chronicle form for imagining how the *Confessio*'s poetics might productively impinge on external reality. To conclude this chapter, I want to examine how the final tale of Book 1 of the *Confessio*, the "Tale of the Three Questions," aligns affective and inventional movements by narrating the sudden emergence of a new chronicle that allows the tale to fictionalize its own invention and, more significantly, to offer a more positive model for imagining the macrocosmic restorative work of the *Confessio*'s poetics.

"STRANGE INTERPRETACIOUNS": CHRONICLE EMERGENCE AND THE "TALE OF THE THREE QUESTIONS"

Like the "Tale of Constantine and Sylvester" that ostensibly presents Charity as a kind of antidote for Envy, the "Tale of the Three Questions" introduces what Olsson calls an "enacted humility" as a countermeasure against the sin of Pride, the focus of Book 1.[49] In the tale, a young daughter saves her father's life by correctly answering three riddles that the king, envious of the father's mental abilities and prideful of his own, has demanded he answer under penalty

---

48. For Nicholson, the mention of the chronicle is but a "historical footnote" that zooms out from Amans to show the effects of bad actions on a larger scale, one "that is so distant from the closed world of emotion in which Amans describes his experience" in the book (*Love and Ethics*, 176); Peck suggests that the overall "historicity of the tale effectively enables Gower to break directly into the lives of his audience without jeopardizing the framework of his fiction" (*Kingship and Common Profit*, 73–74).

49. Olsson, *John Gower and the Structures of Conversion*, 90.

of death. The tale ends happily, with the daughter saving her father, delighting the king with her abilities, and finally engaging in a kind of inventional riddling with the king that elevates her family's social status to the point at which she marries into the royal family, becoming queen. The tale concludes by suddenly introducing a chronicle as the textual source for the narrative, retroactively granting the characters names and the kingdom a physical setting in Spain, but only after the narrative proper has ended. Its plot centers on acts of successful interpretation and invention, and its narrative carefully weaves together these inventional performances among plot points characterized by anticipation and sudden, startling realizations. The final "surprise" revealing of a chronicle source for its narrative embeds this medley of affective and inventional movements in a culturally authoritative genre as a way of imagining how the poetics of the *Confessio* might emerge restoratively—in contrast to Constantine's *venym*—into historical reality.

The tale links desire with invention explicitly in the figure of King Alphonse, whose passion for inventing and solving "Problemes and demandes" (3071), but also "depe ymaginaciouns / And strange interpretaciouns" (3069–70), causes him to "confounde" an inventionally dexterous knight with whatever "strange matiere" he can find (3092–93). When he assigns the riddles to the knight and informs him that he will "lese hise goodes and his hed" should he fail to answer correctly (3116), the knight's despair is immediate, and his reaction equates the action of striving for inventional discovery with flailing about in anxious uncertainty: "The more he caste his wit aboute / The more he stant therof in doute" (3123–24). As he thinks about the implications for himself, "And after that upon his wif," and then "Upon his children ek also" (3130–31), his daughter, Peronelle, watches him weep alone in the garden and compels him to share with her the cause of his sorrow. He does and agrees to let her answer the riddles for him before the king. When they arrive at court, "Tho was ther gret merveile on honde, / That he, which was so wys a knyht, / His lif upon so yong a wyht / Besette wolde in jeupartie" (3234–37). Their appearance at court presents a "gret merveile," a kind of performative corollary to the king's original riddles, the affective potential of which includes not simply the pathos involved in wondering whether the knight will be condemned to die based on his answers, but also the fact that given the conditions of his appearance, no one can be certain what exactly is about to happen.

Peronelle of course answers each of the king's "pointz" correctly (3245), and then she launches into a flurry of inventional activity that at once delights the king and substantially alters the social reality of Spain. She wastes no time after giving the answers and asks the king to honor the pledge he made to her father, "That ye such grace and such justice / Ordeigne for mi fader hiere, / That after this, whan men it hiere, / The world therof mai speke good" (3318–20). Her request appeals to the sense of pride that clearly characterizes the king in the reputation he enjoys with his subjects, but it also essentially transforms the king's imminent action of judgment into the material for future invention, what "the world . . . mai speke" when they "hiere" of his action. In effect, she invokes the societal implications of *fyndyng* so important to Alphonse's vanity and simultaneously relegates the king to the position of a character in a tale to be told in the future.[50] Upon hearing her replies and her request, the king's "wraththe is overgo" and he is "inly glad and so wel paid" (3324–25). He tells Peronelle that if she "were of such a lignage" so as to be "of parage," she could then become his wife (3335–36). Since she is not, however, he will instead grant her any material wish she desires and "schape" her "encress" (3342). She requests a reward for her father, not herself, and in his "freisshe hete," the king makes the knight a peer of the realm, transferring into his name "An Erldom, which thanne of eschete / Was late falle into his hond" (3353–55). When Peronelle reminds him of his marriage pledge, emphasizing that "it is of record" (3363) and that she is now "an Erles dowhter" (3376), she effectively invents from his invention, reshaping the social reality that surrounds her. The king welcomes her gladly because he "was with love hent" (3379)—though the tale appears vague about whether he is in love with Peronelle, or with her inventional abilities, or both. He finally finds himself unable to "asterte" her, that is, to escape either his love for her or the narrative she has constructed in which to secure her family's new station. Emergence spills forward in a seemingly spontaneous cascade of affect and invention to such an extent that it has caused at least one modern reader to label the tale's conclusion "magical."[51] The tale aligns affective and inventional movements to forward a single process, gesturing in its narrative unfolding toward what it might "feel" like to experience a moment of emergence in which inventional action suddenly recreates the surrounding world.

The tale does not end here, however, but initiates a second wave of emergence by fictionalizing how this sensation of energetic potential that is registered at the conclusion of the narrative might impinge on the historical reality outside the *Confessio Amantis*. With the suddenly reformed social strata of Spain still congealing in the background, Genius declares that his source for the story is a "Cronique":

---

50. Kim Zarins notes that Peronelle's use of rime riche in these lines gives her language a feeling of being "proactive—dwelling not on what has happened, but on what will happen, with real and public consequences for the king" ("Rich Words: Gower's *Rime Riche* in Dramatic Action," in Dutton, Hines, and Yeager, *John Gower, Trilingual Poet*, 251).

51. Nicholson, *Love and Ethics*, 148.

> And over this good is to wite,
> In the Cronique as it is write,
> This noble king of whom I tolde
> Of Spaine be tho daies olde
> The kingdom hadde in governance,
> And as the bok makth remembrance,
> Alphonse was his propre name:
> The knyht also, if I schal name,
> Danz Petro hihte, and as men telle,
> His dowhter wyse Peronelle
> Was cleped, which was full of grace:
> And that was sene in thilke place,
> Wher sche hir fader out of teene
> Hath broght and mad hirself a qweene.
> (3387–400)

The Latin gloss furthermore identifies these events as "recent" (*nuper*)—indicating them to be still in the process of coming into form within a broader pattern of history, just as the world of the tale itself still resonates with its own transformative flux.[52] The effect of Genius's delay in naming his source is not simply an assertion of the relevance of the *Confessio*'s narratives to the current state of the world but also the unsettling impression that the *Confessio*'s narratives themselves are in the process of emerging into contemporary reality. Peck has argued that the tale's protagonists receive names only after their story is told so as to suggest that that "true personal identity comes only after selfish love has been put aside and an adult sense of common profit is realized."[53] This illusion of wholeness created by situating the characters and setting historically is essentially conjured by a trick of narrative delay—all of a sudden, these are "real people," not atavistic characters from some ancient exemplum. Moreover, no source for the "Tale of the Three Questions" has been discovered, and the possibility remains that Genius's *cronique*, like Chaucer's elusive legend of Alceste, is in fact not an actual old book at all but Gower's own creation. Its presentation in the *Confessio* is fraught with inventional potential: Gower's invention about invention poses as a chronicle and thus is doubly *founde*, both discovered and poetically *made*, even as it fictionally emerges into the historical world it purports to record. As the *Confessio* appears to make history

---

52. *Complete Works*, ed. Macaulay, 2:119.
53. Peck, *Kingship and Common Profit*, 58.

rather than simply draw from historiography for narrative *materia*, it appears to remake the world.[54]

As the tale thus imagines the invention of a "newe" world through a performatively affective poetics, Gower effectively links his own inventional work in the *Confessio* with Peronelle's in Spain, not only in the capacity of offering advice to princes in the voice of feminine humility[55] but also in producing the very inventional work that results in the *fyndyng* of new historical realities. As Maria Bullón-Fernández carefully shows, the complexities of Peronelle's inventional machinations in "the masculine world" of the tale extend well beyond plot necessities of the narrative.[56] Her ability to best the king and secure an elevated position for her father and, finally, for herself, all while using "her humility as a masquerade with which she hides her use of power,"[57] begins to pull back the curtain covering the masculinist discourse that maintains social arrangements. "Even as it contains it," Bullón-Fernández writes, "the tale shows the potential both for female power and for the disruption of the system of exchange," and Peronelle's use of language "open[s] up the possibility of female agency" in a way that extends beyond the fiction of the tale and into the very "workings of moralistic literature" of the kind that Genius purports to relate.[58] "Peronelle shows that woman is not simply a word," Bullón-Fernández argues, "but a user and manipulator of words too—a generator of signs."[59] Like Medea, Peronelle is not a representation of invention; she is an inventor. The transformation rendered by the end of the story, however, draws on the same masculinist discourse that conditions Constantine's *pité* and the final actions of Medea. A close examination of the cause of the tale's "magical" sensation of emergence reveals that, as Kendall notes, Peronelle's inventional prowess ultimately only facilitates an exchange between two men, her father and the

---

54. Katie Peebles reads the tale in a late-fourteenth-century political environment, arguing that Gower sets it in Spain in order to encourage a positive relationship between England and Castille, as well as to demonstrate effective counseling of kings ("Arguing from Foreign Grounds: John Gower's Leveraging of Spain in English Politics," in *Gower in Context(s): Scribal, Linguistic, Literary and Socio-historical Readings*, ed. Laura Filardo-Llamas, Brian Gastle, and Marta Gutiérrez Rodríguez, special issue of *ES. Revista de Filología Inglesa* 33.1 (Valladolid: Publicaciones Universidad de Valladolid, 2012), 97–113; for a summary of possible analogues for the tale, see 98–99.

55. See Misty Schieberle, "'Thing Which Man Mai Noght Areche': Women and Counsel in Gower's *Confessio Amantis*," *Chaucer Review* 42 (2007): 91–109.

56. Maria Bullón-Fernández, *Fathers and Daughters in Gower's* Confessio Amantis (Cambridge: D. S. Brewer: 2000), 64.

57. Ibid., 66.

58. Ibid., 68, 72, 74.

59. Ibid., 70. See also Schieberle, 93; Claire Banchich, "Holy Fear and Poetics in John Gower's *Confessio Amantis*, Book I," in Yeager, *On John Gower*, 206–7; and McCabe, 123–30.

king.[60] Indeed, just as a second Arion never actually appears in Gower's discordant world, Peronelle never extracts herself from the patriarchal discourses that ultimately characterize the new Spain she invents. Nevertheless, Peronelle emerges into a "newe" world that she herself has invented from the masculinist *materia* available to her, and the overwhelming rush of emergence that concludes the tale provides an affective and inventional matrix in which to observe masculinist discourses and their capacity to structure cultural relations actually coming into form. Peronelle's tale finally leaves us, alongside its newly named characters, immersed in the charged environment of a world still coalescing, creating a momentary space for "getting behind" invented discourses and the "magical" way in which affective experiences attach to them. As they emerge from the *Confessio* and into a chronicle, the tale's "strange interpretaciouns" seem to enact the restorative processes of "a thing ... so strange."

While each of the three tales discussed here—those of Medea, Constantine, and Peronelle—explicitly work to make the *Confessio*'s poetics of emergence constitutive of culture by imagining whole worlds being literally reformed, in none of them is this historico-poetical alignment fully idealized. Medea's and Peronelle's stories are characterized by the realization of the poetics of patriarchy that underscores their tales' fictions of cultural revivification, and the last liquid seeping out of the story of Constantine is the *venym* of materialism that future generations make of his original act of charity. In each instance in which he explores the macrocosmic potential of the *Confessio*'s poetics, Gower more fully reveals the insidiousness of the problem of a discordant present. The *croniques* of Constantine's and Peronelle's tales in particular offer contrasting views of the relationship of chronicles to the *Confessio*. While each conjures the chronicle as a form of cultural authority, the *cronique* of Constantine's tale introduces the corrosive reality of historical progression, the kind strikingly embodied in the Prologue's Statue of Time. The chronicle of Peronelle's story reverses this trajectory, suggesting how poetry might emerge productively into the world outside its lines. The chronicle itself becomes a vexed form for Gower: it registers the corrosive trajectory of history, but it is also perfectly suited for articulating the *Confessio*'s restorative potential. In the next chapter, I explore how Gower reimagines the chronicle as a site for macrocosmic invention, working through the problem of historical degradation encapsulated in its genre by writing his own chronicles and inserting them into the very center of his poem, and finally going so far as to reinvent the *Confessio* as a new kind of affective chronicle.

---

60. Peronelle "determines her own household status (and transfers her dependence from one man to another) in order to reconfigure the political relationship between king and knight" (Kendall, *Lordship and Literature*, 157).

CHAPTER 4

"THE CRONIQUE OF THIS FABLE"

Transformative Poetry and the Chronicle Form in the *Confessio Amantis*

IN THE PREVIOUS CHAPTER, I argued that the *Confessio* works to figuratively represent movements of affect and invention within its narratives and that it begins to imagine how the productive potential that characterizes such movements might actually impinge upon the social "reality" external to the *Confessio* itself. The tales of Constantine and Peronelle provide examples of how this process might work by introducing the form of the chronicle as a culturally authoritative genre that at once narrates and purports to create a sense of historical reality. As the contrasting depictions of chronicles in these tales show, however, the chronicle is a problematic form in the *Confessio*. On the one hand, the *croniques* regularly invoked in the poem, given their purported authority and proximity to historical events, constitute a literary form that would seem best poised to transfer imaginative movements from the text to the world, the kind of productive impingement happily fictionalized at the end of the "Tale of the Three Questions." On the other hand, because their narratives necessarily move from past to present, *croniques* structurally transfer a corrosive progression of history that always ends, to borrow Gower's iconic, anthropomorphic image of this idea, with Nebuchadnezzar's Statue of Time standing unsteadily below an enormous boulder. The chronicle is at once a model and a vehicle for enacting the Arionic gesture imagined in the Prologue, even though it threatens to reintroduce the *venym* of a corrosive historical trajectory that always ends in discord. In addition to invoking chronicles as sources and making them part of *Confessio* narratives, Gower explicitly writes chronicles into his poem, indeed positioning them at its very heart, in Books 4 and 5. In these chronicles, Gower pairs the topic of invention with the form of the chronicle, working to transform the chronicle from simply a culturally authoritative source for exemplary material into a literary form that is itself capable of resonating with the movements of affect and invention that are thematized elsewhere within the narratives of his poem.

Book 4 first breaks the *Confessio*'s general pattern of exemplary narrative, in which chronicles are referred to mainly as sources for Genius's invention, and instead implants a series of chronicles recounting the history of the physical and intellectual labor that led to the greatest "inventions" of human culture, including writing, hunting, agriculture, mercantilism, alchemy, grammar, rhetoric, and poetry. Book 5 then offers a similar chronicle account in the form of a history of religions that culminates chronologically in the present-day discord of a fractured Christendom. As an authoritative repository of cultural knowledge, the chronicles provide a textual form useful to Gower's project of rejuvenating a fallen present moment, but the cumulative effect of these chronicles, embedded as they are within the very framework of the *Confessio*, finally suggests the emergence of a new kind of chronicle, one that encodes the affective energies of inventional movement as an aspect of its form. Gower manipulates the chronicle structure in order both to gesture toward the affect of invention at a larger, structural level and to suggest how that gesture might be extended to the "real" world of human activity—an exercise that is ultimately as fanciful as it is formal, perhaps, but one that presents a model for how a transformative, Arionic poetics might be imagined to operate in the world outside the *Confessio Amantis*.

To explore how Gower creates this new kind of productively emergent chronicle—and what this chronicle actually looks like when it appears in the *Confessio*—I first want to contextualize the chronicles of Books 4 and 5 within Gower's own effort to portray himself as a writer of chronicles and to examine how he draws on common fourteenth-century chronicling practices, in particular those codified in Ranulf Higden's *Polychronicon* (and its English translation by John Trevisa). I turn then to the chronicles of Book 4, where Gower adapts these commonplace structural models in order to combat the chronological corrosion that characterizes chronicle narrative and to suggest how the form of the chronicle might be adapted to forward the *Confessio*'s larger project of cultural renewal. Finally, I examine the chronicles of religion in Book 5, arguing that Gower critiques, deconstructs, and even satirizes the very process he develops in Book 4 in a way that, despite appearing to overturn the hopeful potential expressed through the earlier chronicles of invention, ultimately contributes to the larger project of imagining one of the ways in which the *Confessio* might embed a capacity to transmit potential as a part of its poetic structure and then, fictively at least, graft that structure onto the world outside of the poem.[1]

"THE WORLDES CONSTITUCION": GOWER THE CHRONICLER AND THE PROBLEM OF FORM

Reading the *Confessio Amantis* as a kind of chronicle has precedent in Gower's own authorial self-presentation: throughout his poetic career, he presents himself as a writer of historiography. In the short Latin poem *Quicquid homo scribat*, for example, Gower describes his final, though probably fictionalized, retirement from a career of poetry. "To whatever a man writes," one version of the poem begins, "Nature applies a limit . . . / She has placed a limit on me, so that I am unable / To write any longer, because I am blind" (1–4). As the poem continues, its speaker declares in terms familiar from Book 1 of the *Confessio* his turn away from poetry to "write with my prayers what my hand cannot" (14).[2] Two of the three extant versions of the poem are preceded by prose notes in which Gower characterizes the nature and achievements of the career he is abandoning: "Here in the end it is to be noted how, from the chronicle that is called *Vox clamantis* to the end of the chronicle that is called *Tripertita*, I notably composed different poems, which are necessary to read."[3] This characterization strikingly recasts Gower's poetic career as that of an English chronicler. Moreover, Gower's decision to use the chronicle as the

---

1. That Gower is interested in reproducing the mechanisms of poetic composition as part of the narrative of the *Confessio* has been noted before. Rita Copeland, for example, argues that such metatextual representation is part of Gower's strategy to leverage English vernacular against a Latin academic tradition, all the while using stories from the past to revitalize the present (*Rhetoric, Hermeneutics, and Translation*, 202–20). Kurt Olsson suggests that Genius's movement from topic to topic in Book 4 indicates a kind of slothful invention, but one that leads to "fruitful leisure" by which the poem inspires continued topical discussion (*John Gower and the Structures of Conversion*, 146). R. F. Yeager sees the *Confessio* as a whole as a kind of metachronicle or "poetic history" that is "a narrative of its own making" (*John Gower's Poetic*, 169).

2. "Quicquid homo scribat, finem natura ministrat . . . / Illa michi finem posuit, quo scribere quicquam / Vlterius nequio, sum quia cecus ego" (1–4); "[Scribire] de precibus que nequit illa manus" (14). The Latin text is from *Complete Works*, ed. Macaulay, 4.365–66. The translation is from *The Minor Latin Works*, ed. and trans. R. F. Yeager (Kalamazoo, MI: Medieval Institute, 2005), 49. Line numbers are quoted parenthetically in the text. The poem exists in three different versions in five manuscripts; I have quoted the All Souls Version.

3. *Minor Latin Works*, ed. and trans. Yeager, 49 ("Hic in fine notandum est qualiter ab illa Cronica que Vox clamantis dicitur vsque in finem istius Cronice que tripertita est, Ego . . .

poetic form best suited to transfer productive potential from text to world may also be a decidedly political decision. As Frank Grady has argued, by 1399 chronicles had become one of the genres that replaced the dream vision as a way of addressing the tumultuous events at the turn of the century (particularly from a pro-Lancastrian perspective), and indeed, the later Latin poems, notes, and revisions that retroactively cast Gower's poetic career in terms of chronicles are in part an effort to adapt to the political necessities faced by writers in what Grady calls "The Generation of 1399."[4]

But Gower's appending of the dream vision of Book 1 to the *Vox* provides a much earlier example of this same interest in writing poetry that, as Andrew Galloway puts it, "creates" history,[5] and it furthermore demonstrates a career-long impetus to link his poetic texts with his own public authorial persona, itself one manifestation of a much larger project of imagining how verse might impinge in productively macrocosmic ways on a larger, external, social reality. In the *visio*, as we have seen, Gower depicts what was, for him at least, the nightmarish Rising of 1381 and takes particular pains to place events within a historical context, establishing the first book of the *Vox* as an exemplary text for action in the future.[6] Gower furthermore places a fictionalized version of himself at the center of this historical vision, figuring himself as a poet who is stripped of his ability to speak by the horror of the events he witnesses. The Gower persona of the *Vox* is at once a tongue-tied poet and a historical commentator, a writer who records simultaneously both historical eventuality and the methods by which poets record such events. Maura Nolan argues that the *Vox* in particular uses its form, especially its appropriation of Ovidian material, to create "a poetic line strung taut between the twin poles of past and present, between Ovid and the *Vox* . . . that vibrates with the tension of sameness and difference," and that, in this way, essentially preserves the energetic life of the past, "using the past while allowing it to speak freely" in its own words.[7] As Siân Echard shows, the historiographic Gower is always

---

varia carmina . . . que ad legendum necessaria sunt, notabiliter conscripsi" [Macaulay, 4:365]). This is the note to the All Souls version of the poem.

4. Grady, "The Generation of 1399," in Steiner and Barrington, *Letter of the Law*, 202–29; Grady argues in particular that "a 'Lancastrian' poetic . . . can be defined formally as well as politically," and those forms reflect an "increase of interest in documentary models of discourse, particularly legal texts and representations of parliamentary activity" (206), including the chronicle, which "all[ies] itself to the putatively irrefutable authority of the documentary record" (208).

5. Galloway, "Gower in His Most Learned Role," 332.

6. Ibid., 335.

7. Nolan, "Historicism after Historicism," 77, 82. Nolan refers specifically to Gower's metaphor of gathering seashells in Book 2 of the *Vox* to describe his compilation of source

also the poetical Gower, a writer for whom historical *materia* is to be understood in terms of the language and artistic forms that are used to represent it.[8] Moreover, the larger metafiction of the *Vox,* as I argued in the Introduction, involves Gower's imagining that the emergence of his own transformational poetics occurs concurrently with the mythico-historical founding of Britain itself, as the conclusion to the *visio* suggests. Gower's interest in embedding statements about his own poetics in imagined historical spaces spans his entire career.

While it is perhaps formally more apparent in the *Vox* or the *Cronica,* Gower's self-description as a chronicler also emerges as an inherent component of the *Confessio.* There, "Gower the historian," as Russell Peck rightly labels him, is keenly aware that "history" itself is a discursive construction. Gower, Peck argues, "thinks and acts like a historian," and he "knows that history is culturally produced."[9] Elizabeth Allen furthermore argues that Gower's use of historical sources indicates an author who is also aware of the dangers of resorting too readily to the historically authoritative examples of antiquity, as well as one who actively questions the function of exemplary narrative in his poetry.[10] At the same time, however, Gower consciously works to install his own artistic productions into a historiographic framework: the colophons at the end of the *Confessio,* for example, work with the effigy that Gower himself designed to present the author to posterity in Southwark Cathedral. Furthermore, his various dedications of the *Confessio*—to Richard II, Henry Derby, and England itself—indicate a consistent, if varied, effort to position his English work within imagined political and literary history.[11]

Unlike the *Cronica tripertita,* the *Confessio,* of course, does not present itself explicitly as history, and unlike the *Vox* it does not purport to narrate direct historical experience (the Prologue's original commissioning scene on the Thames notwithstanding). In Books 4 and 5, however, the *Confessio*

---

texts—a metaphor borrowed from Ovid's *Ars amatoria* that itself "constitutes a critique of its Gowerian use" (82), and that thus preserves at once past writers' as well as his own sense of the relationship of past to present.

8. Echard, "Gower's 'bokes of Latin.'"
9. *John Gower: Confessio Amantis,* ed. Peck, 3:6, 9.
10. Elizabeth Allen, *False Fables and Exemplary Truth in Later English Literature* (New York: Palgrave, 2005). Allen focuses specifically on Gower's retelling of the story of Virginia, which she argues Gower read as the endorsement of republican government "at the price of individual life" (63). Overall, Gower makes his "examples depend for their effect upon readers' reception of misalignments and metaphors rather than didactic reiterations" (79).
11. For the complex and shifting impression presented by the *Confessio*'s colophons, see especially Siân Echard, "Last Words: Latin at the End of the *Confessio Amantis,*" in *Interstices: Studies in Middle English and Anglo-Latin Texts in Honour of A. G. Rigg,* ed. Richard Firth and Linne R. Mooney (Toronto: University of Toronto Press, 2004), 99–121.

presents *croniques* of its own—that is, not independent narrative examples that claim historical veracity, but long passages in which chronological progression itself forms the narrative. As part of the poem that is supposed to combat the sins of Sloth and Avarice, these chronicles have presented a problem for critics, some of whom have viewed them as digressive and "tedious."[12] Even thorough critical treatments of Book 4 tend to overlook its chronicles, reading them instead as a kind of exemplary shorthand: they provide a catalogue of individuals whose ingenuity built civilization; they offer shining examples of how productive *besinesse* can successfully combat Sloth.[13] Only rarely have critics taken up the generic aspect of the chronicles themselves. R. F. Yeager argues that part of the reason Book 4 accomplishes its virtuous work is that the "historically-sketched" catalogue emphasizes the development of writing in particular and "culminates in the invention of poetry" by Herodotus and finally by Ovid.[14] Nicola Masciandaro places Gower's chronicles of invention in the context of other Middle English histories of work and argues that Gower's chronicles demonstrate a bourgeois attitude toward work.[15] In reading Book 5's history of religions, critics have noted the almost ethnographic stance

---

12. Peck calls the chronicles of Book 4 "tedious," (*John Gower: Confessio Amantis*, 3:36); Macaulay famously calls the history of religion a "very ill-advised digression" (*Complete Works*, 2:515).

13. Most recent criticism on Book 4 debates the relative success of this strategy of *besinesse*. Olsson argues that while Genius's exemplary method in Book 4 is slothful, it also productively destabilizes the "human tendency to make easy, premature, unwise, and falsely secure judgments" in an unstable world (*John Gower and the Structures of Conversion*, 146). Other critics have worked to resolve the tension by folding the problematic nature of Book 4 back into Gower's larger plan of ethical instruction. Peter Nicholson argues that Genius achieves this lofty goal by making love an impetus for virtuous behavior in the real world (*Love and Ethics*, 210–37). Yeager notes that the discussion of *gentilesse* emphasizes this "real" world and virtue "manifested in deeds. . . . True gentility thus requires effort; achieving it becomes a kind of work" (*John Gower's Poetic*, 161). Similarly, James Simpson argues that Book 4 at first appears to work against its stated goal but ultimately performs productive work by inspiring productive *otium* in the reader of the poem. Like the *Confessio* as a whole, Book 4 offers nothing less than "a model of recreative relaxedness among many books" ("Bonjour Paresse: Literary Waste and Recycling in Book 4 of Gower's *Confessio Amantis*," *Proceedings of the British Academy* 151 [2007]: 284). For Gregory M. Sadlek, Book 4 reflects the changing attitude toward work in fourteenth-century England, and it advocates no single ideology other than that the fruits of work ought to be directed toward the common profit (*Idleness Working: The Discourse of Love's Labor from Ovid through Chaucer and Gower* [Washington, DC: Catholic University of America Press, 2004], 167–207). The work of these critics has itself been extremely productive, showing that Book 4 is not simply an aberrant distraction but rather a wholehearted embodiment of the instructional project of the entire poem—however varied our understandings of that project might be.

14. Yeager, *John Gower's Poetic*, 164.

15. Nicola Masciandaro, *The Voice of the Hammer: The Meaning of Work in Middle English Literature* (Notre Dame, IN: University of Notre Dame Press, 2007), 84–94.

Gower takes as he works to investigate the nonsupernatural origins of classical deities, all the while subtly acknowledging the awkwardness of Genius who, as a priest of a goddess who is the product of "misbelieve" (5.838), suddenly has to admit his own fictionality.[16] While they address the relationship of poetry to work and Gower's historiographic stance toward his topic, these studies do not examine why the chronicle form itself is especially important to Gower's larger project of cultural rejuvenation. Indeed, as passages that result on the one hand in the invention of Latin poetry, and on the other in a metatextual self-commentary on the fictional frame of the *Confessio* as a whole, the chronicles of Books 4 and 5 demand precisely this kind of critical examination.

In claiming the form as well as the matter of history, Gower not only draws on the *materia* of the past but also gives that matter the shape of historiography.[17] In fact, he imagines the *Confessio* as both a record and a part of the past, openly declaring in the Prologue to

> wryte of newe som matiere,
> Essampled of these olde wyse
> So that it myhte in such a wyse,
> Whan we ben dede and elleswhere,
> Beleve to the worldes eere
> In tyme comende after this.
>
> (Pr. 6–11)

Much more than simply compiling examples, Gower presents the *Confessio* as a kind of instructive chronicle for future generations of English readers in a "tyme comende after this." But the chronicle form is at once potentially productive and corrosive for the project of the *Confessio*. On the one hand,

---

16. Nicholson argues that Genius "treats the problem of misbelief more as an intellectual than as a moral issue," and this attitude "aligns him with the chroniclers" who treat the beliefs of classical antiquity (*Love and Ethics*, 298, 300). Gower, Nicholson continues, "betrays a similar reluctance to intrude upon the Christian monopoly on divinity, even for the purposes of fiction" (300–301). Theresa Tinkle argues that Genius's explanation of the history of Venus joins his others in "separat[ing] the deities from an aestheticized discourse, from a culturally elevated mythic register" (*Medieval Venuses and Cupids: Sexuality, Hermeneutics, and English Poetry* [Stanford, CA: Stanford University Press, 1996], 184). Larry Scanlon reads the chronicles of religions as Gower's effort to discover "the extent to which the construction of divine authority can itself be divinely authorized" (*Narrative, Authority, and Power*, 275). For the awkwardness of Genius's realization of his own fictional status, see especially Yeager, *John Gower's Poetic*, 186–87; Nicholson, *Love and Ethics*, 300–302.

17. For the distinction between Gower's use of "forme" and "matiere" in the *Confessio*, see Simpson, *Sciences and the Self*, 2–4.

chronicles promise to import both the edificatory program understood to be a part of medieval historiography (examples to imitate or to avoid) and a textual form that imposes structure and direction on the disparate events of history. As fraught as the strict definition of a medieval "chronicle" may be, the chronicle as a textual form purports to carry cultural authority because it catalogues noteworthy deeds of the past that are at once constitutive of culture and instructive to readers.[18] On the other hand, as records of post-lapsarian human activity, chronicles threaten to reintroduce into Gower's poem the cultural discord that he actively seeks to quell through writing the *Confessio*: the world "In sondry wyse so diversed, / That it welnyh stant al reversed, / As forto speke of tyme ago" (29–31).[19] Moving inexorably, as they must, closer and closer to the present, chronicles define themselves by culminating in the very discord the *Confessio* would attempt to dispel.[20]

Gower presents this problem of corrosion through the history of *gentilesse*, which itself functions as the introduction to the chronicles of Book 4. Genius's presentation of this virtue conforms to most standard definitions of the concept: true *gentilesse* does not originate in money, land, or family name; instead it resides in the heart and is demonstrated by virtuous action.[21]

---

18. As Galloway succinctly puts it, drawing on John of Salisbury, "historical writing both reveals and makes history and society, preserving but also shaping both past and present" ("Writing History in England," in *The Cambridge History of Medieval English Literature*, ed. David Wallace [Cambridge: Cambridge University Press, 1999], 255). Generic debate over exactly what separates a "chronicle" from a written "history" or other forms of historiography dates back to at least Gervase of Canterbury, who establishes a commonplace (if problematic) binary: "histories" are rhetorically more dynamic than chronicles, which present the matter of the past without flourish and in strict chronological order (256). As Chris Given-Wilson notes, however, "chronicle" in the Middle Ages could "describe any work the subject-matter of which claimed to be essentially historical, whether that meant events in the past or events contemporary with the time at which the author wrote" (*Chronicles: The Writing of History in Medieval England* [London: Hambledon and London, 2004], xix). For a cogent summary of the scholarly debate over the development of the chronicle form and its precise definition, see David Dumville, "What is a Chronicle?" in *The Medieval Chronicle II: Proceedings of the 2nd International Conference on the Medieval Chronicle, Friebergen/Utrecht 16–21 July 1999*, Costerus New Series 144 (Amerstdam: Rodopi , 2002), 1–27.

19. Histories of labor in particular illustrate this decline, since the amount of work that characterizes life is proportional to humanity's distance from original, Edenic bliss. Work is closely related to the writing of history, as Masciandaro shows: it is "a sign of exile in the historical world" (60), and it "enables the continuity of human life and is the means of history itself" (62). Gower emblematizes this kind of progression most strikingly in the Statue of Time in Nebuchadnezzar's dream.

20. For Gower's use of this tradition of the discordant present across his three major poems, see James M. Dean, *The World Grown Old in Medieval Literature* (Cambridge, MA: Medieval Academy of America, 1997), ch. 6.

21. See Rozalyn Levin, "The Passive Poet: Amans as Narrator in Book 4 of the *Confessio Amantis*," *Proceedings of the Illinois Medieval Association* 3 (1986), 114–15. For Levin, Amans

Genius, however, makes it a point to introduce *gentilesse* in historical terms and in doing so establishes the significance and the problem of the chronicle form for Book 4. According to Genius,

> The worldes constitucion
> Hath set the name of gentilesse
> Upon the fortune of richesse
> Which of long time is falle in age.
> Thanne is a man of hih lignage
> After the forme, as thou miht hiere,
> Bot nothing after the matiere.
>   (4.2206–12)

Despite their clear connection to a more properly ordered past, those men today who can boast of "hih lignage" resemble the greatness of the past "After the forme . . . Bot nothing after the matiere." Inherently claiming demonstrable, historical ties to an idealized past, contemporary men of "hih lignage" nevertheless demonstrate that same historical narrative to be meaningless for preserving true gentility, being "riche and vertuous also" (2286). Genius's critique of contemporary *gentilesse* introduces the chronicles that follow by establishing the central paradox of chronicle authority in the *Confessio*: the closer to the present moment that any chronicle moves, the greater the degree of cultural discord that it introduces. The historical narrative of *gentilesse* moves not toward the flowering of the virtue but toward its ruin. This, then, is the structural problem presented by chronicles: How can a poet activate the productive aspects of the chronicle form without reintegrating its potentially corrosive elements? If the *Confessio* moves to create a new kind of chronicle that somehow, by virtue of its form and integration into a larger poem, energizes the present by emerging into it, then the poem must first address this corrosive problem apparently inherent in the form itself.

A tentative solution comes in part through the way in which Gower assimilates organizational structures that characterize the shape of historical narratives in other chronicles contemporary with the *Confessio*. Gower draws on practices in late-medieval English chronicles that embed within a historiographic expression a dramatization of the processes of topical invention. The productive, imaginative, and ultimately generative work of invention counteracts the corrupting effects of chronicle narratives. Taken together, the chronicles of invention in Book 4 reinforce the larger regenerative project

---

comes to understand this meaning of *gentilesse* only at the end of Book 8.

of the *Confessio* by refiguring the cultural authority of the chronicle form in terms of poetic production. The *Confessio* presents an effort to dramatize the sensation of unfolding that characterizes inventional activity as a part of the chronicle form, and thus to suggest structurally how this motion of invention might be entirely transmitted, figuratively at least, into the world beyond the poem.

THE "GRETE BESYNESSE OF Þ E WRITERS OF CRONICLES": HISTORIOGRAPHIC INVENTION IN THE *POLYCHRONICON* AND *CONFESSIO*

As he dramatizes this process structurally in the *Confessio,* Gower borrows the forms of contemporary chronicle writing, working with the accepted historiographic vocabulary of the fourteenth century and consciously drawing on chronicles that themselves embed this inventional action as parts of their formal organization. Briefly examining one of the most important chronicles of the fourteenth century reveals some of the methods and structures that Gower adapts for his own poem. Ranulf Higden's *Polychronicon* and its English translation by John Trevisa organize a record of historical progression around the principle of formal invention, arranging events both topically and chronologically. Like Gower's chronicles in Books 4 and 5, the *Polychronicon* synthesizes biblical, legendary, and near-contemporary historical events into a single narrative. The text was in many ways unprecedented: never before in England had a chronicle of its kind covered so much ground so thoroughly, been as widely copied, or inspired as many continuations.[22] The *Polychronicon* removed the need for many other versions of ancient history, simply because the chronicle was so massive, rich, and inclusive—a "supra-history or master genre," as Emily Steiner calls it.[23] Steiner shows how Higden's chronicle functioned not only as "a locus for formal invention," but also as a basis for what she calls a "radical historiography," reinventing ways of looking at contemporary political relations.[24] While the *Polychronicon* may have been a powerful

---

22. Emily Steiner, "Radical Historiography: Langland, Trevisa, and the *Polychronicon*," *Studies in the Age of Chaucer* 27 (2005): 171–211, summarizes the popularity and extensive dissemination of Higden's chronicle; see esp. 174–75, nn. 10–13. See also Antonia Gransden, *Historical Writing in England*, 2 vols. (Ithaca, NY: Cornell University Press, 1982), 2:43–44; 55–56.

23. Steiner, 175.

24. Ibid., 173–74. This "radical historiography," Steiner argues, was especially palatable to writers like John Wyclif and William Langland, who found in Higden triggers for imagining alternatives to the dominant cultural myths of the late fourteenth century (173–74).

tool for inventing subversive political thought, the encyclopedic quality that made it so popular is traceable in part to the practices of invention that it enacts as part of its historical narrative. Higden's chronicle functions as much as a map for topical invention as for historical understanding.

The *Polychronicon* begins traditionally enough with commonplace ideas about the value of history as a model for ethical behavior transmitted by the diligent work of writers: "For in þe making and bookes of stories, þat is to vs i-sent and byqueþe by grete besynesse of þe writers of cronicles, blaseþ and schyneþ clerliche þe riȝt rule of þewes, ensaumple of leuynge, clensynge of goodnes" (1.5).[25] While they describe the value of chronicles to moral instruction, Higden and Trevisa emphasize in particular the work that historiographers do—the "grete besynesse of þe writers of cronicles" (1:5). This virtuous *besinesse* is of course what will earn them a place in Genius's chronicles of invention in Book 4, but Higden and Trevisa are careful to note that the work of the historian is the labor of organization: "For storie is wytnesse of tyme, mynde of lyf, messager of eldnesse; story weldeþ passyng doynges, storie putteþ forth hire professoures. Dedes þat wolde be lost storie ruleþ; dedes þat wolde flee out of mynde, storye clepeþ aȝen; dedes þat wolde deie, storye kepeþ hem euermore" (1:7).[26] While typical of medieval views of history, Higden's and Trevisa's descriptions of the work of historiography do not focus only on acts of memorialization. History is, first and foremost, an organizer, a process that "fugitiva revocat": any "dedes" that would escape memory, "storye clepeþ aȝen." Trevisa's English translation marks this organizing duty even more clearly. History writing "ruleþ" material that otherwise "wolde be lost," and Trevisa's term for this work—*reulen*—encapsulates senses of governing and controlling, but also senses of organizing and putting something into its proper place.

As a result of this organizational work, the *Polychronicon* presents itself as a sourcebook of inventional topics. In essence, Higden transfers his own authorial characteristics—that of the humble compiler—to his audience, hoping that his work will, "ut arbitror, non inutilem studiosis" (1:12). He hopes,

---

25. "In historico namque contextu chronographorum nobis diligentia delegato relucet clarius norma morum, forma vivendi, probitatis incentivum" (1:4). Higden's Latin and Trevisa's English translations are from *Polychronicon Ranulphi Higden monachi cestrensis: Together with the English Translations of John Trevisa and of an Unknown Writer of the Fifteenth Century*, ed. Churchill Babington and Joseph Rawson Lumby, 9 vol., Rerum Britannicarum Medii Ævii Scriptores, 41 (London: Longman, 1865–86). All references are to this edition and will be cited parenthetically in the text by volume and page numbers.

26. "Historia igitur, cum sit testis temporum, memoria vitæ, nuncia vetustatis, dotes possidet præminentes, suosque quam plurimum prærogat professores. Historia namque quadam famæ immortalitate peritura renovat, fugitiva revocat, mortalia quodammodo perpetuat et conservat" (1:6).

that is, that his text will not be useless to the studious reader, whom he characterizes later as someone with the same intentions as his own—to compile the varied works of history together, and who simply lacks the vast library needed to do so (1:14–15). Higden's chronicle simulates for a reader the practice of selecting topics for invention and then organizing those topics productively, enacting the process of topical selection, of formal invention, even as it atomizes it. It distills and consolidates the expanse of source material but ultimately leaves the choice of selection to its imagined auditor. The reader that Higden's prologue creates, then, is an inventor.[27] Higden's methodology follows the trend analyzed in detail by Rita Copeland, who shows how in the Middle Ages, hermeneutical interpretation—manifested especially in the processes of translation and textual exegesis—in fact became a kind of rhetorical invention; the work of reading replicated the work of textual composition.[28] Higden and Trevisa, moreover, call attention to this methodology not only as the chief structuring principle of the *Polychronicon* but also as a source of its beauty. Higden's text will be defined not by "sententiæ subtilitas neque verborum venustas, sed devotionis sinceritas materiæ militabit," or, as Trevisa puts it, not by "sotilte of sentence, noþer faire florischynge of wordes, but swetnesse of deuocion of þe matire [which] schal regne in þis book" (1:14–15). The beauty and pleasure of historiography—its *swetnesse*—can be found in the inventional *besinesse* of selecting topics from a wealth of source material and organizing those topics in a useful way. Writing chronicles becomes joyfully productive work for the chronicler and the reader alike.

This project so shapes the narrative of history that Higden and Trevisa offer in the massive chronicle that the text's value as a source for topical invention threatens to overshadow its veracity as a historical record. For example, as it presents material from a vast array of sources, the *Polychronicon* regularly conflates irreconcilable evidence. Julius Caesar is said to be both the best administrator of the Roman Republic and an implacable tyrant, and Alexander the Great receives inconsistent treatment in the extensive sections dedicated to his life.[29] Higden notably treats Geoffrey of Monmouth's leg-

---

27. In demonstrating how John Wyclif and William Langland drew on the *Polychronicon* as a source for radical political discourse, Steiner also shows that the success of this strategy may not have been the success Higden himself might have envisioned. Higden's reader-as-inventor model also has obvious parallels with the kind of ethical "invention" that J. Allan Mitchell (*Ethics and Exemplary Narrative*), Olsson (*John Gower and the Structures of Conversion*), and Allen ("Newfangled Readers") argue occurs in the minds of readers of the *Confessio*.

28. Copeland, *Rhetoric, Hermeneutics, and Translation*; see also my discussion in the Introduction.

29. See John Taylor, *The Universal Chronicle of Ranulf Higden* (Oxford: Clarendon, 1966), 43. When Caesar defeated Pompey, "Inde Romam rediens imperatorem se vocari fecit, ubi

ends of Arthur only to state how, in Trevisa's translation, "if Arthor hadde i-wonne þritty kyngdoms . . . why lefte alle þe writers of stories of Romayns, Frenschemen, and Saxons, and speke noȝt of so greet (dedes and of so greet) a victor, seþþe þat þey tolde so moche and of so menye lasse men, and of wel lasse dedes?" (5:335).[30] Perhaps most famously, while presenting the history of Carthage, Higden and Trevisa very clearly state that the love affair between Aeneas and Dido could not have taken place historically: "Þan it may nouȝt stonde þat Virgilius and Phrygius Dares in his storie of þe bataille of Troye seiþ, þat Eneas sih þat womman Dido, for Eneas was dede þre hondred ȝere and more or Cartage was i-founded þat Dido foundede" (1:167).[31] The *Polychronicon* furthermore allows for the possibilities that the *Aeneid* may be talking about another Carthage, or even another Dido, while simultaneously maintaining Augustine's assertion that wise men deny that Aeneas ever existed at all.[32] The congruous arrangement of conflicting historical data transforms the *Polychronicon* into something more than an encyclopedic compilation of source material or the chronological arrangement of *res gestae*. It instead becomes a model and inspiration for invention, not only providing material, but also suggesting the implicit motional nature of that material as it fluctuates continually through different historical possibilities.[33]

---

per tres annos et vii menses isolentius agere cœpit contra consuetudines Romanæ libertatis" (4:204); but "nemo melius rempublicam administrasset" (4:214). For Alexander, see 3:382–4:16.

30. "si Arthurus . . . terdena regna acquisivit . . . cur omnes historici Romani, Franci, Saxonici tot insignia de tanto viro omiserunt, qui de minoribus viris tot minora retulerunt?" (5:334). See Gransden, 2:49–50. Trevisa argues against Higden: see Galloway, "Writing History in England," 278; and Given-Wilson, 4–5.

31. "Non ergo poterit ad litteram stare quod tradit Virgilius, et Phrygius Dares in historia sua de bello Trojano, quod scilicet Æneas vidit Didonem, cum Æeneas obierit ante fundationem Carthaginis, quam Dido fundavit, plus quam trecentis annis" (1:166).

32. Higden again presents these mixed sentiments when he repeats the story during the chapter on the wanderings of Aeneas, 2.433. This analysis is a favorite point for modern commentators on the *Polychronicon*. See, for example, Given-Wilson, 114. Higden justifies his topical methodology through the most resilient of proverbs: "Nam et apostolus non, 'Quæcunque scripta sunt vera sunt,' ait; sed, 'Quæcunque scripta sunt, ad nostram doctrinam scripta sunt,' inquit"—as Trevisa translates it, "For þe apostel seith nouȝt, 'All þat is write to oure lore is sooþ,' but he seiþ 'Al þat is i-write to oure lore it is i-write'" (1:18–19). Trevisa's translation gets at the heart of Higden's appropriation of Paul's maxim: the value of history is not that it is true, but that it is written, and that as writing, it can be organized and directed for our learning. Given-Wilson argues that this proverb compels readers and historians alike to assess the value of history, rather than its verisimilitude (55–56).

33. Higden's chronicle prompted many of its readers to generate new historical inventions, and the *Polychronicon* can in part be credited with the resurgence of monastic chronicle writing in the last quarter of the fourteenth century, when monks and canons vigorously began continuations of Higden's chronicle. The emphasis of the *Polychronicon* on invention also reflects new trends in chronicle production in late-fourteenth-century England overall. Chronicle writing

This organizational model of chronicle writing echoes in many aspects of Gower's *Confessio*: its nature as a compilation of exemplary narratives, its staging of the processes of reading between Genius and Amans, and the metatextual emergence of "John Gower" himself in Book 8 as the reader-writer of the entire poem. Among the chronicles of Book 4, however, Gower carefully transforms the historiographic invention characteristic of the *Polychronicon*. He locates and enacts a compositional process that works to restore the productive potential of the chronicle form and to estrange that form from the movement toward discord demonstrated by the history of *gentilesse*. Gower takes this inventional context from the *Polychronicon*, but he also extends and transforms it into, on the one hand, a device that can combat the corrosion of chronology antithetical to his larger poetic project, and on the other hand, a new kind of affective chronicle which conveys the sensation of something new that emerges out of old records via its structure and that thus transmits not simply material but also the sensation of that emergence actually taking place. Situating the chronicles of invention in Book 4 as a performance of productive work thus establishes a powerful gesture toward the affect of invention. It is not simply that hard work makes for honest readers or even results in beautiful and culturally relevant poetry as an end product; the chronicles of invention in Book 4 recharacterize Gower's poetic efforts as chronicle efforts, linking poetry and historiography as part of a common effort to reinvent the world.

Gower begins in the first chronicle of invention by emphasizing the form and labor of historiographic production and then by narrating the simultaneous emergence of poetry and historiography from the chronicle of cultural development. While Genius insists that Amans should "ensample take" of the inventors he presents, Gower makes clear that what Genius is about to relate is historiography, distinct from his other narratives. Genius will "drawe into memoire, / Here names bothe and here histoire" (2359–60), thus asking that Amans note not only the "vertu of her dede" (2361) but also the form of its presentation. While "histoire" in Middle English can refer to anything from actual past events to any narrative or story, Genius uses a standard classification for historical narrative, the notion of the *res gestae*, great deeds done by great people who, as Genius describes them, possess "wittes grete" and "mihtes stronge" (2354).[34] Significantly, "histoire" here is singular: as Genius introduces

---

changed after Edward III's reign, with an emphasis on popular uprisings in 1381, early instantiations of the Wyclifite and Lollard heresies, and, later, events leading up to the Merciless Parliament of 1388 (Gransden, 2:162–63); Given-Wilson notes that chronicles came to emphasize parliamentary proceedings more than crown–magnate relations (174–80).

34. According to Isidore, a history is "a narration of deeds accomplished; through it what occurred in the past is sorted out" (*The Etymologies of Isiodore of Seville*, trans. Stephen A.

them, the chronicles to follow will not provide the individual biography that corresponds to each name, but rather the single *histoire* that emerges from the cumulative litany of individual names.[35] Genius here offers the chronicle itself as the mode of instruction, and the ensuing history of invention is a chronicle narrative, a progressive series of "lyves" that inspires readers because each builds upon the other to construct the present.

Furthermore, that "present" is constructed through the conflation of the specific discourses of historiography and poetry that emerge together at the end of the first chronicle of invention. Gower conflates the emergence of history and the emergence of poetry as forms of discourse and as phenomena of emergence. The chronicle begins with the *res gestae* of Cham and Cadmus, finders of Hebrew and Greek letters respectively, and moves to Theges the augur and Philemon the physiognomist. It centers next on the "ferste . . . Enditours, / Of old Cronique and ek auctours" (2411–12), ranging from the more obscure to the more famous.[36] Civilization first "finds" language, then prophecy, and then physiognomy; it thus establishes written language, and then a language that "reads" both the future (augury) and the individual human being: "Philemon be the visage / Fond to descrive the corage" (2405–6). These macro- and microcosmic scales of reading are finally encoded into a lasting textual form by "Enditours, / Of old Cronique and ek auctours"—that is, by writers of chroniclers and also by "auctours," whose surviving texts in fact constitute for medieval readers the cultures of the past. Not all of the writers in Genius's list are writers of "old Cronique"—some write texts on natural science, some poetry—but the catalogue appropriately culminates in Josephus, the Hebrew historian whom Chaucer also places in the House of Fame for recording the "Jewes gestes" (*House of Fame*, 1434). Genius's chronicle of inventors thus characterizes history writing itself as a *res gesta* performed by great men: the "dede" accomplished here is the composition of history, and

---

Barney, W. J. Lewis, J. A. Beach, and Oliver Berghof [Cambridge: Cambridge University Press, 2006], 67). Cicero in *De inventione* makes a similar claim for *historia* as a category of narrative: "Historia est gesta res, ab aetatis nostrae memoria remota" ["an account of actual occurrences remote from the recollection of our own age"] (1.19.27), qtd. from *De inventione, De optimo genere oratorm, Topica*, ed. and trans. H. M. Hubbell (Cambridge, MA: Harvard University Press, 1949, rpt. 1993). As Peck argues, remembering the names and deeds of industrious men will enable Amans "to grow beyond his infatuation" into something more serious (*Kingship and Common Profit*, 94). See Edwards, *Ratio and Invention*, 76–82, for a discussion of the developing relationship between historical veracity and narrative form in the Middle Ages as it is registered in John of Garland's *Parisiana poetria*.

35. Masciandaro makes a similar observation about the "collective history" of Chaucer's *Former Age* in which all human action contributes to a general cultural decline (104).

36. See Peck's very helpful explanatory notes in his edition of the *Confessio*, 2:395–400.

the work celebrated for combating Sloth is the "grete besynesse of þe writers of cronicles" praised by Higden and Trevisa.

This emphasis on historiography shapes the way in which the chronicle describes the invention of poetry. Before moving to a catalogue of artists, farmers, fishermen, and merchants, Genius pauses to devote three lines to one *enditour* in particular: Herodotus, the supreme example of early *endityng*. "In his science / Of metre, of rime and of cadence," Genius declares, Herodotus "the ferste was of which men note" (2413–15). Genius emphasizes Herodotus's poetic accomplishments, his ability to organize the "lettres of Gregois" wrought by Cadmus into beautiful poetic forms.[37] Herodotus in fact synthesizes the different types of writing pursued by the authors in the preceding catalogue. Music, sculpture, fishing, agriculture, and mercantilism that follow in Genius's chronicle depend for their discovery on the initial imposition of form onto the matter of the past. Herodotus is a special case, moreover, because in the medieval tradition he is both a poet and a historian—the same dual role Gower adopts for his own poetic persona in the *Vox*, the *Quicquid homo scribat*, and here in the *Confessio*, as he writes his chronicles of invention. Through Herodotus, Gower fuses poetic and historiographic production and begins to transform through his poem the historiographic principle structuring the *Polychronicon*.

Gower thus primes his poem to integrate the processes of invention with the chronicle form of history. Over the two subsequent chronicles of invention, those of alchemy and the intellectual and artistic achievements of Rome, Gower carefully works through a solution to the problem of movement toward discord made explicit in the history of *gentilesse*. It is in this way, furthermore, that, in adapting these historiographical practices, Gower expands the definition of invention in his own poetic chronicles to include gestures toward the kinds of pre-inventional, unstructured movements that I have tracked so far throughout this book. As he begins his history of alchemy, however, Gower stages what is essentially a failed integration of history and invention.

"HOU TO MAKE IT, NOU WOT NON": FAILED EMERGENCE IN THE INVENTION OF ALCHEMY

The nature of alchemy as a craft allows Gower to juxtapose directly chronicle form and poetic invention. As he presents them, the structural procedures of

---

37. Yeager argues that Genius credits Herodotus with the invention of poetry, and that the overall emphasis on textual labor in Book 4 speaks to the power Gower credits to words and poetry (*John Gower's Poetic*, 164–66).

alchemy echo those of formal poetic composition. Alchemy is essentially an exercise in ordering and organization: practitioners "to every point a certain bounde / Ordeignen, that a man mai finde / This craft is wroght be weie of kinde, / So that ther is no fallas inne" (2506–9). Like the formal processes of poetic composition, the processes of alchemy change material via arrangement and culminate in profound transformations: alchemy transforms metals; poetry transforms readers.[38] Furthermore, Genius, like Higden and Trevisa, focuses on the "workman"-like aspect of alchemy. The transformations promised by all three crafts—poetry, alchemy, and historiography—are based not on divine inspiration but on careful, repetitive "clergie" or processes (2533). These processes are reflected in the workaday attitude of "the craft so long to lerne" of Horace via Chaucer,[39] but the history of alchemy involves a double act of invention, or *fyndyng*: alchemy "was founde" by its ancient practitioners (2505), but those contemporary men who examine the chronicle also "mai finde" the kind of organizational processes that enable the transformation of metals (2507). The study of the history of alchemy reveals methods for further acts of invention—as would the study of a poem or the *Polychronicon*. As an analogue for poetic invention, then, alchemy would seem to contribute to Gower's chronicles a kind of productive poetry that could *fynde* a way out of the corrosive chronicle form established in the history of *gentilesse*.

But the opposite turns out to be the case. The problem with alchemical craft resembles the problem with any *ars poetica*: while the formal procedures of invention and arrangement can be easily grasped and understood, executing these procedures—actually creating powerful and transformative poetry—requires something more than simply following the straightforward precepts of treatises on verse. In other words, there is something else going on here than simply the recombinative manipulation of forms and materials. This is perhaps an obvious point, but Gower recasts this missing "something" as central to the chronicle structure he builds in the *Confessio*. The "distillacion," "congelacion," and other components of Genius's litany of alchemical procedures all work to attain "the parfit Elixir / Of thilke philosophres Ston" (2513–14, 2522–23), which, he is careful to emphasize, they "mai gete," and "of which that many on / Of Philosophres whilom write" (2524–25). Despite their efforts, alchemists

---

38. Stephanie L. Batkie sees Gower's chronicle of alchemy as an allegory for ethical reading and argues that "through alchemy Gower shows his audience how to become virtuous readers who are able to materially change themselves through the abstract and immaterial world of the text" ("'Of the parfite medicine': *Merita Perpetuata* in Gower's Vernacular Alchemy," in Dutton, Hines, and Yeager, *John Gower: Trilingual Poet*, 157).

39. The line is the first in Chaucer's *Parlement of Foules*. While it refers ostensibly to the craft of love, the poem as a whole suggests that it refers to poetic craft as well.

have generally had more success writing about the stone than actually achieving it. What is worse, the most recent alchemists have proven far less capable than their ancient forbears: nowadays, "it stant al otherwise; / Thei speken faste of thilke Ston, / Bot hou to make it, nou wot non / After the sothe experience" (2580–83). As Yeager notes, contemporary alchemists are "failures" because they cannot understand the language of the great alchemists of old. "Modern alchemists follow the 'forme of wordes,'" Yeager writes, "but lack the insight to evoke their inherent power."[40] The faulty practice of alchemy, like bad poetry, fails to apply language effectively in order to provoke transformation.[41]

The source of this failure can furthermore be traced to alchemical historiography itself. In his discussion of the *Canon's Yeoman's Tale*, Lee Patterson demonstrates that a double standard characterizes medieval discourses of alchemy. On the one hand, a multiplicity of texts and efforts of obfuscation work to protect secrecy; on the other, alchemical treatises emphasize unity, emblematized in the quest for the stone.[42] As Patterson succinctly puts it, "the assertion of the simplicity of alchemical doctrine and the unity of natural processes is designed to provide a point of stability for a discourse always threatening to lose itself in its own elaboration."[43] This tension also resonates in Gower's chronicle, in which the discourse of alchemy constitutes a history marked by the inscrutability of its language and the failure to achieve its goals of unity and clarity. An ideal chronicle of alchemy would progress toward the realization of these goals; its form would thus foreground unity rather than division. In reality, however, the particulars of its procedural failure link alchemy back to the historical failure of *gentilesse*. Alchemy represents at once the failure of historiographic narration and productive invention.

By narrating the history of alchemy among the chronicles of invention, Gower emphasizes that simply "writing about" invention within a chronicle will not reverse its progression toward discord and disparity. The ancient alchemists, Genius reports,

> were of such Auctorite
> That thei ferst founded out the weie

---

40. Yeager, *John Gower's Poetic*, 167.

41. Ibid., 167–68. For T. Matthew N. McCabe, alchemy fails in the present because it depends in part on experience as much as the science contained in old books (200–202).

42. Lee Patterson, "Perpetual Motion: Alchemy and the Technology of the Self," *Studies in the Age of Chaucer* 15 (1993): 25–57; see esp. 39–47. Patterson argues that the *Canon's Yeoman's Tale* reveals the inability to represent truth in alchemical language (35–38). Patterson also views alchemy as an analogue, but for the representation of a modern, shifting subjectivity.

43. Ibid., 44.

> Of al that thou hast herd me seie;
> Wherof the Cronique of her lore
> Schal stonde in pris forevermore.
>
> (2628–32)

A monument to industrious labor it may be, but the "Cronique of her lore" turns out to be useless to modern practitioners of the craft who know of and consult the ancients' "bokes," because "fewe" of the alchemists "understonde" anything those books have to say, despite how "pleinli . . . thei stonde" (2613–14). The work of the past—not merely the accomplishments of the ancient alchemists but also the very procedures by which they made their discoveries—survives in the present in an expansive body of literature. While these old books are able to preserve "pleinli" the form of alchemy—its accomplishments and procedures—they are unable to provide readers with transformed matter. The source of alchemy's failure lies in its historical record. As the practice of the discipline expands chronologically, its textual presence extends as well—but this textual expansion cannot restore the promise of alchemy eroded over time. Placing alchemy in a chronicle only emphasizes the loss of the art's potential rather than rejuvenating the form of the chronicle. We are left instead with the "pris": a monument as beautiful and as empty as present-day *gentilesse*, a chronicle that merely reflects rather than enacts invention.

The "something" missing, then, Gower articulates not as divine inspiration or some lost kernel of true knowledge, but as movement. In the context of Book 4's performance of inventional work as an antidote to Sloth, that movement is articulated at a rhetorical level, a kind of back-and-forth exhibited in the processes that make up even the most formal activities of invention. In the catalogue of Latin artistic achievement, the final chronicle of Book 4, Gower writes historiography that claims the form of a chronicle without necessarily embodying the progress toward cultural discord inherent in that form. It activates the appositional—rather than hierarchical—method of arrangement of the *Polychronicon* and suggests a way in which the generic form of the chronicle and the procedures of poetic invention might work in concert to generate a different kind of historical poetry in the *Confessio*.

"OURE MARCHES HIERE": *CONGRUITE* AND THE NEW *CRONIQUE* OF THE *CONFESSIO*

The final chronicle of Book 4 is something of a restart. It focuses specifically on "oure Marches hiere" (2633), that is, the Roman tradition that produced

Latin grammar, rhetoric, and ultimately Ovid—and, by extension, the *Confessio Amantis*.⁴⁴ In Genius's account, the Latin language made by Carmen is refined by the grammarians Aristarchus, Donatus, and Dindimus, who determined

> the ferste reule of Scole, and thus,
> How that Latin schal be componed
> And in what wise it schal be soned,
> That every word in his degre
> Schal stonde upon congruite.
> (2642–46)

Congruite becomes the operating principle in Gower's Roman chronicle: the idea that like forms should apply to like matter, but also that this very method of appositional placement results in something more than the mere pairing of like properties. While Genius's description of the construction of Latin conveys institutional correctness—how each "schal be soned," according to "his degree"—his arrangement of items within the chronicle also stresses the congruous relationship among Roman inventors. Rather than establishing a rigid hierarchy based on disciplinary importance or even the forward flow of time, the Roman chronicle operates through an appositional, congruous organization that combines the tenets of poetic invention with chronicle form. Gower encodes the process of poetic composition into the structure of the Roman chronicle, replacing chronology with inventional movement. He thereby replaces the temporal discord that characterizes the progression of chronicles with a structural system that, by definition, encourages discovery, choice, and possibility.

Genius first introduces the chronicle through a decidedly congruous motion. He cuts off his discussion of the great alchemists whose work is safely enshrined "in pris for everemore," and moves instead "toward oure Marches hiere, / Of the Latins if thou wolt hiere" (2632–34). The motion signals not only the chronological progression from ancient language (Hebrew and Greek) into authoritative Latin (ostensibly, at least); it also suggests a geographical transplantation of the narrative out from Mesopotamia and Greece.⁴⁵ By "oure

---

44. McCabe equates "our marches hiere" with "the Latin West" (108).
45. Siân Echard has shown that Gower's texts do not necessarily advocate the primacy or authority of Latin. See "Gower's 'bokes of Latin'" and "With Carmen's Help: Latin Authorities in the *Confessio Amantis*," *Studies in Philology* 95 (1998): 1–40. In his Roman chronicle, Gower uses Latin language to outline how a model based on *congruite* might work, rather than actually describing the development of Latin.

Marches hiere," Genius refers simultaneously to the Latin, especially Ovidian, tradition of which the *Confessio* is a part, and to the island of Britain itself: the *Confessio* stands at once alongside and apart from a Latin tradition, just as disciplines as diverse as poetry, fishing, physiognomy, and mercantilism coexist appositionally in the first chronicle of invention.[46] The *marches* Genius invokes are not merely territories or regions, but also the borders and nebulous spaces beyond borders, between nations—a stark contrast to the rigid and "certain" boundaries "ordeignen" by the great, but dead, alchemists.[47] Whisking the discussion "toward" the time-space coordinates of fourteenth-century England, Gower frames the Roman chronicle in a way that emphasizes both *congruite* and the sensations of displacement—of "restarting"—that characterize this new chronicle of Book 4's series.

Gower makes invention a part of Roman history by institutionalizing it as a formative aspect of culture. Unlike the dream vision of the *Vox*, which culminates in a lesson about the diversity of language, the journey toward English *marches* in Book 4 of the *Confessio* reins in language, suggesting the development of Latin to be straightforward and neat.[48] In the historical reality established by this chronicle at least, language is "componed"—textually and syntactically constructed—institutionally through "the ferste reule of Scole" (2642–43). Roman grammarians assert for language the formal control that no longer applies to *gentilesse*: Latin words will be written and spoken, "componed" and "soned," appropriately, each according to "his degre." The chronicle of Latin development does not strive to restrict the ability of language, however. On the contrary, it works to open language to expansion and productivity in a way that celebrates the inventive and translational potential of that expansion. The craft of Roman rhetoricians—here "Tullius with Cithero" (2648)—opens the newly conditioned Latin to inventive choice: "men schal the wordes pike / After the forme of eloquence, / Which is, men sein, a gret prudence" (2650–52). Similarly, just as the rhetoricians taught how to "pike" topics, Jerome "transposed" and "translateden" the Bible and other

---

46. Copeland makes a similar claim about the relationship of the *Confessio* to Latin tradition, arguing that in Book 7, Gower asserts the authority of English vernacular against Latin academic tradition (*Rhetoric, Hermeneutics, and Translation*, 202–20).

47. See *MED*, "march," def. 1, a–d. Gower uses the term to describe either relations between different geopolitical entities or the spaces between them. For the former, see the *Confessio*, 2:2551, 2:2597, 5:1688, 5:3120, 5:3285, 7:555; for the latter, see 1:1417, 2:2570, 2:2618, 3:2367, 3:2649; for both at once, 2:2521, 5:2062. Like many other critics, I am grateful for the work of J. D. Pickles and J. L. Dawson in *A Concordance to John Gower's* Confessio Amantis (Cambridge: D. S. Brewer, 1987).

48. The reality is, of course, much different, as Gower himself is well aware. See Echard, "Gower's 'bokes of Latin'" and "With Carmen's Help."

"bokes wise" out of Hebrew, Aramaic, Arabic, and Greek (2656–60). The result of this inventive and translational explosion is the creation of usable knowledge—"craftes bothe and . . . clergie" (2667)—in a wide variety of forms, the epitome of which is the *lore* of Ovid. Gower's chronicle builds into the Roman tradition a defining emphasis on *inventio,* the technical *fyndyng* of topics around which any literary text is constructed. By the time Genius reaches that Roman conclusion, his *cronica inventionum* has become a *cronica inventionis.* The chronicle begun by the efforts to assign appropriate form to matter results not in the opulent, rigid, and eternal "pris" of the dead alchemists but in the generative enactment of invention.

Here, then, Gower generates a new kind of poetry, one that invests the chronicle form with a vitality that would seem to have productive consequences for the invention of both historiography and poetry. Indeed, Gower's Roman chronicle embodies productive, congruous associations. While the mistaken medieval bifurcation of Cicero into two people is perhaps amusingly fascinating, "Tullius with Cithero" forms a congruous pair that supplements the grammatical pair of Donatus and Dindimus, who themselves work "with" Aristarchus to develop Latin grammar (2641).[49] Tullius and Cithero furthermore do not take up where Donatus and Dindimus leave off. Rather, the rhetoricians operate with an appropriate temporal *congruite* to the Latin grammarians: "And thilke time at Rome also / Was Tullius with Cithero" (2647–48). Tullius and Cithero follow Donatus and Dindimus only in the same way that the forms and sounds of Latin "follow" the matter they signify. Similarly, "at thilke time" during which Jerome works his translations, various other "Latins" are studying "with gret travaile of Scole" to invent books and encode "the lore of the Sciences" in textual form (2661–66). These are the "new" *enditours* who themselves operate in historical *congruite* with Herodotus and the great writers of Gower's first chronicle of invention. The difference here, however, is that the achievement of Roman letters does not occur by each new generation of inventors standing on the shoulders of those who came before. It occurs instead by multiple generations working together, however chronologically impossible that may be. Furthermore, the chronicle makes the single most remarkable "discovery" of Roman culture the procedures of discovery itself. Whereas in the first chronicle the *res gestae* recorded by historians emphasized the composition of history itself, here they are more broadly the processes of invention. Congruous proximity removes the distinction between

---

49. Ann W. Astell argues that Gower splits "Cicero" and "Tullius" purposefully: Gower "embraces" the plain-speaking "political stance" of the former "while rejecting the ornate doctrine" of the latter (*Political Allegory in Late Medieval England* [Ithaca, NY: Cornell University Press, 1999], 91).

forme and *matiere* in the chronicle—that is, between chronological arrangement and the chronicle's component discoveries. Instead, arrangement determines matter in the chronicle. Congruity becomes historical progression.

All of this would be little more than rhetorical trickery, the clever rearranging and restructuring of narrative order, if such dispositional acrobatics were an end in themselves. But as Gower's poetry as a whole overwhelmingly demonstrates, and as much recent criticism has worked to show, the neat *congruite* of the Roman chronicle is an illusion: this isn't how things actually happened, and languages in their development certainly do not follow so neat a chronological route. As Echard shows, not even Gower's own "last words" at the end of the *Confessio* offer the impression of lasting linguistic stability.[50] Instead, all of this reordering gestures in its frantic realigning toward the energies of emergence, toward that "something" missing from the work of the alchemists in their study of invention's mineralogical analogue. The chronicles of Book 4 comprise an elaborate gesture that indicates a scale much larger than the individual reader as it maps the revitalizing project of the *Confessio* onto the world external to it, one that seems to have emerged into "our Marches hiere" in an untraceable way from forces moving before. Appropriately, then, the chronicles of invention present three separate but congruous chronicles; Gower's Roman chronicle appears as the third in a series, encouraging a habit of congruous juxtaposition by the reader and suggesting how this last, new chronicle—"oure" chronicle—might emerge from the others that precede it. This new chronicle constitutes a gesture to something that occurred before—not a lost former age of peace and harmony but rather moments of emergence that only later collapse into records of discord and their concordant anxieties. In the end, Book 4's chronicles do not merely catalogue invention; they generate a sense of impending emergence as an aspect of genre.

"THE CRONIQUE OF THIS FABLE": THE AFFECT OF INVENTION IN BOOK 5'S CHRONICLES

The Roman chronicles are not the last to appear in the *Confessio*: Gower introduces a second series of chronicles in Book 5 when Genius relates, at Amans's prompting, the whole history and development of gods and religions. As Genius charts the development of ancient religions in particular, he essentially works to understand how historical personages grow, through the affective force of *misbelieve,* into deities capable of defining entire cultures

---

50. Echard, "Last Words."

and, indirectly, reflecting the cosmological influences of moving planets. Culminating in fourteenth-century Christian schism, Book 5's chronicles seem to undo the elaborate inventional restructuring of Book 4. Whatever rhetorical maneuverings the previous book's chronicles may have achieved, the chronicles of Book 5 return us to the steady historical deterioration reified in Nebuchadnezzar's fragmented statue. Yet, even so, the chronicles of Book 5 do so humorously, almost satirically, essentially offering an affective component to the inventional work of Book 4 by calling attention to the fictionality of Gower's entire chronicle project. Gower's chronicles of religion do not simply inject a second instantiation of corrosive self-consumption like that of the chronicle of *gentilesse* or alchemy; instead, they replace the inventional gesture of structural *congruite* with a broader gesture toward affect, registered belatedly as an emotional rush of laughter that resonates within and beyond the chronicle narratives of the *Confessio*.

Amans invites the long elaboration on old religions when, after hearing the story of Venus and Mars's affair and the humiliation of Vulcan, he laments the celestial pervasiveness of Avarice. "Mi fader," he says, "this ensample is hard, / Hou such thing to the heveneward / Among the goddes myhte falle" (5.729–31). Indeed, what chance does Amans have if the planets themselves are cobwebbed in avaricious entanglements? He then asks Genius to explain "Hou suche goddes come aplace" (735). Genius replies with a thorough and complex encyclopedic history of world religions, framing his answer with the repeated emphasis that his information comes from "the Cronique" (816ff) and shaping his catalogue as multiple, divergent chronicle histories much as he does in Book 4. *Misbelieve* replaces *fyndyng* as the formal topic for this second series of chronicles, Gower's term for the kind of religious devotion focused along non-Christian vectors, implying not only "false belief" but also a continuing action of devotional misalignment. *Misbelieve* presents, in Gower's orthodox characterization at least, something of a parallel to Lauren Berlant's idea of "cruel optimism," a belief in, and affective attachment to, a discursively constructed cultural narrative of a "good" that in fact causes far more harm than benefit to the believer. In affective terms, *misbelieve* suggests a directing of devotional energies in the wrong "weie," to use one of Gower's favorite terms in the *Confessio* and one that, as we have seen, famously characterizes his entire poetics as a direction or process rather than as a simple description of style or register. As he catalogues them, Genius also chronicles how various species of *misbelieve* grow into institutions; as such, his history of religions traces how affective energies collapse into discursive structures constitutive of social reality and that cumulatively culminate, like Constantine's *venym*, in a fractured present.

Gower's process of establishing the especially destructive corrosiveness of chronicles of religious history is familiar from Book 4, and the incestuous relationships of some of the gods, as metaphors for self-consuming narratives, thematically intensify the recursive corrosiveness of the chronicle form.[51] As they identify the ways in which *misbelieve* provoked the elevation of ordinary mortals to the status of deities, the chronicles also reveal the negative potential contained in Book 4's inventional model. Jupiter was the king of Crete, Genius explains, Neptune was his brother, and Eolus, the son of the king of Sicily, became the god of winds because to those living elsewhere in "lond forein" to it, Sicily, whose insular wards "Leie open to the wynd al plein" (973–74), seemed the source of all of the world's winds. Other instances of Genius's ethnographic inquiry are less generous. After listing Mercury's abilities as a sorcerer, speaker, and "Auctour" of lies (947), for example, he declares simply "And yit thei [i.e., the "Greks" (835)] maden of this thief / A god, which was unto hem lief, / And clepede him in tho believes / The god of Marchantz and of thieves" (949–52).[52] As Genius's examples illustrate the narrative theme of people's deifying human beings and building devotional infrastructures around them, the *Confessio* presents *misbelieve* as a problem of the accumulation of invention, of *makyng* a person into a god through an historical accretion of affective attachments manifested in the discursive apparatus of religion. Book 5's chronicles even take up the topic of invention explicitly, reintroducing important moments of *fyndyng* from Book 4 as part of their chronological progression. Isis, for example, comes to the Egyptians from Greece "To teche hem for to sowe and eere, / Which noman knew tofore there" (819–20); in Greece, Pan "tawhte men the forthdrawinge / Of bestaile, and ek the makinge / Of Oxen, and of hors the same, / Hou men hem scholde ryde and tame" (1021–24); and Saturn, moreover, comes to Crete where "he fond of his oghne wit / The ferste craft of plowh tilinge" and related agricultural practices (1226–27). The familiar terms of invention—*makyng, fyndyng*—resonate in these chronicles just as they do in Book 4. Conversely, however, the chronicles of religion relate the collapse of affect and invention into systems of religious belief, codifying them into false gods, and revealing moments of potential movement and emergence to be illusions resulting from institutionalized misreadings of climatic trends and exceptional liars and thieves.

---

51. For readings of incest themes in the chronicles of religion, see Yeager, *John Gower's Poetic*, 174–75; and Watt, 84–90.

52. Yeager notes that Gower is particularly careful with categorizing the qualities of Greek and Roman gods and imagining them as real people long ago (*John Gower's Poetic*, 176–77).

Part of the reason Genius finds "the Cronique of this fable" (1270), as he calls it, so fascinating is that it presents fiction masquerading as history via a historiographic form. As such, he deconstructs the chronicles, reverse-engineering how they transform affective devotions into institutionalized *makynges,* and he furthermore characterizes his own efforts to locate sources for *misbelieve* as the action of invention. For example, Genius's history of Pallas is a list of what different people "seie" about her, resembling the inventional techniques familiar from chronicles like the *Polychronicon.* There is "sondri speche" why Pallas is called what she is called (1208): "On seith" one reason, "Another seith" another, and "some ek seide" something else (1209–14). Genius's deconstruction of Pallas's history removes the authority of religions based on *misbelieve,* but it also represents Genius's looking for possible inventional topics that might be responsible for generating the culturally pervasive narrative that is the goddess Pallas. Mapping the potential connections between fictions and possible historical realities, Genius's chronicles reveal an interest in how an affective force like *misbelieve* invents narrative structures that build social and emotional realities for real people in the past. History is of course a text for Gower, but in the case of the history of *misbelieve,* that text is charged with a special affective power registered in devotional worship over long stretches of time. The chronicles of *misbelieve* become, in Gower's fourteenth-century Christian perspective, negative models for how the *Confessio* might activate the kind of chronicles sketched out in Book 4 with the energy of movement and emergence we have seen developed thematically in several of the *Confessio*'s narratives. Capitalizing on moments when affective vectors begin to congeal via acts of imaginative invention into cultural forms that become pervasive and institutionalized, the chronicles of Book 5 perform by the same methods—but with opposite effect—the purported rejuvenating project of the entire *Confessio.*

As he does with the chronicles of invention in Book 4, however, Gower installs a corrective into the way he presents these chronicles: in effect, he presents the process as knowingly self-aware and, finally, very funny. As work by Yeager, Peck, Watt, and Nicholson shows, Genius finds these chronicles troubling because they threaten to reveal the profound lack of seriousness with which Amans, or any reader for that matter, ought to take Genius, who himself, as Venus's priest, is a product of "the Cronique of this fable." Peck observes that "as Genius outlines the history of the gods, he himself seems to be embarrassed by them."[53] Nicholson likewise notes that the result of Genius's chronicles is the necessity of denying the reality of Venus in a Christian

---

53. Peck, *Kingship and Common Profit,* 104; see also Watt, 83–84.

universe and thus of "dismiss[ing] the entire fictional frame in which he himself exists"; Genius is "fully aware of the uncomfortableness of his position."[54] Nevertheless, Nicholson argues, calling attention to the falseness of ancient gods and then continuing to tell stories about them demonstrates how the "fiction" of the *Confessio* "has a 'reality' that remains unimpaired.... The excursus thus does not cancel out the rest of the poem: it merely insists on its fictionality."[55] Indeed, the poem is never in any real danger of collapsing, mainly because of the jovial and self-aware tone with which Gower presents the entire section. Peck, extending C. S. Lewis's reading of Genius as only grudgingly admitting Apollo's status as the god of poetry (and thus, by extension, his own craft), argues that "Gower is having an amusing time distorting the hijinks of the gods that he has worked hard with for so many years by means of just such cultural incongruities."[56] The cumulative effect of Genius's relating these chronicles is the coagulation of an emotional experience emerging from a kind of realization on Genius's part that, as a fictive construct, this chronicle of religious history is finally all rather silly. Gower transforms the inventional weakness of the chronicles' structure—cultural *makyng* out of *misbelieve*—into an affective strength, gesturing toward transformational emergence in a way that is strikingly different from Book 4 and that constitutes something of a laugh at the entire process.

Indeed, Genius's grudging narrative leads to several subtly humorous moments. For example, Pluto, Genius tells Amans, is made king of hell not simply because he sacrificed to the gods but because it was "his commun custummance" or habit to "swere his commun oth, / Be Lethen and be Flegeton, / Be Cochitum and Acheron ... Be Segne and Stige" (1117, 1108–13). His reward of reigning in the underworld is appropriate because he likes to swear by its rivers when he is "wroth" (1107): in Genius's chronicle, cursing by rivers qualifies you to rule cursed rivers. Moreover, the entire section on religion is inaugurated with a laughter that echoes within and beyond the confines of the *Confessio*'s fiction. The tale of Vulcan's revenge and subsequent punishment is what prompts Amans's request for the history of religions in the first place, and it is markedly funny. Not only does the sight of the naked Venus and Mars, chained together in bed and exposed to all, prompt a kind of shameful delight, but the gods themselves direct their mirth at Vulcan and "to skorne him lowhen alle" (696). That laughter reverberates through an entire cosmological spectrum, ranging from planetary bodies of Venus to the laughter of

---

54. Nicholson, *Love and Ethics*, 300.
55. Ibid., 301–2.
56. *John Gower: Confessio Amantis*, ed. Peck, 3:394.

Confessio readers. As a kind of bookend of affective emergence, the same sort of humorous dismissal characterizes the conclusion of the chronicle of ancient religions. Genius relates how Dindimus catalogues Greeks' assigning deities to individual parts of the body: Minerva stands in "for the hed . . . for sche was wys" (1460), Bacchus for the throat, Hercules for the arms and shoulders, and Venus for "al doun the remenant" of body parts (1495). Genius's report subtly pokes fun at the very idea of the micro- and macrocosmic structures on which Gower's entire poetics is based: we really shouldn't take seriously the *misbeleve* that "every membre hadden / A sondri god" (1457–58), should we? If laughter marks both the effects and the transformative power of Arion's rejuvenating poetry in the Prologue to the *Confessio*, then in Book 5 Gower conjures laughter from a distinctly non-Arionic source: the very misalignments that constitute the whole of these chronicles of religion. The imaginative pleasure taken in inventing the connections that make up "the Cronique of this fable" Gower registers explicitly, inciting laughter at an extended joke whose punch line is about inventional alignment, of reconciling *misbeleve* with the trajectories of the "false" institutions it has founded and the larger "true" historical trajectory of Christian eschatology depicted in the iconography of Nebuchadnezzar's dream.

Laughter replaces *congruite* in Book 5's history, but both books' series of chronicles work together to suggest a way in which the very movement of Gower's poetics might be seen to emerge, if only imaginatively, into the world beyond the *Confessio*. The laughter that echoes throughout the chronicles of religion in Book 5 provides a model for how affective chronicles might shape historical reality, but it does so ironically, emphasizing the fictions of invention that sprout polytheistic *misbeleve*. If Book 5 is a place in the *Confessio* where, as Nicholson suggests, Gower takes a step back to examine his poetic methods,[57] then he does so in part by having some fun with his poetics—though without ever losing focus of his poem's larger project of imaginatively modeling macrocosmic rejuvenation. What emerges finally from these chronicles is not a simple history of false beliefs or even a rich catalogue of inventional topics. Instead, what emerges is an extended gesture that works to get behind the movements that culminate in laughter and "fable," and one that finally takes the form of a chronicle, whose ultimate focus is not on recording the past but on registering the sensations of movement and emergence that can be found there.

When in the *Quicquid homo scribat* Gower characterizes his career as the work of a chronicler, he does not merely build a textual "pris," a monument to

---

57. Nicholson, *Love and Ethics*, 36.

coincide with his effigy in Southwark. Adapting a fourteenth-century chronicling practice and applying it to his long poem about love, and then self-consciously disrupting that model in a paradoxically generative way, Gower foregrounds the mechanisms of poetic and historiographic composition and turns the force of codified historical progression into a potentially transformative poetry. If in the *House of Fame* Chaucer attempts the impossible by describing what the transformation of *tydynges* might actually look like, then in Books 4 and 5 of the *Confessio*, Gower attempts a similarly impossible feat, reorganizing the historical world by reorganizing the chronicles that record and, by extension, create it. Gower's chronicles establish a kind of support system for thinking about how to generate an affective chronicle, one that somehow manages to gesture toward inventional emergence as an aspect of its form. They furthermore suggest how a massive English poem like the *Confessio* might itself be imagined as an affective chronicle, one self-sustaining and capable of becoming a kind of imaginative algorithm for poetic posterity that also constructs an energizing framework for thinking about "a thing . . . so strange": how poetic structure might impinge upon the structure of reality.

CHAPTER 5

EMPTY SONGS, MIGHTY MEN, AND A STARTLED CHICKEN

Satirizing the Affect of Invention in Fragment VII of the *Canterbury Tales*

I ARGUED in the final section of the previous chapter that Gower essentially satirizes the model of chronicle invention he establishes in the *Confessio*, and that Book 5's self-conscious critique works alongside the chronicles of invention in Book 4 as part of a larger program of imagining poetry's productive potential. In this chapter, I return to Chaucer, arguing that in Fragment VII of the *Canterbury Tales*, Chaucer stages a similar satire and self-critique but that the object of its satire includes Gower's as well as his own explorations of the relationship between affect and invention. The tales of the Prioress and the Monk, bookending the pilgrim Chaucer's contribution to the fragment, exaggerate to an extreme the kinds of gestures I have explored so far in this book. Both of these tales explicitly introduce specific metaphors and themes that convey a sensation of becoming, but they then immediately force the collapse of those moments using the very terms with which they were originally evoked. As with Gower's project of self-satire in the *Confessio*, however, Fragment VII's ultimate aim is not to condemn or render meaningless these metapoetic efforts. Instead, the final tale of the fragment, the *Nun's Priest's Tale*, redirects the poetics of foreclosure of the *Prioress's* and *Monk's* tales along a more productive trajectory. Examining Chaucer's satire of the affect of invention in these three tales of the most self-reflexive fragment of the *Canterbury Tales* shows how a project of critique is part of a much larger exploration of inventional emergence, and it furthermore suggests the overall shape of Chaucer's career-long engagement with affect and invention.

"THER MAY NO TONGE EXPRESSE": SATIRE AND STASIS IN THE *PRIORESS'S TALE*

It seems at first as if there is no better place in Chaucer's opus to examine a concept like the affect of invention than the *Prioress's Tale*. The tale explicitly takes up affective experience and the production of poetry: the *Prologue* opens with an invocation of Mary in a way that characterizes poetic invention in affective and corporeal terms; the young clergeon is instantaneously attracted to some kind of "ineffable" "swetnesse" in the *Alma redemptoris* (555);[1] the widow's anxiety about her missing child intensifies alongside her search to "fynde" him (596); the ugly affects of the tale's anti-Semitism work to generate its sense of an idealized Christian community; and the Canterbury pilgrims are all apparently "sobre" in their reaction to the "wonder" of the *Prioress's Tale* itself (692). Moreover, no other Chaucer text registers so intensely for modern readers the contrasting emotional experiences of the appreciation of its formal beauty and the horror at its violence and anti-Semitism that those qualities lay open for engagement—experiences that have prompted critical discussions not simply of whether the tale's explicit anti-Semitism reflects Chaucer's but also of the ethical and scholarly imperatives of modern literary criticism itself.[2] Indeed, the tale is a complex investigation of the origins of poetry and feeling, so much so, however, that it essentially satirizes the metapoetic study of how affective movements inform invention by amplifying them to an exaggerated

---

1. "Ineffable" is the term J. Stephen Russell uses to describe Chaucer's representation of song in the *Prioress's Tale*. "Song crystallizes emotion," Russell writes, and "the melody and lyric circumlocution serve as signs of the hidden movements of the heart, but they do not—cannot—express them" ("Song and the Ineffable in the *Prioress's Tale*," *Chaucer Review* 33 [1998]: 179). I take up Russell's argument more fully below.

2. Michael Calabrese argues that "there is no more politically charged issue in Chaucer studies" than the response to the tale's anti-Semitism ("Performing the Prioress: 'Conscience' and Responsibility in Studies of Chaucer's *Prioress's Tale*," *Texas Studies in Literature and Language* 44 [2002]: 66). For a cogent summary of this issue, focusing especially on a comparison of Aranye Fradenburg's and Lee Patterson's important articles on the tale, see Hannah Johnson, "Antisemitism and the Purposes of Historicism: Chaucer's *Prioress' Tale*," in *Medieval Literature: Debates and Criticism*, ed. Holly A. Crocker and D. Vance Smith (New York: Routledge, 2014), 192–200. For a comparison and summary of critical approaches to the tale before and after the Holocaust, and to reading the tale with reference to the Prioress's portrait in the *General Prologue*, see Stephen Spector, "Empathy and Enmity in the *Prioress's Tale*," in *The Olde Daunce: Love, Friendship, Sex, and Marriage in the Medieval World*, ed. Robert R. Edwards and Stephen Spector (New York: SUNY Press, 1991), 218–20.

degree. The tale presents a kind of narrative dramatization of the collapse of affect and invention into an emotionally wrought poetry that, by consciously deploying ugly affects to articulate its sense of community, reveals the ease with which a poetic process seemingly capable of defamiliarizing pervasive cultural forms can slide into a project that perpetuates them.

The *Prioress's Tale* has often been identified as a satire, not simply with reference to the Prioress's supposedly inappropriate attraction to courtly rather than to spiritual concerns but also as a critique of the devotional discourses of affective piety itself.[3] While some readers see the tale as an effort to render sincerely particular positive and negative emotional experiences,[4] others detect an overall impression of stasis in the tale and a corresponding sterility or vacuous repetition of its emotional materials. Robert O. Payne argues, for example, that "the story is in effect frozen into a kind of basic situation and the major effort is in the rhetorical elaboration of emotional implications,"[5] and in what remains the most influential critical interpretation of the tale, L. O. Aranye Fradenburg states bluntly that the tale "has in fact been emptied of movement," since any "emotional vividness" it supposedly presents is ultimately achieved only in its "characterization of the Jews," and furthermore that the wonder it narrates "eternalizes" time in the tale, putting "a stop to history, as, indeed, it puts a stop to narrative."[6] For Fradenburg, the tale flees

---

3. Calabrese, for example, sees the tale as "satirizing a narratology, and ideology, and a doctrine of social reformation based solely on the affective," and calls the tale "a deluxe version of the popular genre, bolstered with the emotion of a grizzly local legend" in its concluding reference to Hugh of Lincoln (82). Lee Patterson notes that the particular form of affective devotion that the Prioress seems to be performing here is of "a religious culture of aesthetic formalism, of the performance of external rituals at the expense of internal struggle," and one "sharply at odds" with the work of William Langland, Margery Kempe, or Julian of Norwich ("'The Living Witnesses of Our Redemption': Martyrdom and Imitation in Chaucer's *Prioress's Tale*," *Journal of Medieval and Early Modern Studies* 31 [2001]: 518). Anthony Bale argues that Chaucer gives the tale to the Prioress "as if to test the authority of this kind of miracle" in terms of truth value (*The Jew in the Medieval Book: English Antisemitisms, 1350–1500* [Cambridge: Cambridge University Press, 2006], 81). Lawrence Besserman argues that the tale's anti-Semitism generates "a space for alternative interpretations and assessments of one particular form of affective piety, exposing its religious and moral shortcomings to the light of day" ("Chaucer, Spain, and the Prioress's Antisemitism," *Viator* 35 [2004]: 334). For brief sketches of readings of the tale as satirizing the Prioress, see Florence H. Ridley, *The Prioress and the Critics* (Berkeley: University of California Press, 1965), 30–36; Spector, 218–20; and Calabrese, 75–76.

4. For example, Carolyn P. Collette, "Sense and Sensibility in the *Prioress's Tale*," *Chaucer Review* 15 (1980): 138–50.

5. Payne, *The Key of Remembrance*, 166. See also Robert Worth Frank, Jr., "Pathos in Chaucer's Religious Tales," in *Chaucer's Religious Tales*, ed. C. David Benson and Elizabeth Robertson (Cambridge: D. S. Brewer, 1990), 39–52.

6. L. O. Aranye Fradenburg, "Criticism, Anti-Semitism, and the *Prioress's Tale*," *Exemplaria* 1 (1989): 83, 84, 86. Fradenburg makes this claim in response to Collette in a discussion

not only history but also "meaning" itself: "The empty formality, then, of the Prioress's poetic effects (by which I do not mean that they have no power, for they have the power, precisely, of emptiness) itself demonstrates the dependence of a miraculous poetics upon conscripted substance and narrative and on suspension of disbelief."[7] Movement in the tale is actually only repetition, which Fradenburg links with the cultural work of miracle stories like this one to define community in terms of a vilified other.[8] Fradenburg's totalizing reading of its emotional and narrative stasis chronicles how the tale struggles to legitimate the generation of its poetry and the community that such poetry celebrates by extracting it from the painful realities of historical experience. As Lee Patterson puts it, the tale "witnesses to a drive toward the pure, the immaculate, and the unalloyed—toward, that is, the ahistorical."[9] This is a tale, then, that would move others precisely through its own refusal to move.

At the same time, however, the tale paradoxically makes ambiguity and indeterminacy a part of its stasis. Helen Barr convincingly demonstrates that the tale never commits to either a sincere or satirical presentation of the apparently transformational effects of the boy's and Prioress's songs, arguing that it uses the "prompts" of "generic affiliations, the collocational patterns of . . . diction and their experiential and relational values" to generate in sophisticated late-fourteenth-century readers the realization that numerous and oppositional interpretations are possible in the tale, especially of the

---

of how in the tale "Jews are being drained of life to *give* vitality to the Christians" to create the "*false* vitality" the tale renders in its descriptions, in particular, of the mother and her boy (83; emphasis in original).

7. Ibid., 94, 97-98. Miriamne Ara Krummel likewise argues that the "the pilgrims' (entirely) emotional responses at the close of her tale . . . indicates [sic] that the Prioress's use of affective piety—and bathos appeals to heartfelt responses—was successful" ("The Pardoner, the Prioress, Sir Thopas, and the Monk: Semitic Discourse and the Jew(s)," in *The Canterbury Tales Revisited—21st Century Interpretations*, ed. Kathleen A. Bishop [Newcastle: Cambridge Scholars Press, 2008], 96).

8. Fradenburg, "Criticism, Anti-Semitism," esp. 101-5. Katherine Zieman argues similarly that the tale's images "stress . . . nondirectional, recursive movement (like the passage in the Jewry that is 'free and open at eyther ende')" (*Singing the New Song: Literacy and Liturgy in Late Medieval England* [Philadelphia: University of Pennsylvania Press, 2008], 200).

9. Patterson, "Living Witnesses," 511-12. Like Patterson, many recent critics see the tale as attempting to enact, with varying degrees of success, a kind of fantasy of escape, articulated in particular through its effort to extract a notion of "pure" song from the ideologies of power, especially the masculinized liturgical, Latinate, grammatical, and violent institutional forms of that power, all the while reintroducing patterns of violence and control to forward this very project. On song, see especially Bruce Holsinger, *Music, Body, and Desire in Medieval Culture: Hildegard of Bingen to Chaucer* (Stanford, CA: Stanford University Press, 2001), esp. 265-72); Nicolette Zeeman "The Gender of Song in Chaucer," *Studies in the Age of Chaucer* 29 (2007): 141-82); and Zieman.

workings and value of emotionally powerful song.[10] Similarly, Shannon Gayk argues that the tale's fascination with "wondre" is less about assigning meanings to the miraculous "things" and much more about examining how such "things" generate wonder and consequently construct subjects.[11]

As this critical tradition shows, the *Prioress's Tale* somehow makes both indeterminacy and stasis part of its narrative process. I want to offer a reading of the *Prioress's Prologue* and *Tale* that focuses on how these texts straddle the gap between emotional and narrative stasis on the one hand, and explicit ambiguity and potential on the other. I argue here that the tale's representations of affective occurrences and inventional activity respond to precisely this phenomenological binary, narrating explicit moments of emergence and then working to flatten and cancel the potential productivity of those moments. Indeed, several passages leap out immediately in this regard: the Prioress's invocation of Mary in her *Prologue*, the boy's first encounter with the sound of the *Alma redemptoris mater*, and the widow's discovery of her mutilated son. As I will show, the tale introduces such moments and nullifies their potentiality through a process of exaggeration, using the very language of affect and invention that generated them in the first place.

"HIR LITEL CHILD TO FYNDE": INVENTION THROUGH THE PRIORESS, THE BOY, AND THE WIDOW

The Prioress accomplishes a great deal of work in her tale's miraculously synthesizing *Prologue*. Starting by praising Christ but ultimately invoking Mary as her poetic muse, she uses a humility topos both to legitimate her own vernacular, feminine authority against the institutionalized masculine authority of "men of dignitee" (456) and to equate herself with innocent children like the clergeon of her tale, whose language of praise is presented as pure and

---

10. Helen Barr, "Religious Practice in Chaucer's *Prioress's Tale*: Rabbit and/or Duck?" *Studies in the Age of Chaucer* 32 (2010): 42. Barr's survey of both the positive and pejorative uses of the phrase "by rote," for example, demonstrates the tale's conscious prompting of simultaneous oppositional readings (52–61). She notes in particular that, in its appeal to affective piety characteristic of Marian literature, the tale would thus appear to lead to orthodox "affective excitation" in readers (47); but readers with an awareness of Wycliffite concerns would read it—especially the descriptions of the boy's singing—more suspiciously as ignorance (47–52).

11. Shannon Gayk, "'To wonder upon this thyng': Chaucer's *Prioress's Tale*," *Exemplaria* 22 (2010): 138–56. Gayk draws on "thing theory," which distinguishes between "things" and "objects," the former being materials not yet assimilated into forms of cultural discourse and meaning and thus full of potential. I take up Gayk's argument more fully below.

uncorrupted.¹² The portrait of Mary she presents in the *Prologue* is totalizing. Neither the Father nor the Ghost is given grammatical agency as a subject in the apostrophic stanza devoted to her: she is the "mayde Mooder free" who

> ravyshedest doun fro the Deitee,
> Thurgh thyn humblesse, the Goost that in th'alighte,
> Of whos vertu, whan he thyn herte lighte,
> Conceyved was the fadres sapience.
>
> (467–72)

In this formulation, it is Mary's humility that attracts the Holy Spirit with a kind of virtuous gravitational pull,¹³ and it is her "vertu" in which the "fadres sapience" itself is "conceyved." For many critics, the work of the *Prologue* is the work of a rhetorical and figurative recursion that is as totalizing as Mary herself. For Fradenburg, the *Prologue* demonstrates the tale's signature "emptiness, circularity" and "repetition" as it narrates a series of images in which endings collapse into beginnings and signs fuse with signifieds. Poetry and praise cannot hope to "encressen" Mary's "honour" (464), because, just as Mary gave birth to the entity that created her, everything from Mary's perspective has already been read and sung, and the apparent emergence of new laudatory poetry is actually only repetition.¹⁴ The *Prologue* introduces a project

---

12. Critics have noted the particular way in which the *Prologue* balances a declaration of authority with an explicit effort to displace final authority to Mary. For Lisa Lampert, even as the Prioress "align[s] herself against learned 'men of dignitee,'" asserting feminine authority against masculine institutional power, she nevertheless "asks to become a vessel of praise rather like the clergeon's corpse. She depicts her inspiration as moving through her rather than being generated by her own understanding" (*Gender and Jewish Difference from Paul to Shakespeare* [Philadelphia: University of Pennsylvania Press, 2004], 82–83). Patterson sees a mimetic circularity at work here which culminates in the performance of "mimicking a cultural form without understanding it" ("Living Witnesses," 510). Bale notes that the Prioress's "rhetorical manoeuvres" in the *Prologue* "create an intertext of orthodox authority rendered into affective exclamation" (82). For Bale, because the Prioress describes herself as childlike—and because the *Prologue* and *Tale* appear between generic exaggerations that constitute the tales of the Shipman and Sir Thopas—the *Prologue* questions "the act of articulation and narrative 'truth'" (82). On the Prioress's self-constructed innocence, see also Allen C. Koretsky, "Dangerous Innocence: Chaucer's Prioress and Her Tale," in *Jewish Presences in English Literature*, ed. Derek Cohen and Deborah Heller (Montreal: McGill-Queen's University Press, 1990), 10–24.

13. Bronwen Welch, "'Gydeth My Song': Penetration and Possession in Chaucer's *Prioress's Tale*," in Bishop, *The Canterbury Tales Revisited*, 132; for a discussion of how the Prioress fashions herself as a mouthpiece for Mary, see 130–32.

14. Fradenburg, "Criticism, Anti-Semitism," 91–95. Barr notes that the *Prologue* posits itself as "not just praise, but the reproduction of praise," though her close textual analysis of the *Prologue* and *Tale* reveals that, like the *Tale*'s treatment of "song" itself, this presentation as "recitation" need not necessarily be pejorative (63).

of collapse that the tale itself performs through the clergeon's living—and then undead—performances of the *Alma redemptoris mater*.¹⁵ As she rhetorically empties herself to become the instrument through which the music of Mary is played,¹⁶ the Prioress also empties her poetry of its ability to generate productive ways of meaning.

Even as it performs this exaggerated and religious iteration of the kind of gendered redefinition of subjectivity dictated by discourses of courtly *pité*,¹⁷ the Prioress's rhetoric grants her a poetic authority by figuring her as a kind of Mary. Moreover, the vocabulary of this figuration is inventional, as the Prioress's description of the behavior of prayers, with Mary acting as intercessor for those who pray, provides an analogue for the processes of affective and inventional emergence. In his exploration of how the *Prioress's Tale* explores the representation of song, J. Stephen Russell shows how the *Prologue* works to describe the inaccessible ineffability of song in terms of its depiction of prayer. He notes that the Prioress calls for the performance of "laud," which is something quite distinct from "praise" in that it is pre-cognitive, "paraverbal," and finally performed rather than spoken, since adequately "lauding the Virgin Mary *in words* is literally impossible."¹⁸ The inventional work of this process appears when, in an adaptation of the *Paradiso*, the Prioress states explicitly that "no tonge" can "expresse" Mary's "vertue and . . . grete humylitee . . . in no science":

> For somtyme, Lady, er men praye to thee,
> Thou goost biforn of thy benyngnytee,
> And getest us the lyght, of thy preyere,
> To gyden us unto thy Sone so deere.
>
> (475–80)

---

15. Fradenburg writes that "The desire of the Prioress's Tale is for a language that erases the difference between word and thing, for a language that, in effect, escapes the differences of symbolicity" ("Criticism, Anti-Semitism," 94)—as Zieman puts it, "proclaiming the sufficiency of the signifier alone, thereby eliminating the need for the signified altogether" (191). See also Patterson, "Living Witnesses," 516. For Fradenburg, this recursion is part of a phobic effort to guard against any kind of transformational change that might originate outside of the system of closed meaning that the tale establishes, and she likens it to "what Freud would name the death drive, the desire of the organism to return to its beginnings in its own way" (97).

16. Welch, 130.

17. The Prioress's use of "ravyshedest" for her description of Mary's capturing of the Holy Ghost from heaven suggests this courtly romance association, as, of course, does the courtly-spiritual fusion of *amor* in her portrait in the *General Prologue*. Lampert notes that the *Prologue* "blends the erotic and the pious" (74).

18. Russell, 180, 181. Russell also notes that "Performing laud is absolutely indifferent to the quality or meaning of a verbal utterance" (183).

Russell shows that the passage details an "impressive" and "disturbing" theological process. The performing of laud, he writes, "takes place in the instant between deciding to pray and actually uttering words, the moment 'er men praye to thee.' In this moment, the Blessed Virgin reads the intention of the heart and flies before the spoken or sung words and delivers this intention to the Lord."[19] While Russell reads the Prioress as sincerely acknowledging her inability to praise adequately and instead having to "content herself with performing laud, with demonstrating the sincerity of her doomed will to praise fitly,"[20] the passage in fact positions the Prioress herself as a kind of poetic intercessor. Even as the Prioress empties herself to become the mouthpiece of a totalized Mary, declaring that her "konnyng is so wayk" and that she is "as a child of twelf month oold, or lesse, / That kan unnethes any word expresse" (481–85), she essentially performs the same work with her "song" that she describes Mary doing with what "men praye" to her (487, 477). Mary goes "biforn" the prayers of "men" in order to direct them to Christ, and in the same way, the Prioress, via her *Prologue*'s explicit invocation and characterization of the narrator, goes "biforn" the matter of the tale. The Prioress establishes herself as a textual authority who works inventionally in the same way Mary works: both fly "biforn" the work of invention collapses into form, and even "biforn" affective processes collapse into patterns of emotionally charged devotion. The process thus describes the Prioress's Marian agency in terms of movements that metaphysically precede the formation and reception of a *tydynge*-like proto-discourse on its journey through the upper atmosphere.

The Prioress's insertion of herself as a narrating intercessor collapses this explicit environment of potential and emergence by retroactively assigning the metatextual movement it describes along a recursive and self-fulfilling trajectory. This trajectory is articulated through the corporeal images of the affective model through which the Prioress declares her authority. The discourse she seeks to transmit is, as Bronwen Welch argues, not simply the ethereal stuff of devotional intentions flying through the spheres, but breast milk transferred from mothers to babies at the very start of the *Prologue*:[21]

> For noght oonly thy laude precious
> Parfourned is by men of dignitee,
> But by the mouth of children thy bountee

---

19. Ibid., 181. For Russell, the ineffability of song culminates by the conclusion of the tale in "nothing other than the theological definition of a sacrament" (187).

20. Ibid., 184.

21. Welch, 130. Zieman argues that the image of suckling becomes part of the Prioress's attempt to create a kind of "Latin praise that is somehow innocent of *scientia*" (189).

> Parfourned is, for on the brest soukynge
> Somtyme shewen they thyn heriynge.
> (455–59)

In alignment with the conventions of affective piety of which her tale is a part, the work of the *Prologue* is to make discursive phenomena physical, as the performance of emotion "scripts" generate feeling.[22] The *Prioress's Tale* performs this same work at a larger scale, pitting those who have "Cristen blood" against the "Jewerye" (497, 489), casting religious difference in essentializing biological terms. The image of children "on the brest soukynge" in fact doubles the Prioress's authority as a narrator: she is both the mother and the child, and her tale is the breast milk that passes between them. The image of the Prioress's transferring her textual milk refers to a wordless, discourseless "embodied" process,[23] a sound that itself performs "laud" to God,[24] but because the bodies between which the milk is transferred are in fact the same body—the Prioress's, as both mother and child—this affective process is ultimately the extension of an overarching authorial persona.

The *Prologue* thus directs these affective and inventional gestures toward collapse and foreclosure. The Prioress works to extract a "pure" lyric utterance out from an array of discursive and institutional structures,[25] and to articulate this extraction she asks Mary to serve as a kind of inventional intercessor for her effort while she posits herself as her own inventional intercessor. As an intercessor who invokes an intercessor as her muse, the Prioress conjures an image of invention that appears to echo with the displacement caused by overlapping aerial goings "biforn," but its gesture is ultimately totalizing rather than generatively destabilizing.[26] Even the passage that most explicitly describes the activity of the inventional intercessor is translated from an Italian source. If in the *Legend of Good Women* a Boccaccian text stands in for the narrator's sincerely strummed heartstrings as the producer of poetic utterance and sincere feeling, then here a Dantean text is the Italian "tonge" that "goost biforn" the Prioress's own English *Prologue*. Unlike in the *Legend*, however, the lasting impression is not one of endless reverberation but of inventional and affective preempting. In short, the metanarrative of the *Prologue* chronicles repeated gestures toward something beyond itself—not simply Mary or Christ

---

22. See the discussion of emotion scripts in my Introduction, referring especially to McNamer, *Affective Meditation*.
23. See Fradenburg, "Criticism, Anti-Semitism," 91–92; and Holsinger, 264.
24. Russell, 183.
25. See note 9 above.
26. See also Fradenburg, "Criticism, Anti-Semitism," 92.

but something that is registered bodily in the inherently pre-linguistic but also pre-emotional action of suckling infants, and something described metaphyscially as the flight of unrealized moments of affective emergence that Mary directs toward her son in heaven. The great paradox, indeed the strange "wonder," of the *Prologue* is the way in which these gestures void themselves of the sensation of imminent emergence in their very vocabulary of potentiality.

The clergeon's first engagement with the *Alma redemptoris mater* parallels the kinds of inventional gestures made in the *Prologue,* but the depiction of his learning the song goes so far as to establish the inventional processes described in the *Prologue* as an object worthy of affective devotion. Central to the narrative and thematic material of the tale, the boy's first discovery of the *Alma* is perhaps most remarkable in how unremarkably the experience is presented:

> This litel child, his litel book lernynge,
> As he sat in the scole at his prymer,
> He *Alma redemptoris* herde synge,
> As children lerned hire antiphoner;
> And as he dorste, he drough hym ner and ner,
> And herkned ay the wordes and the noote,
> Til he the firste vers koude al by rote.
>
> (516–22)

The passage posits the *Alma* as an aural, lyric alternative to the discursive drudgery of learning his primer, and indeed, the boy's compulsion to draw himself nearer and nearer to the sound comes at the risk of punishment, just as his later decision to divert his energies toward learning the *Alma* risks his being "beten thries in an houre" (542).[27] The tale defines his engagement with the song in terms of learning and internalization, interacting with the music of the song as a kind of devotional emotion script. It isn't until later—after he has learned the song is about Mary and has internalized it according to the repetitive, emotional rituals that constitute this sort of affective devotion—that the "swetnesse" of the song "his herte perced so" (555).[28] The "something" that attracts the boy to the sound of the *Alma* turns out to be a kind of conditioned behavioral response toward sacred objects, the repetition of the devotional behaviors his mother has taught him to enact before images of Mary,

---

27. Holsinger, 271–72; see also Fradenburg, "Criticism, Anti-Semitism," 105.

28. Zeeman emphasizes that the boy actively works to learn the song, and she argues that this desire reveals the boy to be as much a narcissist regarding song as any other male singer in Chaucer ("Gender of Song," 173).

and one that also defines the boy's consultation with an older "felawe" at the school. Desiring to learn more about the meaning of the *Alma,* the boy "gan" to "preye" his older schoolmate,

> T'expounden hym this song in his langage,
> Or telle hym why this song was in usage;
> This preyde he hym to construe and declare
> Ful often tyme upon his knowes bare.
>
> (525–29)

The boy in fact treats his "felawe" exactly as he treats "th'ymage / Of Cristes mooder": "to knele adoun and seye / His *Ave Marie*" (505–8). The boy's interaction with the *Alma* itself is certainly emotional, but it in no way bespeaks a kind of affective emergence; rather, it is defined in terms of emotional devotional practice.

Yet the Prioress explicitly introduces the language of invention into this repetitive and ritualized environment. As she relates the narrative, she declares that she is prompted to understand the boy's entire devotional behavior typologically: "whan I remembre on this mateere, / Seint Nicholas stant evere in my presence, / For he so yong to Criste did reverence" (513–15). The "mateere" of her own inventional action is revealed to be predetermined by the clergeon's analogue of a young Saint Nicholas, and her aside functions less as an exegetical interpretation of the passage she has just related than as a gesture that bends a moment of potential inventional emergence back toward a preconceived design. The boy himself becomes the premeditated expression of a saintly *archetypus,* not an indicator of the pre-inventional movements that precede such expression. The Prioress then repeats the term "mateere" some twenty lines later, placing it on the tongue of the boy's "felawe" as he says to the clergeon, after telling him all he can about the *Alma,* "I kan namoore expounde in this mateere. / I lerne song; I kan but smal grammeere" (535–36). While the discussion of inventional terms appears to gesture toward something outside of institutionalized experience—a "pure" song free of the discursive baggage and trappings of control that are conceived and buttressed by the resonances of a term like "grammeere"—it ultimately points toward the intercessional inventional doubling performed in the *Prologue.*[29] Indeed, both Nicholas and the older "felawe" go "biforn" the boy in the Prioress's

---

[29] This moment is often read as key to the tale's efforts to extract a "pure" song from variously institutional and gendered discourses: see, for example, Russell, 184; Holsinger, 265–67; and Elizabeth Robertson, "Aspects of Female Piety in the *Prioress's Tale,*" in Benson and Robertson, *Chaucer's Religious Tales,* 155.

presentation of the inventional "mateere" of both the *Alma* and her own tale. Given the additional fact that the words of the *Alma redemptoris* are themselves absent from the tale, and that the word "mater" is frequently dropped when the title is named,[30] the focus of the song shifts from Mary to the doubled, recursive inventional activity of the *Prologue*. The context in which the song is introduced and learned suggests the alternatives inherent in affective and inventional potential, but that same context ultimately directs the indeterminate "laud" of the song back to the recursive inventional intercession of the *Prologue*.

Nowhere is this process made more explicit than in the moment when the panicked widow discovers her son, undead and singing in a pit. When the clergeon does not return home from school, she, "With moodres pitee in her brest enclosed" (593), searches everywhere for him as if "she were half out of hir mynde," looking in "every place where she hath supposed / By liklihede hir litel child to fynde" (594–96). Unable to *fynde* him anywhere, she at last inquires among "the cursed Jues" (599), and after "every Jew" answers her with "nay,"

> Jhesu of his grace
> Yaf in hir thoght inwith a litel space
> That in that place after hir sone she cryde,
> Where he was casten in a pit bisyde.
> (601–606)

In place of a moment of *fyndyng*—a nexus of emergence in which the culmination of the mother's intensifying affective experience materializes alongside the sound of the *Alma*—the tale narrates a process by which Jesus implants the knowledge of the boy's whereabouts in the mother's brain, after which she cries out for her son, and he, "with throte ykorven lay upright" and "gan to synge" (611–12). The passage carefully combines affective and inventional moments: Jesus implants a spatial location, the mother calls for the boy, and the boy answers with the sound of a supernaturally amplified rendition of the *Alma*. But the tale actively disrupts this series, inserting at the moment that affect and invention intersect an apostrophe that introduces the reanimated boy in language explicitly echoing the inventional formulation of the *Prologue*: the Prioress interjects, almost as "Jhesu" does in the mother's "thought,"

---

30. William A. Quinn, "The Shadow of Chaucer's Jews," *Exemplaria* 18 (2006): 299–326, notes this frequent omission, included only when it is needed for a rhyme (310), and he links it to the Prioress's "rather juvenile comprehension of comprehension itself" (309).

"O grete God, that parfournest thy laude / By mouth of innocentz, lo, heere thy myght!" (607–8). In this moment of narrative displacement, the Prioress, via her inventional apostrophe, essentially goes "biforn" the literal *fyndyng* of the boy, subsequently presenting him in his new, bejeweled form: a "gemme of chastite," an "emeraude," an object perfectly completed, well beyond any stage of invention (609). When her stanza of apostrophe concludes, it is "The Cristene folk" in general who crowd the streets to "coomen for to wondre upon this thyng" (614–15), and the mother is not mentioned again until she performs her typological role as "This newe Rachel" to whom the people have already carried her exhumed, singing son (627). The tale thus stages a metaphorical moment of inventional discovery—the *fyndyng* of a boy who, in his new, divinely controlled body, is at once singer and song—but then removes the actual moment of emergence and replaces it with the language of the *Prologue* and then the whole of the Christian community that floods in instead.

What is most striking about the anti-emergent process laid out here is its construction in terms of affect and invention. The passage offers a powerful emotional experience, one that Carolyn P. Collette argues allows readers "to experience the religious significance of her tale through the same, intense emotional reaction she obviously has to the action of her own story."[31] As Welch puts it, "We wait with her all night. . . . Nowhere else in the tale does the audience so intensely participate in the human emotions of one of the characters."[32] Fradenburg rightly qualifies such readings by emphasizing that these emotional portraits of Christians gain their vitality by vampirically sucking it out of Jews.[33] Indeed, the tale remains emotionally powerful because of its depiction of the mother's anxiety via its hateful villainizing of the city's Jews. It is the tale's attention to emotion and invention—and not the institutionalized, masculine "grameere" of the boy's *prymer* or the abbot's impromptu mass and burial service—that shuts down the possibility for gestures toward affective emergence.[34]

---

31. Collette, "Sense and Sensibility," 145. Collette argues that in this way the Prioress privileges emotional experience over even doctrinal content. Frank sees the presentation of this emotional experience in the tale as outdoing even the devotion to Mary ("Pathos in Chaucer's Religious Tales," 45).

32. Welch, 135.

33. Fradenburg, "Criticism, Anti-Semitism," 83–84.

34. Lampert argues that the actions of men in the tale "become very significant, even dominant," only after the discovery of the boy's body (75), and that "the martyrdom unites the Christian community behind the boy and against the Jews, strengthening a sense of Christian community and identity at the same time that it contains and checks the maternal power of the Virgin, harnessing those for use by the Church. Feminine forces are subsumed within the universal Church, controlled by men" (76). For other readings of how the tale constructs a

The *mateere* of this would-be inventional discovery is the singing of a cadaverous automaton whose undead incantations are what, as many readers have noted, the *Prioress's Prologue* aspires to in its longing for, as Katherine Zieman puts it, an "ethically pristine utterance."[35] Shannon Gayk's reading of the tale holds out the possibility of affective potential in the way in which the tale explores "inassimilable things"—that is, "things" that are not easily (or, sometimes, ever) assimilated into "objects" via the imposition of meaning and understanding. Such "things" resonate with affective potential before they collapse into assimilated "objects," and for Gayk, the boy's undead, singing body "is characterized by ontological excess; it is pure potentiality, both subject and object, not quite living but not yet dead."[36] As Gayk shows, the tale explicitly takes wonder and its circulation as topics for invention, effectively stretching out miraculous moments for extended periods: the boy, after all, is in public view for a long time, singing through the mass and taking a break only to explain in clear, narrative discourse the explicit cause and nature of his condition.[37] Despite his apparent capacity to generate wonder, however, the undead boy is never quite an embodiment of pure potentiality. On the contrary, his extended, singing physicality makes him a material analogue of the exaggerated, satirical gestures toward the affect of invention that I have attempted to trace through the tale. What is embodied here is the prescribed narrative discourse itself. Never quite afforded the opportunity to be the manifestation of "pure potentiality" in the terms Gayk introduces,[38] the boy, along with his grain, is a materialization—an incarnation, perhaps—of the tale's own satirical metapoetic analysis. Generating emotional responses and marked by the grain's inventional symbolism, the boy is nevertheless void of sensations of

---

Christian community at the expense of the tale's Jewish community, see Denise L. Despres, "Cultic Anti-Judaism and Chaucer's Litel Clergeon," *Modern Philology* 91 (1994): 413–27; and Greg Wilsbacher, "Lumiansky's Paradox: Ethics, Aesthetics, and Chaucer's '*Prioress's Tale,*'" *College Literature* 32 (2005): 1–28.

35. Zieman, 197.

36. Gayk, 143; Gayk also emphasizes the sense of stasis created by the miracle, arguing that "Chaucer's representation of wonder in the tale is oddly static" and finally "forestalls interpretation; it insists on the limits of cognition; it emphasizes receptivity over agency; and it results in the silencing and objectification of the things that produced it in the first place" (149). Patterson likewise argues that "the 'greyn' represents a significance that is self-identical and self-present, one that requires no interpretation—nor even, one might suppose, symbolic representation. Just as the song that passes through the clergeon's throat solicits no interpretive effort, so the *Prioress's Tale* as a whole aspires to a similar transparency" ("Living Witnesses," 516).

37. Holsinger notes that the clergeon's explanation of his own miracle in fact interrupts the song he is singing, and he thus actually "*disobeys* the careful instructions of the Virgin" (288; emphasis in original).

38. Gayk, 143.

emergence in his resilient fixity; he is a wonder because the tale finally labels him as one.

"BUT A LITEL WHILE AGO": THE EFFECTS OF EXAGGERATION

The nature of the tale's satire is exaggerated amplification of multiple affective and inventional movements in the *Prologue* and, most vividly, in the speaking image of a mutilated child whose mouth has been stuffed with a mysterious grain posited as a material source for the generation of song. The effects of this exaggeration are subtle and complex. It does not prompt an implicit reexamination of how we might fold ourselves into dominant cultural narratives so easily in the same way as the *Legend of Good Women* does, since it never provides the moments of rupture and emergence that might compel such reassessment. Instead, the exaggeration illustrates how quickly gestures toward affective and inventional emergence can be redirected to perpetuate rather than question pervasive cultural discourses.[39] Because of the way in which her inventional work in the prologue and tale goes "biforn" the tale's narrative, as well as the way in which satire is couched in the particular brand of affective devotion that is the Prioress's Marian narrative (explicitly cordoned off as such by the repetition of "quod she" in the *Prologue* and the *Tale*),[40] Chaucer fashions the Prioress as the source of this redirection: it is she who becomes the usurper of emergent moments. The tale thus functions as more than a satire of a worldly prioress or a critique of devotional narrative. Instead, via its intentionally stunted narratives of discovery, the tale draws out a process that implicates readers in the "dumping" of negative affects on the Prioress.[41] In other words, it is not simply that she is vain and her tale self-serving and emotionally hollow; it is also that the metatextual gestures so thoroughly

---

39. Wilsbacher argues that the aesthetic appreciation of the *Prioress's Tale* (in Kantian terms), dramatized by the pilgrims' silent reaction to the story, demonstrates its success at making ideology seem rationally correct (16). See 15–16 for the implications for the aesthetic appreciations of modern criticism of the tale.

40. Winter S. Elliott argues that the dialogic interjections emphasize the juxtaposition of a feminine speaker with the masculine authority of "oure lord" ("Eglentyne's Mary/Widow: Reconsidering the Anti-Semitism of *The Prioress's Tale*," in Bishop, *The Canterbury Tales Revisited*, 115). Patterson argues that they emphasize that the "perfect" singing of the clergeon is rendered in the Prioress's voice, making her "breathless sequence of exclamations ... unintentionally parodic" ("Living Witnesses," 516).

41. This is the kind of affective "dumping" that Teresa Brennan describes as having characterized Western notions of the feminine (6).

exaggerated in the tale map out and compel us to follow a process that generates and directs negative affects at the figure of the Prioress, precisely because of the inventional and affective nexus she enacts. The tale's anti-Semitism becomes an essential part of this process, since it functions in the overall narrative as a means of inventing a Christian community by vilifying Jews.[42] The Prioress's effort to forge an imagined Christian community through violence and anti-Semitism parallels the tale's formation of a second kind of "community" of readers whom the tale implicitly encourages to separate themselves affectively from the Prioress and her totalizing inventions. If the *Legend* offers rupture and break to prompt a kind of pre-cognitive shock that results in subsequent and productive reexamination, then the *Prioress's Tale* works oppositely, folding readers into a process of affective and inventional perpetuation, enacting what the Prioress does even as they work to separate themselves from her. The tale thus makes the perpetuators of pervasive cultural discourses its readers: they participate in the logic of anti-Semitism that constructs its narrative and its community of readers, and they are then implicitly compelled to make the Prioress the focus of the resulting emotional capture that emerges from this process.

Modern criticism about the *Prioress's Tale*'s representation of anti-Semitism, however, reveals the tale to engage readers in a way Chaucer perhaps never could have intended, one that, in defiance of the tale's project, prompts a sudden, surprised urgency for reexamination, not only of the contemporary pervasiveness of the hatred and violence complicit in the formation of emotional communities as they are rendered in the tale, but also of the ethical and moral responsibility that the professional literary critic and teacher has to texts, to the past, and to the present.[43] Indeed, for twenty-first-century

---

42. Patterson notes the intensification of the anti-Semitism in the tale compared to other examples from the genre ("Living Witnesses," 519–20); as Besserman succinctly puts it, Chaucer writes "a typical Miracle of the Virgin . . . with atypical antisemitic fervor" ("Chaucer, Spain," 334). Besserman argues that it is "unlikely" that Chaucer would "have subscribed wholeheartedly to the demonizing view of Jews that he attributes to the Prioress and subtly critiques in her tale-telling performance" (332). Alternatively, Roger Dahood, citing the connections of Chaucer's coterie audience to the story of Hugh of Lincoln, argues that the tale most likely does not satirize the Prioress's anti-Semitism ("The Punishment of the Jews, Hugh of Lincoln, and the Question of Satire in Chaucer's *Prioress's Tale*," *Viator* 36 [2005]: 465–91). Showing the Prioress to be the originator of the tale's anti-Semitism becomes a way of liberating Chaucer from accusations of prejudice or hatred, and it is important to remember that the tale's implicit criticism of affective discourses of anti-Semitism (if that criticism exists) does not necessarily preclude Chaucer's own anti-Semitism. Quinn, for example, argues that while "the spectacular anti-Semitism of the Prioress needs revision," the *Parson's Tale* "finally reaffirms an explicit doctrinal opposition to the Jews" ("Shadow of Chaucer's Jews," 322).

43. Emily Stark Zitter argues that "the greatest ironies of the tale . . . were not intended by Chaucer" ("Anti-Semitism in Chaucer's Prioress's Tale," *Chaucer Review* 25 [1991]: 282).

readers, the Prioress's phrase "but a litel while ago" in reference to the martyrdom of Hugh of Lincoln becomes the most profound line in the tale (686): the phrase registers not simply the medieval conception of an eternal Christian timeframe but also *litotes,* a deeply ironic understatement, amid the realization that what generates the kind of community building presented in the tale resonates even more strongly today.[44] This "litel while ago" is, it turns out, also right now. As Greg Wilsbacher puts it, modern readers of the tale must "struggle" simultaneously "with two distinct temporal absolutes: one that places [the tale's anti-Semitism] comfortably within an accepted medieval context and one that gathers around that reading the much more modern context of the Shoah."[45] Similarly, the experience of reading a text by a canonical author whose name is for many students (and critics) pregnant simultaneously with cultural authority and perennial subversive potential seems to be affectively mismatched, causing, as A. B. Friedman puts it, many readers to have "panicked in reaction to" what Friedman calls, I think inaccurately, "the poem's incidental anti-Semitism."[46] Whatever the tale might implicitly compel its readers to perform, the response in modern criticism has indeed been productive. It has produced calls for ethically and morally centered approaches to teaching and writing about the tale that are conscious of the "two distinct temporal absolutes" of the tale and that, in the welcoming space of a classroom community, have the potential to be as personally and culturally productive as the tale is haltingly disturbing.[47] The process of finding productive means of engagement with the emotionally difficult text of Chaucer's *Prioress's Tale* is thus profoundly characterized by the intersection of affect and invention.

Especially since Fradenburg's article, many critics acknowledge how the perception of medieval alterity shapes ethical engagement with the tale; see Johnson's summary, 195–96.

44. See Calabrese's reading of the Prioress's understanding of this line, which registers a particular relationship of the past, present, and future (76–77).

45. Wilsbacher, 19.

46. A. B. Friedman, "The *Prioress's Tale* and Chaucer's Anti-Semitism," *Chaucer Review* 9 (1974): 127.

47. Most influential in this regard has been Fradenburg. Calabrese warns against the dangers he sees as implicit in Fradenburg's call for an affective critical engagement with medieval texts, arguing that critics who write "affective criticism" of anti-Semitic medieval narratives like the *Prioress's Tale* run the risk of replicating "the same, potentially sterile, emotionalism that we indict in the Prioress herself" (74); see also Besserman, "Ideology, Antisemitism, and Chaucer's *Prioress's Tale,*" *Chaucer Review* 36 (2001): 48–72. Zitter advocates "a stronger and more explicitly moral approach" to teaching the tale (282). Wilsbacher notes that "the feelings of pleasure and of anxiety produced in modern readers" are crucial for forming ethical responses for the future (20). Reconciling Fradenburg's and Patterson's influential essays, Johnson calls for a methodology that combines theory and historicism "in terms of medieval cultural memory *and* in terms of the continuities and ruptures that characterize the long Western history of Jewish-Christian relations" (199; emphasis in original).

THE MONK'S "CERTEYN STORIE" AND TRAGIC CHRONICLE

If the *Prioress's Tale* exaggerates moments of affective experience and inventional emergence, then the *Monk's Tale* abbreviates them through a narrative processes characterized by intensified terseness and repetition. Moreover, the tale's emphasis on "tragedies" as the genre for the exploration of this narrative process (1971), relating a compounding series of short, historical narratives, invokes methods similar to those we have seen Gower employ in his efforts to imagine a kind of poetics capable of productively impinging on the historical reality in which they are intended to intercede. Whereas in the *Confessio* the idea of an affective chronicle of invention offers the potential for the generation of a culturally transformative poetics, the Monk's tragic chronicle actively works to dispel the possibility of any such transformative potential. As I explore the *Monk's Tale*'s dismantling of productive invention, my argument here will not be that the tale is a mini-*Confessio* and the Monk a satirized mini-Gower who has a limited, overly moralized view of human activity in history. Rather, I want to suggest how the *Monk's Tale* approaches the affect of invention and its culturally transformative potential in a way similar to parts of the *Confessio* but that the tale satirizes that approach, reaching a diametrically opposite conclusion.

The *Monk's Tale* is unique among the Canterbury collection because it comprises not one but seventeen separate narratives as well as the most detailed description of its own proposed genre, a twelve-line explanation of the "manere of tragedie" (1991), specifically its content and form. As the Monk presents it, this genre consists exclusively of terse historical narratives that relate the falls of great men and women from prosperity into wretchedness. He pulls his seventeen narratives from the full spectrum of history: biblical, classical, and contemporary sources provide the *materia*, and his tragedies thus include personages as diverse as Lucifer, Adam, Samson, Caesar, Zenobia, Bernabò Visconti, and Ugolino of Pisa.[48] As a tale collection, it resembles not only the *Canterbury Tales* as a whole but the *Confessio Amantis* as well.[49]

---

48. The overall frame for the *Monk's Tale*, and the narratives of several of the protagonists, are apparently derived from Boccaccio's *De casibus virorum illustrium*, an attribution that many manuscripts preserve in the title. See Thomas H. Bestul, "The Monk's Tale," in *Sources and Analogues of the "Canterbury Tales,"* gen. ed. Robert M. Correale, vol. 1 (Cambridge: D. S. Brewer, 2002), 410–11; Piero Boitani, "The *Monk's Tale*: Dante and Boccaccio," *Medium Aevum* 45 (1976): 50–54; and Peter Godman, "Chaucer and Boccaccio's Latin Works," in *Chaucer and the Italian Trecento*, ed. Piero Boitani, (Cambridge: Cambridge University Press, 1983), 269–81.

49. Jahan Ramazani, for example, calls the Monk's tragedies "a negative inverse image of Chaucer's" *Canterbury Tales*, "a disturbing and crowded miniaturization of the tales of which

In fact, in its *compilatio* structure and apparent pedagogical intentions, the *Monk's Tale* employs an approach similar to—but exaggeratedly satirical of—Gower's *Confessio*, ostensibly citing examples from history to educate readers in the present.[50] If the *Confessio*'s narratives render thinkable the complexities and practicalities of ethical subjectivity, however, then the tragedies of the *Monk's Tale* flatten this pedagogical project to the simple lesson to "Be war" of the fickleness of Fortune (1998).[51] Indeed, a distinctive characteristic of the *Monk's Tale* is its excessive paring down of the often rich and complex narrative development that characterizes the sources' versions of the stories, and the tale ends only because the Knight and the Host demand that the Monk change the topic of his invention and the mode of his narration.[52] As part of an ongoing effort to recuperate the tale from a tradition of scholarly dismissals of its art, recent critics identify the Monk's narrative brevity as a condition of his views of history and poetic invention.[53] Richard Neuse, for example, argues that "the Monk seeks to banish from history the specters of a grand design," emphasizing the importance of human agency,[54] and Ann W. Astell argues that through the tale Chaucer "weds the Monk's reduction of art to *materia* with the materialistic philosophy he espouses," resulting finally in the bleak notion that "there is no final cause, no intentionality, only formless *materia*."[55] The Monk's narratives link the reason for invention with a view of

they form a part" ("Chaucer's Monk: The Poetics of Abbreviation, Aggression, and Tragedy," *Chaucer Review* 27 [1993]: 260). Similar claims might be made of the tale's resemblance to the *Confessio*.

50. Many readers of the tale have slotted the Monk's tragedies into a subgenre of the moral exemplum. For Godman, the tale adheres to the "exemplary force, moral authority and historical veracity" of Boccaccio's Latin works (291); Boitani notes that the Monk identifies the tragedies as "authoritative *exempla*" (*The Tragic and the Sublime in Medieval Literature* [Cambridge: Cambridge University Press, 1989], 41); and Larry Scanlon calls the tale "a miniature exemplum collection" that "foregrounds the compression already built into the genre," and each tragedy "is the negative exemplum in its most distilled form" (*Narrative, Authority, and Power*, 215).

51. Henry Ansgar Kelly notes that the Monk's introduction informs the pilgrims that "by taking precautions against falls, one may sometimes avoid or prevent them" (*Chaucerian Tragedy* [Cambridge: D. S. Brewer, 1997], 71).

52. A similar effect of paring down might be assigned to the *Confessio* as well, and "narrative economy" seems to be one of the defining characteristics of Gower's method in his English poem (Robert R. Edwards, "Gower and the Poetics of the Literal," in Dutton, Hines, and Yeager, *John Gower, Trilingual Poet*, 59).

53. For a review and analysis of such dismissals, as well as an assessment of the importance of the *Monk's Tale* to the English vernacular tradition, see Scanlon, *Narrative, Authority, and Power*, 216–20.

54. Richard Neuse, *Chaucer's Dante: Allegory and Epic Theater in "The Canterbury Tales"* (Berkeley: University of California Press, 1991), 149.

55. Ann W. Astell, *Chaucer and the Universe of Learning* (Ithaca, NY: Cornell University Press, 1996), 191–92.

historical process, focusing on the event of the tragic transition itself, the precise moment of the fall from prosperity into wretchedness; indeed, they define themselves existentially as narratives based on this singular focus.

This focus fashions the Monk's stories into tragic chronicles, narratives stripped down to their "chronicle" essence of the report of events themselves. Like Gower's chronicle of inventions in Book 4 of the *Confessio*, which repeatedly narrates a process of discovery, the Monk's tragedies suggest a broad temporal sweep defined by decline, from the original falls of Lucifer and Adam through to "modern instances" like Bernabò and Ugolino and, by extension, the eventual ruinous endpoint of human chronological progression that leads, inevitably, to apocalypse.[56] The Monk's explanation of the genre emphasizes this point:

> Tragedie is to seyn a certeyn storie,
> As olde bookes maken us memorie,
> Of hym that stood in greet prosperitee,
> And is yfallen out of heigh degree
> Into myserie, and endeth wrecchedly.
> (1973–77)

"Tragedie," the Monk specifies, "is a certeyn storie": that is, as Patterson notes, a certain kind of history, and, as the Knight and Host in particular quickly come to realize, this historical form consists solely of the singular movement of the tragic transition itself, the fall from prosperity into wretchedness.[57]

---

56. I follow in my reading here the order presented in the Hengwrt and Ellesmere manuscripts, which place the modern instances at the end of the tragedies rather than in the middle, as is the case in most of the surviving manuscripts of the *Canterbury Tales*. For a concise discussion, see Helen Cooper, *The Canterbury Tales*, Oxford Guides to Chaucer (Oxford: Oxford University Press, 1989), 325–26; see also the brief discussion in Daniel Pinti, "The *Comedy* of the *Monk's Tale*: Chaucer's Hugelyn and Early Commentary on Dante's Ugolino," *Comparative Literature Studies* 37 (2000): 294 n19. Donald K. Fry argues that the latter placement of the modern instances helps explain the Knight's interruption ("The Ending of the *Monk's Tale*," *JEGP* 71 [1972]: 355–68).

57. Patterson writes that "tragedy deals with the world of public events—of history—in which the socially exalted enact their inevitable fate" ("'What Man Artow?'", 121); he elsewhere surveys classical and medieval scholarship that links tragedy with "public," summarizing that "the epic of Antiquity was in the Middle Ages called tragedy. And for the Middle Ages tragedy dealt with history" ("Genre and Source in *Troilus and Criseyde*," in *Acts of Recognition: Essays on Medieval* Culture [Notre Dame, IN: University of Notre Dame Press, 2010], 201–2, qt. on 202). For a thorough discussion of Chaucer's understanding of tragedy in the *Monk's Tale*, see H. Kelly, 65–79, who also notes that in the *Polychronicon*, Trevisa translates Higden's *tragedia* into "geste" but apparently "saw no difference in content between tragedy and comedy, for he defines comedy as 'a song of gestes'" (41).

The tragedies are concerned less with explaining why or how history's tragic falls occurred or their places in a larger historical field, and more with maintaining with virtually no variation that these falls simply *did* occur: William C. Strange notes that "it is still the fall alone that fascinates this Monk," Jahan Ramazani calls the Monk's focus "a monomaniacal obsession" indicating a "state of mind," and Neuse suggests that in the Monk's view, history itself "can be regarded as a form of tragedy whose pattern is set by the fall of Lucifer and includes the Crucifixion, which generically is not different from Caesar's or Pompey's assassination or Cato's suicide."[58] If tragedies, at least as the Monk presents them, provide a means of transporting narratives of the past into the present—to "maken memorie" from the stories of "olde books"—then they presume to do so without lugging along any corresponding hermeneutical baggage.[59] The Monk's formulation of tragedy strives to preserve the event, the moment of narrative movement when the force of Fortune suddenly and unexpectedly emerges in the tale's narrative continuum, without the teleology of exemplary morality or the complexities of Boethian philosophy from which its definition was originally derived. Tragedy is a poetic means of representing the idea of historical progression whose only "meaning" is realized in the moment of sudden transition from prosperity to wretchedness.[60] Because they scarcely offer anything other than the scantest moralizations of each of the stories and instead merely list moral or ethical defects as already folded into

---

58. William C. Strange, "The '*Monk's Tale*': A Generous View," *Chaucer Review* 1 (1967): 171; Ramazani, 265; Neuse, 193. In contrast to Neuse, Monica E. McAlpine argues that for Chaucer "the tragic concept of the fall is incompatible with the theological concept of *the* Fall" (*The Genre of* Troilus and Criseyde [Ithaca, NY: Cornell University Press, 1978], 105; emphasis in original).

59. Winthrop Wetherbee, "The Context of the Monk's Tale," in *Language and Style in English Literature: Essays in Honour of Michio Masui*, ed. Masui Kawai (Hiroshima: English Research Association of Hiroshima, 1991), 159–77, sees Fortune "function[ing] at times as a sort of hermetic vessel in which the prince's fall occurs in total isolation" (164) and argues that the *Monk's Tale* is actually an "anti-*De casibus*," because its tragedies "rob" the original stories "of the moral and historical complexities inherent in their biblical and classical sources" (167); McAlpine argues that "although the Monk's stories are dressed out in all sorts of moralistic trappings, they are fundamentally amoral" (108); and Kurt Olsson argues that the Monk "seems intent on ridding tragedy of what he deems narrative or doctrinal chaff" ("Grammar, Manhood, and Tears: The Curiosity of Chaucer's Monk," *Modern Philology* 76 [1978]: 4).

60. Neuse sees in this the Monk's celebration of human agency in history: "The Monk's Tale thus represents, I would say, an emphatic repudiation of any system of otherworld justice as something that does violence to the fabric of human existence" (177). Of course, the *Monk's Tale* is filled with explicit references to moral, prudential, or ultimately misogynistic "causes" for the falls of its protagonists, and the Monk never completely extinguishes ethics and morality from his narratives, nor does he merely dismiss their more complex moral meanings by simplifying the context of his sources. For a concise "census" of the causes of the falls of the Monk's protagonists, see H. Kelly, 71; see also Boitani, *Tragic and the Sublime*, 42–43.

the event of the fall itself, the Monk's tragedies present a view of history that attempts to preserve the event somehow independently of its representation. The point is simply that this happened, and that point is made via chronicle repetition, whose topic—the tragic fall—doubles as historical process.

The Monk's details of the genre's formal and affective elements likewise emphasize the singular movement that defines the narrative as a genre. Tragedies, the Monk says,

> ben versified communely
> Of six feet, which men clepen *exametron*.
> In prose eek been endited many oon,
> And eek in meetre in many a sondry wyse.
> (1978–81)

His description of how one can compose tragedies is so inclusive as to be almost meaningless: while tragedies are concerned with only the most specific, localized, "certeyn" instances of a singular motion of historical progression, they can, on the other hand, take almost any kind of written form imaginable.[61] As such, the Monk's metrical definition actively directs attention toward the genre's defining criterion of transitional movement, the moment of tragic fall. A similar logic applies to the Monk's characterization of the essential emotional component of the genre. "Tragedies," he reports at the end of the story of Croesus,

> in noon oother maner thyng
> Ne kan in syngyng crie ne bewaille
> But that Fortune alwey wole assaille
> With unwar strook the regnes that been proude.
> (2761–64)

Patterson shows how this definition of tragedies, emphasizing their pathos, demonstrates the Monk's misunderstanding of Philosophy's critique of tragedy as a genre in Boethius's *Consolation*, in which she faults tragedy for its reliance on emotional effect rather than rational understanding.[62] Whatever Boethius

---

61. Patterson cites Skeat's early note which clarifies that Chaucer here is referring to Latin, not English, poetry, especially that of Virgil, Statius, and Lucan ("Genre and Source," 201).

62. Ibid., 200–201. Patterson emphasizes that Chaucer understood this definition in the terms with which Lady Philosophy dismisses it as a viable form of philosophical discourse in the *Consolation*, and that its use in the *Monk's Tale* is certainly satirical; see also Jane Dick Zatta, "Chaucer's Monk: *A Mighty Hunter before the Lord*," *Chaucer Review* 29 (1994): 117; and

really meant, the Monk's tragedies, even as they focus on moments when the sudden "unwar strook" of tragic transition first occurs, make this kind of phenomenological eruption a marker of historical movement and generic form; they express a necessarily predetermined outcome rather than gesture toward a sudden emergence of unstructured potentiality. The Monk's tripartite definition of tragedy makes affective and inventional emergence codependent on the expressly historical event of the protagonist's fall.[63] It thus encodes moments of emergence into a kind of chronicle framework, one defined by an unceasing progression of fall after fall that begins with Satan and continues all the way to contemporary Spain and Italy.[64] In this way, even despite their emphasis on the event of tragic fall, the tragedies of the *Monk's Tale* seem to elide the kind of "eventful" complexities that J. Allan Mitchell has shown to be inherent in medieval ideas about Fortune.[65] Focusing on the moment of tragic movement itself as the nexus of affective occurrence and poetic invention, the Monk's tragedies are nevertheless defined by and folded into their essential trajectory of decline, the same trajectory that generates the event of the fall in the first place.[66]

What emerges from the narrative processes of these short stories, then, is a paradox of chronicle progression similar to the one Gower introduces and works to unravel in Book 4 of the *Confessio*. The Monk's tragedies fixate on movement, on the event of transition itself, but they exaggerate that focus to such an extreme that the potential for productive transformation of the kind imagined in Gower's chronicles is completely erased. The tragedies of the *Monk's Tale* function satirically by conceptualizing poetic invention as a kind of force of movement that coincides with affective unfolding in historical

---

H. Kelly, 50–65. Boitani notes that Chaucer's definition of tragedy is "more complex" than the Monk's (*Tragic and the Sublime*, 42). For the importance of lamentation to medieval understandings of tragedy, see Renate Haas, "Chaucer's *Monk's Tale*: An Ingenious Criticism of Early Humanist Conceptions of Tragedy," *Humanistica Lovaniensia* 36 (1987): 52–53.

63. David Wallace charts a similar sensational experience when he notes that part of the appeal of the Monk's Tale is that its stories were taken "*as* a contemporary text. Great men have fallen; *great men are falling*" (299; emphasis in original). The fall of a mighty man, Wallace argues, revises the meaning of his entire life, and Chaucer exhibits "a willingness to suggest that such renarration is always imminent; that it may already be in progress," especially "for English people living under, or in sight of, Richard II or any 'myghty man'" (300); see also McAlpine, 107–8.

64. For some critics, it continues even to the immediate present of England in its implicit critique of, and warning to, Richard II: see, for example, Wallace, 329–31; and Astell, *Political Allegory*, 102–9.

65. Mitchell, *Ethics and Eventfulness*, esp. 1–26.

66. Wallace observes that the same rule applies to the human lives that these tragedies narrate: "The moment of the fall will become the narrative *telos* of the life, prompting a rewriting of every earlier 'accounte'" (330).

reality, only to restrict severely the scope of that movement along the unidirectional trajectory essential to the Monk's definition of the genre into which he folds all of his narrative material.

Consequently, the Monk finally defines poetry's ability to impinge on historical reality in these intensely limited terms. The tragedies achieve this satirical gesture by presenting the event of a protagonist's fall as the endpoint rather than the origin of the Monk's invention. That is, instead of composing poetry that has been "inspired" by an event "trewe and olde" (1998), the tale reverses the trajectory of this process and presents events as appearing to emerge from the process of invention. In the end, the larger hermeneutic paradigm that replaces the providential, moral, and ethical frames dismissed by the Monk's view of history is a mechanical presentation of poetic invention itself. Like Gower's chronicles, the Monk's tragedies imagine a way in which poetic structure might somehow impinge on the structure of reality, but unlike in the *Confessio,* they actively work to stifle invention in the very process of representing it, making invention an end rather than a beginning. The process begins with the Monk's somewhat unusual choice for his first tale.

"AT HYM WOL I BIGYNNE": EVENT AND INVENTION IN THE MONK'S TRAGEDIES

The Monk's decision to begin with Lucifer, out of the hundred or so tragedies he keeps in his mind, is remarkable because it introduces the only protagonist who is not a human being and is therefore untouchable by Fortune:

> At Lucifer, though he an angel were
> And nat a man, at hym wol I bigynne.
> For though Fortune may noon angel dere,
> From heigh degree yet fel he for his synne
> Doun into helle, where he yet is inne.
> O Lucifer, brightest of angels alle,
> Now artow Sathanas, that mayst nat twynne
> Out of miserie, in which that thou art falle.
>
> (1999–2006)

The Monk's provocative beginning establishes the pattern to which the rest of the tragedies adhere. As Larry Scanlon argues, the fact that Lucifer's fall occurs outside of history complicates this tragedy's relationship with the human tragedies that follow. For Scanlon, a structural resemblance "remains as the only evidence available in purely temporal terms of the cosmic link between Lucifer's fall and the process of human history. The story cannot provide the Monk with the central authority of an origin, but that is precisely the point. It distills the figural authority of Fortune to an irreducible doubleness, confirming at once its universality and its incompleteness."[67] In terms of historical precedent, then, the first of the Monk's tragedies establishes a view of history that overlooks causes—moral or otherwise—in favor of the simple teleology of progression. Beginning "At Lucifer" does not illustrate a cause, source, or origin but instead establishes a narrative pattern that stands in place of historical cause.[68]

The Monk's narratological bait-and-switch—first apologizing for not telling his tragedies in natural order ("I by ordre telle nat thise thynges" [1985]) but then starting at the beginning after all—posits his signature historical event, the tragic transition, as the result of formal activities of invention. The choice to begin with Lucifer's fall intentionally confuses natural and artificial beginnings, and the Monk's very first word emphasizes this confusion: "*At* Lucifer ... wol I bigynne," he declares, and his inaugural preposition is important. "At" transforms Lucifer into a kind of event, a point in time along a chronicle of fall after fall. At the same time, "At" renders Lucifer a topic for invention, one of the many "thynges" that the Monk stores in his "celle" (1985, 1972).[69] In starting with "At," the Monk posits an artificial order that is also natural order, and as such he appears to render natural order, that is, chronological history, a product of its invention.[70] At the same time, however, the Monk also emphasizes that the moment of this event is caught in an eternal state of perpetual emergence. "Now artow Sathanas," the Monk announces, noting in his miniature apostrophe that the event of this fall still continues, even into the very moment of his own narration. Occurring outside of time,

---

67. Scanlon, *Narrative, Authority, and Power*, 223; see also Neuse, 193.

68. Critics have tended to view the Monk's narrative arrangements in terms of authority. For Scanlon, this process becomes a way of exhibiting the social power of exemplary narrative, which, Scanlon argues, is apparent in particular through the Monk's depiction of Fortune; see p. 177 below. Wallace argues that the tragedies as a whole work to destabilize the authority of humanistic understandings of the past and the political ideologies that those understandings support; see esp. 313–31.

69. It is worth noting as well that Chaucer uses the term "thyng" elsewhere to refer, if nebulously, to inventional topics and the act of *fyndyng*. See, for example, the "certeyn thing" and "som thyng for to fare / The bet" of *Parlement of Foules* (20, 698–99).

70. Astell argues more generally that the Monk's "misordering of the tragedies should alert us to Chaucer's use of artificial, rather than natural, order" and causes readers "to supply other 'Modern Instances,'" of murdered men, and to think of Edward II, whose tale the Host originally requested; thinking of Edward would make them think also of Richard, who worked to associate himself with Edward (*Political Allegory*, 108).

this tragedy is never over: it is still happening, even "Now."[71] In its slight detail and incisive treatment of the single occurrence of Lucifer's fall, the Monk's narrative carefully constructs a scaffolding of inventional references that attempts to render the event of Lucifer's fall the product of poetic invention. On the face of it, then, the tragedy of Lucifer imaginatively posits an event emerging from the mechanics of inventional play, but an event evacuated of any trace of generative potentiality.

The *Monk's Tale* pairs this reversal of inventional trajectory with an active effort to introduce and then dispel alternative moments of potential invention. This pattern repeats throughout the Monk's tragedies, including even those that present relatively greater narrative amplification and development. As in the *Prioress's Tale,* these narratives emphasize a sense of inventional stagnation by explicitly introducing moments of potential invention only to quash them, but they furthermore direct this effort toward the genre's pervading narrative trajectory. In the first longer narrative, for example, that of Samson, the Monk presents a one-stanza "argument" of Samson's case,[72] describing how the man who was once "to God Almyghty consecrat" soon "slow hymself for wrecched-nesse" (2017, 2022), and then amplifies this summary in nine stanzas in which we learn the details of the state of Samson's prosperity, the specific conditions of his wretchedness, and the particulars of his downfall, especially how,

> Unto his lemman Dalida he tolde
> That in his heeris al his strengthe lay,
> And falsly to his foomen she hym solde.
> And slepynge in hir barm upon a day,
> She made to clippe or shere his heres away,
> And made his foomen al his craft espyen;
> And whan that they hym foond in this array,
> They bounde hum faste and putten out his yen.
>   (2063–70)

Even as it fills out the "skeletal" framework of its opening stanza,[73] the narrative locates the source of Samson's tragic transition in an action charged with

---

71. McAlpine argues that the name change to "Satan" in the narrative "suggests his continuing role as an agent of evil" (104). Wallace locates a sense of presentism in readers' inclination to relate past tragedies to contemporary events; see 299–300, and note 63 above.

72. I borrow the useful term "argument" from H. Kelly's description of the stanzaic summaries in the *Monk's Tale* (75).

73. The term "skeletal" I adapt from Wallace, who describes the modern instances as "the shadow or skeleton of a text" (330).

inventional resonance. Dalida "made his foomen al his craft espyen," and the Monk's terms, both "made" and "craft," explicitly invoke the process of poetic invention. The Monk's subsequent moralization—"Beth war by this ensample oold and playn / That no men telle hir conseil til hir wyves" (2091–92)—urges the prevention of further acts of *makyng* by folding them into a misogynistic proverb and sealing off the potential for any inventional and affective rupture that might provoke the sudden urge to reexamine the silencing cultural narrative that the tragedy repeats. The Monk's story of Samson turns on its simultaneous treatment of poetic invention and the moment of tragic transition, bending the one into the service of the other in a way that makes historical event the result of exposing the inventional procedures of "craft."

Transforming Fortune herself into a kind of author-figure perpetuates this process. She appears for the first time in the tragedy of Hercules as a historical force and an inventor of glosses.[74] Though it is Dianira and the poisoned shirt that undo Hercules, the Monk's larger claim is that when "Fortune list to glose, / Thanne wayteth she her man to overthrowe / By swich a wey as he wolde leest suppose" (2140–42). Fortune tricks "her man" Hercules by bringing him down by the method he least expects, and she does so by glossing on Hercules' life. Scanlon notes that this discursive characterization of Fortune illustrates "the thoroughness of Fortune's domination over human existence," and that, more significantly, "like Boccaccio, the Monk has given Fortune a voice, or more precisely, *he has made her disruptiveness discursive. That is, he has constructed a narrative field where disruption, narrative's characteristic assertion of its own autonomy, becomes the sign of discursive control without ceasing to be narrative.*"[75] As Scanlon helps us to see, the Monk's Fortune is not so much an agent in her own right as a placeholder for a broader discursive process which, for Scanlon, demonstrates the cultural power of textual authority,[76] and this is precisely the way in which, as Rita Copeland has shown, ver-

---

74. For other efforts to trace the Monk's portrayal of Fortune across the tragedies, see Edward M. Socola, "Chaucer's Development of Fortune in the 'Monk's Tale,'" *JEGP* 49 (1950): 159–71; Strange; Douglas L. Lepley, "The Monk's Boethian Tale," *Chaucer Review* 12 (1978): 162–70; and Peter C. Braeger, "The Portrayals of Fortune in the Tales of the *Monk's Tale*," in *Rebels and Rivals: The Contestive Spirit in the Canterbury Tales*, ed. Susanna Greer Fein, David Raybin, and Peter C. Braeger (Kalamazoo, MI: Medieval Institute Press, 1991), 223–36.

75. Scanlon, *Narrative, Authority, and Power*, 224–25; emphasis in original. Neuse's reading of the Monk's Fortune takes its discursive nature to the extreme: "As a catchall term for all sorts of political and other factors, [Fortune] can mean just about anything—or nothing at all" (160).

76. For Scanlon, the tragedies' "endings underline Fortune's disruptive power by depicting misfortune at its most invasive. . . . She deprives the most powerful of people even the simple control of their own bodies. The complete loss of personal autonomy drives home the essential uncontrollability of political power" (*Narrative, Authority, and Power*, 225); ultimately, then, resistance to this narrative, as demonstrated by the Knight's interruption of the Monk, only

nacular writers could assert authorial agency in the face of tradition as medieval hermeneutical practices of scriptural exegesis evolved into *inventio*.[77] In another sense, though, Fortune becomes for the Monk a shorthand that registers the way in which potential inventional emergence is put in service of the tale's reproduction of a singular historical event. As it transfers historical and inventional agency to Fortune, the *Monk's Tale* reassigns agency not to an authorial figure, but to the very process of invention itself.

A similar pattern holds for the "modern instances" of the *Monk's Tale*, the tragic narratives of historical people drawn not from "olde bokes" but from recent cultural memory.[78] The modern instances appear to remove any mention of inventional potential whatsoever, as if the change in temporality emphasizes the historical veracity of their accounts. The exception is the last of the group, the tragedy of Hugelyn, which deploys a pathos reminiscent of the *Prioress's Tale*, relating the deaths of Hugelyn's "litel children thre," the eldest of whom "scarsly fyf yeer was of age" (2411–12).[79] The most openly pathetic of the tragedies, Hugelyn's tale makes it a point to emphasize that its intensification of emotional experience results in the halting of further invention. Not only does the story cause the Knight to stop the *Monk's Tale* with a cry of "Hoo!" (2767), but, as Winthrop Wetherbee notes, the pathos generated by the innocent selflessness of Hugelyn's starving children is immediately directed back to Hugelyn himself, "substitut[ing] maudlin self-pity for the emotional void so starkly depicted in Dante's version, and . . . remind[ing] us of the self-indulgence that is an ever-present danger for those who practice the art of Gothic pathos."[80] What Wetherbee reads as a critique of pathos may also be seen as the result of the Monk's centralization of the moment of tragic transition: even the potential for affective emergence is preemptively arced backward toward the singularity of the tragic event itself. A similar arc conditions the poetic source for the tragedy: "the grete poete of Ytaille / That highte Dant" (2460–61). The Monk's concluding reference emphasizes that Dante has not only told the story of Hugelyn but told it "Fro point to point," and that interested readers will find that in "nat o word wol he faille" (2462). Daniel Pinti reads the Monk's totalizing reference to Dante ironically, arguing that the sprawling Trecento

---

illustrates further the "instability" that "defines human history. . . . The Knight's resistance itself is a characteristic instance of that instability, for it is nothing less than the resistance of political power to textual authority" (226).

77. Copeland, *Rhetoric, Hermeneutics, and Translation*; see also my discussion in the Introduction.

78. Sylvia Federico, "Chaucer and the Matter of Spain," *Chaucer Review* 45 (2011): 300. Wallace argues that the modern instances are "the only narratives that can hope for independent, extratextual verification" (307).

79. Helen Cooper, "Four Last Things," 51; see also Boitani, "*Monk's Tale*," 63.

80. Wetherbee, 171.

commentaries, "which along with Dante's poem itself together constituted the *Comedy* of fourteenth-century literary history, are the surest indication that even Dante could not narrate *everything*."[81] While the reference to Dante could, as Pinti suggests, offer readers interpretive alternatives in terms of both historical understanding and poetic invention, the narrative structure of the *Monk's Tale* actually locks out any such possibility. Through its short narrative, the Monk's version of the Hugelyn story, which is also the culminating tragedy of his tale, presents itself as the chronicle source of Dante's poem—the "trewe and olde" version of what occurred in the case of Ugolino of Pisa, and the text from which the "grete poete of Ytaille" invents his own wordier version that does not fail to convey a single detail as it invents on the event.[82]

The *Monk's Tale* thus directs the phenomenological potential of moments of tragic transition toward capture and collapse, evacuating them of any sense of emergence or becoming.[83] Furthermore, the tragedies narrate a repetitive fiction in which poetic invention impinges on historical reality, postulating the historical event of tragic transition itself to be the result of poetic invention; as such, they satirically engage the kind of affective chronicle that Gower imagines in the *Confessio*. The image of the Monk himself as the corporeal nexus of these narrative patterns compounds the satire of this inventional expression. In particular, the Host's rhetorical construction of the Monk, when considered alongside the cumulative effect of his tragedies, goes so far as to envision in the Monk a satirical version of Gower's iconic Statue of Time, the figure which, as it pervades Gower's English and Latin poetry, represents a paradoxically stable image of temporal instability.

"MYGHTY" MEN AND THE MONSTER OF TIME

While readers who link the tragedies to their narrator have often noted how the Monk himself appears to embody or enact metaphorical versions of the

---

81. Pinti, *Comedy of the Monk's Tale*, 290; emphasis in original. Boitani carefully catalogues the differences between Dante's and Chaucer's versions of the story ("*Monk's Tale*," 55–64).

82. Pinti identifies a similar relationship in terms of the commentary tradition surrounding the *Commedia*, arguing that "Chaucer's version of the Ugolino story assumes the role of 'commentary' which asks to be glossed by 'authoritative' poetry, creating a text that appropriates Dante as both authoritative poet *and* authoritative commentator for an English text" (*Comedy of the Monk's Tale*, 289); Pinti relates his reading to Copeland's argument about commentary and invention. Though arguing that the Monk recognizes the authority of Dante's version over his own, Boitani notes that the Monk's term for Dante's activity, "devises," implies invention in particular: "Dante invents a tragic fiction, Chaucer reads it" (*Tragic and the Sublime*, 55).

83. Scanlon succinctly puts it in historical terms: "The fall becomes the normative form of change" in the Monk's understanding of history (*Narrative, Authority, and Power*, 223).

tragic falls he narrates, falling short, for example, of the monastic life to which he has sworn himself or of the poetics and style with which he intends to move his audience,[84] it is an active process of reading by the Host that creates the persona of the Monk. The Host imagines a name for him: "lord daun John, / Or daun Thomas, or elles daun Albon" (1929–30). He guesses at his station in the monastery: "Upon my feith, thou art som officer, / Som worthy sexteyn, or som celerer . . . Thou art a maister whan thou art at hoom" (1935–38). And he exaggerates the apparent conflict between the Monk's virile appearance and his devotional vocation: "I pray to God, yeve hym confusion / That first thee broghte unto religioun! / Thou woldest han been a tredefowel aright" (1943–45). As he glosses the Monk's body and attire, the Host invents the Monk via a kind of Ciceronian *notatio* that, embedded in the fictional frame of the Canterbury pilgrimage, appears to take place in real life, in real time. His rhetorical "fantasies," as David Wallace refers to them,[85] in fact graft onto the Monk a Ciceronian hierarchy of narrative classification that builds up the Monk by alluding first to the lowest or most fictional form of narrative, *fabula,* and finally to the highest and "truest" form, *historia,* the category that includes the Monk's own genre of choice.[86] The names that the Host postulates demonstrate this process: first, "Daun John," the name of the lecherous monk from the *Shipman's Tale*'s fabliau from the beginning of the fragment; next, "Daun Thomas," a name that invokes Thomas à Becket but also St. Thomas the Apostle, whose reputation as the doubting apostle conjures the fictional-but-plausible narratives of *argumentum,* the second classification of Ciceronian narrative; and finally, "Daun Albon," a name that resonates historically as much as ecclesiastically or spiritually: Saint Alban, martyred

---

84. Wallace, for example, argues that "the narratives he tells . . . point to the logic of his own fall as a narrator" (312), and the tale itself "falls, or moves uncertainly, between its attempt to develop and sustain an elevated 'heigh style' that approximates humanist Latin and the pull of a narrative vernacular" (313); Scott Norsworthy argues that the Ellesmere order essentially narrates the Monk's descent into Hell ("Hard Lords and Bad Food-Service in the Monk's Tale," *JEGP* 100 [2001]: 326). For additional examples of the Monk's failings, see R. E. Kaske, "The Knight's Interruption of the *Monk's Tale*," *ELH* 24 (1957): 249–68; David E. Berndt, "Monastic *Acedia* and Chaucer's Characterization of Daun Piers," *Studies in Philology* 68 (1971): 435–50; Robert B. White Jr., "Chaucer's Daun Piers and the Rule of St. Benedict: The Failure of an Ideal," *JEGP* 70 (1971): 13–30; Olsson, "Grammar, Manhood, and Tears"; Douglas J. Wurtele, "Chaucer's Monk: An Errant Exegete," *Journal of Literature and Theology* 1 (1987): 191–209; and Yoshiko Kobayashi, "Chivalry and History in the 'Monk's Tale,'" *Poetica* 55 (2001): 83–104. Paul E. Beichner, "Daun Piers, Monk and Business Administrator," *Speculum* 34 (1959): 611–19, offers a more complimentary reading of the Monk.

85. Wallace, 309.

86. Cicero classifies these three types of narratives in the *De inventione,* 1.27, pp. 54–55 in the Hubbell edition.

during the tumultuous conversion period of English history, functions as a kind of patron saint of England, a function institutionalized in his namesake, St. Albans, north of London.[87] In true tragic fashion, the Host brings this rhetorical construction crashing right back down into the realm of *fabula*, first by imagining for the Monk the sexual enactment of an almost overpowering masculine virility, and making, as Peter Godman puts it, "bawdily obvious what is ambiguous and double-edged in the description of the Monk in the General Prologue,"[88] before finally apologizing for his suggestion, calling it nothing more than a "game" (1964). His game articulates a tragic narrative trajectory in explicitly inventional terms—from *fabula* to *historia* and back to *fabula* again—and focuses it in the singular person of the Monk himself. In this way, the Host's inventional teasing reflects the individualized focus of the Monk's tragedies that makes each individual protagonist the site at which historical narrative develops. Each individual mighty man or woman becomes a single anthropomorphic icon of the only "trewe" narrative possible: the fall from prosperity to wretchedness. The Host's assessment of the Monk likewise characterizes his "myghty" masculinity in terms of chronological corrosion (1951), noting not only that "Religioun hath take up" all the truly manly men (1954), leaving only "shrympes" among the laypeople (1955), but also that the fact that "Of fieble trees ther comen wrecched ympes," and "This maketh that oure heires been so sklendre / And feble that they may nat wel engendre" (1956–58).[89] As a figure to be seen and glossed, the Monk, in the Host's view, indicates very clearly the corrosion of temporal belatedness that characterizes his own condition, an impression his tragedies narratively reinforce.

Indeed, the Host, Harry Bailey, sees in the monk a chronicle image of historical decline. He sees, in a joking, exaggeratedly satirical way, a living, breathing version of Gower's Statue of Time, the anthropomorphic figure that appears before the dreaming Nebuchadnezzar and that Gower includes in

---

87. See, for example, the narrative in Bede's *Historia Ecclesiastica*, 1.7. St. Albans is also the residence of another monastic Thomas, Thomas of Walsingham, who was writing his own chronicle, itself a continuation of Higden's *Polychronicon*, at the very moment that Chaucer's fictional pilgrims rode toward Canterbury. See Neuse for a discussion of monks as producers of historiography in relation to the *Monk's Tale* (142–43).

88. Godman, 279. Godman argues that the Monk tells his entire tale in order to "deflate" the Host (281). Michael D. Sharp argues that "the Host sees the Monk in part through the lens of the medieval fabliau tradition" ("Reading Chaucer's 'Manly Man': The Trouble with Masculinity in the *Monk's Prologue* and *Tale*," in *Masculinities in Chaucer: Approaches to Maleness in the* Canterbury Tales *and* Troilus and Criseyde, ed. Peter G. Beidler [Cambridge: D. S. Brewer, 1998], 175). The Host finally settles on the name "Daun Piers" for the Monk only after the tale is interrupted by the Knight (2792), but this name also echoes the exclamation "Peter!" of the merchant of the fabliau of the *Shipman's Tale* (214).

89. See Sharp.

both the *Confessio* and the *Vox Clamantis* as a symbol that merges the corrosive decline of temporal progression with the microcosmic form of a human being whose choices affect that progression. The Statue symbolically depicts world history in the form of an embodied chronology of metals of decreasing value, from a head of gold to feet of an unstable and potentially self-destructive mixture of steel and clay, and, in the *Confessio*, it stands ever on the verge of obliteration by a giant boulder, presumably representing apocalypse. The Statue fuses the macrocosmic whole of human history with a microcosmic human form, presenting an image of a "myghty man" that at once embodies and displays the movement of an inevitable and impending historical fall (1951).[90] In the same way, the persona of the Monk anthropomorphizes the corrosive inventional and historical trajectory of his tragedies. Like Gower's Statue of Time, the Monk is created on the one hand by his own narratives, representing along with the metals on the Statue a singular historical process that cannot be countered or diverted. On the other hand, the figure of the Monk is created by the Host's invention, which, like Daniel's own glossing of Nebuchadnezzar's dream in the *Confessio*'s version of the story, makes the Monk into a figure representing a process in which movement and emergence are unremittingly collapsed back into an inescapable trajectory. Like the Statue of Time, the Monk is an icon of movement and potential that, somehow, does not move.

The central difference, of course, between these two "myghty" men is that while Gower's Statue stands outside of time and is representative of it, the Monk stands firmly planted within time, as an element of a particular late-fourteenth-century English moment in which the necessary duality of someone like an *outridere* Monk could become a sign that calls into question anagogic cosmic meaning. The Monk becomes a living, breathing, but ultimately nonallegorical example of what the Statue of Time might "actually" have looked like, had it existed in—instead of as—history. He thus satirizes iconically the notion of chronicles' impingement into social reality that Gower imagines in the *Confessio*. Again, my final claim here is not that the Monk represents John Gower. Furthermore, in likening the Monk to the Statue of Time, rather than to Gower himself, I do not wish simply to characterize the Monk's tragedies as a misreading of history and ascribe that misreading to a

---

90. See Peck, "John Gower and the Book of Daniel"; and Arner, who reads the statue in the context of the Rising of 1381 to argue that it "becomes a nexus of contradictory ideologies about historical processes," presenting history "both as a teleological progression into ruin and as a homogeneous, static mass" (74). Dean notes in passing that in the Statue's figuration, "the driving forces of change seem to be large and impersonal, as in Chaucer's Monk's Tale" (258); McAlpine briefly mentions Gower to emphasize the Monk's worldly focus (102).

character fault in the Monk himself. Rather, my point has been to illustrate how the relationship between the Host's discursive creation of the Monk and the Monk's tragic inventions satirize in Gower's own terms the *Confessio*'s faith in the culturally transformative potential of invention.

But Fragment VII does not conclude simply with critique. Rather, just as Gower directs his own self-satire in Book 5 of the *Confessio* toward an imagined capacity of poetry to affect the world, Chaucer makes the stultifying satire of the Prioress's and Monk's tales part of a larger exploration of poetry's productive potential and situates it within the most explicitly self-referential and experimental fragment of the *Canterbury Tales*. To close this chapter, I want to turn briefly to the *Nun's Priest's Tale*, which, by capping this fragment and functioning as a microcosm for the generic and vocal variety and self-reflexive narrative play that characterizes the fragment as a whole, redirects Chaucer's earlier critiques toward a renewed and productive exploration of affect and invention, and furthermore suggests how this process of redirection itself brings into new focus Chaucer's career-long exploration of affective and inventional movements.

THE "HEIGH YMAGINACIOUN" OF PRODUCTIVE FANTASY IN THE *NUN'S PRIEST'S TALE*

It is something of a commonplace in modern criticism of the *Nun's Priest's Tale* to locate its meaning at a metatextual level, especially in how the tale adapts, fuses, positions, organizes, and satirizes different voices and literary genres, so it is not surprising that a motional vocabulary tends to characterize this critical work. For Derek Pearsall, for example, the tale's defining characteristic is "elusiveness"; for Larry Scanlon, the tale moves back and forth via complex dialectic, as allegories, satires, and their various referents become discourses in motion, speaking to one another in specific, historically and ideologically situated contexts; for John Finlayson, the tale's "energy" emerges from its "shifts" and the way in which genres and hermeneutic points of view "mix and clash"; and in his stunningly thorough reading of the tale as Chaucer's ultimate *ars poetica*, Peter W. Travis frequently refers to this inter- and metatextual back-and-forth as "crisscrossing."[91] Yet amid this well-demonstrated field of

---

91. Derek Pearsall, ed., *The Nun's Priest's Tale*, vol. 2, pt. 9 of *A Variorum Edition of the Works of Geoffrey Chaucer* (Norman: Oklahoma University Press, 1984), 3; Larry Scanlon, "The Authority of Fable: Allegory and Irony in the *Nun's Priest's Tale*," *Exemplaria* 1 (1989): 43–68; John Finlayson, "Reading Chaucer's *Nun's Priest's Tale*: Mixed Genres and Multi-Layered Worlds of Illusion," *English Studies* 86 (2005): 498, 493, and 506; Peter W. Travis, *Disseminal*

movement and transformation, the tale, like those of the Prioress and Monk, explicitly introduces mechanisms for removing the sensation of precisely that movement: it loads itself up with references to prescriptive and determinant authorities; its protagonist experiences a dream vision that turns out to be a precisely accurate prediction of a future encounter; and the overall plot of the tale itself repeats the commonplace narrative of a chicken encountering a fox so that the central event of the tale comes as no surprise to its readers. Consequently, when the tale narrates episodes of *fyndyng*, it embeds them within this elaborately prescriptive framework, removing from them metadiscourses about affective occurrences and the sense of an "event" of *fyndyng* delivered via a metaphorical narrative of discovery.

For instance, the most detailed of the dream examples that Chauntecleer cites for Pertelote relates precisely a narrative metaphor for *fyndyng*. In the anecdote, one of two pilgrims who are traveling together has a dream in which his companion comes to him to tell him he has been murdered. After waking up, the pilgrim walks to the place where the dream told him he could expect to find his friend's corpse. He goes "Unto the west gate of the toun, and fond / A dong-carte . . . arrayed in that same wise / As ye han herd the dede man devyse" (3035–38). The tale's language makes this a narrative about invention, about *fyndyng* something, and it uses the familiar narrative trope of relating a literal act of discovery to gesture toward the metatextual act of poetic making. As a singularly framed and narratively concise example of the prophetic truth of dreams, however, Chauntecleer's story of the pilgrim's *fyndyng* distinctly lacks any sensation of the imminence of an event of discovery, emphasizing not a moment of potential emergence but a fully rendered narrative structure. As Travis notes, the predetermined trajectory of this and the other examples that Chauntecleer relates makes them very different from Chaucer's own dream visions, and "the reader is so confident" of their prescribed outcome "that he also finds himself predicting the literary future."[92] The example thus reenacts the structures of foreclosure from the tales of the Prioress and the Monk: narratives that consciously introduce but then actively nullify efforts to represent potential, and that then define their trajectory in the overly wrought terms of a specific, unambiguous, and ultimately unnuanced narrative outcome.

This structural logic extends into Chauntecleer's own narrative, not only in the fact that the dream he had the previous night likewise turns out to be

---

Chaucer: Rereading The Nun's Priest's Tale (Notre Dame, IN: University of Notre Dame Press, 2010), 157 and 249, for two different contexts for this metatextual movement.

92. Travis, 318.

prophetic but also in that his experience of meeting the fox is in fact cast in terms of one of the Monk's chronicles. After Chauntecleer abandons the discussion of discursive authorities and has "fethered" and "trad" Pertelote and started strutting through the yard (3177–78), the impending realization that "For evere the latter ende of joye is wo" made manifest in the sudden discovery of the fox is an event that, "if a rhetor koude faire endite, / He in a cronycle saufly myghte it write" (3205–8). This formulation of the story of Chauntecleer as the rhetorically moving chronicle of a fall of course directly invokes the *Monk's Tale*—even punning on "myghte" and "myghty."[93] By extension, the tale also makes the social reality on which this Gowerian type of chronicle invention impinges the "reality" of an ordinary farmyard. Taken as a whole, then, these stunted narratives of *fyndyng* and their deployment as part of the tale's own narrative process remove more nebulous sensations of emergence while still preserving the framework of imminent discovery, exactly as both the Prioress's and Monk's tales had. This trajectory is compounded by the careful and explicit layering of other controlling discourses, including not only Chauntecleer's position as the avian protagonist of the conventional chicken-and-fox story but also the brief and satirical allusions to Augustine's and Bradwardine's ideas about causality and the Nun's Priest's misogynistic jab. If the tale introduces but never settles on any single hermeneutical model for making meaning out of narrative—as the narrator's own immediate dismissal of these (and all of the tale's) authorities and cultural discourses insinuates—then its multiple and shifting vantage points nevertheless share a general trajectory of collapse.

But a moment of sudden affective occurrence does arrive when Chauntecleer realizes that there is there is something potentially dangerous lying in wait for him among the cabbages. When his eyes happen upon the fox, "Nothyng ne liste hym thanne for to crowe, / But cride anon, 'Cok! Cok!' and up he sterte / As man that was affrayed in his herte" (3276–78). Chauntecleer experiences this fear "natureelly" (3279)—that is, as an animal would as a condition of its *kynde,* and the animal parallel allows Chaucer to circumscribe human ratiocination in describing what seems to be a nonrational affective occurrence that is registered only physiologically. Chauntecleer, as L. A. J. R. Houwen shows, reacts in complete accordance with medieval understandings of the instinctive capacities of the "sensitive soul" of animals (in Aquinas's terms), a faculty defined, as Houwen puts it, by the "subtle

---

93. Finlayson goes so far as to argue that the entire tale is a response in particular to the *Monk's Tale* that results "almost" in the creation of "a new genre, the comedy of Fortune, to refute the Monk's tragedy of Fortune" ("Reading Chaucer's *Nun's Priest's Tale,*" 508).

interaction between the apprehensive and motive parts of the sensitive soul" that allows animals to discern immediately the intentions of an object (or a fox) and then to react affectively to them.[94] Chauntecleer utters his "Cok! Cok!", as Travis notes, "at precisely the same instant that his estimative powers apprehend the fox."[95] The simile that completes the sentence, however, marks the scene as a representational fantasy: the phrase "As a man that was affrayed in his herte" exposes before the entire moment is even fully narrated the artificiality of Chauntecleer's animal experience. This is, finally, a narrative account in which a human imagines what a pre-conscious affective experience might look like, a "heigh ymaginacioun" to be sure (3217), and one that occurs within the blurred and shifting generic space of an animal fable in which the nonhuman characters think and act like humans as much as animals.

Indeed, the vacillation between being a chicken and being a chicken-as-human (or human-as-chicken)—what Lesley Kordecki deftly describes as the tale's "species confusion," resulting in what Finlayson calls "the comedy of displacement"[96]—links the fantasy of discursively representing pre-rational affective emergence to representing the movements of poetic invention. Because conceptualizing the movement in the tale between animal and human souls is facilitated by the tale's own pervasive emphasis on the movement between voices, genres, registers, and authorities, examining the initial, pre-conscious movements of affective emergence becomes inseparable from examining the movements registered in the tale as shifts between literary types. Here, then, is where the *Nun's Priest's Tale* preserves the possibility for imagining potential even among the overly scripted discursive fields in which it grounds its satire. The gesture toward an unstructured event of affective emergence—Chauntecleer's reaction to seeing the fox—manifests at the moment in which metafictional and generic play folds into *natureel* affective occurrences registered physiologically. Chauntecleer's autonomic jolt occurs within a multilayered intertextual field, and its depiction conveys a sensation of surprise that

---

94. L. A. J. R. Houwen, "Fear and Instinct in Chaucer's *Nun's Priest's Tale*," in *Fear and Its Representations in the Middle Ages and Renaissance*, ed. Anne Scott and Cynthia Kosso, Arizona Studies in the Middle Ages and the Renaissance 6 (Turnhout: Brepols, 2002), 26. Houwen also notes that the brief commentary on Chauntecleer's "natureel" reaction to the fox is in fact one of Chaucer's additions to his source in the *Roman de Renart* story (20n4).

95. Travis, 328. See 318–25 for Travis's reading of the encounter in terms of medieval faculty psychology, which Travis directs toward the tale's efforts to deconstruct the ways in which language means.

96. Kordecki, 110; Finlayson, "Reading Chaucer's *Nun's Priest's Tale*," 502. As Kordecki continues, "Through beast literature, we both *are* animals and *are* dominant over animals, but by constructing the story's animal as a dreaming subject, the text deconstructs along genre lines" (120; emphasis in original).

seems somehow authentic because it is expressed at once physically and metatextually. The result is not only the deconstruction of the pervasive discourses and authorities invoked in the tale but also the sudden "feeling" of what that sort of realization might involve physiologically. This is a complex gesture of displacement: the narrative posits a pre-conscious, nonrational affective occurrence through self-conscious generic shifts that themselves occur amid, and are constructed by, a crowded field of intertexts. *The Nun's Priest's Tale* thus uses the strategies of satire from the Prioress's and Monk's tales to regenerate a sensation of impending emergence, one that locates both affective and inventional movements as aspects of a single emergent process, even amid the very narrative discourses that would seem to actively foreclose such gestures.

What follows in the tale is an outpouring of rhetorical eloquence deployed to produce "feelynge" (3293) in auditors, including Chauntecleer's own music and each animal's appeals to the other's vanity. Subsequent physiological descriptions are likewise made an aspect of the tale's rhetorical machinations, as the way in which Chauntecleer prepares to sing is presented not in terms of the sudden manifestations of affective phenomena but as the conscious movements and positioning of body parts for the premeditated and routine generation of song. These rhetorical and bodily elaborations, moreover, focus on an emphatically masculinist need to outdo the father, to prove oneself as a maker of music who operates independently of authority while at the same time becoming the new authority. As such, the discourses that spring forth when the moment of affective and inventional emergence collapses are familiar conceptualizations of poetic invention in terms of authorial politics registered as masculinist usurpation.

The climax of this satirical outpouring of eloquent augmentation arrives in the tale's redeployment of Geoffrey of Vinsauf's lament for the death of Richard I to describe Chauntecleer's sudden downfall. Travis views Chaucer's satirical use of the *Poetria Nova* here as a declaration of self-liberation that also exposes the masculinist assertions that underwrite Geoffrey's *ars poetica* (and the twelfth- and thirteenth-century *artes poetriae* more generally) through the hypermasculine Chauntecleer (and Nun's Priest), and as what he sees to be Chaucer's own "pushing back against the pressure to imitate one's forebears."[97]

---

97. Travis, 90. See Chapter 1, in which Travis argues that "Fragment VII's metapoetic quest for a fully realized supreme fiction" manifested in the *Nun's Priest's Tale* is one "complemented, recoded, and parodied by Harry Bailey's quest throughout this fragment for the supremely masculine male" (30); Chaucer, Travis argues, does not "destroy these medieval masculinist aesthetic ideals" but rather "has managed to diagnose and decenter the phallocentric presuppositions of a complex European aesthetic tradition" (44). Kordecki extends the tale's self-reflexive masculinist framework beyond authorial politics to epistemology more broadly, arguing that Chauntecleer "personifies masculinized and masculinist Chaucerian subjectivity" (106) and that

The Nun's Priest's Tale is for Travis Chaucer's most complex and nuanced *ars poetica,* but also one that maps a poetics by comically undermining previous authoritative *artes poetriae*. As Camargo shows, when Chaucer here comically invokes the death of Richard I, his rendering of the event conjures it not as "an independent historical artifact" but as a chronicle account firmly embedded in Geoffrey's *ars poetica*.[98] Chaucer's use of Geoffrey explicitly emphasizes the aftereffects of inventional movement, the carefully crafted motions of a practiced rhetorical poet rather than the unstructured, pre-inventional movements of a would-be poet's "impetuous hand." As it makes an *ars poetica* one of its intertexts, the *Nun's Priest's Tale* folds the productive potential of inventional emergence—what was gestured toward in the *House of Fame* and *Legend,* for example—into the scripted appeals of rhetorical eloquence. Geoffrey's Ricardian apostrophe is itself a self-conscious exaggeration for the purpose of illustrating a rhetorical technique,[99] and Chaucer's additional layer of satirical redeployment furthermore frames this recently discovered (by Chaucer, at least) *ars poetica* as a sophisticated guide for generating rhetorical and stylistic effects rather than exploring inventional and affective origins. The tale finally narrates the way in which a formal treatise on making poetry itself emerges as an aftereffect, a byproduct, it turns out, of whatever affective and inventional movements underwrite Chauntecleer's "Cok! Cok!"[100]

As this cascade of satirized prescriptive poetics becomes the "noyse" of the fox chase (3493), the *Nun's Priest Tale* concludes with one final allusive act that carefully situates a second, wholly unexpected affective occurrence within a framework of chronicle invention. Chaucer's reference at the end of the tale to the Rising of 1381—the farmyard din so loud that "Certes, he Jakke Straw and his meynee / Ne made nevere shoutes half so shrille / Whan that they wolden

---

the *Canterbury Tales* as a whole depicts a project in which the "censorship of nonhumans [is] clearly shadowed by the censorship of women" (104). Scanlon also sees the tale as appropriative, satirizing ecclesiastical discourse via the vernacular, asserting literary and cultural authority via ironic critique, an authority that Scanlon likewise notes is expressed in gendered terms via the "male and royal" Chauntecleer ("Authority of Fable," 56), since "sexual dominance was the *sine qua non* of noble power in the Middle Ages" (57).

98. Camargo, 202.

99. Travis notes that Geoffrey's apostrophe "is a knowing and serious self-parody" (86), which Chaucer redeploys to parody "the very act of literary imitation itself" (89).

100. Travis argues that something similar happens through the tale's use of sound, specifically that the noise of the tale is meant to trigger exactly this sort of higher-level, self-reflexive analysis: it "is meant ultimately not to muffle thinking but to heighten our awareness of what goes on when we think *about* language, and when we think *in* language about language and thought," in particular to make readers think "independently and energetically about . . . how the sounds and sense of words are processed and created in the mind" (250–51; emphasis in original).

any Flemyng kille" (3394–96)—likewise provides one last example of how discourses of critique can be turned toward productive invention. The fleeting allusion to so local and recent an event smashes together two strikingly different affects for readers: the joy of the comic scene of the beast fable and the fear caused by the sudden remembrance of a traumatic event—traumatic not simply because of its violence but also, from the conservative perspectives of both Chaucer and Gower, each of whom apparently witnessed it, because of its existential threat to traditional social hierarchies.[101] Moreover, this jarring affective misalignment is implicitly grounded in Gower's own meditation on poetic invention in Book 1 of the *Vox Clamantis*. Steven Justice has shown how the *Nun's Priest's Tale* draws on specific language from the *Vox*, but rather than savagely criticize Gower and his poem as Justice suggests,[102] Chaucer's tale makes far more productive use of this allusion, doubling it to refer at once to the Rising and to Gower's poem. As I argued in the introduction, Gower's *Vox* dramatizes metapoetic discourse emerging from the dreaming narrator's angst-ridden stasis in the *media via* of his own chronicle account of the events of the Rising. Chaucer's invocation of those events here creates a sensation of affective dissonance—pairing joy with terror—and it links that sensation to Gower's own earlier inventional representation. The result is not simply satire or critique, but an unexpected jolt—at once affective and doubly metatextual—that compels readers to think about the larger cultural discourses at play around the events of the Rising, even before they realize why they have done so. Furthermore, that jolt prompts them to think simultaneously about the relationship of those discourses to how both the resulting emotions and poetry come into being.[103] Chaucer delivers this jolt by explicitly devaluing the voices of the lower classes involved in the Rising, a perspective he shares with Gower, but at the same time he revalues the ability of poetry to generate moments of sudden and unexpected compulsions to examine

---

101. Justice argues that the memory of the Rising is written through much of the geography of the *Canterbury Tales* itself but that Chaucer's aim is to ensure that "the memory of the rising would not be the grim companion of their travel" (230). The one reference to the Rising "emerges in esoteric play" and "in the minutely textual encoding of a coterie joke" (230–31). Travis, however, notes the stunning power the reference may have had: "It is a subtle piece of professional violence—as if a film editor had neatly sliced out a few frames of the My Lai episode of the movie *Platoon* and spliced them into the middle of a Wile E. Coyote and Road Runner chase scene" (260).

102. Justice, 208–18.

103. Travis argues that Chaucer's goal here is the constant consideration of the Rising itself: Chaucer places his only reference to the Rising amid the noisiest part of the poem, "to fine-tune the reader's powers of audition so that the Peasants' Revolt, an historical event dangerous to recount in any other way than by hegemonic condemnation, serves as the subject of sustained critical interpretation" (264).

discourses of cultural power. The sensation of something new emerging that is triggered by this carefully constructed narrative moment depends for its success on an allusion not only to the Rising but also to Gower's earlier metapoetic meditation. In this way, the satirical sidestepping that characterizes the tale turns critique into a moment suddenly filled with metapoetic allusion and potential.

Chaucer's final formal exploration of his own poetics in the *Nun's Priest's Tale* thus becomes a clear example of what we have come to understand to be "Chaucerian": any gestures it makes are produced ironically, satirically, and indirectly, and its generation of new poetic utterance comes from innovative compilation, translation, and transformation.[104] What I want to emphasize here, however, is how the tale focuses these notions in particular on a conspicuously artificial narrative account of something suddenly emerging: the fantasy of imagining an affective occurrence happening in a chicken. Chauntecleer's affective *fyndyng*, the tale suggests, is the structural analogue of any poet's process of *fyndyng*. It is finally also deeply satirical: poets invent in the same way chickens feel. Itself also a commentary on a career-long exploration of the relationship between affect and invention, the *Nun's Priest's Tale* effectively throws into relief Chaucer's own earlier efforts by presenting them satirically, prompting a final, wholesale gesture of displacement that is paralleled, though in a very different way, by the Retraction. The *Nun's Priest's Tale* thus works in concert with the other tales of Fragment VII, especially the tales of the Prioress and the Monk, to demonstrate, as Gower does in Book 5 of the *Confessio*, how self-conscious satire is an essential part of conceptualizing affective and inventional movements. Moreover, this broader self-satire—spanning Fragment VII and referring more nebulously to both Chaucer's and Gower's variegated explorations of affect's relationship to invention over the course of many years—itself becomes a kind of emergent phenomenon, multivalent and nonlocalized, that attempts to enact the poetics it explores.

---

104. As Scanlon puts it in his reading of the tale, for example, "Chaucerian authority is critical yet profoundly conservative, ironically self-conscious yet deferential to the status quo. It is precisely his examination of previous authority which enables him to appropriate it" ("Authority of Fable," 64).

CONCLUSION

FROM ASHES ANCIENT COME

Affective Intertextuality in Chaucer, Gower, and Shakespeare

THROUGHOUT THIS BOOK I have worked to show how Chaucer and Gower conceptualize affect and poetic invention in terms of each other: specifically, how the movements and energies that precede the formal, prescriptive actions of poetic composition parallel similar movements, shifts, and sensations of potential that precede the collapse of affect into emotion. This examination has identified a variety of approaches in the work of both poets: aligning descriptions of affective occurrences with narratives that metaphorically relate moments of discovery and invention; manipulating narrative and generic forms to metatextually simulate affective movements as a way of gesturing indirectly toward pre-conscious and formal activities of invention; and engaging in self-satire as an important component of a larger metapoetic examination that redirects critique toward further invention. I have argued that a common goal of these varied approaches is to generate moments that cause readers suddenly to want to reexamine or ask questions about the ways in which pervasive cultural discourses shape reality, social structures, and individual experience.

I have also argued that Chaucer's and Gower's treatment of the affect of invention is ultimately derived from a commonly received tradition of thinking about poetic invention that can be traced back to elements of classical rhetoric, through medieval *artes poetriae,* to commonplaces of Middle English narratives of *fyndyng* that receive their fullest self-reflexive vernacular and secular expression in the poetic productions of the late fourteenth century. The poetry of Chaucer and Gower joins in and continues to shape an expanded definition of poetic invention itself, understanding *fyndyng* as a metapoetic category that includes not only the relegation of inventional "brainstorming" to the strictures of a pre-determined *archetypus*, the formal rhetorical exercises of invention in terms of description or augmentation, and variously expressed manifestations of authorial politics, but also the energies and movements that occur before and alongside these more formal activities. As it tries to "get behind" the formal structures of generating poetry, the work of Chaucer and Gower also tries to get behind the discursive logic that generates structures of culture. Both poets locate the productively transformative potential of poetry—its ability to somehow affect people and the historical points in which they live—in moments of inventional emergence.

While their explorations of affect and invention have much in common, Chaucer and Gower of course differ in their approaches as well. Chaucer's explorations manifest more ambiguously in carefully crafted moments of rupture and displacement, working to trigger moments in which affective responses appear to be misaligned with the expectations of culturally determined emotional scripts—a kind of realization for which *Parlement*'s transition from an inventional "certeyn thyng" to "som thyng" provides a shorthand. Chaucer imagines an alignment of affective and inventional movements most fully by distilling them to an individualized point of focus and locating the expression of inventional emergence more closely to individuated affective experience. Gower takes a similar approach, but he also works to redirect an individuated focus toward much larger, macrocosmic structures—what he refers to in the *Confessio* as "a thing . . . so strange"—going so far as to imagine how generic and narrative forms of poetry might impinge upon social structures outside a poem. He accomplishes this first metaphorically by writing narratives in which macrocosmic transformations take place as the direct result of affective and inventional transformations on a smaller scale, and second by imagining chronicles as a genre authoritatively capable of affecting the social worlds they purport to describe.

The resulting image of the literary relationship between Chaucer and Gower that emerges from this study is as necessarily fleeting and tenuous as these writers' gestures toward the affect of invention itself. It includes critical viewpoints that see Chaucer and Gower as careful and serious readers of each other's work, recognizing both interpretive nuance and implications of modes of reading, viewpoints that are typically offered in analyses of the more immediately recognizable moments of literary engagement that punctuate the poets' work, including, for instance, the *Man of Law's Introduction* and *Tale*, and the likelihood that the *Confessio* and the *Legend of Good Women* initially emerged from a common literary impetus, perhaps even a royal commission.[1] The image of literary engagement that this study does not support is one that is centrally defined by reaction and opposition, that imagines parts of Chaucer's opus as organized as a systematic objection to Gower's (or vice versa), tracing a chronology of various rewritings and abandonments of particular poetic projects, and that too often relies for its efficacy on reinscriptions of an overtly "moral Gower."[2] My argument throughout this book suggests that both writers locate in the exploration and articulation of an expanded view of poetic invention the productively transformative potential for poetry. It also attempts to demonstrate the possibility of different forms of political and cultural engagement attempted by Chaucer's and Gower's poetry, forms that not only involve direct political commentary but also offer more speculative, imaginative, and admittedly ambiguous forms of engagement. Chaucer and Gower install moments of affective and inventional resonance into their

---

1. For a recent argument for the common impetus for the *Confessio* and the *Legend*, see Joyce Coleman, "'A bok for king Richardes sake': Royal Patronage, the *Confessio*, and the *Legend of Good Women*," in Yeager, *On John Gower*, 104–23. John H. Fisher dispels the eighteenth-century idea of a "quarrel" between Gower and Chaucer and proposes, probably correctly, a long and serious literary relationship between the two poets. He traces what seem to him to be indirect allusions to Gower throughout Chaucer's entire poetic career (*John Gower: Moral Philosopher and Friend of Chaucer* [New York: New York University Press, 1964], 204–302). R. F. Yeager ("'O Moral Gower': Chaucer's Dedication of Troilus and Criseyde," *Chaucer Review* 19 [1984]: 87–99), productively redefines the "moral" of Chaucer's "moral Gower" dedication to refer to Gower's status as an authoritative and prolific trilingual poet at the time when Chaucer had completed the *Troilus*. Elizabeth Allen convincingly argues that Chaucer's jab at Gower in the introduction to the *Man of Law's Tale* is actually a jab at misreadings of both Gower's and his own texts: Gower is as morally complex as Chaucer, and the authorial engagements both in the *Man of Law's Introduction* and at the end of *Troilus and Criseyde* reveal moments of intersection in a long and complex poetic relationship ("Chaucer Answers Gower: Constance and the Trouble with Reading," *ELH* 64 [1997]: 627–55). Carolyn Dinshaw ("Rivalry, Rape, and Manhood: Gower and Chaucer," in *Chaucer and Gower: Difference, Mutuality, Exchange*, ed. R. F. Yeager [Victoria: University of Victoria Press, 1991], 130–52, reveals the inherently gendered component both of a possible Chaucer–Gower competition and of scholarly efforts to locate and describe the alleged quarrel between the two poets.

2. For examples of reading Chaucer's and Gower's poetic projects as oppositional, see Robert W. Hanning, "'And countrefete the speche of every man / He koude, whan he sholde telle a tale': Toward a Lapsarian Poetics for *The Canterbury Tales*," *Studies in the Age of Chaucer* 21 (1999): 29–58; B. W. Lindeboom, *Venus' Owne Clerk: Chaucer's Debt to the Confessio Amantis* (Amsterdam and New York: Rodopi, 2007); Andrew Galloway, "Gower's Quarrel with Chaucer, and the Origins of Bourgeois Didacticism in Fourteenth-Century London Poetry," in *Calliope's Classroom: Studies in Didactic Poetry from Antiquity to the Renaissance*, ed. Annette Harder, Alasdair A. MacDonald, and Gerrit J. Reinink (Leuven: Peeters, 2007), 245–67; John M. Bowers, "Rival Poets: Gower's *Confessio* and Chaucer's *Legend of Good Women*," in Dutton, Hines, and Yeager, *John Gower, Trilingual Poet*, 276–87; and Arner, *Chaucer, Gower, and the Vernacular Rising*.

poetry as a way of triggering a dynamic reexamination of the way in which culture and experience get constructed.

Particularly interesting is how Chaucer's and Gower's differing foci in fact become central to what later English writers think of as "the Chaucerian" or "the Gowerian." By way of concluding this study, I wish to look forward some 200 years to a writer whose assimilation and adaptation of Chaucerian and Gowerian materials demonstrate an understanding of these writers' works in the terms I have explored in this book. I'd like to end by speculating about how two works by William Shakespeare draw upon—but also help to perpetuate—Chaucer's and Gower's diverging conceptualizations of the relationship between affect and invention. Shakespeare's short lyric "The Phoenix and Turtle" and his later romance *Pericles, Prince of Tyre* (which most critics agree Shakespeare co-wrote with George Wilkins) respectively invoke Chaucer and Gower, and as they do so they consciously craft an intertextual relationship that is grounded in Chaucer's and Gower's varying approaches to the alignment of affect and invention. My goal in briefly turning to these two early-seventeenth-century texts is threefold. First, I want to demonstrate how these early modern texts register specifically "Chaucerian" and "Gowerian" attitudes toward affect and invention in order to show that the analyses I have offered in this book are in fact those that later writers detect when exploring inventional themes in the works of these medieval writers—in other words, that the affect of invention as I've traced it in Chaucer's and Gower's poetry is in large part what characterized these poets for late Elizabethan and early Jacobean writers. Second, I want to propose that Shakespeare develops a kind of "affective intertextuality" in these works, a paradigm of textual borrowing that parallels affective movement and emergence. Third, I want to suggest how this affective intertextuality provides modern readers with an alternative model for thinking about how early-modern English writers may have engaged late-medieval English poets, a model that is not grounded in authorial politics or periodization alone. In essence, I want to begin to explore here how, when an early-modern writer like Shakespeare invented new material from the work of Chaucer and Gower, he did so in part by recognizing and then perpetuating these medieval poets' own conceptualizations of affect and invention.

INTERTEXTUAL "PERTURBATIONS" IN "THE PHOENIX AND TURTLE"

Shakespeare's lyric poem "The Phoenix and Turtle" describes an avian funeral procession for a phoenix and turtledove who, before the poem begins, have died in a fire of mutual and perfectly reciprocal love. Appearing in Robert Chester's 1601 poem collection *Love's Martyr*, "Phoenix" is noteworthy in part because its structure is so unlike the rest of Shakespeare's work: it consists of thirteen quatrains of rhymed iambic tetrameter and a concluding *"Threnos"* of five iambic-tetrameter tercets. Two commonplaces characterize criticism of the poem: declarations of the lyric's stunning affective power, and a general acknowledgment that one of its sources is Chaucer's *Parlement of Foules*. Yet few critics focus on this affective register directly, studying what Lynn Enterline calls "the emotional work" of the poem, and a similar lack of critical attention characterizes the treatment of Chaucer's influence on "Phoenix."[3] In an important exception to this trend, Patrick Cheney argues that the "dearth of commentary" on the poem's Chaucerian intertext is "unfortunate,"[4] and he frames the relationship in terms of authorial politics, asserting that Shakespeare ultimately draws on Chaucer in the poem "almost certainly to represent the art of Spenser,"[5] using Chaucer's authorial "self-effacement" as

---

3. Lynn Enterline, "'The Phoenix and the Turtle,' Renaissance Elegies, and the Language of Grief," in *Early Modern English Poetry: A Critical Companion*, ed. Patrick Cheney, Andrew Hadfield, and Garrett A. Sullivan Jr. (Oxford: Oxford University Press, 2007), 148. Enterline argues that "Phoenix" follows early-modern emotion scripts that connect classical elegy with mourning and stand in for the banished Catholic mass for the dead as a means of regulating grief. Representative of general comments on the poem's emotional power, for example, F. T. Prince argues that Shakespeare "compressed all his feeling for pure passion and loyalty in human love" into the poem (F. T. Prince, ed. *The Poems*, 3rd ed. [London: Methuen, 1960], xlvi); Richard C. McCoy argues that the power of the poem's "figures and images" comes from their "capacity . . . to stimulate emotion" ("Love's Martyrs: Shakespeare's 'Phoenix and Turtle' and the Sacrificial Sonnets," in *Religion and Culture in Renaissance England*, ed. Claire McEachern and Debora Shuger [Cambridge: Cambridge University Press, 1997], 204); James P. Bednarz worries that the powerful "emotional souvenir" generated by these figures threatens to impede the poem's promised transcendence (*Shakespeare and the Truth of Love: The Mystery of "The Phoenix and Turtle"* [New York: Palgrave, 2012], 155); and Patrick Cheney concludes that the final "wonder" of the poem is nothing short of its commemoration of "the affective authority of human inwardness" (*Shakespeare, National Poet-Playwright* [Cambridge: Cambridge University Press, 2004], 197). Since Arthur H. R. Fairchild's detailed structural comparison of "Phoenix" and the *Parlement of Foules* over a century ago ("*The Phoenix and Turtle*: A Critical and Historical Interpretation," *Englische Studien* 33 [1904]: 337–84), very few readers have offered any real consideration of Chaucer's influence on the poem beyond the most cursory resemblances: Bednarz's detailed and rewarding study of the poem devotes only a few general references to Chaucer, concluding finally that "the direct importance" of Chaucer "has been exaggerated" (227 n42). For similar dismissals, see, for example, Ronald Bates, "Shakespeare's 'The Phoenix and Turtle,'" *Shakespeare Quarterly* 6 (1955), 19 and 25; and Enterline, 155. Despite Bednarz's claim, critics have on the whole tended to dismiss anything more than a cursory resemblance between the poems.

4. Patrick Cheney, "The Voice of the Author in 'The Phoenix and Turtle,'" in *Shakespeare and the Middle Ages*, ed. Curtis Perry and John Watkins (Oxford: Oxford University Press, 2009), 108.

5. Cheney (*Shakespeare, National Poet-Playwright* 187).

a counterweight to "Spenserian self-crowning" as a means of presenting his own authorial voice.[6] While Cheney convincingly demonstrates the nuance with which "Phoenix" engages Chaucer's poem, I want to suggest that the work of *Parlement* in Shakespeare's lyric extends beyond rewriting, continuing, or appropriating Chaucer in a hierarchical context of authorial careers. "The Phoenix and Turtle" interacts with the affective potential explicitly signaled in *Parlement of Foules*, generating a framework of affective intertextuality that articulates its relationship to this earlier English poem in terms specific to early-modern understandings of affective experience.

"The Phoenix and Turtle" itself signals that it should be read in affective terms. Describing the funeral for the two birds who have burned up together in a "mutuall flame" of love and sacrifice (24),[7] the poem makes the central event of its slight narrative action the effort to conceptualize the birds' absolute commingling. The love of these birds, marked by the affective circulation between them, is perfectly reciprocal:

> So between them Loue did shine,
> That the *Turtle* saw his right,
> Flaming in the *Phœnix* sight;
> Either was the others mine.[8]
> (33–36)

The first critic to read this mutual love—in which the birds are each "two distincts," even though their distinctiveness reveals "Diuision none" between them (26–27)—appears in the poem itself. Reason, the only fully allegorized entity attending the funeral, suddenly finds "it selfe confounded" to see "Diuision grow together" (41–42), and it finally acknowledges its inability to understand rationally what it sees, exclaiming,

---

6. Cheney ("Voice of the Author," 113). Bednarz also (briefly) compares Chaucer's *Parlement* with "The Phoenix and Turtle" in terms of authorial self-presentation, arguing that, unlike Chaucer's narrator in *Parlement*, Shakespeare's authorial voice is not "baffled by his vision" and maintains absolute control over the content of the poem (144). Bednarz takes Shakespeare's level of authorial control to the extreme, essentially equating Shakespeare with the voice of god in Genesis (145).

7. All quotations from "The Phoenix and Turtle" are from Robert Chester, *Loues Martyr: or, Rosalins complaint. Allegorically shadowing the truth of Loue, in the constant Fate of the Phœnix and Turtle* (London, 1601). Line numbers are cited parenthetically in the text.

8. Colin Burrow notes that "mine" can refer to the birds' mutuality as well as "a source of riches for the other" (*The Complete Sonnets and Poems* [Oxford: Oxford University Press, 2002], 375n36).

> "how true a twaine,
> Seemeth this concordant one,
> Loue hath Reason, Reason none,
> If what parts can so remaine."
> (45–48)

The poem explicitly signals the shift in interpretive authority from rational analysis to affective experience. It gives "Loue," an affective agent, the interpretive reins and leaves Reason to lament the loss of its own defining characteristic. In a gesture that shows the poem's analytic agent moving from rational to affective engagement, Reason then turns to poetry, "Whereupon it made this *Threne*," a song of lamentation, to grieve for the "dead Birds" (49, 67).[9]

In seeing the "wonder" that is the birds' indescribable fusion—what James P. Bednarz calls "incorporate selves" in which individual identities "remain *essentially* relational"—Reason witnesses a poetic analogue to an affective occurrence.[10] Like poetry itself, emotion is a retrospective reconstruction of affect, the relics of a necessarily inaccessible initial phenomenon. Reason's experience in "The Phoenix and Turtle," then, imaginatively acknowledges that the effort to understand affect is to transform it into emotion and poetry, to fix as utterance and emotional memory an event characterized by movement, potential, and emergence. Moreover, the affect of "Phoenix" is thoroughly embodied. It is Reason who in the *Threnos* introduces the idealizing vocabulary of "Truth," "Beautie," and the accoutrements of apparent transcendence (64), but the earlier description of the birds' love emphasizes its physical qualities. "Propertie was thus appalled" by their union, for example, not because property as a defining characteristic evaporates but because the same property applies to two different bodies rather than exclusively to one (37). Contributing to the feeling of embodiment is the temporal distance between the birds' past fusion and the poem's present. Richard C. McCoy notes that the birds' "love *was* indeed a wonder . . . but it occurs entirely in the past tense."[11] Moreover, the mutual flame never burned in isolation from the avian bodies it physically, literally immolated. As G. Wilson Knight puts it, in fact, if the phoenix is a "transcendent" animal, it is so "without ceasing to be physical."[12]

---

9. See the explanatory note for "Threnos" in Burrow's edition (376n52.1).

10. Bednarz, 15; emphasis in original. Bednarz argues that the phoenix and turtledove "inhabit the nonrational experience at the heart of both religion and love" (115).

11. McCoy, 195.

12. G. Wilson Knight, *The Mutual Flame: On Shakespeare's* Sonnets *and* The Phoenix and the Turtle (London: Methuen, 1955), 151.

The embodied experience of affect—as distinct from emotion—was itself theorized in the vernacular in early-modern England, and early-modern notions of "the passions" or "affections" emphasize flow and circulation in a way that is often quite distinct from modern, post-Cartesian emotion scripts that emphasize isolated, individual, and self-contained subjects. The passions were, in fact, physical movements among bodily fluids, what Thomas Wright called "perturbations" in his 1601 treatise on *The Passions of the Minde*.[13] Likewise, the movements of these perturbations were also intersubjective, as the important work of Gail Kern Paster has shown: "consciousness in the humoral body," she writes, "might actually function in relation to the analogously constructed universe," and "subjectivity in the humoral body is regularly breached and penetrated by its phenomenological environment."[14] The passions themselves are thus liminal phenomena defined by movement and intersubjectivity. As Wright describes them, they "stand betwext these two extreames" of "internall" and "external" realms, and "border vpon them both."[15] And as Bruce Smith puts it, "the passions 'hear' sensations before reason does. The sensations circulate throughout the body as an aerated fluid on which reason's imprint is always insubstantial."[16]

Shakespeare's poem works to convey this movement of affect, functioning as a kind of affective treatise that investigates its subject by performing the movement itself. It does so only belatedly, however, by using images of stasis and fixity to gesture backwards to impressions of movement and potential. In its effort to gesture toward a representation of affective experience, "Phoenix" offers a paradoxical poetics of fixed movement, and it is in precisely this way that Shakespeare's poem draws on Chaucer's own avian poetry.

---

13. Thomas Wright, *The Passions of the Minde* (London, 1601), 14. Gail Kern Paster, Katherine Rowe, and Mary Floyd-Wilson argue that "early modern psychology only partially shares the priority we place on inwardness, alongside very different conceptions of the emotions as physical, environmental, and external phenomena," and in fact, "early modern Europeans had not yet separated the mind from the changeable body, or the body from the world" (*Reading the Early Modern Passions: Essays in the Cultural History of Emotion* [Philadelphia: University of Pennsylvania Press, 2004, 15–16). For helpful discussions of the similarities and differences between modern cognitive science and early-modern, pre-Cartesian, Galenic materialism, see also Gail Kern Paster, *Humoring the Body: Emotions and the Shakespeare Stage* (Chicago: University of Chicago Press, 2004), 21–22, and Mary Thomas Crane, *Shakespeare's Brain: Reading with Cognitive Theory* (Princeton, NJ: Princeton University Press, 2001), esp. 17–19, 27.

14. Gail Kern Paster, "Melancholy Cats, Lugged Bears, and Early Modern Cosmology: Reading Shakespeare's Psychological Materialism across the Species Barrier," in Paster, Rowe, and Floyd-Wilson, *Reading the Early Modern Passions*, 116).

15. Wright, 12.

16. Bruce Smith, "Hearing Green," in Paster, Rowe, and Floyd-Wilson, *Reading the Early Modern Passions*, 168.

The Parlement of Foules becomes a source for "Phoenix" not simply because it represents an earlier example of an English poem about a congregation of birds, but moreover because of how *Parlement* also represents moments of paradoxically fixed movement as a way of indicating the emerging potential that characterizes both affective experience and the pre-conscious work of poetic invention. As I argued in the Introduction, *Parlement* figures this paradox most vividly in its anxious narrator, who finds himself immobile as the result of being pulled equally in opposite directions by two powerful magnetic fields beneath a literally intertextual gate. It explicitly emphasizes moments of the coemergence of affect and invention, articulating its poetic quest for "som thyng" in terms of movement and potential. Its plot, ending in the deferral of the formel and the narrator's quest for new invention, further articulates this overarching sense of potential as an aspect of the poem's structure, a prolongation that Shakespeare himself dramatizes in his anthropomorphized version of Chaucer's poem in *Love's Labour's Lost*.[17] "Phoenix," representing Shakespeare's later revisiting of the dream vision, does not adapt or restructure specific passages of *Parlement* but instead draws on this vivid Chaucerian sensation of representing the emergence of new poetic utterance in terms of affective occurrence. Capturing such moments and directing them toward a death scene of lyric memorialization, Shakespeare transforms deferral into death and, most significantly, presents its relationship to Chaucer's poetry as an affective intertextuality rather than exclusively in terms of authorial politics. That intertextual relationship functions analogously to the ways in which the passions themselves were thought to move and to register the "perturbations" that afterwards are understood discursively as emotional experiences.

Like *Parlement*'s depiction of its magnetically stranded narrator, "Phoenix" presents both movement and stasis simultaneously, depicting movement only in terms of capture, and capture only in terms of movement. The poem opens with an explicit call for movement as it orders the "chaste wings" of birds who will attend the funeral of the phoenix and turtle to "obay" the cry of "the bird of lowdest lay" (1–4). This call is hardly the raucous cacophony of birdsong and flapping wings that concludes *Parlement of Foules*; instead, the poem's present moment consists of movement defined in terms of its own restriction. The Eagle's task is to "Keep the obsequie so strict," relegating avian movement to sanctioned ritual and the funeral procession itself (5–12),[18] and the poem concludes not with "som thyng" newly sought after but only with the softly

---

17. See Krier, "The Aim Was Song."
18. See also Marjorie Garber, "Two Birds with One Stone: Lapidary Re-Inscription in *The Phoenix and Turtle*," *Upstart Crow* 5 (1984): 8.

sighed prayers of the attendees.[19] Also like *Parlement*, "Phoenix" embeds this sensation of captured movement as an aspect of its structure, especially as the poem moves through its individual sections of the opening funereal call, the "Antheme" sung to the birds (21), and Reason's concluding *Threnos*.[20] Each new section of *Parlement* takes up and transforms the material of the previous sections, and in "Phoenix," I. A. Richards sees "each part of the poem being included in and produced by" another, each part being "put into a mouth created in the part before it," and argues that this process of unfolding enclosure "has a lot to do with the power and spring" of the poem.[21] In her analysis of the poem's "extremely original sound" and "particularly haunting and original rhythm," Barbara Everett observes that "the Anthem flows out of the Invocation, which uses the first line of the sixth stanza as introduction, a fine irregular ripple-effect which gives liquidity" to its verse.[22] Indeed, we might consider Everett's metaphor of liquidity in a more literal sense, in terms of the "perturbations" registered in the poem's own humoral makeup, a fantasy of embodied poetry that is detectable only retrospectively through the analysis of its lyric movement. In this way, then, the poem's structure itself gestures toward movements and emergence, of sections growing out of sections, even while its subject matter remains the static rigidity of a funeral procession.

The same affective motion characterizes the poem's mechanics of reference. Enterline notes that the poem's use of deictics contributes to the ambiguity surrounding the identity of its birds. Its deictics, she writes, "are local and concrete while at the same time strangely floating. . . . Each 'this' and 'here' anchors the poem in a specific context and at the same time detaches it from such reference."[23] More than merely transforming the poem into "a rite or monument,"[24] these processes actually internalize movement within the poem itself, providing a paradox of fixity in motion. The poem thus becomes, as Bednarz neatly puts it, "resonant without being referential."[25] Denying satisfactory referents for its supposed topical allusions and clear objects for its deictic gestures, the poem emphasizes relational movement itself, the potential of becoming conveyed in the journey toward—but impossibility of arrival at—any referent, internal or

---

19. For a summary of the critical debate over whether a new phoenix has risen from the ashes in Shakespeare's poem, see Bednarz, 123–24 and 130–38.

20. See Cheney ("Voice of the Author," 119–24).

21. I. A. Richards, "The Sense of Poetry: Shakespeare's 'The Phoenix and the Turtle," *Dædalus* 87 (1958): 90.

22. Everett, "Set upon a golden bough to sing: Shakespeare's Debt to Sidney in 'The Phoenix and Turtle,'" *TLS* (16 Feb. 2001): 13–14.

23. Enterline, 153.

24. Ibid., 154.

25. Bednarz, 84

external. What we are left with is the impression of unceasing movement and circulation, not of the now-dead birds themselves but of the very process of imagining what their particulate union must have been like.

"Phoenix" finally literalizes this impression of felt movement though its images of breath and breathing. Marjorie Garber notes that the actions of each of the birds "requires utterance, or at least the giving and taking of breath," which she reads as a figure for poetic composition,[26] and Bednarz likewise cites the birds' breath as a marker of invention: "the poem's medium is also air, as the breath of its creator becomes the breath of its mourners."[27] Indeed, the poem concludes with the almost inaudible sound of soft breathing as the birds are called to "sigh a prayer" to the urn of ashes, but these prayers are not in fact portrayed as poetic utterance. As Richards notes of these final lines, the prayer itself "is wordless . . . sighed only, not spoken."[28] The quiet undulation of breath offers an overarching sensation that is best felt—that is, felt literally as soft, hot breath on the skin—rather than heard or understood. Described in a vocabulary of embodiment and noise that is familiar to—but also different from—*Parlement*'s conclusion of birdsong and flapping wings, the breathing of the birds of "Phoenix" embodies and echoes the affective movements and emergent circulations that the poem elsewhere presents metrically and referentially, but only ever as retrospective gestures that follow the death of the titular birds.

In its final image and invocation, then, "The Phoenix and Turtle" offers an affective paradox of fixed mobility, of unceasing, transformative movement that is somehow embedded in the poem's sarcophagal subject matter and that stubbornly refuses to open out into anything beyond the poem itself. Through these echoes and resonances, the poem metrically, structurally, and thematically offers an analogue for the movement of affect. Even while they culminate in the "monument" that turns out to be the printed poem itself, these affective movements are never quite captured by the poem, defying the analysis of readers like Reason and conveying the impression of an ultimately ineffable— but a felt and embodied—experience. The poetics of "The Phoenix and Turtle" operates analogically to the movement of the passions, and it explicitly fuses these affective movements with a sensation of poetry being invented as an inseparable part of this process. What emerges from the poem's movements are structures and utterances of poetic discourse—innovative stanza forms and the mysterious, nonhuman sounds of birds' sighing and mumbling prayers.

---

26. Garber, 8.
27. Bednarz, 145.
28. Richards, 93.

In this way, the poem opens itself to the possibility of an affective intertextuality, a means of connecting texts through affective movement rather than through direct allusion or invocation. Rather than directly invoke Chaucer, as Spenser might, or mine Chaucer's poems for phrases or structure, Shakespeare sees in *Parlement* a new vantage point from which to displace and express the affective "wonder" that Reason witnesses in the "mutuall flame" of the phoenix and turtledove. This affective intertextuality is characterized first by Shakespeare's recognition of, and attention to, passages in Chaucer's poetry that themselves stage moments of affective and inventional emergence, and second by the way in which Shakespeare re-presents those moments as textual equivalents of Wright's affective "perturbations," as motions or disturbances that explicitly invite continued poetic entanglement. Defined by its intertextual registering of affect and by its conscious incompleteness, *Parlement* establishes itself as an affective body able to engage in a kind of intertextual affective circulation.[29] In short, Shakespeare recognizes moments of affective and inventional potential that are built into *Parlement* and that demand intertextual engagement in equally affective terms. "The Phoenix and Turtle" resonates with these moments of capture, engaging *Parlement* indirectly, without besting, rewriting, or completing it. "Phoenix" instead offers gestures, generates echoes, and conveys a sensation of interpretive movement that the vagaries of the poem never allow to close or stop completely, generating a model of intertextuality grounded in affective circulation. In commemorating its dead birds it also remembers the affective energy of Chaucer's poem, suggesting a felt connection with a sense of the past that is at once distant and familiar. Shakespeare transfers through "Phoenix" a Chaucerian poetics that feels different, an engagement with a sixteenth-century Chaucer who is both distant and a contributing part of English literary culture, and who, as he is presented in sixteenth-century printed editions, invites readers to form communal relationships.[30] Rather than adapt antiquated style and language that had increasingly

---

29. It is possible to imagine how these poems might offer an intertextual analogue to the kinds of biological "transmission of affect" studied by Teresa Brennan in *The Transmission of Affect*—Chaucer's poems not only invite structural completion by future poets but also "infect" those subsequent inventions with their own affective encodings. Katherine Rowe sketches a map of this sort of "affective contagion" in terms of emotional exchange between characters in Shakespeare's drama ("Minds in Company: Shakespearean Tragic Emotions," in *A Companion to Shakespeare's Works*, ed. Richard Dutton and Jean E. Howard, vol. 1. [Oxford: Blackwell, 2003], 58).

30. As Tim William Machan writes in his discussion of Thomas Speght's 1598 edition, "the Chaucer of the Renaissance is decidedly paradoxical, simultaneously the father that English literary traditions needed to validate themselves but also a figure whose origins in the *medium aevum* necessarily rendered his language and style obscure and rough" ("Speght's Works and the Invention of Chaucer," *Interdisciplinary Journal of Textual Studies* 8 [1995]: 157). Critics have

come to characterize Chaucer by the seventeenth century, or insert "The Phoenix and Turtle" into a line of English literary succession, Shakespeare develops a Chaucerian model that resonates with the intersubjective "mystery" of the Phoenix and Turtle's indescribable relationship, linking intertextual movement with the "wonder" of their union and the mobile poetics used to describe it.

GOWER AND THE "UNBORN EVENT" IN *PERICLES*

If the idea of the Chaucerian in "The Phoenix and Turtle" is registered (and perpetuated) in terms of shifts and movements, then in *Pericles,* a collaboration between Shakespeare and George Wilkins first performed at the Globe perhaps as early as 1606, Gower appears directly, rising like a very different kind of phoenix from "ashes ancient" in the opening chorus (1.0.2), and remaining an integral part of the entire play, introducing dumb shows and main action in no fewer than eight different chorus sections throughout its five acts, standing, as he puts it, "i'th'gaps to teach you / The stages of our story" (4.4.8–9).[31] "There is no parallel for such a character or effect anywhere else in Shakespeare," David F. Hoeniger writes of Gower's striking presence in *Pericles,* and Helen Cooper likewise notes that "None of his other plays does anything like this."[32] Furthermore, the Gower who appears is thoroughly

---

noted how Speght's edition of Chaucer's works implicitly invites readers to build communities around an affective relationship with an imagined Chaucer: Stephanie Trigg argues that professions of "love" for Chaucer in the prefatory material of Speght's edition work to construct imagined communities in which authors, editors, and readers are part of the same gentlemanly and masculine cohort (*Congenial Souls: Reading Chaucer from Medieval to Postmodern* [Minneapolis: University of Minnesota Press, 2002], 129–40); and David Matthews sees a desire in Speght's edition for a private relationship with Chaucer, one that Speght's (apparently forced) move to print seems to violate ("Public Ambition, Private Desire, and the Last Tudor Chaucer," in *Reading the Medieval in Early Modern England,* ed. Gordon McMullan and David Matthews [Cambridge: Cambridge University Press, 2007], 83–84). As Trigg and Matthews show, in Speght's edition Chaucer becomes a nexus to which strong affective energies can be directed in order to construct communities that are understood to convey gentlemanly status, and to whom a reader's engagement is framed in terms of love.

31. All quotations from *Pericles* are from the edition by Suzanne Gossett, Arden Shakespeare (New York: Bloomsbury, 2004). Act, scene, and line numbers will be cited parenthetically in the text. Richard Hillman and Paul Dean both note that Gower's materialization out of ashes resembles the mythical phoenix, but neither connects this image to "The Phoenix and Turtle" (Hillman, "Shakespeare's Gower and Gower's Shakespeare: The Larger Debt of *Pericles,*" *Shakespeare Quarterly* 4 [1985]: 437; Dean, "Pericles' Pilgrimage," *Essays in Criticism* 50 [2000]: 126). See Gossett's introduction for a full discussion of critical views on the relative contributions of Shakespeare and Wilkins to *Pericles,* as well as other sources for the plot of the play.

32. David F. Hoeniger, "Gower and Shakespeare in *Pericles,*" *Shakespeare Quarterly* 33 (1982): 463; Helen Cooper, "'This worthy old writer': *Pericles* and Other Gowers," in *A Companion*

"medieval" when compared to the audiences "born in these latter times" to whom he speaks (1.0.11).[33] Yet, as Richard Hillman shows, the play is clearly informed by a nuanced consideration of the whole of the *Confessio Amantis* itself: Pericles' travels parallel not only those of Gower's Apollonius in Book 8 but also the "torturous psychic voyage of Amans toward self-discovery" and even more broadly "the painful journey toward the rebuilding of selfhood" that forms the ostensible ethical component of Gower's project.[34] The thoroughness of *Pericles*' treatment of the *Confessio* is also apparent in the play's elaboration of a decidedly Gowerian view of poetic invention: how the alignment of affective and inventional movements can impinge upon extratextual worlds as part of a larger project of imagining widespread cultural rejuvenation. In the *Confessio*, as I have argued, the "real" Gower imagines extending his poem's own inventional poetics into the world it explicitly seeks to reshape. In *Pericles*, that process of extension is refigured as the transformation of poetic text into dramatized event. What I mean to say is not simply that the play dramatizes Gower's Apollonius narrative but rather that the

---

to *Gower*, ed. Siân Echard (Cambridge: D. S. Brewer, 2004), 107. Martha Driver notes that "Shakespeare gives no other medieval poet this attention," including Chaucer ("Conjuring Gower in *Pericles*," in Dutton, Hines, and Yeager, *John Gower, Trilingual Poet*, 318). For surveys of Gower's relative popularity in the sixteenth and seventeenth centuries and the editions in which Shakespeare may have encountered his poetry, see Cooper, "'This worthy old writer'"; R. F. Yeager, "Shakespeare as Medievalist: What It Means for Performing *Pericles*," in *Shakespeare and the Middle Ages: Essays on the Performance and Adaptation of the Plays with Medieval Sources or Settings*, ed. Martha Driver and Sid Ray (Jefferson, NC: McFarland, 2009), 215–31; and N. W. Gilroy-Scott, "John Gower's Reputation: Literary Allusions from the Early Fifteenth Century to the Time of 'Pericles,'" *Yearbook of English Studies* 1 (1971): 30–47.

33. Several critics have approached the Gower of *Pericles* as variously representative of what we might call an early-seventeenth-century medievalism. Yeager argues that though "Shakespeare's encounters with Gower were varied in kind and must have been numerous" ("Shakespeare as Medievalist," 218), given his reading of Gower in Thomas Berthelette's 1532 edition and Gower's appearance in other fictions, such as *Greene's Visions*, Shakespeare would have found Gower to be "an ancestral figure whose language(s), poetic expressions, and moral ethos were of the Middle Ages" (217); Stephen J. Lynch argues that Shakespeare makes Gower even "more antiquated than the *Confessio* would suggest" ("The Authority of Gower in Shakespeare's *Pericles*," *Mediaevalia* 16 [1993]: 366); Felix C. H. Sprang argues that *Pericles*, like *Two Noble Kinsmen*, posits "that modern audiences have a privileged perspective on the workings of fate within God's providence. The ideological stance that this privileged perspective spawns is exactly the frame that serves for the construction of the 'medieval'" ("Never Fortune Did Play a Subtler Game: The Creation of 'Medieval' Narratives in *Pericles* and *The Two Noble Kinsmen*," *European Journal of English Studies* 15 [2011]: 122). Much recent criticism demonstrates that sixteenth- and seventeenth-century distinctions between "the medieval" and "the early modern" were not as neatly drawn as once thought, especially by early-modern literary critics: see the introductions to the essay collections edited by McMullan and Mathews, and by Perry and Watkins.

34. Hillman, 430, 436.

larger metanarrative concern of *Pericles* is to dramatize on stage an almost metaphysical process in which Shakespeare and Wilkins's Gower watches as his poetry moves into, and becomes constitutive of, the physical world of the play's fiction. In other words, *Pericles* is not simply Book 8 of the *Confessio* adapted for the stage; it is a performative process in which self-conscious comments on poetic invention materially encroach on and affect the external world they claim to represent.

Shakespeare and Wilkins's reanimated Gower emerges from antiquity in the opening chorus as the physical embodiment of the potentially transformative project of the *Confessio*. "From ashes ancient Gower is come," he declares of himself at the start of the play, "Assuming man's infirmities," singing "a song that old was sung" (1.0.1–3). Gower appears here in the same way he appears as "John Gower" in Book 8 of the *Confessio*: old, tired, and characterized by physical limitations.[35] His "song" of Apollonius/Pericles, he says, was "sung at festivals" long ago, but it was also "read" by "lords and ladies in their lives . . . for restoratives" (5–8), that is, not simply for pleasure or entertainment but also as a component of a larger project of personal reformation.[36] Addressing now an audience "born in these latter times / When wit's more ripe" (11–12), Gower acknowledges an inventional position defined by temporality as much as by textuality, locating himself, as Paul Dean puts it, "both later than the past which he is retelling, and earlier than those to whom he now tells it"[37] and mediating what his own ancient "authors say" (20) and what the "latter times" of Jacobean theatrical culture might require. *Pericles* intensifies the *middel weie* that Gower would go, extending it beyond binaries of lust and lore or past and present to include Gower's position between his own self-recognized pastness, the future-as-present moment in which he now appears, and his future's future, indicated in his closing lines' wish that a "New joy" might "wait on" his audience after they leave the performance (Epi. 18). The emergent potential of Gower's poetics is made explicit via his sensitivity to his temporal displacement, but that poetics is channeled more directly toward its larger goal: if the Gower of the *Confessio* imagines what the future might make of his poetry "In tyme comende after this," the Gower of *Pericles* emerges within that future to manage once again how audiences might engage his work. The self-fictionalized Gower in Book 1 of the *Confessio Amantis* "may noght strecche up to the hevene / Min hand" to make macrocosmic adjustments to reality, but

---

35. Hillman also argues for the relevance to the play of Gower's appearance in Book 8 as someone transformatively affected by hearing the Apollonius story (428–30).

36. Cooper writes that "Pleasurableness, restorative power and antiquity . . . together make up the virtues of the 'song' to follow" ("'This worthy old writer,'" 106).

37. P. Dean, 126.

Shakespeare and Wilkins's Gower can do exactly that, stretching forth a hand to alter "events"—that is, the actions and speeches of the play—as a kind of playwright and director. Gower in fact initiates the whole of the play's action with a literal gesture of his hand. Introducing the very first scene, he tells the audience simply, "This Antioch, then" (1.0.17), and his words indicate an inaugural physical gesture toward the unfolding events that materialize adjacently onstage. In *Pericles,* the stretching of Gower's hand makes Antioch and starts the entire play.

That *makyng* itself emerges alongside the self-conscious metatextual alignment of affect and invention, triggering the play's sweeping geographical and temporal movements with an initial act of *fyndyng* as Pericles realizes the answer to Antiochus's riddle and immediately understands that it also functions as a veiled confession describing Antiochus's incestuous relationship with his daughter. Perceiving Pericles' awareness of his riddle's significance, Antiochus exclaims in an aside, "Heaven, that I had thy head! He has found the meaning," (1.1.110). Antiochus uses technical inventional vocabulary here: Pericles "has found the meaning" of the riddle, that is, discovered its solution as well as the self-consumptive *archetypus* that the riddle poetically expresses. The sprawling romance narrative that follows organizes itself, as does Gower's version of the story, around a series of repetitions, rebirths, and reformations that works to counteract the destructively recursive narrative structure of the riddle and the socially destructive effects of its referent, incest. The play's narrative thus springs forth from an explicit metafictional moment of invention that is then immediately paired with Pericles' sudden and inexplicable affective transformation. The very next scene finds Pericles analyzing his unexpected "change of thoughts" (1.2.2) in precise terminology:

> the passions of the mind,
> That have their first conception by misdread,
> Have after-nourishment and life by care;
> And what was first but fear what might be done
> Grows elder now, and cares it not be done.
> And so with me.
>
> (1.2.11–16)

The *OED* cites this passage as the only use of "misdread" as a noun,[38] and it functions here to render as a past event the now irrecoverable moment in

---

38. "Misdread," definition 1; Gossett makes this important observation in the gloss on this word in her Arden edition (195).

which "the passions of the mind" are first registered as a physiological process of fluidic displacement—what Thomas Wright would label a "perturbation." The actual affective occurrence itself happens, quite literally, offstage before the scene begins. As Stephen J. Lynch argues, Pericles' "melancholy, which he is quick to interpret and define, seems far more mysterious, far more of a riddle, than he comprehends,"[39] and, after its initial gesture toward an ineffable moment of affective movement, Pericles' soliloquy concentrates on the emotional performance script of melancholy that characterizes its "elder" stages, whose "after-nourishment" consists of the continuous fear of impending death.

A similar gesture occurs in the reciprocal scene in Act 5 in which Pericles again finds himself affectively changed after meeting a woman whom he will soon discover to be his long-lost daughter, Marina. The two meet in the dark hold of Pericles' ship, and, as in the *Confessio*, they feel some kind of affinity but are unable to pinpoint its source. That feeling causes Pericles to break his long self-imposed silence, and he is moved not only by his desire to know the identity of this stranger who has come to sing to him but also by an overwhelming urge to locate the source of his affective change: "Tell me," he demands of Helicanus, "if thou canst / What this maid is, or what is like to be, / That thus hath made me weep" (5.1.173–75). *Pericles* brings its narrative full circle, dispelling the recursive effect of the incest riddle through a scene that purports to stage an occurrence of pre-conscious recognition, aligning moments of affect and invention, folding the one into the other. Moreover, at the moment of recognition, Pericles suddenly hears "The music of the spheres" (5.1.217) playing around him, indicating not simply the near-completion of the play's narrative arc but also the proper realignment of the cosmos itself. What emerges from ancient ashes, then, is an image of a Gowerian poetics that seems capable of materially altering the physical reality of human interaction and experiential event, a transformative power that extends beyond simply creating ethical subjects in readers to include constructing, organizing, and activating event itself. Extending this Gowerian power from the hold of Pericles' ship upward to the spheres themselves, *Pericles* incorporates as an aspect of its mode and genre an image of how poetry might stretch forth and affect a macrocosmic "thing . . . so strange."

The play thus aligns affect and invention in a way that it explicitly labels "Gowerian," making these metadramatic moments sites in which to explore how the coemergence of affect and poetic invention might somehow productively impinge on external reality. Perhaps the most nuanced exploration

---

39. S. Lynch, 370.

occurs alongside a dumb show in the middle of Act 4, where Gower narrates as a silent Pericles discovers what he takes to be Marina's tomb. Unaware that the tomb is in fact a deception constructed by the Tarsian rulers Cleon and Dionyza, Pericles mimes his woe, and Gower instructs the audience to "See how belief may suffer by foul show. / This borrowed passion stands for true-owed woe" (4.4.23–24). The "borrowed passion" refers to Cleon and Dionyza's dissimulation, but as Suzanne Gossett glosses in her edition of the play, the line registers a potential metatheatrical reading as well, in "the actor who *borrows* or portrays an emotion (*passion*) that can only *stand for* a real feeling."[40] This borrowing of passions quickly fuses with textual appropriation in a way that fractures any clear sense of affective or inventional origin. Whatever Cleon and Dionyza may have "borrowed" for their deception, Gower's own description of Pericles' woe in this scene is "borrowed" from that woe's "real" depiction next to him on stage. Similarly, Shakespeare and Wilkins's own staging of Gower's narration is likewise "borrowed" from Apollonius's woe in the *Confessio*—a narrative that, of course, Gower's poem itself had already "borrowed" from the *cronique* relating the history of the Tyrian king. The resulting confusion about the original source of this woe generates a ceaseless back and forth that culminates in an explicitly staged fusion of poetry and event. In the lines that immediately follow, Gower, along with the audience, watches Pericles in the dumb show silently read the inscription on Marina's tomb, but it is Gower himself who literally reads the words aloud. In this process, Gower's "source" text is transposed to the physical action on the stage, and Gower reads poetry—his own poetry—that has now become inseparable from the event of its own performance as part of the physical structure of Tarsian architecture. His poetry here has literally become part of the material world that it is explicitly shown to represent.

Gower's interactions with the play's dumb shows and the main acts comprise the central phenomenological theme of *Pericles:* a tension between word and event that intensifies to such an extent that the play's narrative appears almost to gain a life of its own and operate independently of Gower's initial inventional actions.[41] In the opening dumb show of Act 2, for example, the relevant action is "brought to your eyes," Gower admits, so "what need speak

---

40. *Pericles,* ed. Gossett, 343; emphasis in original.
41. Critics typically attribute this phenomenon to the fictionalized Gower's inability to effectively do his job as chorus: Stephen J. Lynch goes so far as to argue that Gower becomes "a myopic foil to a text that proves too slippery and suggestive for choric authority or control" (374); see also Walter F. Eggers Jr., for whom the play's "wonders . . . have outstripped [Gower's] narrow view" ("Shakespeare's Gower and the Role of the Authorial Presenter," *Philological Quarterly* 54 [1975]: 438).

I?" (2.0.16). In Act 3, Gower declares that "What's dumb in show I'll plain with speech" (3.0.14), but in his introduction to the main action of the following scene, Gower essentially transfers inventional agency to the action itself:

> And what ensues in this fell storm
> Shall for itself itself perform.
> I nill relate, action may
> Conveniently the rest convey,
> Which might not what by me is told.
> (3.0.53–57)

As Gower frames it, the narrative of *Pericles* invents itself without any need for Gowerian oversight: it "Shall for itself itself perform," wrapping both inventional imperative and action together in a spiraling moment of autonomous self-production. This impression of emerging event intensifies in Act 4, which Gower introduces by declaring,

> The unborn event
> I do commend to your content,
> Only I carry winged time
> Post on the lame feet of my rhyme,
> Which never could I so convey
> Unless your thoughts went on my way.
> (4.0.45–50)

Inventional agency here again lies with the "unborn event" rather than with Gower's "lame feet," and Gower's poetic task is not to organize narrative but simply to emphasize the potential emergence of that as yet "unborn event" itself. The "lame feet" pun draws, of course, on a familiar modesty topos, but it also registers a phenomenological imperative as the defining characteristic of the transformative potential of Gowerian poetry.

Shakespeare and Wilkins thus present a fully embodied Gower who himself presents his own poetry in terms of emerging potential and who is explicitly aware of his own displaced historicity. This Gower does not exert overarching authorial control but instead stands in as a nexus for movement and potential transformation, a kind of performative glossator whose "lame feet" point toward and emphasize the imminent emergence of "unborn event." Shakespeare and Wilkins likewise recognize and deploy Gower's large-scale focus as constitutive of the play's theme and narrative structure: for the Gowers of both the *Confessio* and *Pericles*, poetic invention involves imagining at a macrocosmic scale how a project of cultural revivification might actually become part of historical reality.

Pericles may even playfully confuse this impinging of the poetic world on the historical by reflecting on the geographical proximity of the play's Gower onstage at the Globe to the tomb and effigy of the real John Gower, just down the street from the theater in St. Saviour's, now Southwark Cathedral. Indeed, the connection between St. Saviour's and the King's Men was not insubstantial: not only did the church serve the theaters in the area but Shakespeare also had his brother Edmund interred there.[42] The referent for the play's Gower thus includes not only the abstract authorial presence transmitted in Berthelette's edition of the *Confessio*, or a vague sense of an English literary history, but also the "real" Gower who once lived and worked just south of London and whose tomb is only a short walk away. The idea of "Gower" in *Pericles* becomes an embodied inventional force that is historically, geographically, and materially imminent to the performance of the play itself, a Gower who, as Kelly Jones puts it, is a liminal entity "born of the fusion of both literary and performance culture"[43] and who stretches an impetuous hand between two existentially divergent worlds. The kind of affective intertextuality realized in *Pericles*, then, not only invokes Gower's tranformative poetics but also performs it, on and beyond the stage.

ENGAGING EMERGENCE

What I have tried to show in this brief look at "Phoenix" and *Pericles* is that these works define their self-conscious interactions with Chaucer and Gower not only in terms of source material, medieval alterity, and authorial politics but also in ways that recognize and build on Chaucer's and Gower's self-conscious representations of inventional emergence. Similar explorations might be productively extended to other sixteenth- and seventeenth-century writers: it is in the affective movements of lyric poetry, for example, that Wyatt locates his own interactions with Chaucer's work, and Spenser depicts a crucial moment of metatextual *fyndyng* via Calidore's discovery of a fragment of

---

42. Driver, 317; Yeager, "Shakespeare as Medievalist," 218. Yeager notes as well that "almost half the actors whose names appear in the First Folio are to be found listed in St. Saviour's registers" (218).

43. Kelly Jones, "'The Quick and the Dead': Performing the Poet Gower in *Pericles*," in Driver and Ray, *Shakespeare and the Middle Ages*, 206. For Jones, this liminality ultimately complicates "Gower as a literary authority" by demonstrating "a playful concern with the unstable, vulnerable, and unreservedly performative nature of authorship itself" (203).

Chaucerian narrative—the *Wife of Bath's Tale*—in the woods of Mount Acidale in Book 6 of the *Faerie Queene*. Such engagements suggest the potential for the study of what we might think of as affective intertextualities among early modern and medieval vernacular writings and their personal and cultural work. Indeed, an idea of affective intertextuality—one defined by emergence, imminence, movement, and an inescapably inherent tenuousness and fleetingness—provides access to moments of poetic contact that need not necessarily be predetermined by (but likewise need not exclude) the manifold tensions of authorial politics. It becomes a versatile model defined as much by poetic forms as by social and cultural pressures. Whatever the future critical applications, it is my hope that this book has helped to show the affect of invention to be, as it must always be, an emergent potentiality, coalescing in particular points of resiliency and then dissipating among the many inventional moments in the poetry of Chaucer and Gower.

BIBLIOGRAPHY

Aers, David. "*The Parliament of Fowls*: Authority, the Knower, and the Known." In *Chaucer's Dream Visions and Shorter Poems*, edited by William Quinn, 279–88. New York: Garland, 1999.
———. "Reflections on Gower as '*Sapiens* in Ethics and Politics.'" In Yeager, *Re-Visioning Gower*, 185–201.
Ahmed, Sara. *The Cultural Politics of Emotion*. New York: Routledge, 2004.
Allen, Elizabeth. "Chaucer Answers Gower: Constance and the Trouble with Reading." *ELH* 64 (1997): 627–55.
———. *False Fables and Exemplary Truth in Later English Literature*. New York: Palgrave, 2005.
———. "Newfangled Readers in Gower's 'Apollonius of Tyre.'" *Studies in the Age of Chaucer* 29 (2007): 419–64.
Arner, Lynn. *Chaucer, Gower, and the Vernacular Rising: Poetry and the Problem of the Populace after 1381*. University Park, PA: Pennsylvania State University Press, 2013.
Astell, Ann W. *Chaucer and the Universe of Learning*. Ithaca, NY: Cornell University Press, 1996.
———. *Political Allegory in Late Medieval England*. Ithaca, NY: Cornell University Press, 1999.
Australian Research Council Centre of Excellence for the History of Emotions. Aug. 5, 2014. <http://www.historyofemotions.org.au>.
Bakalian, Ellen Shaw. *Aspects of Love in John Gower's Confessio Amantis*. New York: Routledge, 2004.
Bale, Anthony. *The Jew in the Medieval Book: English Antisemitisms, 1350–1500*. Cambridge: Cambridge University Press, 2006.
Banchich, Claire. "Holy Fear and Poetics in John Gower's *Confessio Amantis*, Book I." In Yeager, *On John Gower*, 188–215.
Barr, Helen. "Religious Practice in Chaucer's *Prioress's Tale*: Rabbit and/or Duck?" *Studies in the Age of Chaucer* 32 (2010): 39–62.
Baswell, Christopher. *Virgil in Medieval England: Figuring the Aeneid from the Twelfth Century to Chaucer*. Cambridge: Cambridge University Press, 1995.

Bates, Ronald, "Shakespeare's 'The Phoenix and Turtle.'" *Shakespeare Quarterly* 6 (1955): 19–30.
Batkie, Stephanie L. "'Of the parfite medicine': *Merita Perpetuata* in Gower's Vernacular Alchemy." In Dutton, Hines, and Yeager, *John Gower, Trilingual Poet*, 157–68.
Bednarz, James P. *Shakespeare and the Truth of Love: The Mystery of "The Phoenix and Turtle."* New York: Palgrave, 2012.
Beichner, Paul E. "Daun Piers, Monk and Business Administrator." *Speculum* 34 (1959): 611–19.
Benson, C. David, and Elizabeth Robertson, eds. *Chaucer's Religious Tales*. Cambridge: D. S. Brewer, 1990.
Berlant, Lauren. *Cruel Optimism*. Durham, NC: Duke University Press, 2011.
Berndt, David E. "Monastic *Acedia* and Chaucer's Characterization of Daun Piers." *Studies in Philology* 68 (1971): 435–50.
Besserman, Lawrence. "Chaucer, Spain, and the Prioress's Antisemitism." *Viator* 35 (2004): 329–53.
———. "Ideology, Antisemitism, and Chaucer's *Prioress's Tale*." *Chaucer Review* 36 (2001): 48–72.
Bestul, Thomas H. "The Monk's Tale." In *Sources and Analogues of the "Canterbury Tales*,*"* general editor Robert M. Correale, vol. 1, 409–47. Cambridge: D. S. Brewer, 2002.
Bishop, Kathleen A., ed. *The Canterbury Tales Revisited—21st Century Interpretations*. Newcastle: Cambridge Scholars Press, 2008.
Blamires, Alcuin. "A Chaucer Manifesto." *Chaucer Review* 24 (1989): 29–44.
Boccaccio, Giovanni. *Famous Women*. Edited and translated by Virginia Brown. Cambridge, MA: Harvard University Press, 2001.
———. *Filostrato. Tutte le opere*. Edited by Vittore Branca. Vol. 2. Milan: Mondadori, 1964.
Boboc, Andreea. "Se-duction and Sovereign Power in Gower's *Confessio Amantis* Book V." In Dutton, Hines, and Yeager, *John Gower, Trilingual Poet*, 126–38.
Boitani, Piero. *Chaucer and the Imaginary World of Fame*. Cambridge: D. S. Brewer, 1984.
———. "The Monk's Tale: Dante and Boccaccio." *Medium Aevum* 45 (1976): 50–69.
———. *The Tragic and the Sublime in Medieval Literature*. Cambridge: Cambridge University Press, 1989.
Bolens, Guillemette. *The Style of Gestures: Embodiment and Cognition in Literary Narrative*. Baltimore: Johns Hopkins University Press, 2012.
Bowers, John M. "Rival Poets: Gower's *Confessio* and Chaucer's *Legend of Good Women*." In Dutton, Hines, and Yeager, *John Gower: Trilingual Poet*, 276–87.
Braeger, Peter C. "The Portrayals of Fortune in the Tales of the *Monk's Tale*." In *Rebels and Rivals: The Contestive Spirit in the* Canterbury Tales, edited by Susanna Greer Fein, David Raybin, and Peter C. Braeger, 223–36. Kalamazoo, MI: Medieval Institute, 1991.
Brennan, Teresa. *The Transmission of Affect*. Ithaca, NY: Cornell University Press, 2004.
Brewer, D. S., ed. *The Parlement of Foulys*. London: Thomas Nelson, 1960.
Brownlee, Kevin, Tony Hunt, Ian Johnson, Alastair Minnis, and Nigel F. Palmer. "Vernacular Literary Consciousness c. 1100-c.1500: French, German, and English Evidence." In *The Cambridge History of Literary Criticism*, vol. 2, edited by Alistair J. Minnis and Ian Johnson, 422–71. Cambridge: Cambridge University Press, 2005.
Bullón-Fernández, Maria. *Fathers and Daugthers in Gower's* Confessio Amantis. Cambridge: D. S. Brewer, 2000.
Bundy, Murray Wright. *The Theory of Imagination in Classical and Mediaeval Thought*. Champaign: University of Illinois Press, 1927.
Burke, Linda Barney. "Genial Gower: Laughter in the *Confessio Amantis*." In Yeager, *John Gower: Recent Readings*, 39–63.
Burrow, Colin, ed. *The Complete Sonnets and Poems*. Oxford: Oxford University Press, 2002.
Calabrese, Michael. "Performing the Prioress: 'Conscience' and Responsibility in Studies of Chaucer's *Prioress's Tale*." *Texas Studies in Literature and Language* 44 (2002): 66–91.

Camargo, Martin. "Chaucer and the Oxford Renaissance of Anglo-Latin Rhetoric." *Studies in the Age of Chaucer* 34 (2012): 173–207.
Cannon, Christopher. "Form." In Strohm, *Middle English*, 177–90.
Carruthers, Mary. *The Book of Memory: A Study of Memory in Medieval Culture.* Cambridge: Cambridge University Press, 1990.
———. *The Craft of Thought: Meditation, Rhetoric, and the Making of Images, 400–1200.* Cambridge: Cambridge University Press, 1998.
———. *The Experience of Beauty in the Middle Ages.* Oxford: Oxford University Press, 2013.
———. "Italy, Ars Memorativa, and Fame's House." *Studies in the Age of Chaucer: Proceedings* 2 (1987): 179–87.
Chaucer, Geoffrey. *The Riverside Chaucer.* General editor Larry D. Benson. Boston: Houghton Mifflin, 1987.
Cheney, Patrick. *Shakespeare, National Poet-Playwright.* Cambridge: Cambridge University Press, 2004.
———. "The Voice of the Author in 'The Phoenix and Turtle.'" In Perry and Watkins, *Shakespeare and the Middle Ages*, 103–25.
Chester, Robert. *Loues Martyr: or, Rosalins complaint. Allegorically shadowing the truth of Loue, in the constant Fate of the Phœnix and Turtle.* London, 1601.
Cicero, Marcus Tullius. *De inventione, De optimo genere oratorm, Topica.* Edited and translated by H. M. Hubbell. Cambridge, MA: Harvard University Press, 1949. Reprinted 1993.
Clough, Patricia Ticineto. Introduction to *The Affective Turn: Theorizing the Social,* edited by Patricia Ticineto Clough and Jean Halley, 1–33. Durham, NC: Duke University Press, 2007.
Cohen, Jeffrey J. "Time Out of Memory." In Scala and Federico, *The Post-Historical Middle Ages*, 37–61.
Coleman, Joyce. "'A bok for king Richardes sake': Royal Patronage, the *Confessio*, and the *Legend of Good Women.*" In Yeager, *On John Gower*, 104–23.
Coley, David K. "'Withyn a Temple Ymad of Glas': Glazing, Glossing, and Patronage in Chaucer's House of Fame." *Chaucer Review* 45 (2010): 59–84.
Collette, Carolyn P., ed. *The Legend of Good Women: Context and Reception.* Cambridge: D. S. Brewer, 2006.
———. "Rethinking the *Legend of Good Women:* Context and Reception." In Colette, *The Legend of Good Women*, vii–xviii.
———. "Sense and Sensibility in the *Prioress's Tale.*" *Chaucer Review* 15 (1980): 138–50.
———. *Species, Phantasms, and Images: Vision and Medieval Psychology in* The Canterbury Tales. Ann Arbor: University of Michigan Press, 2001.
Cooper, Helen. *The Canterbury Tales.* Oxford Guides to Chaucer. Oxford: Oxford University Press, 1989.
———. "Four Last Things in Dante and Chaucer: Ugolino in the House of Rumor." *New Medieval Literatures* 3 (1999): 39–66.
———. "'Peised Evene in the Balance': A Thematic and Rhetorical Topos in the *Confessio Amantis.*" *Medievalia* 16 (1993): 113–39.
———. "'This worthy old writer': *Pericles* and Other Gowers." In Echard, *A Companion to Gower*, 99–113.
Copeland, Rita. "*Pathos* and Pastoralism: Aristotle's *Rhetoric* in Medieval England." *Speculum* 89 (2014): 96–127.
———. *Rhetoric, Hermeneutics, and Translation in the Middle Ages.* Cambridge: Cambridge University Press, 1991.
Copeland, Rita, and Ineke Sluiter, eds. *Medieval Grammar and Rhetoric: Language Arts and Literary Theory, AD 300–1475.* Oxford: Oxford University Press, 2009.

Crane, Mary Thomas. *Shakespeare's Brain: Reading with Cognitive Theory*. Princeton, NJ: Princeton University Press, 2001.

Crocker, Holly A. "Affective Politics in Chaucer's *Reeve's Tale*: 'Cherl' Masculinity after 1381." *Studies in the Age of Chaucer* 29 (2007): 225–58.

Dahood, Roger. "The Punishment of the Jews, Hugh of Lincoln, and the Question of Satire in Chaucer's *Prioress's Tale*." *Viator* 36 (2005): 465–91.

Dean, James M. *The World Grown Old in Medieval Literature*. Cambridge, MA: Medieval Academy of America, 1997.

Dean, Paul. "Pericles' Pilgrimage." *Essays in Criticism* 50 (2000): 125–44.

Delany, Sheila. *Chaucer's House of Fame: The Poetics of Skeptical Fideism*. Chicago: University of Chicago Press, 1972.

———. *The Naked Text: Chaucer's* Legend of Good Women. Berkeley: University of California Press, 1994.

Desmond, Marilynn. *Reading Dido: Gender, Textuality, and the Medieval Aeneid*. Minneapolis: University of Minnesota Press, 1994.

Despres, Denise L. "Cultic Anti-Judaism and Chaucer's Litel Clergeon." *Modern Philology* 91 (1994): 413–27.

Dinshaw, Carolyn. *Chaucer's Sexual Poetics*. Madison: University of Wisconsin Press, 1989.

———. *Getting Medieval: Sexualities and Communities, Pre- and Postmodern*. Durham, NC: Duke University Press, 1999.

Donavin, Georgiana. "Rhetorical Gower: Aristotelianism in the *Confessio Amantis*'s Treatment of 'Rethorique.'" In Urban, *John Gower*, 155–73.

Driver, Martha. "Conjuring Gower in *Pericles*." In Dutton, Hines, and Yeager, *John Gower, Trilingual Poet*, 315–25.

Driver, Martha, and Sid Ray, eds. *Shakespeare and the Middle Ages: Essays on the Performance and Adaptation of the Plays with Medieval Sources or Settings*. Jefferson, NC: McFarland, 2009.

Dumville, David. "What is a Chronicle?" In *The Medieval Chronicle II: Proceedings of the 2nd International Conference on the Medieval Chronicle, Friebergen/Utrecht 16–21 July 1999*, 1–27. Costerus New Series 144. Amsterdam: Rodopi, 2002.

Duncan, Pansy. "Taking the Smooth with the Rough: Texture, Emotion, and the Other Postmodernism." *PMLA* 129 (2014): 204–22.

Dutton, Elizabeth M., John Hines, and Robert F. Yeager, eds. *John Gower, Trilingual Poet: Language, Translation, and Tradition*. Cambridge: D. S. Brewer, 2010.

Echard, Siân, ed. *A Companion to Gower*. Cambridge: D. S. Brewer, 2004.

———. "Gower's 'bokes of Latin': Language, Politics, and Poetry." *Studies in the Age of Chaucer* 25 (2003): 123–56.

———. "Last Words: Latin at the End of the *Confessio Amantis*." In *Interstices: Studies in Middle English and Anglo-Latin Texts in Honour of A. G. Rigg*, edited by Richard Firth and Linne R. Mooney, 99–121. Toronto: University of Toronto Press, 2004.

———. "With Carmen's Help: Latin Authorities in the *Confessio Amantis*." *Studies in Philology* 95 (1998): 1–40.

Edwards, Robert R. *The Dream of Chaucer: Representation and Reflection in the Early Narratives*. Durham, NC: Duke University Press, 1989.

———. *The Flight from Desire: Augustine and Ovid to Chaucer*. New York: Palgrave, 2006.

———. "Gower and the Poetics of the Literal." In Dutton, Hines, and Yeager, *John Gower, Trilingual Poet*, 59–73.

———. *Ratio and Invention: A Study of Medieval Lyric and Narrative*. Nashville: Vanderbilt University Press, 1989.

Eggers, Walter F., Jr. "Shakespeare's Gower and the Role of the Authorial Presenter." *Philological Quarterly* 54 (1975): 434–43.

Elliott, Winter S. "Eglentyne's Mary/Widow: Reconsidering the Anti-Semitism of *The Prioress's Tale.*" In Bishop, *The Canterbury Tales Revisited*, 110–26.
Enterline, Lynn. "'The Phoenix and the Turtle,' Renaissance Elegies, and the Language of Grief." In *Early Modern English Poetry: A Critical Companion*, edited by Patrick Cheney, Andrew Hadfield, and Garrett A. Sullivan Jr., 147–59. Oxford: Oxford University Press, 2007.
Evans, Ruth. "Chaucer in Cyberspace: Medieval Technologies of Memory and the *House of Fame.*" *Studies in the Age of Chaucer* 23 (2001): 43–69.
Evans, Ruth, Andrew Taylor, Nicholas Watson, and Jocelyn Wogan-Browne. "The Notion of Vernacular Theory." In *The Idea of the Vernacular: An Anthology of Middle English Literary Theory, 1280–1520*, edited by Jocelyn Wogan-Browne, Nicholas Watson, Andrew Taylor, and Ruth Evans, 314–30. University Park: Pennsylvania State University Press, 1999.
Everett, Barbara. "Set upon a golden bough to sing: Shakespeare's Debt to Sidney in 'The Phoenix and Turtle.'" *TLS*. 16 Feb. 2001. 13–14.
Fairchild, Arthur H. R. "*The Phoenix and Turtle*: A Critical and Historical Interpretation." *Englische Studien* 33 (1904): 337–84.
Fanger, Claire. "Magic and the Metaphysics of Gender in Gower's 'The Tale of Circe and Ulysses.'" In Yeager, *Re-Visioning Gower*, 204–19.
Federico, Sylvia. "Chaucer and the Matter of Spain." *Chaucer Review* 45 (2011): 299–320.
Finlayson, John. "Reading Chaucer's *Nun's Priest's Tale*: Mixed Genres and Multi-Layered Worlds of Illusion." *English Studies* 86 (2005): 493–510.
———. "Seeing, Hearing and Knowing in *The House of Fame*." *Studia Neophilologica* 58 (1986): 47–57.
Fisher, John H. *John Gower: Moral Philosopher and Friend of Chaucer*. New York: New York University Press, 1964.
Fox, George C. *The Mediaeval Sciences in the Works of John Gower*. New York: Haskell, 1966.
Fradenburg, L. O. Aranye. "Beauty and Boredom in *The Legend of Good Women*." *Exemplaria* 22 (2010): 65–83.
———. "Criticism, Anti-Semitism, and the *Prioress's Tale*." *Exemplaria* 1 (1989): 69–115.
———. "Living Chaucer." *Studies in the Age of Chaucer* 33 (2011): 41–64.
———. *Sacrifice Your Love: Psychoanalysis, Historicism, Chaucer*. Minneapolis: University of Minnesota Press, 2002.
Frank, Robert Worth, Jr. *Chaucer and* The Legend of Good Women. Cambridge, MA: Harvard University Press, 1972.
———. "Pathos in Chaucer's Religious Tales." In Benson and Robertson, *Chaucer's Religious Tales*, 39–52.
———. "Structure and Meaning in the *Parlement of Foules*." *PMLA* 71 (1956): 530–39.
Friedman, A. B. "The *Prioress's Tale* and Chaucer's Anti-Semitism." *Chaucer Review* 9 (1974): 118–29.
Fry, Donald K. "The Ending of the *Monk's Tale*." *JEGP* 71 (1972): 355–68.
Fyler, John M. *Chaucer and Ovid*. New Haven, CT: Yale University Press, 1979.
———. *Language and the Declining World in Chaucer, Dante, and Jean de Meun*. Cambridge: Cambridge University Press, 2007.
Galloway, Andrew. "Chaucer's *Legend of Lucrece* and the Critique of Ideology in Fourteenth-Century England." *ELH* 60 (1993): 813–32.
———. "Gower in his Most Learned Role and the Peasants' Revolt of 1381." *Mediaevalia* 16 (1993): 329–47.
———. "Gower's Quarrel with Chaucer, and the Origins of Bourgeois Didacticism in Fourteenth-Century London Poetry." In *Calliope's Classroom: Studies in Didactic Poetry from Antiquity to the Renaissance*, edited by Annette Harder, Alasdair A. MacDonald, and Gerrit J. Reinink, 245–67. Leuven: Peeters, 2007.

———. "The Literature of 1388 and the Politics of Pity in Gower's *Confessio Amantis*." In Steiner and Barrington, *The Letter of the Law*, 67–104.

———. "Reassessing Gower's Dream Visions." In Dutton, Hines, and Yeager, *John Gower, Trilingual Poet*, 288–303.

———. "Writing History in England." In *The Cambridge History of Medieval English Literature*, edited by David Wallace, 255–83. Cambridge: Cambridge University Press, 1999.

Garber, Marjorie. "Two Birds with One Stone: Lapidary Re-Inscription in *The Phoenix and Turtle*." *Upstart Crow* 5 (1984): 5–19.

Gayk, Shannon. "'To wonder upon this thyng': Chaucer's *Prioress's Tale*." *Exemplaria* 22 (2010): 138–56.

Geoffrey of Vinsauf, *Poetria Nova. Les Arts Poétiques du xxe et du xxiiie siècle*. Edited by Edmond Faral. Paris: Champion, 1924.

———. *Poetria Nova of Geoffrey of Vinsauf*. Translated by Margaret F. Nims. Toronto: Pontifical Institute of Mediaeval Studies, 1967.

Getty, Laura J. "'Other smale ymaad before': Chaucer as Historiographer in the 'Legend of Good Women.'" *Chaucer Review* 42 (2007): 48–75.

Gilroy-Scott, N. W. "John Gower's Reputation: Literary Allusions from the Early Fifteenth Century to the Time of 'Pericles.'" *Yearbook of English Studies* 1 (1971): 30–47.

Given-Wilson, Chris. *Chronicles: The Writing of History in Medieval England*. London: Hambledon and London, 2004.

Godman, Peter. "Chaucer and Boccaccio's Latin Works." In *Chaucer and the Italian Trecento*, edited by Piero Boitani, 269–95. Cambridge: Cambridge University Press, 1983.

Gordon, R. K., ed. and trans. *The Story of Troilus*. New York: Dutton, 1964.

Gould, Deborah. "On Affect and Protest." In *Political Emotions*, edited by Janet Staiger, Ann Cvetkovich, and Ann Reynolds, 18–44. New York: Routledge, 2010.

Gower, John. *The Complete Works of John Gower*. Edited by G. C. Macaulay. 4 vols. Oxford: Clarendon Press, 1899–1902.

———. *The French Balades*. Edited and translated by R. F. Yeager. Kalamazoo, MI: Medieval Institute, 2011.

———. *John Gower: Confessio Amantis*. Edited by Russell A. Peck. 3 vols. Kalamazoo, MI: Medieval Institute Publications, 2000–2004.

———. *The Major Latin Works of John Gower*. Edited and translated by Eric W. Stockton. Seattle: University of Washington Press, 1962.

———. *The Minor Latin Works*. Edited and translated by R. F. Yeager. Kalamazoo, MI: Medieval Institute, 2005.

Grady, Frank. "The Generation of 1399." In Steiner and Barrington, *The Letter of the Law*, 202–29

Gransden, Antonia. *Historical Writing in England*. 2 vols. Ithaca, NY: Cornell University Press, 1982.

Grennen, Joseph E. "Science and Poetry in Chaucer's *House of Fame*." *Annuale Mediaevale* 8 (1967): 38–45.

Guerin, Dorothy. "Chaucer's Pathos: Three Variations." *Chaucer Review* 20 (1985): 90–112.

Haas, Renate. "Chaucer's *Monk's Tale*: An Ingenious Criticism of Early Humanist Conceptions of Tragedy." *Humanistica Lovaniensia* 36 (1987): 44–70.

Hanning, Robert W. "'And countrefete the speche of every man / He koude, whan he sholde telle a tale': Toward a Lapsarian Poetics for *The Canterbury Tales*." *Studies in the Age of Chaucer* 21 (1999): 29–58.

Hansen, Elaine Tuttle. *Chaucer and the Fictions of Gender*. Berkeley: University of California Press, 1992.

Harvey, Elizabeth D. "Speaking in Tongues: The Poetics of the Feminine Voice in Chaucer's *Legend of Good Women*." In *New Images of Medieval Women: Essays Toward a Cultural Anthropology*, edited by Edelgard E. DuBruck, 47–60. Lewiston, NY: Edwin Mellen, 1989.

Havely, Nicholas R., ed. *The House of Fame*. Durham, UK: Durham Medieval Texts, 1994.
Higden, Ranulf. *Polychronicon Ranulphi Higden monachi cestrensis: Together with the English Translations of John Trevisa and of an Unknown Writer of the Fifteenth Century*. Edited by Churchill Babington and Joseph Rawson Lumby. 9 vols. Rerum Britannicarum Medii Ævii Scriptores 41. London: Longman, 1865–86.
Hillman, Richard. "Shakespeare's Gower and Gower's Shakespeare: The Larger Debt of *Pericles*." *Shakespeare Quarterly* 4 (1985): 427–37.
Hoeniger, David F. "Gower and Shakespeare in *Pericles*." *Shakespeare Quarterly* 33 (1982): 461–79.
Holley, Linda Tarte. *Reason and Imagination in Chaucer, the* Perle-*Poet, and the* Cloud-*Author: Seeing from the Center*. New York: Palgrave, 2011.
Holsinger, Bruce. *Music, Body, and Desire in Medieval Culture: Hildegard of Bingen to Chaucer*. Stanford, CA: Stanford University Press, 2001.
Houwen, L. A. J. R. "Fear and Instinct in Chaucer's *Nun's Priest's Tale*." In *Fear and Its Representations in the Middle Ages and Renaissance*, edited by Anne Scott and Cynthia Kosso, 17–30. Arizona Studies in the Middle Ages and the Renaissance 6. Turnhout: Brepols, 2002.
Irvin, Matthew W. *The Poetic Voices of John Gower: Politics and Personae in the* Confessio Amantis. Cambridge: D. S. Brewer, 2014.
Irvine, Martin. "Medieval Grammatical Theory and Chaucer's *House of Fame*." *Speculum* 60 (1985): 850–76.
Isidore of Seville. *The Etymologies of Isiodore of Seville*. Translated by Stephen A. Barney, W. J. Lewis, J. A. Beach, and Oliver Berghof. Cambridge: Cambridge University Press, 2006.
John of Garland. *The Parisiana poetria of John of Garland*. Edited and translated by Traugott Lawler. New Haven, CT: Yale University Press, 1974.
Johnson, Hannah. "Antisemitism and the Purposes of Historicism: Chaucer's *Prioress' Tale*." In *Medieval Literature: Debates and Criticism*, edited by Holly A. Crocker and D. Vance Smith, 192–200. New York: Routledge, 2014.
Jones, Kelly. "'The Quick and the Dead': Performing the Poet Gower in *Pericles*." In Driver and Ray, *Shakespeare and the Middle Ages*, 201–14.
Justice, Steven. *Writing and Rebellion: England in 1381*. Berkeley: University of California Press, 1994.
Kaske, R. E. "The Knight's Interruption of the *Monk's Tale*." *ELH* 24 (1957): 249–68.
Kelly, Douglas. *The Arts of Poetry and Prose*. Typologie des Sources du Moyen Age Occidental 59. Turnhout: Brepols, 1991.
———. *Medieval Imagination: Rhetoric and the Poetry of Courtly Love*. Madison: University of Wisconsin Press, 1978.
———. "Theory of Composition in Medieval Narrative Poetry and Geoffrey of Vinsauf's *Poetria Nova*." *Mediaeval Studies* 31 (1969): 117–48.
Kelly, Henry Ansgar. *Chaucerian Tragedy*. Cambridge: D. S. Brewer, 1997.
Kendall, Elliott. *Lordship and Literature: John Gower and the Politics of the Great Household*. Oxford: Clarendon Press, 2008.
———. "Saving History: Gower's Apocalyptic and the New Arion." In Dutton, Hines, and Yeager, *John Gower, Trilingual Poet*, 46–58.
Kennedy, Thomas. "Rhetoric and Meaning in the *House of Fame*." *Studia Neophilologica* 68 (1996): 9–23.
Kiser, Lisa J. *Telling Classical Tales: Chaucer and the* Legend of Good Women. Ithaca, NY: Cornell University Press, 1983.
Knapp, Peggy A. *Chaucerian Aesthetics*. New York: Palgrave, 2008.
Knight, G. Wilson. *The Mutual Flame: On Shakespeare's* Sonnets *and* The Phoenix and the Turtle. London: Methuen, 1955.
Knuuttila, Simo. *Emotions in Ancient and Medieval Philosophy*. Oxford: Clarendon Press, 2004.

———. "Medieval Theories of the Passions of the Soul." In *Emotions and Choice from Boethius to Descartes*, edited by Henrik Lagerlund and Mikko Yrjonsuuri, 49–83. Boston: Kluwer Academic Press, 2002.

Kobayashi, Yoshiko. "Chivalry and History in the 'Monk's Tale.'" *Poetica* 55 (2001): 83–104.

———. "*Principis Umbra*: Kingship, Justice, and Pity in John Gower's Poetry." In Yeager, *On John Gower*, 71–103.

Kolve, V. A. *Chaucer and the Imagery of Narrative: The First Five Canterbury Tales*. Stanford, CA: Stanford University Press, 1984.

———. *Telling Images: Chaucer and the Imagery of Narrative II*. Stanford, CA: Stanford University Press, 2009.

Kordecki, Leslie. *Ecofeminist Subjectivities: Chaucer's Talking Birds*. New York: Palgrave, 2011.

Koretsky, Allen C. "Dangerous Innocence: Chaucer's Prioress and Her Tale." In *Jewish Presences in English Literature*, edited by Derek Cohen and Deborah Heller, 10–24. Montreal: McGill-Queen's University Press, 1990.

Krier, Theresa M. "The Aim Was Song: From Narrative to Lyric in the *Parlement of Foules* and *Love's Labour's Lost*." In *Refiguring Chaucer in the Renaissance*, edited by Theresa M. Krier, 165–88. Gainesville: University Press of Florida, 1998.

———. *Birth Passages: Maternity and Nostalgia, Antiquity to Shakespeare*. Ithaca, NY: Cornell University Press, 2001.

Kruger, Steven F. "Imagination and the Complex Movement of Chaucer's *House of Fame*." *Chaucer Review* 28 (1993): 117–34.

———. "Passion and Order in Chaucer's *Legend of Good Women*." *Chaucer Review* 23 (1989): 219–35.

Krummel, Miriamne Ara. "The Pardoner, the Prioress, Sir Thopas, and the Monk: Semitic Discourse and the Jew(s)." In Bishop, *The Canterbury Tales Revisited*, 88–109.

Lampert, Lisa. *Gender and Jewish Difference from Paul to Shakespeare*. Philadelphia: University of Pennsylvania Press, 2004.

Le Guin, Ursula K., and Brian Attebery, eds. *The Norton Book of Science Fiction: North American Science Fiction, 1960–1990*. New York: Norton, 1993.

Lepley, Douglas L. "The Monk's Boethian Tale." *Chaucer Review* 12 (1978): 162–70.

Levin, Rozalyn. "The Passive Poet: Amans as Narrator in Book 4 of the *Confessio Amantis*." *Proceedings of the Illinois Medieval Association* 3 (1986): 114–30.

Lewis, C. S. "Gower." In Nicholson, *Gower's Confessio Amantis*, 15–39.

Leyerle, John. "Chaucer's Windy Eagle." *University of Toronto Quarterly* 40 (1971): 247–65.

Leys, Ruth. "The Turn to Affect: A Critique." *Critical Inquiry* 37 (2011): 434–72.

Lindeboom, B. W. *Venus' Owne Clerk: Chaucer's Debt to the Confessio Amantis*. New York: Rodopi, 2007.

Lowes, John L. "The Prologue to the *Legend of Good Women* as Related to the French *Marguerite* Poems and to the *Filostrato*." *PMLA* 19 (1904): 593–683.

Lynch, Kathryn L. *Chaucer's Philosophical Visions*. Cambridge: D. S. Brewer, 2000.

Lynch, Stephen J. "The Authority of Gower in Shakespeare's *Pericles*." *Mediaevalia* 16 (1993): 361–78.

Machan, Tim William. "Speght's Works and the Invention of Chaucer." *Interdisciplinary Journal of Textual Studies* 8 (1995): 145–70.

Mann, Jill. *Geoffrey Chaucer*. Atlantic Highlands, NJ: Humanities Press International, 1991.

Masciandaro, Nicola. *The Voice of the Hammer: The Meaning of Work in Middle English Literature*. Notre Dame, IN: University of Notre Dame Press, 2007.

Massumi, Brian. *Parables for the Virtual: Movement, Affect, Sensation*. Durham, NC: Duke University Press, 2002.

Matthew of Vendôme. *Ars versificatoria. Les Arts Poétiques du xxe et du xxiiie siècle*. Edited by Edmond Faral. Paris: Champion, 1924.

———. *Ars versificatoria (The Art of the Versemaker)*. Translated by Roger P. Parr. Milwaukee: Marquette University Press, 1981.

Matthews, David. "Public Ambition, Private Desire, and the Last Tudor Chaucer." In McMullan and Matthews, *Reading the Medieval in Early Modern England*, 74–88.

McAlpine, Monica E. *The Genre of* Troilus and Criseyde. Ithaca, NY: Cornell University Press, 1978.

McCabe, T. Matthew N. *Gower's Vulgar Tongue: Ovid, Lay Religion, and English Poetry in the* Confessio Amantis. Cambridge: D. S. Brewer, 2011.

McCoy, Richard C. "Love's Martyrs: Shakespeare's 'Phoenix and Turtle' and the Sacrificial Sonnets." In *Religion and Culture in Renaissance England*, edited by Claire McEachern and Debora Shuger, 188–208. Cambridge: Cambridge University Press, 1997.

McDonald, Nicola F. "Chaucer's *Legend of Good Women*, Ladies at Court and the Female Reader." *Chaucer Review* 35 (2000): 22–42.

———. "Games Medieval Women Play." In Collette, The Legend of Good Women, 176–97.

McKinley, Kathryn. "Lessons for a King from Gower's *Confessio Amantis* 5." In *Metamorphosis: The Changing Face of Ovid in Medieval and Early Modern Europe*, edited by Alison Keith and Stephanie Rubb, 107–28. Toronto: Centre for Reformation and Renaissance Studies, 2007.

McMullan, Gordon, and David Matthews, eds. *Reading the Medieval in Early Modern England*. Cambridge: Cambridge University Press, 2007.

McNamer, Sarah. *Affective Meditation and the Invention of Medieval Compassion*. Philadelphia: University of Pennsylvania Press, 2010.

———. "Feeling." In Strohm, *Middle English*, 241–57.

Minnis, Alistair J., ed. *Gower's* Confessio Amantis: *Responses and Reassessments*. Cambridge: D. S. Brewer, 1983.

———. "Langland's Ymaginatif and Late-Medieval Theory of Imagination." *Comparative Criticism* 3 (1981): 71–103.

———. "Medieval Imagination and Memory." In *Cambridge History of Literary Criticism*, edited by Alistair J. Minnis and Ian Johnson, vol. 2, 239–74. Cambridge: Cambridge University Press, 2005.

———. *Medieval Theory of Authorship: Scholastic Literary Attitudes in the Later Middle Ages*. 2nd ed. Philadelphia: University of Pennsylvania Press, 2010.

Minnis, Alistair J., with V. J. Scattergood and J. J. Smith. *The Shorter Poems*. Oxford Guides to Chaucer. Oxford: Clarendon Press, 1995.

Mitchell, J. Allan. *Ethics and Eventfulness in Middle English Literature*. New York: Palgrave, 2009.

———. *Ethics and Exemplary Narrative in Chaucer and Gower*. Cambridge: D. S. Brewer, 2004.

Morse, Ruth. *The Medieval Medea*. Cambridge: D. S. Brewer, 1996.

Murphy, James J. *Rhetoric in the Middle Ages: A History of Rhetorical Theory from Saint Augustine to the Renaissance*. Berkeley: University of California Press, 1974.

Neuse, Richard. *Chaucer's Dante: Allegory and Epic Theater in "The Canterbury Tales."* Berkeley: University of California Press, 1991.

Nicholson, Peter, ed. *Gower's* Confessio Amantis: *A Critical Anthology*. Cambridge: D. S. Brewer, 1991.

———. *Love and Ethics in Gower's* Confessio Amantis. Ann Arbor: University of Michigan Press, 2005.

Nolan, Maura. "Agency and the Poetics of Sensation in Gower's *Mirour de l'Omme*." In *Answerable Style: The Idea of the Literary in Medieval England*, edited by Frank Grady and Andrew Galloway, 214–43. Columbus: The Ohio State University Press, 2013.

———. "Historicism after Historicism." In Scala and Federico, *The Post-Historical Middle Ages*, 63–85.

———. "Making the Aesthetic Turn: Adorno, the Medieval, and the Future of the Past." *Journal of Medieval and Early Modern Studies* 34 (2004): 549–75.

———. "The Poetics of Catastrophe: Ovidian Allusion in Gower's *Vox Clamantis*." In *Medieval Latin and Middle English Literature: Essays in Honour of Jill Mann*, edited by Christopher Cannon and Maura Nolan, 113–33. Cambridge: D. S. Brewer, 2011.

Norsworthy, Scott. "Hard Lords and Bad Food-Service in the Monk's Tale." *JEGP* 100 (2001): 313–32.

Oatley, Keith, and Jennifer M. Jenkins. *Understanding Emotions*. Oxford: Blackwell Press, 1996.

Olson, Glending. "Making and Poetry in the Age of Chaucer." *Comparative Literature* 31 (1979): 272–90.

Olsson, Kurt. "Grammar, Manhood, and Tears: The Curiosity of Chaucer's Monk." *Modern Philology* 76 (1978): 1–17.

———. *John Gower and the Structures of Conversion: A Reading of the* Confessio Amantis. Cambridge: D. S. Brewer, 1992.

———. "Poetic Invention and Chaucer's 'Parlement of Foules.'" *Modern Philology* 87 (1989): 13–35.

Paster, Gail Kern. *Humoring the Body: Emotions and the Shakespeare Stage*. Chicago: University of Chicago Press, 2004.

———. "Melancholy Cats, Lugged Bears, and Early Modern Cosmology: Reading Shakespeare's Psychological Materialism across the Species Barrier." In Paster, Rowe, and Floyd-Wilson, *Reading the Early Modern Passions*, 113–29.

Paster, Gail Kern, Katherine Rowe, and Mary Floyd-Wilson, eds. *Reading the Early Modern Passions: Essays in the Cultural History of Emotion*. Philadelphia: University of Pennsylvania Press, 2004.

Patterson, Lee. "Genre and Source in *Troilus and Criseyde*." In *Acts of Recognition: Essays on Medieval Culture*, 198–214. Notre Dame, IN: University of Notre Dame Press, 2010.

———. "'The Living Witnesses of Our Redemption': Martyrdom and Imitation in Chaucer's *Prioress's Tale*." *Journal of Medieval and Early Modern Studies* 31 (2001): 507–60.

———. "Perpetual Motion: Alchemy and the Technology of the Self." *Studies in the Age of Chaucer* 15 (1993): 25–57.

———. "'What Man Artow?': Authorial Self-Definition in *The Tale of Sir Thopas* and *The Tale of Melibee*." *Studies in the Age of Chaucer* 11 (1989): 117–75.

Payne, Robert O. *The Key of Remembrance: A Study of Chaucer's Poetics*. New Haven, CT: Yale University Press, 1963.

———. "Making His Own Myth: The Prologue to Chaucer's *Legend of Good Women*." *Chaucer Review* 9 (1975): 197–211.

Pearsall, Derek. "Gower's Narrative Art." *PMLA* 81 (1966): 475–84. Reprinted in Nicholson, *Gower's Confessio Amantis*, 62–80.

———, ed. *The Nun's Priest's Tale. A Variorum Edition of the Works of Geoffrey Chaucer*. Vol. 2. Pt. 9. Norman: Oklahoma University Press, 1984.

Peck, Russell A. "Chaucerian Poetics and the Prologue to the *Legend of Good Women*." In *Chaucer in the Eighties*, edited by Julian N. Wasserman and Robert J. Blanch, 39–55. Syracuse, NY: Syracuse University Press, 1986.

———. "John Gower and the Book of Daniel." In Yeager, *John Gower: Recent Readings*, 159–87.

———. "John Gower: Reader, Editor, and Geometrician." In Urban, *John Gower*, 11–37.

———. *Kingship and Common Profit in Gower's* Confessio Amantis. Carbondale: Southern Illinois University Press, 1978.

Peebles, Katie. "Arguing from Foreign Grounds: John Gower's Leveraging of Spain in English Politics." In *Gower in Context(s): Scribal, Linguistic, Literary and Socio-historical Readings*, edited by Laura Filardo-Llamas, Brian Gastle, and Marta Gutiérrez Rodríguez, 97–113. Special issue of *ES. Revista de Filología Inglesa* 33. Valladolid: Publicaciones Universidad de Valladolid, 2012.

Percival, Florence. *Chaucer's Legendary Good Women.* Cambridge: Cambridge University Press, 1998.
Perry, Curtis, and John Watkins, eds. *Shakespeare and the Middle Ages.* Oxford: Oxford University Press, 2009.
Pickles, J. D., and J. L. Dawson. *A Concordance to John Gower's Confessio Amantis.* Cambridge: D. S. Brewer, 1987.
Pinti, Daniel. "The *Comedy* of the *Monk's Tale*: Chaucer's Hugelyn and Early Commentary on Dante's Ugolino." *Comparative Literature Studies* 37 (2000): 277–97.
———. "Commentary and Comedic Reception: Dante and the Subject of Reading in *The Parliament of Fowls*." *Studies in the Age of Chaucer* 22 (2000): 311–40.
Porter, Elizabeth. "Gower's Ethical Microcosm and Political Macrocosm." In Minnis, *Gower's Confessio Amantis*, 135–62.
Prince, F. T., ed. *The Poems.* 3rd ed. London: Methuen, 1960.
Quinn, William A., ed. *Chaucer's Dream Visions and Shorter Poems.* New York: Garland, 1999.
———. "Chaucer's Recital Presence in the *House of Fame* and the Embodiment of Authority." *Chaucer Review* 43 (2008): 171–96.
———. "The Shadow of Chaucer's Jews." *Exemplaria* 18 (2006): 299–326.
Ramazani, Jahan. "Chaucer's Monk: The Poetics of Abbreviation, Aggression, and Tragedy." *Chaucer Review* 27 (1993): 260–76.
Richards, I. A. "The Sense of Poetry: Shakespeare's 'The Phoenix and the Turtle." *Dædalus* 87 (1958): 86–94.
Ridley, Florence H. *The Prioress and the Critics.* Berkeley: University of California Press, 1965.
Robbins, William. "Romance, Exemplum, and the Subject of the *Confessio Amantis*." *Studies in the Age of Chaucer* 19 (1997): 157–81.
Robertson, Elizabeth. "Aspects of Female Piety in the *Prioress's Tale*." In Benson and Robertson, *Chaucer's Religious Tales*, 143–60.
Rosenfeld, Jessica. *Ethics and Enjoyment in Late Medieval Poetry: Love after Aristotle.* Cambridge: Cambridge University Press, 2011.
Rosenwein, Barbara H. *Emotional Communities in the Early Middle Ages.* Ithaca, NY: Cornell University Press, 2006.
Rowe, Donald. *Through Nature to Eternity: Chaucer's Legend of Good Women.* Lincoln: University of Nebraska Press, 1988.
Rowe, Katherine. "Minds in Company: Shakespearean Tragic Emotions." In *A Companion to Shakespeare's Works,* edited by Richard Dutton and Jean E. Howard, vol. 1, 47–72. Oxford: Blackwell, 2003.
Rowland, Beryl. "The Art of Memory and the Art of Poetry in *The House of Fame*." *Revue de l'Université d'Ottawa* 51 (1981): 162–71.
———. "Bishop Bradwardine, the Artificial Memory, and the *House of Fame*." In *Chaucer at Albany,* edited by Russell Hope Robbins, 41–62. New York: Burt Franklin, 1975.
Runacres, Charles. "Art and Ethics." In Minnis, *Gower's Confessio Amantis*, 106–34.
Russell, J. Stephen. "Song and the Ineffable in the *Prioress's Tale*." *Chaucer Review* 33 (1998): 176–89.
Sadlek, Gregory M. *Idleness Working: The Discourse of Love's Labor from Ovid through Chaucer and Gower.* Washington, DC: Catholic University of America Press, 2004.
Salisbury, Eve. "Remembering Origins: Gower's Monstrous Body Poetic." In Yeager, *Re-Visioning Gower*, 159–84.
Sanok, Catherine. "Reading Hagiographically: *The Legend of Good Women* and its Feminine Audience." *Exemplaria* 13 (2001): 323–54.
Scala, Elizabeth and Sylvia Federico, eds. *The Post-Historical Middle Ages.* New York: Palgrave, 2009.

Scanlon, Larry. "The Authority of Fable: Allegory and Irony in the *Nun's Priest's Tale*." *Exemplaria* 1 (1989): 43–68.

———. *Narrative, Authority, and Power: The Medieval Exemplum and the Chaucerian Tradition*. Cambridge: Cambridge University Press, 1994.

Schibanoff, Susan. *Chaucer's Queer Poetics: Rereading the Dream Trio*. Toronto: University of Toronto Press, 2006.

Schieberle, Misty. "'Thing Which Man Mai Noght Areche': Women and Counsel in Gower's *Confessio Amantis*." *Chaucer Review* 42 (2007): 91–109.

Schmitz, Götz. "Rhetoric and Fiction: Gower's Comments on Eloquence and Court Poetry." In Nicholson, *Gower's* Confessio Amantis, 117–42.

Sedgwick, Eve Kosofsky. *Touching Feeling: Affect, Pedagogy, Performativity*. Durham, NC: Duke University Press, 2003.

Seigworth, Gregory J., and Melissa Gregg. "An Inventory of Shimmers." In *The Affect Theory Reader*, edited by Melissa Gregg and Gregory J. Seigworth, 1–25. Durham, NC: Duke University Press, 2010.

Shakespeare, William. "The Phoenix and Turtle." In Chester, *Loves Martyr*.

Shakespeare, William, and George Wilkins. *Pericles*. Edited by Suzzane Gossett. Arden Shakespeare. New York: Bloomsbury, 2004.

Sharp, Michael D. "Reading Chaucer's 'Manly Man': The Trouble with Masculinity in the *Monk's Prologue* and *Tale*." In *Masculinities in Chaucer: Approaches to Maleness in the* Canterbury Tales *and* Troilus and Criseyde, edited by Peter G. Beidler, 173–85. Cambridge: D. S. Brewer, 1998.

Shouse, Eric. "Feeling, Emotion, Affect." *M/C Journal* 8 (2005). <http://journal.media-culture.org.au/0512/03-shouse.php>.

Simpson, James. "Bonjour Paresse: Literary Waste and Recycling in Book 4 of Gower's *Confessio Amantis*." *Proceedings of the British Academy* 151 (2007): 257–84.

———. "Ethics and Interpretation: Reading Wills in Chaucer's *Legend of Good Women*." *Studies in the Age of Chaucer* 20 (1998): 73–100.

———. *Sciences and the Self in Medieval Poetry: Alan of Lille's* Anticlaudianus *and John Gower's* Confessio amantis. Cambridge: Cambridge University Press, 1995.

Smith, Bruce. "Hearing Green." In Paster, Rowe, and Floyd-Wilson, *Reading the Early Modern Passions*, 147–68.

Smith, D. Vance. "The Application of Thought to Medieval Studies: The Twenty-First Century." *Exemplaria* 22 (2010): 85–94.

———. "Chaucer as an English Writer." In *The Yale Companion to Chaucer*, edited by Seth Lerer, 87–121. New Haven, CT: Yale University Press, 2006.

Socola, Edward M. "Chaucer's Development of Fortune in the 'Monk's Tale.'" *JEGP* 49 (1950): 159–71.

Spector, Stephen. "Empathy and Enmity in the *Prioress's Tale*." In *The Olde Daunce: Love, Friendship, Sex, and Marriage in the Medieval World*, edited by Robert R. Edwards and Stephen Spector, 211–28. New York: SUNY Press, 1991.

Sprang, Felix C. H. "Never Fortune Did Play a Subtler Game: The Creation of 'Medieval' Narratives in *Pericles* and *The Two Noble Kinsmen*." *European Journal of English Studies* 15 (2011): 115–28.

Steiner, Emily. "Radical Historiography: Langland, Trevisa, and the *Polychronicon*." *Studies in the Age of Chaucer* 27 (2005): 171–211.

Steiner, Emily, and Candace Barrington, eds. *The Letter of the Law: Legal Practice and Literary Production in Medieval England*. Ithaca, NY: Cornell University Press, 2002.

Stewart, Kathleen. *Ordinary Affects*. Durham, NC: Duke University Press, 2007.

Strange, William C. "The *"Monk's Tale*: A Generous View." *Chaucer Review* 1 (1967): 167–80.

Strohm, Paul, ed. *Middle English*. Oxford: Oxford University Press, 2007.

Taylor, John. *The Universal Chronicle of Ranulf Higden*. Oxford: Clarendon, 1966.
Tinkle, Theresa. "The Case of the Variable Source: Alan of Lille's *De Planctu Naturae*, Jean de Meun's *Roman de la Rose*, and Chaucer's *Parlement of Foules*." *Studies in the Age of Chaucer* 22 (2000): 341–77.
———. *Medieval Venuses and Cupids: Sexuality, Hermeneutics, and English Poetry*. Stanford, CA: Stanford University Press, 1996.
Travis, Peter W. *Disseminal Chaucer: Rereading* The Nun's Priest's Tale. Notre Dame, IN: University of Notre Dame Press, 2010.
Trigg, Stephanie. *Congenial Souls: Reading Chaucer from Medieval to Postmodern*. Minneapolis: University of Minnesota Press, 2002.
Urban, Malte, ed. *John Gower: Manuscripts, Readers, Contexts*. Turnhout: Brepols, 2009.
Wallace, David. *Chaucerian Polity: Absolutist Lineages and Associational Forms in England and Italy*. Stanford, CA: Stanford University Press, 1997.
Watson, Nicholas. "Desire for the Past." *Studies in the Age of Chaucer* 21 (1999): 59–97.
———. "The Phantasmal Past: Time, History, and the Recombinative Imagination." *Studies in the Age of Chaucer* 32 (2010): 1–37.
Watt, Diane. *Amoral Gower: Language, Sex, and Politics*. Minneapolis: University of Minnesota Press, 2003.
Welch, Bronwen. "'Gydeth My Song': Penetration and Possession in Chaucer's *Prioress's Tale*." In Bishop, *The Canterbury Tales Revisited*, 127–50.
Wetherbee, Winthrop. "The Context of the Monk's Tale." In *Language and Style in English Literature: Essays in Honour of Michio Masui*, edited by Masui Kawai, 159–77. Hiroshima: English Research Association of Hiroshima, 1991.
White, Robert B., Jr. "Chaucer's Daun Piers and the Rule of St. Benedict: The Failure of an Ideal." *JEGP* 70 (1971): 13–30.
Wickert, Maria. *Studies in John Gower*. Translated by Robert J. Meindl. Washington, DC: University Press of America, 1981.
Wilsbacher, Greg. "Lumiansky's Paradox: Ethics, Aesthetics, and Chaucer's *"Prioress's Tale."* College Literature* 32 (2005): 1–28.
Wimsatt, James I. *Chaucer and His French Contemporaries: Natural Music in the Fourteenth Century*. Toronto: University of Toronto Press, 1991.
Woods, Marjorie Curry. *Classroom Commentaries: Teaching the* Poetria nova *across Medieval and Renaissance Europe*. Columbus: The Ohio State University Press, 2010.
Wright, Thomas. *The Passions of the Minde*. London, 1601.
Wurtele, Douglas J. "Chaucer's Monk: An Errant Exegete." *Journal of Literature and Theology* 1 (1987): 191–209.
Yeager, R. F. "Did Gower Write Cento?" In Yeager, *John Gower: Recent Readings*, 113–32.
———, ed. *John Gower: Recent Readings*. Kalamazoo, MI: Medieval Institute, 1989.
———. *John Gower's Poetic: The Search for a New Arion*. Cambridge: D. S. Brewer, 1990.
———. "'O Moral Gower': Chaucer's Dedication of Troilus and Criseyde." *Chaucer Review* 19 (1984): 87–99.
———, ed. *On John Gower: Essays at the Millennium*. Kalamazoo, MI: Medieval Institute, 2007.
———, ed. *Re-Visioning Gower*. Asheville, NC: Pegasus Press, 1998.
———. "Shakespeare as Medievalist: What It Means for Performing *Pericles*." In Driver and Ray, *Shakespeare and the Middle Ages*, 215–31.
Zarins, Kim. "From Head to Foot: Syllabic Play and Metamorphosis in Book I of Gower's *Vox Clamantis*." In Yeager, *On John Gower*, 144–60.
———. "Rich Words: Gower's *Rime Riche* in Dramatic Action." In Dutton, Hines, and Yeager, *John Gower, Trilingual Poet*, 239–53.

Zatta, Jane Dick. "Chaucer's Monk: *A Mighty Hunter Before the Lord.*" *Chaucer Review* 29 (1994): 111–33.

Zeeman, Nicolette. "The Gender of Song in Chaucer." *Studies in the Age of Chaucer* 29 (2007): 141–82.

———. "Imaginative Theory." In Strohm, *Middle English*, 222–40.

Zieman, Katherine. *Singing the New Song: Literacy and Liturgy in Late Medieval England.* Philadelphia: University of Pennsylvania Press, 2008.

Zitter, Emily Stark. "Anti-Semitism in Chaucer's Prioress's Tale." *Chaucer Review* 25 (1991): 277–84.

INDEX

abbreviatio, 84
Aeneas, 37, 59, 60n68, 61–63, 65, 66n77, 67–68, 83–84, 134
aesthetics, 10n16, 13n27, 17n45, 21, 23, 27, 28, 29n81, 37, 39, 45n20, 59, 77, 90, 92
affect, 1–2, 13–18; and displacement, 4–5, 31, 75–76, 107, 112, 202, 207; and emergence, 1–2, 15n37, 28, 32, 37, 39, 47, 73–80, 85, 100, 109, 116, 157, 160–61, 163, 165, 173, 186–87, 202, 207; and emotion, 1–2, 7, 25, 31–33, 36, 38, 58, 62, 70–76, 78, 80, 99, 102, 109, 191–92, 197–98; of invention, 1–2, 12, 13–35, 39, 42, 59–68, 73, 77, 80, 86–92, 109, 123, 135, 144–50, 152, 191–92, 194, 211; and movement, 7, 22, 28, 32, 39, 42, 48, 58, 73, 85–86, 94, 97, 99, 102–4, 107–9, 115–18, 122–23, 152, 165, 183, 186–88, 190, 191, 192, 194, 198, 201–2, 204, 207, 210–11. *See also* displacement; emotion; invention
affective piety, 109n38, 111, 153, 154n7, 155n10, 159
Ahmed, Sara, 15n39, 90–91
Alan of Lille, 3
Alban, Saint, 180–81
Albertus Magnus, 44, 46n28
alchemy, 123, 137–40, 142, 144–45
Alexander the Great, 133

Alighieri, Dante, 3, 37, 38n5, 41–42, 55–56, 60, 159, 179; *Commedia*, 41, 179n82; and Trecento commentaries, 178–79
allegory, 3n1, 7–10, 43, 48–49, 55, 138n38
Allen, Elizabeth, 95n5, 126, 133n27, 193n1
Anselm, 23
antifeminism, 34, 70, 73, 80
anti-Semitism, 152, 153n3, 166–67
apostrophe, 51, 162–63, 175, 188
Aquinas, Thomas, 44n17, 45, 46n28, 56n53, 185
archetypus, 22–24, 27, 36, 42, 90, 98, 161, 192, 206
argumentum, 180
Arion, 11, 96–99, 109, 114–15, 121, 122–23, 149
Aristarchus, 141, 143
Aristotle, 18–19, 27, 44, 56–57
Arner, Lynn, 30, 89n50, 182n90, 193n2
ars poetica, 1, 37, 58, 70, 71n6, 138, 183, 187–88
artes poetriae, 19–25, 27, 32–33, 64n74, 187–88, 191
Arthur, King, 134
Astell, Ann W., 143n49, 169, 173n64, 175n70
auctoritas, 21, 30
Augustine, 20, 23, 46n27, 47, 87–88, 97, 134, 185
authorial politics, 1, 21, 73, 77, 192, 187, 192, 194, 195–96, 199, 211. *See also* displacement

227

Averroes, 115
Avicenna, 44, 47n31

Bacon, Roger, 44n17
Bakalian, Ellen Shaw, 100–101, 106n33
Bakhtin, Mikhail, 37n2
Bale, Anthony, 153n3, 156n12
Barr, Helen, 154, 155n10, 156n14
Bartolomaeus Anglicus, 44n17
Baswell, Christopher, 49, 59–60, 66n77, 67n81
Batkie, Stephanie L., 138n38
Becket, Thomas à, 10, 180
becoming, 1, 7, 14n33, 16, 22, 31, 36, 37n2, 40, 45, 48, 55, 61, 98, 116, 151, 179, 200
Bede, the Venerable: *Historia Ecclesiastica*, 181n87
Bednarz, James P., 195n3, 196n6, 197, 200–201
beginnings, 7, 39, 40–42, 47, 63–64, 156, 174–75. See also *gynnynges*
Benoît de Sainte-Maure, 100
Bergson, Henri, 48, 50, 55, 61
Berlant, Lauren, 15–16, 17n45, 145
Bernardus Sylvestris, 23
Berthelette, Thomas, 204n33, 210
Besserman, Lawrence, 153n3, 166n42, 167n47
Blamires, Alcuin, 71n4, 75n18
Boboc, Andreea, 102–3, 106n32
Boccaccio, Giovanni, 3, 10n16, 159, 169n50, 177; *De casibus virorum illustrium*, 168n48; *De mulieribus claris*, 88n47; *Filostrato*, 75–76
Boethius, 1, 19, 56–57, 171; *Consolation of Philosophy*, 172–73
Boitani, Piero, 37n2, 40n8, 49n40, 54, 168n48, 169n50, 171n60, 172n62, 178n79, 179nn81–82
Bolens, Guillemette, 17, 86n39, 87n44
Bradwardine, Thomas, 185
Brennan, Teresa, 15n39, 90, 165n41, 202n29
Brewer, D. S., 6n6
Brownlee, Kevin, 27n79, 29n82
Bullón-Fernández, Maria, 120
Bundy, Murray Wright, 44, 46n25
Burke, Linda Barney, 97n14
Burrow, Colin, 196n8, 197n9
Bynum, Caroline Walker, 17n47

Calabrese, Michael, 152n2, 153n3, 167n44, 167n47
Camargo, Martin, 64, 188
Cannon, Christopher, 10n16, 27
Carmen, 141

Carruthers, Mary, 20, 25n72, 29n81, 38n5, 43, 45–47, 54n49
Carthage, 83, 134
Cato, 171
Caxton, William, 67n79
Chaucer, Geoffrey, 1–2, 28–33, 72, 191–94, 202–3, 210–11; and Boccaccio, 75–76; *The Book of the Duchess*, 26, 31, 36; *The Canterbury Tales*, 31–32, 34, 64n72, 151–90; *The Canon's Yeoman's Tale*, 139; *Former Age*, 136n35; and Geoffrey of Vinsauf, 23, 64; *The Man of Law's Introduction and Tale*, 192; *The Miller's Tale*, 68n82; *The Nun's Priest's Tale*, 35, 151, 183–90; *The Parlement of Foules*, 2, 3–7, 10–12, 17, 37, 138, 175n69, 192, 195–96, 198–202; *The Reeve's Tale*, 85n38, 87n44, 91; *The Shipman's Tale*, 156n12, 180, 181n88; *The Squire's Tale*, 26; *The Tale of Sir Thopas*, 156n12; *Troilus and Criseyde*, 23, 68, 75n18, 193n1; *The Wife of Bath's Tale*, 211. See also *The House of Fame*; *The Legend of Good Women*; *The Monk's Tale*; *The Prioress's Tale*
"Chaucerian," 35, 190, 194, 199, 202–3
Cheney, Patrick, 195–96, 200n20
Chester, Robert: *Love's Martyr*, 195, 196n7
chronicle, 33–35, 93, 99, 110, 114, 116–17, 119, 121–51; affective, 34, 121, 135, 150, 168, 179; arrangement determining matter in, 144; and corrosion, 123, 128–29, 145; as culturally authoritative genre, 93, 122–23, 129, 131, 135; tragic, 168–74
Cicero, 1, 3, 19, 21–22, 46nn26–27, 142–43, 180; *De inventione*, 19, 135n34, 180n86; *Topica*, 19
Clough, Patricia Ticineto, 15n35, 16n42
Cohen, Jeffrey Jerome, 50n42
Coley, David K., 38n5
Collette, Carolyn P., 46, 48n38, 70n3, 153n4, 163
Confessio Amantis (Gower), 2, 11–12, 21, 29, 31–34, 91–92, 93–150, 151, 168–70, 173–74, 179, 181–83, 190, 192–93, 204–5, 207–10; *abreidynge*, 111–13; Alphonse, 117–19; Amans, 95n6, 97n10, 104, 106–7, 114, 116n48, 129n21, 135, 136n34, 144–45, 147–48, 204; Apollonius, 31, 204–5, 208; Arion, 11, 96–99, 109, 114–15, 121, 122–23, 149; Avarice, 108n36, 127, 145; Cadmus, 136–37; Cham, 136; Charity, 107, 109, 112, 113, 116, 121; colophons, 126; *congruite*,

140–44, 145, 149; Creusa, 100, 107; and cultural rejuvenation, 28, 30, 34, 92, 93, 95–100, 101, 103, 105, 110, 114, 121, 123, 128, 147, 149, 204; Daniel, 182; Envy, 110, 114–15, 116; Eson, 103–5; Genius, 97n10, 103–4, 106–7, 114, 118–19, 123, 124n1, 127n13, 128–30, 132, 135–39, 141–42, 144–49; *gentilesse*, 127n13, 129–30, 135, 137–39, 142, 145; laughter, 97, 145, 148–49; liquids, 109–16; macrocosmic emergence in, 93–121; *marches*, 140–44; *middel weie*, 11–13, 97n13, 99, 205; *misbelieve*, 128, 144–49; Nebuchadnezzar's dream, 98, 105, 112, 122, 129n19, 145, 149, 181–82; Pallas, 147; Peronelle, 100, 117–18, 120–21, 122; Philemon, 136; *pité*, 106–7, 112–13, 120; Pride, 116; Prologue, 11, 32, 94, 96–97, 98n15, 100, 121, 122, 128, 149; religion, 123, 127, 144–50; Rome, intellectual and artistic achievements of, 137, 140–44; Sloth, 127, 137, 140; Statue of Time, 179 (see also *Confessio Amantis*, Nebuchadnezzar's dream); "Tale of Constantine and Sylvester," 34, 99, 109–16, 120–21, 122, 145; "Tale of Jason and Medea," 32, 34, 99, 100–109, 113, 115, 120–21; "Tale of the Three Questions," 32, 34, 99, 116–21, 122; Theges, 136; *venym*, 110, 113–16, 117, 121, 122, 145; *weie*, 99, 145
Constantine. See *Confessio Amantis*, "Tale of Constantine and Sylvester"
Cooper, Helen, 42n13, 64n72, 97n12, 98n15, 170n56, 178n79, 203, 205n36
Copeland, Rita, 18n49, 19–22, 23n65, 72, 124n1, 133, 142n46, 177–78, 179n82
Crane, Mary Thomas, 198n13
Crocker, Holly A., 85n38, 87n44, 91

Dahood, Roger, 166n42
Dean, James M., 129n20, 182n90
Dean, Paul, 203n31, 205
deconstruction, 37, 42, 123, 147, 186n95, 187
Delany, Sheila, 37n2, 38nn4–5, 40, 54n52, 56n53, 56n55, 57n60, 60, 71, 75–76, 77n24, 79, 87n44
delectatio, 47
Deleuze, Gilles, 13, 16
Derby, Henry, 126
Deschamps, Eustache, 74
desire, 2, 3–6, 13, 17, 17n47; personified, 5
Desmond, Marilynn, 59n66, 60, 66, 67n81
dialectic, 20, 183

Dido, 31, 33, 37–39, 58, 59–68, 69–70, 78, 83–84, 134
Dindimus, 141, 143, 149
Dinshaw, Carolyn, 17, 71, 78n26, 87n45, 193n1
displacement: authorial politics and, 21; narrative, 163; sensation of, 27, 39–40, 51, 53–66, 72–80, 89–91, 103, 115, 142, 159, 187, 190, 192. See also affect
Donatus, 141, 143
Donavin, Georgiana, 95n6
dream theory: medieval, 40–41
dream visions, 3, 8n8, 12, 32–33, 37, 40, 69, 76, 79, 125, 142, 184, 199
Driver, Martha, 203n32, 210nn42–43
ductus, 45n21
Duncan, Pansy, 13, 15

Echard, Siân, 11, 12n25, 125–26, 141n45, 142n48, 144
Edward II, 175n70
Edward III, 134n33
Edwards, Robert R., 3n1, 4n4, 5n5, 6n7, 17n47, 21–23, 25n72, 26, 38n5, 39, 40n8, 42n13, 47n29, 56, 57n63, 87n45, 97n12, 135n34, 169n52
Eggers, Walter F., Jr., 208n41
elision, 80–86, 91
Elliott, Winter S., 165n40
emergence. See affect; invention; *Confessio Amantis*
emotion, 1, 2, 4–5, 7, 11, 12, 13–18, 21, 25, 31–32, 33, 35–38, 58–60, 62–63, 67–68, 69–76, 78, 80–85, 89–91, 95, 97, 99, 102–3, 107–8, 112–13, 115–16, 145, 147, 148, 152–55, 160–61, 163, 164, 165–67, 172, 178, 189, 195, 197, 198–99, 202n29; as movements of the soul, 18, 46; and *propassio*, 47; scripts, 17, 159, 192, 207. See also affect; feeling(s); passion(s)
empathy, 17n47, 31, 90–91
endityng, 136–37
engyn, 41–42, 43–48, 51
Enterline, Lynn, 195, 200
erasure, 15n39, 90–91, 157n15
ethics, 3, 17n47, 91, 171; emergent, 95; invention and, 133n27; modern critics and, 152, 166–67; ethical instruction, 12, 97, 108, 127n13, 138n38, 174, 204; ethical subjectivity, 18, 29, 95–96, 109, 169, 207; and work, 132
Evans, Ruth, 25–26, 38n5, 43, 45
eventuality, 10, 18n48, 54, 112
Everett, Barbara, 200
exegesis, 20, 72n9, 133, 178

exemplary instruction, 8n10, 29, 175n68
exemplary narrative, 95n6, 123, 125, 126, 135, 175n68
exemplum/exempla, 67–68, 93, 106n32, 108, 119, 169n50

faculty psychology, 20, 23, 41, 44–45, 46n27, 67, 69, 186n95
Fairchild, Arthur H. R., 195n3
Fanger, Claire, 104n30
Federico, Sylvia, 178n78
feeling(s), 1, 13, 35, 40, 41, 43, 46, 60, 68, 69, 71n5, 74, 76, 78, 87, 91n56, 152, 159, 187, 207
Finlayson, John, 52n45, 183n91, 185n93, 186
Fisher, John H., 193n1
Fortune, 18, 96, 111, 169. See also *The Monk's Tale*
Fox, George G., 115
Fradenburg, L. O. Aranye, 17, 71–72, 77, 78n26, 79n32, 87n41, 152n2, 153–54, 156, 157n15, 159n23, 159n26, 160n27, 163, 166n43, 167n47
Frank, Robert Worth, Jr., 3, 71, 80, 87n44, 153n5, 163n31
Froissart, Jean, 73, 79n32
Fry, Donald K., 170n56
Fyler, John, 38, 39, 40n7, 56, 57n62, 60n68, 62, 77n24, 79, 81
fyndyng, 7, 12, 33, 37, 55, 82–83, 88–89, 92, 113, 118–20, 138, 143, 145–46, 152, 162–63, 175n69, 184–85, 190, 191–92, 206, 210

Galen, 44
Galloway, Andrew, 8n10, 10, 11n21, 86n39, 87n44, 107n34, 112n43, 125, 129n18, 134n30, 193n2
Garber, Marjorie, 199n18, 201
Gayk, Shannon, 155, 164
gender, 2, 34, 65–66, 69, 72, 78, 80, 85–91, 107n34, 108, 111n40, 120, 155, 156n12, 157, 161n29, 165n40, 187n97, 193n1; form/matter and, 66–67, 88, 105; masculinist definition of, 15n39, 78, 88–90, 165n41; and masculinist discourse, 120–21, 187
Geoffrey of Monmouth, 133–34
Geoffrey of Vinsauf: *Poetria nova*, 22–25, 63–66, 187–88
Gervase of Canterbury, 129n18
Getty, Laura J., 81n34, 87n45
Given-Wilson, Chris, 129n18, 134n30, 134nn32–33
Godman, Peter, 168n48, 169n50, 181

Gossett, Suzanne, 203n31, 206n38, 208
Gould, Deborah, 14n33, 15
Gower, John, 1–2, 28–33, 191–94, 210–11; *Cronica tripertita*, 124, 126; as chronicler, 122–50; and *media via*, 11–12, 189; and *middel weie*, 11–12, 97n13, 99, 205; "moral," 193; *Mirour de l'Omme*, 94; and *Pericles*, 203–10; *Quicquid homo scribat*, 124, 137, 149; and Southwark Cathedral, 126, 150, 210; *Traite*, 96n8; *Vox Clamantis*, 2, 7–13, 94, 124–26, 137, 142, 182, 189. See also *Confessio Amantis*
"Gowerian," 35, 194, 207
Grady, Frank, 125
Green, André, 15
Greene's Visions, 204n33
Gregg, Melissa, 14, 28, 43n16, 44
Grennen, Joseph E., 56n54
Guattari, Félix, 13
gynnynges, 40–43, 48–51, 55. See also beginnings

Hansen, Elaine Tuttle, 65–66
Harvey, Elizabeth D., 89n50
Havely, Nicholas R., 67n79
Hercules, 84, 149, 177
hermeneutics, 20–22, 42, 50, 111, 133, 171, 174, 178, 183, 185
Herodotus, 127, 137, 143
Higden, Ranulf: *Polychronicon*, 123, 131–37, 138, 140, 170n57, 181n87
Hillman, Richard, 203n31, 204, 205n35
historicity, 29, 209
historiography, 120, 124–29, 138–40, 150; beauty and pleasure of, 133; and invention, 131–37, 143. See also chronicles; Gower, John, as historiographer; history
history, 12, 114, 119, 125–26, 128–29, 131–34, 147, 153–54, 182; of Church, 109–10, 112; corrosive progression of, 122, 128–29; and tragedy, 167–74. See also chronicles; Gower, John, as chronicler; historiography
Hoeniger, David E., 203
Holley, Linda Tarte, 29n81, 37n2, 45n21
Holsinger, Bruce, 154n9, 159n23, 160n27, 161n29, 164n37
Horace, 138
The House of Fame (Chaucer), 16n43, 20n55, 31, 33, 35, 36–68, 69–70, 73, 75, 76, 78, 80, 84, 92, 136, 150, 188; Aventure, 54; eagle's lecture, 55–58, 60; Geffrey, 35, 39, 41, 49, 51–58, 59–68, 69–70, 78; House of Rumor, 43, 49–55, 102; imagination,

37–51; laughter in, 41, 58; Pepys 2006 manuscript, 67; "pitee," 59–60; proems of, 39–42, 51, 66; proverbs in, 61–67; Temple of Glass, 37, 59–60, 69; thought, 41–42, 43–48, 51; *tydynges*, 33, 36–38, 43, 49–55, 58, 65, 68–69, 102, 150, 158
Houwen, L. A. J. R., 185, 186n94
Hugelyn (Ugolino) of Pisa, 168, 178–79
Hugh of Lincoln, 153n3, 166n42, 167
Hunt, Tony, 27n79
Hypsipyle, 68, 84–85

imagination, 16n43, 17n47, 20–21, 23, 29n81, 33, 54n49, 67, 69, 77, 114, 186; and *House of Fame*, 37–51
incest, 146, 206–7
intentio/intentiones, 44–46, 49, 57
intersubjectivity, 13, 198, 203
intertextuality, 3–5, 7, 21, 41, 42, 73, 77, 183, 186–88; affective, 35, 194–211
inventio, 7, 12, 19, 20, 143, 178
invention, 1–2, 4–7, 12–13, 16, 18–28, 36, 39, 42, 48, 51, 55, 59, 64, 66, 69, 71, 73, 75–77, 79, 94, 98, 100, 104, 112, 138, 140–42, 152, 155–65, 169, 173–74, 176–77, 186–87, 191–93, 194, 199, 204–5, 207, 209; affect of (*see* affect, of invention); as affective force, 1, 70; chronicle and, 123, 129, 135–44, 168; as emergence, 4, 5, 7, 12, 13, 18, 22, 24–25, 28, 32–35, 36–37, 39, 42, 51, 54–55, 58, 59–68, 72, 79, 82–86, 89–90, 98–99, 103, 105, 108–9, 112–13, 116, 118, 120–21, 144, 149–50, 151–52, 155, 157, 161–62, 165, 168, 173–74, 178, 184–85, 187, 192, 199, 200–201, 207–11; formal processes of, 22–25, 55, 131, 133, 138, 175, 191; historiographical, 131–37, 143; medieval idea of, 18–28; and movement, 26, 28, 29, 32, 36–68, 72, 89, 103, 123, 130, 141, 165, 187–88, 204; slothful, 124n1, 127n13. *See also* affect; *fyndyng*; *inventio*; *makyng*; rhetoric
Irvin, Matthew W., 11n21, 101n23, 107n34, 108n37
Irvine, Martin, 49nn39–40
Isidore of Seville, 10n16, 135n34

Jason, 84–85, 100–109
Jerome, Saint, 142–43
John of Garland, 64; *Parisiana poetria*, 25n72, 135n34
John of Salisbury, 129n18
Johnson, Hannah, 152n2, 166n43, 167n47
Johnson, Ian, 27n79

Jones, Kelly, 210
Julian of Norwich, 153n3
Julius Caesar, 133, 168, 171
Justice, Steven, 9n13, 189

Kelly, Douglas, 19n52, 20, 21, 23, 24n70
Kelly, Henry Ansgar, 169n51, 170n57, 171n60, 172n62, 176n72
Kempe, Margery, 153n3
Kendall, Elliot, 97n9, 97n11, 98n15, 100, 102n25, 106n32, 120, 121n60
Kennedy, Thomas, 37n2
Kiser, Lisa J., 70n2, 71, 77, 87n45
Knapp, Peggy A., 28–29, 41n12, 45
Knight, G. Wilson, 197
Knuuttila, Simo, 46n28, 47n29
Kolve, V. A., 44n17, 78n27
Kordecki, Leslie, 3n1, 5n5, 37n2, 52n45, 54, 66n77, 186, 187n97
Krier, Theresa M., 3n1, 6n7, 199n17
Kruger, Steven F., 37, 38n5, 42n13, 62n70, 71n5
Krummel, Miriamne Ara, 154n7

labor, 123, 129n19, 132, 135, 137n37, 140
Lampert, Lisa, 156n12, 157n17, 163n34
Langland, William, 131n24, 133n27, 153n3; *Piers Plowman*, 53n47
The Legend of Good Women (Chaucer), 21, 31, 33–34, 64n72, 68, 69–92, 99, 101, 113, 159, 165–66, 188, 193; Alceste, 77n24, 78–79, 119; *allas*, 80–86, 91; Antony, 80–83; Cleopatra, 80–83, 113; daisy, 70–75, 77–79, 86; Dido, 83–84; elision, 80–86, 91; Hercules, 84; Hypsipyle, 84–85; Jason, 84–85; Lucrece, 86–89; Piramus, 82–83; *pité*, 78, 85, 90; Prologue, 71–72, 73–80; Tarquinius, 86–89; Thisbe, 80, 82–83
Le Guin, Ursula K., 35n85
Levin, Rozalyn, 129n21
Lewis, C. S., 103n28, 148
Leyerle, John, 57
Leys, Ruth, 14–15, 91n57
litotes, 167
Lollard heresies, 134n33
Lucan, 172n61
Lydgate, John, 29
Lynch, Kathryn L., 37n2, 40n10, 41n11, 56n54, 87n44
Lynch, Stephen J., 204n33, 207, 208n41
lyric poetry, 46, 78, 96n8, 97, 159–60, 210

Macaulay, G. C., 9n14, 127n12
Machan, Tim William, 202n30

Machaut, Guillaume de, 74
Macrobius, 3
makyng, 29, 60, 75, 81–82, 89, 113, 119, 146–47, 148, 177, 206
Mann, Jill, 71n4, 78n26, 81
Mary (Virgin), 77n24, 152, 155–60, 162, 163n31
Masciandaro, Nicola, 127, 129n19, 136n35
Massumi, Brian, 13–14, 17n45, 43, 47–48, 55, 61, 74
Matthew of Vendôme, 64; *Ars versificatoria*, 25n72
Matthews, David, 202n30
McAlpine, Monica E., 171nn58–59, 173n63, 176n71, 182n90
McCabe, T. Matthew N., 108n37, 109, 110–11, 113, 120n59, 139n41, 141n44
McCoy, Richard C., 195n3, 197
McDonald, Nicola F., 70n3
McNamer, Sarah, 17, 73–74, 78n26
Medea, 68. See also *Confessio Amantis*, "Tale of Jason and Medea"
medievalism, 204n33
memory, 20, 22, 25n72, 37n2, 38, 43–46, 132, 178, 189n101, 197
Merciless Parliament (1388), 134n33
metachronicle, 124n1
metadrama, 207
metafiction, 58, 126, 186, 206
metanarrative, 3n1, 37, 74–75, 101, 159, 205
metaphysics, 58, 158, 205
metapoetics, 9, 31, 35, 65, 76–77, 84, 152, 164, 189–90, 191–92
metatextuality, 51, 62–63, 67–68, 76, 78, 99, 104n30, 124n1, 128, 135, 158, 165, 183–84, 187, 189, 191, 206, 210
metatheater, 208
Minnis, Alistair, 3n1, 27n79, 38n5, 41n12, 44n17, 40, 45, 48n38, 49n40, 53n47, 57n60, 60n68, 68n83, 70n3, 71n5, 74n11, 81n34, 86n40, 87nn43–44, 90n52, 95n5
misogyny, 34, 66, 68, 70, 72, 80, 89, 90, 171n60, 177, 185
Mitchell, J. Allan, 18, 95, 133n27, 173
The Monk's Tale (Chaucer), 34, 151, 168–83, 184–85, 187, 190; Adam, 168, 170; Caesar, 168, 171; Dalida, 176–77; Dianira, 177; Fortune, 169, 171–75, 177–78; Hercules, 177; and the Host, 169–70, 175n70, 179–83; Hugelyn (Ugolino) of Pisa, 168, 170, 178–79; and the Knight, 169–70, 177n76, 178, 181n88; Lucifer, 168, 170–71, 174–76; and the Statue of Time, 179–83; Samson, 168, 176–77; as tragic chronicle, 168–74; Zenobia, 168; Visconti, Bernabò, 168, 170
monstrosity, 10n16, 100, 108
Morse, Ruth, 100, 106, 107n34
movement. *See* affect, and movement; invention, and movement

Neuse, Richard, 169, 171, 175n67, 177n75, 181n87
Nicholson, Peter, 94n2, 95, 100, 101n21, 104n29, 106nn31–32, 107, 108n35, 116n48, 118n51, 127n13, 128n16, 147–49
Nolan, Maura, 10n16, 11, 28–29, 50n42, 125
Norsworthy, Scott, 180n84

occupatio, 82
Olson, Glending, 29
Olsson, Kurt, 4, 95, 108, 109n38, 116, 124n1, 127n13, 133n27, 171n59, 180n84
Ovid, 9n13, 10–11, 37, 39, 60, 67, 72, 79, 96, 100, 106n32, 125, 127, 141–43; *Ars amatoria*, 125n7; *Metamorphoses*, 105

Palmer, Nigel F., 27n79
passion(s), 13, 15n35, 117, 198–99, 201, 207–8
Paster, Gail Kern, 198
pathos, 80, 117, 172, 178
Patterson, Lee, 29, 139, 152n2, 153n3, 154, 156n12, 157n15, 164n36, 165n40, 166n42, 167n47, 170, 172
Payne, Robert O., 19n53, 70n2, 71n6, 79, 153
Pearsall, Derek, 100n18, 183
Peck, Russell, 70n2, 71, 74n14, 76–77, 94n1, 95n5, 98n16, 101, 102n26, 114, 116n48, 119, 126, 127n13, 135n34, 136n36, 147–48, 182n90
Peebles, Katie, 120n54
Percival, Florence, 74, 79, 81n34, 87
perturbation(s), 65, 194, 198, 200, 202, 207
Petrarch, 47n34
phantasia, 44
phantasms, 50, 67
Pinti, Daniel, 3n2, 170n56, 178–79
pité, 59–60, 78, 85, 90, 106–7, 112–13, 120, 157
Plato, 27; *Timaeus*, 23
Pompey Magnus, 133n29, 171
postmodernism, 13n27, 38n5
poststructuralism, 38n5
praeteritio, 84
Prince, F. T., 195n3
The Prioress's Tale (Chaucer), 34, 151, 152–67, 168, 176, 178, 183, 184, 187, 190; *Alma redemptoris mater*, 152, 155, 157, 160–62;

anti-Semitism, 152, 153n3, 166–67; laud, 157–59, 162; Mary, 155–60, 162; *pité*, 157; *Prologue*, 152, 155–62, 164–65
Proba, A. Faltonia: *Cento Virgilianus*, 10n16
process, 31
propassio, 47

Quinn, William A., 40n8, 67n80, 70n3, 162n30, 166n42

Ramazani, Jahan, 168n49, 171
ratio, 39
rhetoric, 2, 123, 141; bodily, 111–13, 115; Ciceronian, 19, 21–22; classical, 19–20, 27, 31, 50, 143, 191, 192; in *Confessio Amantis*, 142; eloquence, 187–88; rhetorical invention, 1, 7, 133, 142, 192; rhetorical poetics, 18–19
Rhetorica ad Herennium, 19
Richard I, 188
Richard II, 126, 173nn63–64, 175n70
Richards, I. A., 200–201
Rising of 1381, 8, 125, 134n33, 182n90, 188–90
Roman de la Rose, 3
Rosenwein, Barbara H., 17
Rowe, Donald, 71n4
Rowe, Katherine, 198n13, 202n29
Rowland, Beryl, 49n40, 50–51, 53n46
Runacres, Charles, 95n6
Russell, J. Stephen, 152n1, 157–58, 159n24

Sadlek, Gregory M., 127n13
Saint Alban's, 180–81
Salisbury, Eve, 10n16
Samson, 168, 176–77
Sanok, Catherine, 66, 74, 89, 90
satire, 55–58; of affect of invention, 151–90, 191; estates, 8n8, 10n16, 94
Scanlon, Larry, 104n30, 109, 113, 128n16, 169n50, 169n53, 174–75, 177, 179n83, 183, 187n97, 190n104
Schibanoff, Susan, 38n5, 57n62, 60n68, 66n77
Schmitz, Götz, 94
Sedgwick, Eve Kosofsky, 13, 14n32, 15–16
Seigworth, Gregory J., 14, 28, 43n16, 44
Seneca, 47, 114–15
sensus communis, 44
Shakespeare, Edmund, 210
Shakespeare, William, 35, 194–95; *Love's Labour's Lost*, 199; *Pericles: Prince of Tyre*, 35, 194, 203–10; "The Phoenix and Turtle," 35, 194–203, 210; *Two Noble Kinsmen*, 204n33

Shouse, Eric, 13
Simpson, James, 77, 89n50, 94–95, 96n7, 97n10, 111, 127n13, 128n17
Sir Gawain and the Green Knight, 26
Smith, Bruce, 198
Smith, D. Vance, 36, 91n57
sound(s), 33, 39, 49, 52, 54–58, 76, 105, 112, 143, 159, 201, 188n100
Speght, Thomas, 202n30
Spenser, Edmund, 195–96, 202, 210; *The Faerie Queene*, 211
Sprang, Felix C. H., 204n33
Statius, 172n61
Steiner, Emily, 131, 133n27
Stewart, Kathleen, 16, 17n45, 43n16
Stockton, Eric, 9n14
Stoicism, 47
Strange, William C., 171, 177
St. Saviour's, 210
Sylvester I, Pope 34, 112. See also *Confessio Amantis*, "Tale of Constantine and Sylvester"

Taylor, Andrew, 25–26
Taylor, John, 133n29
Thomas, Saint, the Apostle, 180
Thomas of Walshingham, 181n87
Tinkle, Theresa, 5n5, 128n16
tragedy, 168–79. See also *The Monk's Tale*
translation, 20–21, 42, 75–76, 133, 142–43, 190
Travis, Peter W., 183–84, 186–88, 189n101, 189n103
Trevisa, John, 123, 131–34, 137, 138, 170n57
Trigg, Stephanie, 202n30
Troy, 10, 59–60, 83, 85, 107–8, 134; London as New, 8–9
tydynges. See *House of Fame*

Ugolina of Pisa. See Hugelyn of Pisa

vernacular, 11n20, 19, 20–21, 25–27, 29–31, 35, 39, 53n47, 60, 71–72, 73, 75, 80, 142n46, 169n53, 178, 187n97, 191–92, 198, 211
Vincent of Beauvais, 81n34
Virgil, 37, 42, 59n64, 60–61, 134, 172n61; tradition of, 67. See also Aeneas
vis imaginativa, 44–45

Wallace, David, 75n18, 76, 173nn63–64, 173n66, 175n68, 176n71, 176n73, 180
Watson, Nicholas, 16n43, 17n47, 25–26, 38n5, 43, 44n17, 45n20, 47–48, 50, 54, 90n52

Watt, Diane, 95n5, 96n7, 146n51, 147
Welch, Bronwen, 156n13, 157n16, 158, 163
Wetherbee, Winthrop, 171n59, 178
Wilkins, George, 35, 194, 203, 205–6, 208–9
Wilsbacher, Greg, 163n34, 165n39, 167
Wogan-Browne, Jocelyn, 25–26, 26n73
Woods, Marjorie Curry, 64–65
Wright, Thomas: *The Passions of the Minde,* 198, 202, 207
Wyatt, Thomas, 210
Wyclif, John, 131n24, 133n27, 134n33; Wycliffites, 155n10

Yeager, R. F., 8n8, 10n16, 96–97, 98n15, 101n22, 103n28, 104, 124n1, 127, 128n16, 137n37, 139, 146nn51–52, 147, 193n1, 203n32, 204n33, 210n42

Zarins, Kim, 9n13, 11n24, 118n50
Zeeman, Nicolette, 26, 51, 154n9, 160n28
Zieman, Katherine, 154nn8–9, 157n15, 158n21, 164
Zitter, Emily Stark, 166n43, 167n47

INTERVENTIONS: NEW STUDIES IN MEDIEVAL CULTURE
Ethan Knapp, Series Editor

Interventions: New Studies in Medieval Culture publishes theoretically informed work in medieval literary and cultural studies. We are interested both in studies of medieval culture and in work on the continuing importance of medieval tropes and topics in contemporary intellectual life.

Chaucer, Gower, and the Affect of Invention
STEELE NOWLIN

Fragments for a History of a Vanishing Humanism
EDITED BY MYRA SEAMAN AND EILEEN A. JOY

The Medieval Risk-Reward Society: Courts, Adventure, and Love in the European Middle Ages
WILL HASTY

The Politics of Ecology: Land, Life, and Law in Medieval Britain
EDITED BY RANDY P. SCHIFF AND JOSEPH TAYLOR

The Art of Vision: Ekphrasis in Medieval Literature and Culture
EDITED BY ANDREW JAMES JOHNSTON, ETHAN KNAPP, AND MARGITTA ROUSE

Desire in the Canterbury Tales
ELIZABETH SCALA

Imagining the Parish in Late Medieval England
ELLEN K. RENTZ

Truth and Tales: Cultural Mobility and Medieval Media
EDITED BY FIONA SOMERSET AND NICHOLAS WATSON

Eschatological Subjects: Divine and Literary Judgment in Fourteenth-Century French Poetry
J. M. MOREAU

Chaucer's (Anti-)Eroticisms and the Queer Middle Ages
TISON PUGH

Trading Tongues: Merchants, Multilingualism, and Medieval Literature
JONATHAN HSY

Translating Troy: Provincial Politics in Alliterative Romance
ALEX MUELLER

Fictions of Evidence: Witnessing, Literature, and Community in the Late Middle Ages
JAMIE K. TAYLOR

Answerable Style: The Idea of the Literary in Medieval England
EDITED BY FRANK GRADY AND ANDREW GALLOWAY

Scribal Authorship and the Writing of History in Medieval England
MATTHEW FISHER

Fashioning Change: The Trope of Clothing in High- and Late-Medieval England
ANDREA DENNY-BROWN

Form and Reform: Reading across the Fifteenth Century
EDITED BY SHANNON GAYK AND KATHLEEN TONRY

How to Make a Human: Animals and Violence in the Middle Ages
KARL STEEL

Revivalist Fantasy: Alliterative Verse and Nationalist Literary History
RANDY P. SCHIFF

Inventing Womanhood: Gender and Language in Later Middle English Writing
TARA WILLIAMS

Body Against Soul: Gender and Sowlehele *in Middle English Allegory*
MASHA RASKOLNIKOV

www.ingramcontent.com/pod-product-compliance
Lightning Source LLC
Chambersburg PA
CBHW020648230426
43665CB00008B/358